INSIDERS' GUIDE® TO
DENVER

HELP US KEEP THIS GUIDE UP TO DATE

We would love to hear from you concerning your experiences with this guide and how you feel it could be improved and kept up to date. Please send your comments and suggestions to:

editorial@GlobePequot.com

Thanks for your input, and happy travels!

INSIDERS' GUIDE® SERIES

INSIDERS' GUIDE® TO

DENVER

NINTH EDITION

LINDA CASTRONE

INSIDERS' GUIDE®

GUILFORD, CONNECTICUT
AN IMPRINT OF GLOBE PEQUOT PRESS

All the information in this guidebook is subject to change. We recommend that you call ahead to obtain current information before traveling.

INSIDERS' GUIDE®

Copyright © 2002, 2004, 2005, 2007, 2009 Morris Book Publishing, LLC
A previous edition of this book was published by Falcon Publishing, Inc., in 1999.

Interior design: Sheryl Kober
Maps: XNR Productions, Inc. © Morris Book Publishing, LLC
Layout artist: Maggie Peterson

ISSN 1534-2166
ISBN 978-0-7627-5030-6

Printed in the United States of America
10 9 8 7 6 5 4 3 2 1

CONTENTS

Denver and Surrounding Area

Downtown Denver

PREFACE

Welcome to the Mile High City. Whether you're relocating or just visiting, I'm sure you'll love it here. With sweeping Rocky Mountain vistas and casual hospitality, Denver is a place rich in history, beauty, and excitement. *The Insiders' Guide to Denver* is designed to help you make the most of your time here.

For starters, chances are good that if you're already in Denver reading this book, the sky will be a startling shade of blue for at least part of the day. The sun shines 300 days a year here, and sunglasses are highly recommended. In fact, bad weather is perhaps the biggest misconception about Denver. Put simply, snowcapped peaks in the Rockies don't mean snow-covered streets in Denver. We do get the occasional blizzard, but most snows melt within a day or two, leaving fresh, clean air and sunny weather in their wake.

Beyond the great climate, Denver is a vibrant, growing city. It's no surprise that Democrats chose it as the site of their 2008 National Convention, nor did all that national attention hurt Denver's reputation as a great place to stage a mammoth party. Regardless why you're visiting, one of the first landmarks many visitors see is Denver International Airport (DIA), Denver's gateway to the rest of the world. In addition to its spectacular tented terminal building, DIA is known for its beautiful stonework, whimsical artwork, great views of both mountains and open plains, and a location that provides easy access to Colorado's interstate system.

Even die-hard Denver lovers like me find new things to treasure about our city. For instance, our city parks are vast expanses of green cut with walking and biking trails and flower beds. If what you really want is great shopping, you're in luck there too. The Cherry Creek Shopping Center stands as the area's top attraction, surpassing even the Mint, Coors Brewery, and the Denver museums in tourist draw, but it shares the retail arena with other regional shopping centers strewn throughout the Metro Denver area. Park Meadows to the southeast has been a high-end hit since it opened in August of 1996. FlatIron Crossing has served the northwest quadrant since 2000, and Colorado Mills filled another niche in the western suburb of Lakewood when it opened in 2002. Among the newest additions is NorthField at Stapleton, a 1.2-million-square-foot lifestyle, entertainment, and retail center located just north of I-70 at Quebec Street. Early tenants include Bass Pro Shops, SuperTarget, a Harkins 18-screen theater, and Macy's.

Denver is also a sports town, with modern venues for all its professional teams. Coors Field in Lower Downtown houses the Colorado Rockies baseball team. The glass and steel Pepsi Center, also in Lower Downtown, is shared by the Colorado Avalanche hockey team and Denver's basketball team, the Nuggets. The Denver Broncos play nearby at INVESCO Field at Mile High, and the Colorado Rapids, a professional soccer team, plays its games at the new Dick's Sporting Goods Park in Commerce City. A new facility called the Broomfield Events Center was built on the northwestern edge of Metro Denver for two minor league clubs—the Rocky Mountain Rage hockey team and the Colorado 14ers basketball team.

There are so many things to do in or near downtown these days that boredom is out of the question. Elitch Gardens amusement park is located in the once-abandoned Platte Valley area just west of downtown. Brewpubs are a way of life—in or out of baseball season. And Larimer Square (Larimer Street between 14th and 15th Streets downtown) is a year-round destination where visitors can experience Denver's flavor and appreciation for historical buildings and the lore that accompanies them.

And more development is yet to come. Denver's Union Station is set to become a regional transit/retail/housing center similar to Union Station in Washington, D.C., and the Ferry Building in San Francisco. Commons Park continues to grow on the western edge of the transit site, and the metropolitan governments continue the expansion of one of the best urban trail systems in the country. If cultural experiences are also your interest, the Denver Art Museum opened the new Frederic C. Hamilton Building in 2006, completing its seven-year, $90.5 million expansion project.

While no book can ever capture everything great about a metropolitan area as diverse as Denver, this one attempts to distill the best of everything into a format that will give newcomers the inside scoop, offer visitors a guide on what to see and experience, and bring even more wisdom to longtime Denverites. So go forth and tour, buy a pair of cowboy boots, picnic in the park, gaze at the mountains from the middle of the city and savor the beauty.

ACKNOWLEDGMENTS

Two sets of authors preceded me in writing the *Insiders' Guide to Denver*—Bob Ebisch and Laura Caruso, who wrote the original manuscript; then Sally Stich and Jana Miller, who took it through several more editions. By now the book has taken on a life of its own—no longer their work but not entirely mine either. I'd like to thank them for building a strong foundation. Acknowledgments go to Rich Grant, director of the Denver Metro Convention & Visitors Bureau, and my husband, Jim, whose meticulous editing skills left the eighth edition in fine shape for future rewrites.

HOW TO USE THIS BOOK

The *Insiders' Guide to Denver* is designed to let you flip easily through the pages, either looking for something specific or simply finding something that catches your eye. For overall subject areas, such as nightlife or shopping, go to the Contents. To find information on specific places, such as the name of a restaurant or a ski resort, consult the Index.

The book is a guide, not a directory. So while I've made sure to include all the leading tourist attractions, restaurants, hotels, and natural wonders in Metro Denver, to a great extent my choices are personal. But that's one of this guide's strong points—honest, knowledgeable insider-based information on Denver and five of the six surrounding counties. Boulder County has enough of its own attractions to warrant a separate book, *Insiders' Guide to Boulder and Rocky Mountain National Park*.

Nor is this book a novel. It's designed to be read selectively, on a need-to-know or want-to-know basis, rather than all in one sitting. Each chapter stands alone and has its own introduction. If you are new to the area, you'll want to start by reading through the Area Overview and Getting Here, Getting Around chapters. Then carry the book in your backpack as you explore, or tuck it in the glove box of your car. When you want to know where to stop for lunch, or whether the Denver Zoo is open on Sunday (it is), you'll be glad you have it nearby.

Throughout the book wherever you see an **i** you'll find Insiders' Tips, handy hints from those in the know for those who want to be.

Enjoy your stay, whether it be for a few hours or a lifetime.

AREA OVERVIEW

Denver is, today, as it has been for more than 100 years, the largest metropolis between California and Missouri. An expansive self-regard still comes easily to the present inhabitants of Metro Denver, just as it did when the town was being established in the mid-1800s.

Most are proud of its agricultural roots, and many keep a pair of cowboy boots in the closet for times when hootin' and hollerin' are just what the doctor ordered. Even so, residents are well aware that Metro Denver is an economic powerhouse with a thriving cultural community, strong recreational offerings, and the best shopping in a seven state region. The metropolitan area is defined by the city and county of Denver and its five suburban counties: Adams, Arapahoe, Broomfield, Douglas, and Jefferson. Boulder County is close by but regarded as having its own identity. Only about 40 percent of Greater Denver's present citizens were born here. Natives and newcomers alike are uneasy about recent growth, and its threats to their quality of life, but boosterism runs rampant.

Because of its geographic location near the nation's center, Denver is already a major hub of the railroad, airline, and highway systems. Denver International Airport helped secure the city's potential as a focus of worldwide trade and transportation, playing on its location midway between Munich and Tokyo, Canada and Mexico.

Geography also has much to do with the city's self-image. No matter where you are in Denver, you have only to look west to see the Rocky Mountains running north and south like a wall dividing west from east. Yet as the "Queen City of the Plains," Denver has an urban fabric that extends into the mountains on the west and overlays the first swells of the Great Plains to the east. The mountains drew Paleolithic hunters to the sheltering slopes and fertile hunting grounds of the foothills. Between the housing developments of Jefferson County on Denver's southwest fringe, archaeologists have found 10,000-year-old remains of mammoths and camels that appear to have been killed by human hunters. Modern Indians, principally the Ute, Comanche, Apache, Arapaho, Cheyenne, and Kiowa, later gravitated to the area for hunting, trade, and war.

SETTLING THE LAND

European settlers first came from the south, beginning with Spanish explorers and soldiers in the 1600s. During the next two centuries, a slow movement of mostly agrarian colonists from Mexico and New Mexico gave a distinctly Hispanic culture to the southern part of the state. The city of Pueblo, less than a two-hour drive south of Denver, and all points south were Mexican territory until the United States grabbed them the 1848 war with Mexico. As Colorado grew, the ancestors of today's Hispanic citizens generated much of the sweat that built the state's mining, railroads, and agriculture.

Invaders from the east came faster and hit harder. In 1858, little more than 50 years after the first mountain men began trapping furs in the Rockies, a party of prospectors panned gold from the Platte River in what is now the city of Englewood on Denver's southern edge. Their discovery earned each man no more than about $10 a day, but it was enough to start the rush.

The history of modern Denver began at the confluence of the South Platte River with tiny Cherry Creek, where cottonwood groves sheltered the camps of Indians and early explorers such as John C. Frémont. By the beginning of 1859, the city of Denver had been established there by friends of James W. Denver, then governor of the Kansas Territory. Within months, the cottonwood groves had been axed into oblivion and replaced by some 400 cabins and a lot of bare dirt and mud. Today new life has been breathed into that area as a new breed of pioneer reclaims the industrial wasteland for use as an elegant creekside neighborhood.

STRIKING GOLD

Gold strikes in the mountains brought not just a growing swarm of fortune seekers from the east but also merchants, industrial entrepreneurs, and other citizens of a real city, including the bad elements. Denver had "more brawls, more pistol shots with criminal intent … than in any community with equal numbers on Earth," according to Horace Greeley. "Uncle Dick" Wootton, an early merchant, later recalled that "stealing was the only occupation of a considerable portion of the population, who would take anything from a pet calf, or a counterfeit gold dollar, up to a saw mill."

As Denver matured it acquired a certain air of refinement, becoming the capital of the new Colorado Territory in 1867 and capital of the State of Colorado in 1876. "A shooting affray in the street is as rare as in Liverpool," noted British traveler Isabella Bird in 1872, "and one no longer sees men dangling to the lamp posts when one looks out in the morning." Still, she noted, Denver was not a very pretty sight. It was a city that "lay spread out, brown and treeless, upon the brown and treeless plain, which seemed to nourish nothing but wormwood and the Spanish bayonet."

The kind of money needed to polish the city's rough edges was soon to come from Colorado's growing cattle, mining, railroad, steel, banking,

and other industries. Journalistic accounts of the time were filled with news about gambling houses and painted ladies, but a new class of aristocrat began decorating Denver's Capitol Hill neighborhood with mansions that have now become tourist destinations. Silver strikes in the mountains in the late 1870s caused another mining boom that poured money into the city until the silver market collapsed in 1893 and threw Denver into a depression. Yet more gold strikes in the mountains, along with the growth of Colorado's agriculture and manufacturing industries, brought Denver citizens into the 20th century, making them more prone to creating parks than cavorting in bawdy houses.

Still, the Queen City of the Plains was more plain than queenly, as one visitor put it. Major credit for developing her assets generally goes to Mayor Robert Speer, who pursued his dream of a "City Beautiful" during the first two decades of the 20th century. He created parks both in the city and the mountains, planted thousands of trees, and is credited with laying hundreds of miles of sewers and paving streets that turned Cherry Creek from a garbage dump into the centerpiece of what is today Speer Boulevard. The Denver Civic Center is the culmination of his planning, a popular downtown park located between the capitol and city and county buildings that was completed nearly two decades after his 1918 death.

WAR SPURS GROWTH

Despite the Great Depression, Denver's population grew by more than 50 percent between 1910 and 1940. World War II initiated the area's greatest surge when fear of attack on the nation's coasts transformed the area into a center of military and other government functions. Within a year after Pearl Harbor, major employment bases appeared in facilities such as the Denver Federal Center, the Rocky Mountain Arsenal, and the Fitzsimons Army Medical Center. Those who came for war-related opportunities stayed on when the war was done, and Metro Denver now contains some 50 percent of Colorado's population.

Close-up

A 19th-Century Perspective of Denver

In 1873, British traveler Isabella Bird spent time in Denver and other areas of Colorado. *A Lady's Life in the Rocky Mountains,* her account of those travels, is still in print and can easily be found at Denver book stores and libraries.

An intrepid traveler and keen observer, Isabella came to town after spending a summer in Estes Park that included a dramatic climb up 14,255-foot-high Longs Peak in what is now Rocky Mountain National Park. The peak had been scaled for the first time only five years before a true character named Rocky Mountain Jim hauled Isabella to the summit. If she had gone three weeks earlier, Isabella could have been the first woman to stand there, but she was beaten by American writer and orator Anna Dickinson.

Isabella was surprised by Denver, which she called a "great, braggart city." Here, as recounted with permission from the biography *Amazing Traveler: Isabella Bird,* is her description of the streets of Denver: "Hunters and trappers in buckskin clothing; men of the Plains with belts and revolvers, in great blue cloaks, relics of the war; horsemen in fur coats and caps and buffalo-hide boots with the hair outside; Broadway dandies in light kid gloves; rich English sporting tourists, clean, comely and supercilious-looking; and hundreds of Indians on their small ponies, the men wearing buckskin suits sewn with beads, and red blankets, with faces painted vermilion, and hair hanging lank and straight, and squaws much bundled up riding astride with furs over their saddles."

Readers interested in learning more about Isabella Bird and her adventures are directed to *Amazing Traveler: Isabella Bird* by Boulder author Evelyn Kaye (Blue Panda Publications, 1999).

OPTIMISM AND DIVERSIFICATION

Since World War II the local economy has had its ups and downs, but Metro Denver has never lost that growth momentum. The city's economy endured the after effects of an oil bust in the 1980s as well as the dotcom bust in 2002, but in each case the recessions were short lived. They were followed by unprecedented spending on transportation infrastructure, including Denver International Airport, a major expansion and installation of light-rail lanes along Interstate 25, and an even more ambitious light-rail project nicknamed FasTracks that will take another decade to complete.

Perhaps nowhere is revitalization more evident than in the area known as the Central Platte Valley, the city's birthplace at the confluence of the South Platte River and Cherry Creek. As Denver grew up and outward in the 1870s, the Central Platte Valley became the rail and warehousing district; by the 1970s it had become an urban wasteland best known for the trash-strewn vacant fields that were criss-crossed by railroad tracks. The area is now rebounding as the focal point of the new Denver, a planned community of green spaces and residential, retail, office, and entertainment developments. Much of the vision is already under way, led by the early developments of anchor projects that included Coors Field, the 50,000-seat home to Denver's major league Colorado Rockies; Elitch Gardens, a 60-acre amusement park; and high-rise residential projects clustered around Commons Park.

Lower Downtown, a warehouse district along the valley's edge that is best known for its turn-of-the-century red brick buildings, was the first to rebound. Since Coors Field opened in 1995, it has become a hotbed of restaurants, brewpubs, prestigious offices, condominiums, and lofts around Denver's historic railroad terminal, Union Station.

BIG CITY PAINS

Of course, not everything is perfect about Metro Denver.

Tourists strolling amid the stately buildings and flower gardens of Denver's Civic Center might well be asked for money by transients who lounge in the shade. While crime is no more prevalent in Denver than in any midsize city, it pays to stay alert when visiting downtown and fringe neighborhoods. Rush hour traffic can also be annoying, especially on I-25 and I-70. Special carpool lanes ease the pain, but watch the signs carefully along I-25. Lanes that bring commuters into the downtown area change direction in mid-afternoon so they can carry travelers back home at the end of the work day.

Denver also is plagued by seasonal weather patterns that trap visible layers of yellow-brown haze in the air. Warm summer breezes carry them away, but during the months when a crackling fire would be most welcome, wood-burning bans are often in effect.

Even without air pollution, visitors may temporarily find it a bit more difficult to breathe at a mile above sea level. They may also feel headachy and strangely out of sorts, but at higher elevations the symptoms of altitude sickness can become acute, signaling a collapse of the body's ability to take in and metabolize oxygen. Those who plan to exert themselves in the mountains should take a few days to acclimate and drink an abnormally large amount of water.

It's also important to distinguish between weather patterns in Denver and in the nearby mountains. Snow can be piling up on ski slopes in Vail or Aspen at the same time golfers and joggers are enjoying 70-degree weather in Denver. Periodic cold spells do set in between November to February, and Denver does get some whopping winter snowstorms. But within a few days, most of the snow has melted and people are back out walking their dogs and working in their yards. Snow melts particularly fast during the late winter and early spring when Chinook winds come roaring down from the mountains at speeds that have been clocked as high as 143 miles per hour.

These warm, dry "snow-eaters" suck moisture out of the snow and have been known to raise Front Range temperatures by as much as 36 degrees within two hours. They've also been known to tear the roofs off houses, topple trees, and blow semitrailers right off the interstate.

The National Center for Atmospheric Research is studying those weather extremes from its mountainside campus in nearby Boulder, and meteorologists joke that the area is an ideal place to be stationed because they can golf in the morning and chase thunderstorms in the afternoon. Both play into the common observation: "If you don't like the weather, just wait five minutes."

DENVER SUBURBS

Much of what we've already said about Metro Denver has focused on the city itself, but the suburban counties have their own lives and characters. While Metro Denver was home to 2.76 million people in July 2007, only 581,388 of them lived in the City and County of Denver. The rest are settled in suburban counties that ring the core city.

Jefferson County, West of Denver

Among Metro Denver counties, Jefferson is the third largest, with 542,152 residents. It serves as Metro Denver's gateway to the mountains, wrapping around the western end of the metropolitan area and including the mountain communities of Evergreen and Conifer. Jefferson tends to attract residents motivated by quality of life who can afford to locate in or near the mountains. Not surprisingly, its population is highly educated and includes a high percentage of dual-income families. Skiers, sightseers, mountaineers, and other motorists travel west through Jefferson County on I-70 or US 6 through scenic Clear Creek Canyon, the historic main thoroughfare to the gold and silver meccas of the 1800s. Many of these passersby notice little more than the city of Golden to the north or the upscale homes that dot the hills alongside the road.

But "Jeffco," in the local slang, is also an urban county in which cities such as Arvada, Edgewater,

Westminster, Wheat Ridge, and Lakewood represent a continuum of the urban fabric that reaches out from Denver.

Jefferson County is highly industrialized, with an emphasis on high technology. Golden, the county seat, claims Metro Denver's highest percentage of technology Ph.D.s, and up to a third of Colorado School of Mines' graduates stay in the county. The region's geotechnology, materials, mining, and energy businesses are clustered in Jefferson County. The federal government is its largest employer, with the mammoth Denver Federal Center in Lakewood and the National Renewable Energy Laboratory in Golden.

i If you're a low-altitude person like many new arrivals in Denver, you may wonder why you have a nagging slight headache. Don't worry; it's just the altitude. Drink lots of water and your physiology should be Denverized within a week.

Arapahoe County, East and South of Denver

The Arapahoe County of the Kansas Territory once covered nearly half the present state of Colorado, but nowadays the county covers only about 800 square miles. Reaching halfway from Denver to the Kansas border, Arapahoe County claims 561,388 residents in cities that include Englewood, Greenwood Village, Centennial, and Littleton, the county seat.

Arapahoe contains most of the city of Aurora, the state's biggest city by area and its third-largest in population. Since World War II, Aurora has been heavily influenced by the military. It contains the sites of two former military bases: Fitzsimons Army Medical Center, which is being redeveloped into a new research center and campus for the University of Colorado's Health Sciences Center; and Lowry Air Force Base, which has been redeveloped into a residential neighborhood. Buckley Air Force Base (the city's largest employer) is still in use on the east.

The county's second- and third-largest cities are Englewood and Littleton. Littleton still has something of a small-town feel, but its school system has produced Scholastic Aptitude Test scores that rank among Metro Denver's highest. Englewood was a prairie when Colorado's first gold was discovered there in 1858. By the late 1800s, its fruit orchards gave the city its modern name, derived from the Old English words for "wooded place." Denver's ladies and gentlemen often made it their destination for Sunday carriage drives and picnics. Today Englewood boasts more jobs and businesses per square mile than any other city in the Rocky Mountains. The small communities of Glendale and Sheridan also are part of Arapahoe County.

Adams County, Northeast of Denver

Adams County, population 433,267, ceded 53 of its approximately 1,200 square miles to the City of Denver in the 1990s for the construction of a new airport. But Adams is still Metro Denver's largest county by area. Lying north of Arapahoe County, Adams County is perhaps Greater Denver's most economically diverse county, hosting agriculture, heavy industry, transportation, and high-tech companies. It does have an image as Metro Denver's big-shouldered, blue-collar county, thanks to the spread of warehouses, smokestack industries, and oil refineries that can be seen along I-70 and I-270. At the same time, it has its share of communications, biopharmaceutical, and computer software and hardware companies in the urbanized eastern region. The county seat is in Brighton. Other cities and towns in the county include Northglenn, Thornton, Bennett, Federal Heights, and parts of Arvada and Westminster.

Anyone who looks at a map will see a large blank space east of Commerce City with a scattering of lakes and the words "Rocky Mountain Arsenal (Restricted Area)." During World War II the Rocky Mountain Arsenal was located on 17,000 acres of land 10 miles northeast of downtown Denver, where the U.S. Army manufactured chemical weapons such as mustard gas, white phosphorus, and napalm. Contaminated

Metro Denver Vital Statistics

Denver was named for James W. Denver, governor of the Kansas Territory when the city was founded.

Denver became the capital of the new Colorado Territory in 1867 and capital of the State of Colorado in 1876.

Population: As of 2007, the U.S. Census Bureau estimated the city and county of Denver at 581,388, Adams County at 433,267, Arapahoe County at 561,388, Broomfield County at 49,686, Douglas County at 284,144, and Jefferson County at 542,152.

Location: The city sits at the base of the Rocky Mountains about a third of the way between Wyoming and New Mexico.

Terrain: Rocky Mountain foothills on the west, rolling plains on the east.

Altitude: A bronze disk imbedded on one of the western steps of the State Capitol building proclaims, ELEVATION 5,280 FEET. The words ONE MILE ABOVE SEA LEVEL are chiseled just above.

Climate: Mild. Dry heat in summer makes days bearable and nights pleasantly cool. Snow seldom stays long on the ground during winter. Average maximum temperature in the summer is 85 degrees; minimum is 56. Average maximum winter temperature is 45 degrees; minimum is 18. Average annual rainfall is 11 inches. Average annual snowfall is 60 inches. Average number of days with snow, ice pellets, or hail of 1 inch or more in depth is 18. Clear days: 115. Partly cloudy days: 130. Cloudy days: 120.

Denver government consists of a mayor and a city council. The current mayor is John Hickenlooper.

groundwater began to cause crop damage in the mid-1950s, so production stopped and cleanup began. More than half the acreage has been scrubbed, with the project projected to be done by 2011. In the meantime it has become the most impressive wildlife refuge in Metro Denver. A continuous flow of weekend visitors and weekday school groups visit to view eagles, elk, and other wildlife that call the arsenal home.

While dealing gracefully with its past, Adams County is well positioned for its future. In exchange for land on which DIA was built, Adams was promised economic growth as it developed around the airport. It has been a primary beneficiary of economic spin-offs. Thanks to residential and commercial development on the county's western side, Adams is also home to some of the Denver metro area's best new golf courses (see our Parks and Recreation chapter for details) and an entertainment complex at Church Ranch Road and US 35 that rivals any in the area. More growth

is occurring between Brighton and DIA, bringing housing, retail, and industrial parks.

Adams County's own Front Range Airport is just 3 miles southeast of Denver International Airport, having begun operations in 1983. The abundance of air transportation has enhanced basic industries such as metalworking, food processing, and wood products in Adams County's southwestern corner, as well as high-technology companies along the 120th Avenue corridor in the county's northwestern corner.

Douglas County, South of Denver

Flowing through the Pike National Forest southwest of Denver, the South Platte River has some of the most celebrated trout fishing on Colorado's Front Range, once described by *Time* magazine as "the St. Peter's Basilica of trout fishing." That distinction is just one of the things that make Douglas County such an attractive place that 284,144 people call it home.

Many are housed in Highlands Ranch, one of Metro Denver's most popular planned communities because of its mountain views, abundant parks, and looping pedestrian trail system. The unincorporated community's population is expected to reach 100,000 by the year 2015. The county also includes Castle Rock, Lone Tree, Larkspur, and Parker as well as a piece of Littleton. Although Douglas County is the only metro county that does not share a boundary with the City and County of Denver (it is separated by a slice of Arapahoe County that wraps under the city's south side), it serves as Metro Denver's southern frontier. Douglas is the only Metro Denver county in which the vast majority of its population lives in unincorporated communities such as Castle Pines. It also is one of the area's prestigious ZIP codes, with the region's highest median income and home prices, and by far the highest ratio of people commuting outside the county to reach their jobs.

As the focus of what local planners call the Denver/Colorado Springs Development Corridor, Douglas also a turn as Colorado's fastest-growing county, with a population that grew 191 percent between 1990 and 2000. That rate has slowed considerably in recent years, but with 29 planned communities and 319 subdivisions covering nearly 18 percent of the county, Douglas anticipates a half-million new residents by 2030.

Meanwhile, the county plans to protect as much as 70 percent of its 841 square miles as open space, in the form of ranches, greenbelts, and public parks. Its county seat of Castle Rock, so named for the monolith-capped hill that towers above it, is just short of halfway to Colorado Springs, and most of its workers commute to one metropolis or the other.

GETTING HERE, GETTING AROUND

If you get lost, look at the mountains. That's the mantra when it comes to getting your bearings in Denver. The mountains to the west can orient even the most turned-around traveler, so take advantage of them as you're navigating the region. The second vital fact about Denver is that its historic core parallels Cherry Creek, while the rest of its streets were laid out in north-south and east-west grids. At times that can make downtown's diagonal streets feel like a confounding mistake in the midst of otherwise neatly planned neighborhoods.

Cherry Creek cuts through the town from northwest to southeast, and that's where the city's founders planted their roots. Later generations corrected the slap-dash planning, orienting their streets to match more traditional compass points. It helps to look at a Denver map to understand the orientation. In general, from downtown Denver, Aurora is to the east; the Denver Tech Center, Englewood, and Greenwood Village are to the south; Littleton is southwest; Lakewood, Wheat Ridge, and Golden are to the west; Arvada, Broomfield, and Westminster are to the northwest; and Commerce City, Northglenn, and Thornton are to the north.

"Downtown" refers to the area that is roughly bounded by 13th Avenue on the south, Speer Boulevard (which follows Cherry Creek) on the west, the South Platte River on the north, and Grant Street on the southeast. Most downtown streets run one way. Seventeenth Street, where most of the banks and big office buildings are located, is in many ways the heart of downtown. The 16th Street Mall is also an important pedestrian thoroughfare, as free MallRide shuttle buses run up and down its one-mile length, connecting the two RTD (Regional Transportation District) bus terminals on Broadway and Market Street. The shuttle buses operate between about 5 a.m. and 1:30 a.m. on weekdays, from about 5:30 a.m. to 1:30 a.m. on Saturdays, and from 6 a.m. to 1:30 a.m. on Sundays and holidays. Frequency depends on the time of day and ranges from one every ten minutes to almost one a minute during the morning and afternoon rush hours. The 16th Street Mall is closed to auto traffic between Market Street and Broadway. Bikes and in-line skates also aren't allowed.

Somewhere around Market Street, downtown becomes Lower Downtown, or "LoDo" (say "low-dough"). Dana Crawford, who spearheaded the Larimer Street rejuvenation, defines the area narrowly as Larimer and Market Streets west to Union Station, from 20th Street to Cherry Creek. A broader definition extends farther west to the Platte River. Capitol Hill is the name given to the area just east of downtown.

Our Area Overview chapter, which talks about the different counties that make up Metro Denver, should help you orient yourself. For descriptions of neighborhoods see our Relocation chapter.

LOGISTICS: FINDING AN ADDRESS

In central Denver the streets are laid out on a sort of grid: Broadway runs north-south and serves as the dividing line between east and west addresses. Ellsworth Avenue runs east-west and serves as the dividing line between north and south streets and addresses. Broadway and Ellsworth Avenue are the "zero hundred blocks." As streets travel away from them, address numbers go up.

Close-up

Art at the Airport

When Denver International Airport (DIA) was built in the mid-1990s with a construction budget of more than $3.2 billion, the funding for art was equally impressive. That's because Denver, like many other cities, has a percent-for-art ordinance that requires developers of city projects to set aside an amount equal to 1 percent of the total costs for art at the site. At DIA, that amounted to about $7.5 million that was divided among 26 art projects.

That sounds like a lot of money and a lot of art, but it isn't always easy to find. The main areas to look for art are in the center of each concourse, along the underground train passages, and throughout the main terminal.

Here are a few of our favorite pieces:

A 30-foot-high fiberglass blue mustang is the first piece of art people see as they come into the airport via Peña Boulevard. Made by well-known New Mexico artist Luis Jiminez, the rearing horse has eyes that shoot laserlike beams of red light.

Near the carousels in the baggage claim area, check out the two whimsical suitcase gargoyles by Terry Allen. They go by the name Notre Denver.

Also in the baggage claim area are two colorful murals painted by Denver artist Leo Tanguma, a Chicano activist/artist who likes to involve the community in creating his murals. He calls them *In Peace and Harmony with Nature*, and *The Children of the World Dream of Peace*.

Across the main terminal from Tanguma's murals is Gary Sweeney's *America, Why I Love Her*, two photomural maps of the United States with the artist's small framed snapshots of odd bits of Americana (ever seen the Frog Fantasies Museum in Eureka Springs, Arkansas?) tacked onto the appropriate locations. Sweeney used to work as a baggage handler for Continental Airlines. On the spot occupied by Denver, he included a little sign that says: "You are here . . . but your luggage is in Spokane." Needless to say, not everybody was amused, especially in the early 1990s, when glitches in the automated baggage system caused multiple delays in the airport's opening date.

Above escalators that connect Level 5 and Level 6 in the main terminal are 28 glossy, vibrant ceramic vases by internationally known ceramicist Betty Woodman, titled Balustrade. Although Woodman has exhibited widely in the United States and Europe, this was her first public commission.

Another favorite piece is *Interior Garden*, an installation created by Michael Singer in Concourse C. These mossy ruins are visible from above in the concourse and from below as you exit the train.

Artists have worked on the floors of DIA in several places, including the main terminal and Concourse B, so if you watch where you're walking, you'll see pictographs and fossils inlaid in the terrazzo floor. In the food court areas in Concourse A, you'll notice colorful tile patterns that appear to be abstract—but go up the escalator, take a look from above and you'll see that they form foreshortened figures of people. Barb McKee and Darrell Anderson collaborated on this project.

Finally, on the way out of the airport, you may notice a line of rusted farm implements. It's not that there wasn't time to clean up—this is an art installation called *Fenceline Artifact* created by Sherry Wiggins and Buster Simpson to acknowledge that agriculture was historically one of the primary uses of the land on which DIA was built.

Curious passersby can get a brochure that identifies and locates the art at DIA in the information booths in the main terminal and in Concourses A and C.

MAPSCO, 800 Lincoln Street, (303) 830-2373, has every kind of map you'll ever need to find your way around—topographic, recreational, and illustrated. They also stock guidebooks.

MAIN THOROUGHFARES

I-25 runs north-south through Denver in a line from Cheyenne to Colorado Springs (and farther in each direction, of course). Just north of downtown, it intersects I-70, the major route to the mountains that runs east-west through the northern edge of the city. I-225 cuts diagonally across Aurora, running northeast to southwest and connecting with I-70 just west of Peoria Street and with I-25 near the Denver Tech Center.

The so-called Denver Beltway is comprised of three separate highways (with a fourth segment planned) that form a loop around the city. The Northwest Parkway is a toll road that cuts across the north between US 36 at Broomfield and I-25.

The second segment, a toll road called E-470, runs east from I-25 to I-76. There it turns south, passes Denver International Airport (take the Peña Boulevard exit to reach DIA), and rejoins I-25 near Park Meadows Shopping Center. The final section begins there. Called C-470, it's the only piece that doesn't charge a toll. It serves the metro area's south and west sections, stretching from I-25 at the Arapahoe County/Douglas County border west past Littleton, then north to I-70. The final segment—intended to connect C-470 at I-70 with the Northwest Parkway—is the subject of a hotly contested debate in the northwest communities of Golden and Arvada. Plans remain in place but are under vigorous discussion.

Other major thoroughfares are 6th Avenue (US 6), which joins up with I-70 at Golden; Santa Fe Drive (US 85), a north-south route that can be a good alternative to I-25; and Broadway. Colfax Avenue (Highway 40) is an east-west route but, like Broadway, it has a lot of traffic and can be a slow pathway from one side of town to another. Speer Boulevard runs parallel to Cherry Creek and connects Downtown Denver with the Cherry Creek shopping area.

Rush hour comes early in Denver. Assuming all goes well, the highways have cleared in the mornings by 9 a.m., but the evening rush hour starts as early as 3:30 p.m.

HOV (high-occupancy vehicle) lanes encourage carpooling on several of Denver's major commuter routes, including South Santa Fe Drive, eastbound US 36, and I-25 north of downtown. Watch for them and use them; they'll save you 15 to 20 minutes of stop-and-go in rush hours. To use these lanes, you must have at least two occupants per vehicle.

Downtown parking is tight but not impossible and is much cheaper than in other big cities. Options for drivers are on-street meters and parking lots. Bring coins and small bills; you'll need to spend anywhere from $6 to $15 for an afternoon shopping spree.

FASTRACKS TRANSPORTATION EXPANSION PROJECT

If you're visiting or new to Denver, you might hear newscasters talking about FasTracks, a 12-year plan that will add 119 miles of new light-rail lines, 18 new miles of express bus service, 21,000 new parking spaces at rail and bus stations, and expanded bus service throughout Denver. Construction began in 2008 and is expected to take about a decade to complete. It was originally expected to cost $4.7 billion, part of which will come from a 0.4 percent sales tax increase approved by voters that began in 2005.

PUBLIC TRANSPORTATION

REGIONAL TRANSPORTATION DISTRICT
1600 Blake Street
(303) 299-6000
www.rtd-denver.com
The Regional Transportation District (RTD) provides bus and light-rail service throughout the city and suburbs.

Light Rail—RTD operates six light-rail routes in Denver and its southern suburbs, five of which begin their routes in the downtown core and run north and south along a central corridor that roughly parallels I-25. The sixth provides spur service on the southeastern edges of the system, between Lincoln Avenue and the Nine Mile station. Light-rail lines serve the Five Points neighborhood, downtown Denver, the Auraria campus, the University of Denver, Englewood, Littleton, Aurora, Greenwood Village, Centennial, Lone Tree, and Parker. Feeder buses serve all stations, providing mass transit from the central corridor into suburbs on either side of I-25. Fares range from $2.00 to $4.50 each way, depending on how far you travel on the train. Seniors 65 and over, people with disabilities, Medicare recipients, and students ages 6 to 19 pay roughly half price.

Buses—RTD runs local, express, and regional bus service. Local buses operate on many routes downtown and cost $2. Express routes travel longer distances without as many stops; the basic fare is $3.50. Regional routes run to Boulder and other outlying areas; the fare is $4.50 The regional buses are comfortably upholstered, with reclining seats and air-conditioning. In all cases, exact change is required. Tokens, ticket books, and monthly passes are available at RTD stations and supermarkets, and many discounts apply (for senior citizens, students, and the disabled). RTD also provides transportation to and from the airport (for more information, see the Airports section later in this chapter), as well as to and from professional football and baseball games (details are provided in our Spectator Sports chapter). Information about routes, schedules and fares is available at (303) 299-6000, www.rtddenver.com, and all RTD stations.

i   Ski traffic on I-70 is a major problem during winter months. Prepare for a long, slow trip through the Eisenhower Tunnel on most days, especially during peak hours. A trip from Denver to Breckenridge can take three or more hours on heavy traffic days.

TAXIS

Generally you don't just wave down a cruising taxi on Metro Denver streets, although it is sometimes possible downtown. Plan to call ahead when you need a ride, usually about 30 minutes before you need to leave. All taxi companies are allowed to take you out of the city if you wish, but it gets expensive. Rides to and from Denver International Airport cost $46.50.

All companies have similar rate structures: $2.60 entry fee and $2.20 a mile: Metro Taxi, (303) 333-3333 or www.metrotaxidenver.com; Yellow Cab, (303) 777-7777; Freedom Cab, (303) 292-8900 or www.freedomcabs.com.

LEAVING TOWN: PLANES, TRAINS, AND BUSES

Airports

DENVER INTERNATIONAL AIRPORT
8500 Peña Boulevard
(303) 342-2000
www.flydenver.com

Denver residents are fond of their airport, even if it is 24 miles from downtown, and based on passenger traffic, they aren't the only ones. DIA served a record fifty-one million passengers in 2008, making it the nation's sixth and the world's eleventh busiest airport. Its six runways can land three aircraft at once using state-of-the-art radar, and with 53 square miles of land, it is large enough to hold several more if air traffic demands them. DIA is situated to the north and east of Denver and is bisected by Peña Boulevard. To reach it, take I-70 to exit 284 or, from the north, take 104th Avenue to Tower Road, and then drive south to Peña Boulevard. Two toll roads, the Northwest Parkway and E-470, also serve DIA. Take the Peña Boulevard exits off either road.

Charges for short-term parking run from $1 to $3 an hour, depending on location, up to a twenty-four-hour maximum of between $9 and $18. Long-term parking costs $5 a day.

You could let RTD do the driving. SkyRide operates seven major routes to DIA from stations throughout Metro Denver. One-way fare for the suburban routes is $12; from downtown, $10; and from the former Stapleton Airport, which is just south of DIA and offers free parking to SkyRide passengers, $8. SkyRide information is available at (303) 299-6000 or www.rtd-denver.com/skyRide_SubHome.shtml.

DIA's unique terminal has a dramatic tented roof of Teflon-coated fiberglass that has been fashioned into 34 peaks that symbolize the Rocky Mountains. From a distance, the roof also looks like an encampment of tepees, a nod to the American Indians who regularly used the site for temporary encampments. Inside, many surfaces are brushed steel, and $7.5 million worth of commissioned art adorns the floors, walls, and ceilings. (See our Close-up in this chapter for a more complete description of the art.)

DIA has three concourses and a main terminal, all of which are connected by underground trains. A pedestrian bridge also connects Concourse A with the main terminal, offering passengers a close-up view of the airfield as well as a soothing soundtrack of authentic Indian chants.

Travelers appreciate the well-planned variety of retail shops and restaurants within the terminal. Airport administrators work hard to attract local businesses that add color to the more typical national chain stores.

Ground transportation from DIA into Metro Denver is plentiful. Taxis can be hailed outside the baggage claim area and cost $46.50 to downtown, more if you're going farther (see the Taxis section in this chapter). Shuttle buses are provided by many major hotels, so check with yours. Otherwise, a number of other shuttle companies provide service from DIA to Metro Denver locations as well as major mountain ski towns. More information about ground transportation is available at (303) 342-4059. You must have a destination in order to get a price quote, but shuttle service to downtown Denver will cost about $19 or $20 per person. Out

of Colorado, you can call (800) AIR-2-DEN to make arrangements ahead of time.

All major rental car companies service DIA, with customer service counters located near the baggage claim carousels. Rental agents recommend making arrangements before you arrive, as many run out of cars during peak times.

ADVANTAGE RENT-A-CAR
(800) 777-5500

ALAMO RENT A CAR
(800) GO ALAMO

AVIS RENT A CAR
(800) 331-1212

BUDGET CAR AND TRUCK RENTAL
(800) 527-0700

DOLLAR RENT A CAR
(800) 800-4000

ENTERPRISE RENT-A-CAR
(800) RENT A CAR

HERTZ RENT A CAR
(800) 654-3131

NATIONAL CAR RENTAL
(800) 227-7368

PAYLESS CAR RENTAL
(800) PAY LESS

THRIFTY CAR RENTAL
(800) 367-2277

COLORADO SPRINGS AIRPORT
7770 Milton E. Proby Parkway, Colorado Springs
(719) 550-1972
www.flycos.com

This small airport is about 90 miles south of Denver that provides service to and from 10 U.S. cities as well as Denver. Travelers whose end destination is located in Denver's southern suburbs may find it handier to use this airport, although many of its flights also land in Denver. Shuttle and van service is available to a variety of locations in the Denver area at rates that start at about $30 per person.

CENTENNIAL AIRPORT
7800 South Peoria Street, Englewood
(303) 790-0598
www.centennial-airport.com
This suburban airport southeast of Denver is among the busiest general aviation airports in the country. It features three lighted runways and an instrument-landing system for bad weather. Two full-service fixed-base operators are on hand for fueling. Private, corporate and charter planes are welcomed at this airport, although no commercial carriers provide service. Ground transportation is limited to taxis, rental cars and crew cars for corporate pilots.

Trains

DENVER UNION STATION
1701 Wynkoop Street
(303) 534-2812
www.denverunionstation.org
Like many cities in the West and Midwest, Denver has a Union Station that dates from the 19th century and fell upon hard times once planes and interstates provided other ways to travel. A consortium of planners, politicians, and developers are in the process of bringing the old dame back to life. Once the redevelopment is completed, Union Station will be the hub for ingoing and outgoing buses and light-rail trains. Restaurants and retail shops will fill its cavernous terminal, and mixed use high-rises will surround it with housing, office, and retail units. The completion date depends on several variables, not the least of which is an improvement in economic conditions that will free up construction funding. Until then, Union Station welcomes two different kinds of trains on a regular basis. The famous *California Zephyr* still runs through Denver on its east-west route between Chicago and the San Francisco Bay. It travels an amazingly scenic route across the Continental Divide and through Glenwood Canyon on its way to Salt Lake City and, eventually, Oakland, California. In the winter a ski train makes the round-trip to Winter Park (see our Ski Country chapter for details). Union Station is in Lower Downtown at Wynkoop and 17th Streets. For Amtrak information call (800) USA-RAIL. For recorded information about Amtrak departures and arrivals in Denver, call the Denver Amtrak ticket office at (303) 534-2812.

Buses

GREYHOUND BUS TERMINAL
1055 19th Street
(303) 293-6555, (800) 231-2222
www.greyhound.com
The Denver terminus for Greyhound and other private bus lines is at 20th and Curtis Streets, only a few blocks away from RTD's Market Street Station. Generally RTD provides bus service to points less than an hour away, such as Boulder and Longmont, while Greyhound passengers travel longer distances. Buses to such places as Fort Collins and the mountains originate at this 20th and Curtis station. For online fare and schedule information, visit Greyhound's Web site at www.greyhound.com, then click on station locator and follow the prompts to Colorado and Denver.

ACCOMMODATIONS

Greater Denver is a community of travelers: those who made their way here to live, those who come for vacations, and, increasingly, those who are sent here on business or for conventions. It's one of those places residents seldom have trouble convincing friends and relatives from other states to come and visit. About 12.2 million overnight visitors came to Denver in 2007, spending $2.6 billion in the process. The city's tourism bureau marked that as a record year, up 4 percent from 2006's tally. Statewide figures were also up in 2007, with twenty-eight million visitors who spent $9.8 billion.

The appetites of travelers for good accommodations are well matched by more than 45,000 hotel and motel rooms in the Denver area. Whether your tastes tend toward the magnificent or the humble, you'll find plenty of choices.

OVERVIEW

One good general source of hotel information is Visit Denver, the city's convention and visitors bureau. Its Web site is the region's best for one-stop shopping, with information about lodging options throughout Metro Denver as well as an online booking engine. It also compiles deals and seasonal specials.

Lodging prices in the mountain resorts show amazing bargains in the off-seasons of spring and fall, but Denver hotels tend to be less vacation-driven and more commerce-oriented, so don't expect much price variation from month to month. They do tend to give much better rates on weekends than during the week—a boon for the working person who wants a weekend getaway.

The average room rate is not what you'll pay all the time, of course. Most hotels have a wide range of rates on any specific day, and, in addition to good weekend rates, most offer special package deals that might include such things as tickets and a limousine ride to a show, carriage rides, or dinner at a local fine restaurant.

Business travelers tend to gravitate toward hotels near the airport, in downtown Denver, and around the Denver Tech Center to the southeast.

Those hotels in are closer to Denver International Airport than they might seem thanks to I-225, which provides a direct easterly connection with I-70 and Peña Boulevard. They also are closer than it would seem to the mountains via C-470, the beltway that loops around Denver's congested core and joins I-70 on its way west into the foothills.

Tourists will generally stay anywhere they can get a good price, but downtown is the preferred location for seeing the sights of Denver. Those interested in seeing Rocky Mountain National Park and want Denver to be part of their trip might want to choose lodgings in Denver's northwest quadrant. The near-east side of Denver is the most convenient place to stay for those visiting the Denver Museum of Nature and Science. Lodgings on the west side of Denver provide the best access to Golden, home of the Coors Brewery. The west side also allows fast access to downtown and makes for a speedy mountain getaway via I-70. Sporting events are another big attraction, and downtown or the near-west side are prime lodging locations for ready access to the Colorado Rockies at Coors Field or the Denver Broncos at INVESCO Field at Mile High.

Many hotels offer free continental breakfasts, transportation, newspapers, attached parking, and free or discounted access to nearby athletic clubs. In most of our listings, we haven't detailed all the freebies, so make a point of asking when you check in.

All hotels, bed-and-breakfasts, and hostels in this chapter accept credit cards.

To save yourself confusion and possible grief, be aware that many Englewood addresses are not actually located in Englewood. They are in unincorporated parts of Arapahoe County (which includes Englewood). We've noted this in each such listing.

HOTELS

Price Code

Our listings rate hotels according to a three-symbol price key, representing average room cost per night during the week for a double occupancy.

$.................less than $100
$$ ....$101 to $150
$$$ .... more than $150

Denver

ALOFT DENVER INTERNATIONAL AIRPORT $$
16470 East 40th Circle, Aurora
(303) 371-9500
www.starwoodhotels.com

Geared toward younger, hipper travelers, the Aloft hotel chain is known for contemporary design and online capabilities in every corner. This 144-room site near Denver International Airport doesn't disappoint, with reasonably priced loft-like rooms that offer, among more standard features, plug & play stations for charging electronics and linking them to LCD televisions. Internet access is available in the 24/7 gym, the lobby, the bar, the pool, and even at the check-in desk, where kiosks allow guests to serve themselves if they prefer. Pets and kids have programs of their own, and food is available round the clock at re:fuel, a self-service eatery.

BEST INN & SUITES AT STAPLETON $
4950 Quebec Street
(303) 320-0260, (877) 813-9355
www.bestinndenver.com

Well located in east Denver near the Stapleton neighborhood and Denver International Airport, this former Days Inn is a good bet for air travelers on a budget, business travelers on extended stays, and anyone who is relocating and needs a weekly or monthly rental. All rooms come with full kitchens and access to an outdoor pool and exercise room. Parking is free.

Ancient Secrets of the Brown Palace Hotel

The Navarre Building, 1727 Tremont Place, across the street from the Brown Palace, was built in 1890 as the Brinker Collegiate Institution, the first coeducational college west of the Missouri River. Nine years later it was converted into the Hotel Richelieu, the city's most elegant gambling house and brothel. In its basement you can still see rails disappearing into the wall where rail carts once traveled a tunnel beneath Tremont Place, delivering fine foods from the Brown Palace kitchens. Legend has it that these carts also delivered Brown Palace patrons too discreet to be seen entering and leaving the Hotel Richelieu.

BROWN PALACE HOTEL $$$
321 17th Street
(303) 297-3111, (800) 321-2599
www.brownpalace.com

This is Denver's most famous hotel, and deservedly so. If you want a central downtown location, prestigious accommodations, and a historic experience all in one, you can't do better than the Brown Palace. The list of celebs and potentates who have stayed here since Henry C. Brown opened the doors in 1892 includes the Beatles, Elvis Presley, Snoop Dogg, British royalty, kings from Sweden and Romania, Japan's emperor, U.S. presidents that stretch back to Teddy Roosevelt, and entertainment industry names ranging from Lionel Barrymore to Bruce Willis. Flo Ziegfeld wanted to stay here, but stormed off in a huff once he was told he couldn't bring in his dog.

When the Brown Palace opened, it represented the state of the art in Italian Renaissance hotel design, with a sunlit eight-story atrium lobby and tiers of balconies above white onyx walls. Today has earned Mobil's four-star and AAA's four-diamond ratings, and is a member of the National Trust Historic Hotels of America. Its 241 rooms and suites feature all the modern conveniences required by business and pleasure travelers alike, as well as pure artesian water from the deep spring that flows beneath the hotel. Executive rooms on the top two floors are equipped with Roman bathtubs and enough business equipment to outfit a home office, and two have in-room fitness machines. Three of the suites are legends in themselves, named for Presidents Ronald Regan, Teddy Roosevelt, and Dwight D. Eisenhower and decorated to reflect their namesakes. The hotel offers more than 13,000 square feet of meeting space that can accommodate groups of up to 800; three elegant restaurants and a cigar bar (the Palace Arms is described in our Restaurants chapter; the rest are covered in the Nightlife chapter); a full-service 5,200-square-foot spa; and traditional afternoon tea, served daily in the atrium lobby much as it was served a century ago. Valet parking is available for $26 a night.

THE BURNSLEY HOTEL $$
1000 Grant Street
(303) 830-1000, (800) 231-3915
www.burnsley.com
Equipped for and specializing in the extended stay, the Burnsley also compares with the finest Denver hotels. All the rooms are apartment-style

suites, and each unit has a fully equipped kitchen, separate living room, dining area, and bedroom with king-size bed. The Burnsley also has an on-site self-serve business center, an outdoor pool, and complimentary parking. If you'd prefer not to cook in your kitchen, contemporary American cuisine is available in the Burnsley Dining Room. The Lounge hosts live piano music, and live jazz on Friday and Saturday nights.

CHERRY CREEK HOTEL $$
600 South Colorado Boulevard
(303) 757-3341
www.cherrycreekhotel.com
On Colorado Boulevard in the heart of the Cherry Creek Shopping District, this hotel offers fast access to downtown as well as the district's upscale shops, restaurants, and movie theaters. Guests in its 210 rooms have access to a twenty-four-hour fitness center, a beauty salon, outdoor swimming pool, a business center, meals service at the Boulevard Bistro, and complementary parking. The hotel also can accommodate groups of up to 300 in its 12,000-square-foot meeting space.

COMFORT INN DOWNTOWN $
401 17th Street
(303) 296-0400
www.comfortinn.com
You can see the big yellow letters "Comfort Inn" high on the side of this 231-room downtown hotel. Although it's an economy hotel, it's connected by a skywalk across Tremont Place to the Brown Palace Hotel, one of Denver's luxury inns. That means guests have access to many of the same amenities, including twenty-four-hour room service, valet parking ($17 a day), and close proximity to the Brown's elegant restaurants, lounges, meeting spaces, and lobby. The Comfort Inn is pet-friendly and provides its guests with free high-speed Internet service and full American breakfasts. The State Capitol, Civic Center, and Denver Art Museum are a short walk away, as are free shuttles that provide service along the 16th Street Mall to Larimer Square and Lower Downtown.

Close-up

Denver's Most Famous Hotel

Quite simply, the Brown Palace—known locally as "The Brown"—is Denver's most famous hotel. Opened on August 12, 1892, it has conducted business every day since—never stopping to catch its breath during any of its many renovations.

The hotel was the brainchild of Henry Brown, a real estate mogul from Ohio who came to Denver in 1860 and purchased acres of land, including the triangular plot at the corner of Broadway, Tremont, and 17th Street where the hotel stands today. (Not surprisingly, the building also is triangular.)

Brown decided Denver needed a grand hotel, and, sparing no expense, he hired Denver architect Frank Edbrooke, who had also designed the State Capitol. Edbrooke chose the Italian Renaissance style, matching the grand exterior with an equally grand interior. The lobby boasted the country's first atrium, with balconies rising eight floors above ground. Cast-iron railings with ornate grillwork surround each floor. (Two of the grillwork panels are upside down—no one knows if this was an accident or intentional.)

The hotel opened with 400 guest rooms that rented for between $1 and $4 a night. It had no restaurants, but it did have at least 18 stores (most have been replaced by the two-story spa). The Brown has always had its own water supply, using deep artesian wells that provide water to every faucet in the hotel. The hotel also produces its own baked goods in a carousel oven that is one of only three in the world, including the melba toast that is considered to be a house specialty.

Over the years The Brown has housed its share of famous guests. President Dwight Eisenhower left a dent in the fireplace mantle when his erratic golf ball hit the wall. When the Beatles stayed in 1964, the hotel received a slew of applications from young girls wanting to work as housekeepers. Even the singer once-again-known-as Prince spent a few days at The Brown. He requested that the bed be stripped to the frame so that he could install his own water-filled mattress pad.

Naturally, a hotel of this caliber has had its share of unusual situations. At one time, pets were allowed in the hotel. One of the first canine visitors was a fox terrier from Philadelphia who'd inherited $50,000 from his owner and on the advice of his veterinarian came to the Rocky Mountains to cure his consumption. The pooch and the daughter of his master, as well as a nursemaid, took a seven-room suite for an indefinite period.

Another wealthy visitor arranged for his dog to be fed on hotel china with silver domes. The pampered canine did, however, have to eat on the sidewalk since his visit came after dogs were prohibited from sleeping in the hotel. Where'd this pup take naps? In a rented limo outside the hotel.

The hotel is still the palace that Henry Brown envisioned. But even those without deep pockets can enjoy it. The sophisticated afternoon tea served daily in the lobby is open to anyone willing to pay for the tea, pastries, sandwiches, and wines. If you don't want to drop a dime, free tours are offered every Wednesday and Saturday at 2 p.m.

COMFORT INN & SUITES $
4685 Quebec Street
(303) 388-8100
www.comfortinn.com
This Comfort Inn offers 138 rooms near the new Stapleton neighborhood, just 17 miles south of Denver International Airport. While full development of the former airport site will take years to complete, Stapleton already boasts a full complement of shopping and dining destinations. It also

is close to Northfield Stapleton, an outdoor shopping center built on land that once was used as landing strips. Guests of this hotel have access to a fitness center, wireless high-speed Internet service, and a free continental breakfast.

COURTYARD $$
Denver Airport
6901 Tower Road
(303) 371-0300
www.marriott.com

Billing itself as one of the hotels closest to Denver International Airport, this Courtyard property has 196 rooms and six suites, 2,900 square feet of meeting space, an indoor pool and fitness center, a full-service restaurant and bar, and complimentary parking and airport shuttle service. It also offers long-term park and fly packages.

COURTYARD DENVER DOWNTOWN $$
934 16th Street
(303) 571-1114, (888) 249-1810
www.marriott.com

Located on Denver's downtown 16th Street Mall, this elegant Courtyard gets extra points for its proximity to just about everything, including the Colorado Convention Center, federal buildings, and the University of Colorado at Denver. It has 166 rooms and 11 suites on six floors that overlook the city's lively pedestrian mall. Amenities include 3,200 square feet of meeting space, valet parking ($22 a day), a fitness center, and the Rialto Cafe, a favorite hang-out for actors and musicians booked into theaters at the nearby Denver Performing Arts Center.

COURTYARD DENVER STAPLETON $$
7415 East 41st Avenue
(303) 333-3303, (888) 238-8240
www.marriott.com

Positioned off I-70 on Denver's northeast side, this Courtyard is adjacent to the new Stapleton neighborhood and 17 miles from Denver International Airport. It offers 134 rooms, 12 suites, 1,274 square feet of meeting space, and free on-site parking. Pets are welcome. Guests have access to

an indoor pool, a fitness center, free parking, and a cafe that is open only for breakfast.

CROWNE PLAZA—DENVER INTERNATIONAL AIRPORT $$
15500 East 40th Avenue
(303) 371-9494
www.ichotelsgroup.com

Renovated in 2008, this airy hotel has 255 rooms and three suites on six floors. Meals are served in The Terrace, a full-service restaurant, and at the Mountain Terrace, the lobby lounge. Located north of the Chambers Avenue exit from I-70, it also has nearly 80,000 square feet of meeting and exhibit space, an indoor pool, whirlpool, sauna, and fitness room. Free parking is provided, as is free shuttle service to DIA and Stapleton shops. Pets are allowed.

✓ CROWNE PLAZA HOTEL DENVER $$$
1450 Glenarm Place
(303) 573-1450
www.ichotelsgroup.com

This centrally located downtown hotel was fully renovated in 2007, leaving it with 364 guest rooms and 32 suites on 16 floors. That plays up its key location within easy walking distance to the Denver Art Museum, the Denver Center for the Performing Arts, Lower Downtown, and the State Capitol. Amenities include an outdoor pool, fitness center, Off Sixteenth Restaurant, a lobby bar called The Place, and 7,387 square feet of meeting space. Self-parking is available for $10 a day.

CRYSTAL INN HOTEL & SUITES AT DIA $$
3300 North Ouray Street, Aurora
(303) 340-3800
www.crystalinns.com

Opened in 1997 to serve Denver International Airport, the Crystal Inn has 157 rooms, 17 of which are suites with a living area, refrigerator, and microwave; some have Jacuzzis. Amenities include 3,500 square feet of meeting space, an indoor pool and Jacuzzi, laundry facilities, and a fitness area. Breakfast is served daily. Free shuttle service is provided to and from DIA.

DENVER MARRIOTT CITY CENTER $$$
1701 California Street
(303) 297-1300, (800) 228-9290
www.marriott.com

Marriott's flagship hotel in the city, the Denver Marriott City Center lies in the heart of Denver's financial district, but also is less than two blocks from the city's pedestrian mall and less than four blocks from the Colorado Convention Center. It is among the city's largest hotels, with 601 rooms and 14 suites on 20 floors and 27,000 square feet of meeting space, which often is booked with high-profile fund-raisers, galas and national conferences. Allie's American Grille is open for breakfast and lunch; the subterranean D-Spot Lounge serves lunch, dinner, and cocktails. The Marriott also offers its guests a fitness center, an indoor pool, and valet parking ($27 a day).

DENVER MARRIOTT TECH CENTER $$$
4900 South Syracuse Street
(303) 779-1100
www.marriott.com

Alongside I-25 and on the edge of the city of Denver's farthest southeast corner, this hotel provides excellent access to businesses located in the Denver Tech Center. With 616 rooms and 12 suites spread across 11 floors, this hotel offers its guests breathtaking views of the mountains to the west, the plains to the east, and Denver's skyline to the northwest. It also is a favorite spot for fund-raisers and galas that make use of the 42,000 square feet usually reserved for meetings and conventions. Guests can choose from Italian food at Compari's, American dinners at The Lift, and deli foods at the Front Range Trading Post. Recreational facilities include a workout room, indoor pool, outdoor pool whirlpool and spa, steam room, and racquetball and handball courts. Valet parking is $15 a day.

DOUBLETREE HOTEL DENVER $$$
3203 Quebec Street
(303) 321-3333
www.doubletree.com

One of the finer "airport hotels," the Doubletree is just off I-70 near the developing Stapleton neigh-

borhood and offers free shuttle service to Denver International Airport as well as the Northfield Stapleton shopping center. It has an outdoor hot tub, an indoor pool, and exercise equipment for the guests in its 561 rooms. As with other large hotels, it's a major meeting venue with 32,000 square feet of meeting space, The Cafe, two lounges, an indoor pool, and a renovated fitness center.

DRURY INN DENVER EAST $
4380 Peoria Street
(303) 373-1983
www.druryhotels.com

A well-situated inn for the price-conscious traveler, the Drury Inn is off I-70 near Denver International Airport. A free breakfast bar and evening cocktails and snacks are available in the lobby. The hotel also has a heated indoor-outdoor pool and meeting rooms.

EMBASSY SUITES DENVER—AURORA $$
4444 North Havana Street
(303) 375-0400
www.embassysuites.com

While a new generation of airport hotels is springing up around Denver International Airport, this property is 12 miles west, across the Aurora city line, but it offers fine accommodations with quick access to I-70 and I-225. It has 210 two-room suites, 10,000 square feet of meeting and banquet space, Northfield's restaurant and lounge, indoor pool and whirlpool, a fitness center, 12 executive meeting suites. Guests also have access to free cooked-to-order breakfasts, evening cocktails and nonalcoholic beverages, parking, and airport shuttles.

EMBASSY SUITES DENVER SOUTHEAST $$
7525 East Hampden Avenue
(303) 696-6644
www.embassysuites.com

Of the Embassy Suites hotels in Metro Denver, this one is nearest the Denver Tech Center, with fast access to downtown as well. Each of its 206 suites has a living room and bedroom, with food service available at the Creekside Bar & Grille. Guests also can enjoy exercise facilities, an indoor pool, free cooked-to-order breakfast, and complementary evening cocktails and nonalcoholic beverages. Up to 5,750 square feet of meeting space is available.

FOUR POINTS BY SHERATON DENVER
SOUTHEAST $$$
6363 E. Hampden Avenue
(303) 758-7000
www.starwoodhotels.com

The Four Points by Sheraton Denver Southeast is about halfway between downtown Denver and the Denver Tech Center. It's a big place, with 475 rooms, and nearly 16,000 square feet of meeting space. Inside the hotel there are two restaurants and a sports bar, indoor and outdoor pools, a hydrotherapy pool, and an exercise room. You've got the Wellshire Municipal Golf Course a little more than a mile west and a lot of theaters and restaurants within easy reach.

GRAND HYATT DENVER $$$
1750 Welton Street
(303) 295-1234
www.granddenver.hyatt.com

Denver's first Hyatt is still among the city's nicest downtown hotels, earning the AAA four-diamond rating. In addition to housing guests in 513 elegant rooms, all with city views, it often hosts civic gatherings and fundraising galas in the 58,000-square-foot meeting area. Thanks to an $8 million renovation a few years back, all rooms have large flat-screen TVs, plus stereos with iPod docks and wired work stations. Meals and twenty-four-hour room service are available from 1876 Restaurant. For cozy drinks and socializing, Fireside Terrace provides the perfect venue. Its outdoor jogging track, tennis court, and swimming pool are unique to the Grand Hyatt, letting guests sample Denver's famous sunshine from within the privacy of its rooftop setting.

HOLIDAY INN DENVER—CENTRAL $$
4849 Bannock Street
(303) 292-9500
www.ichotelsgroup.com

You'll see this Holiday Inn on the west side of I-25

as you drive just north of I-70. While not the most scenic place in the area, it's well located at dead-center of Metro Denver. It's convenient for visits to the Denver Merchandise Mart, the National Western Stock Show, or for trips that could take you to all four points of Metro Denver's compass. In addition to 200 rooms and six two-bedroom suites, the hotel has an outdoor heated pool, a full-service dining room, a deli, and Teddy's Bar, a tavern that heats up whenever cowboys come to town.

HOLIDAY INN SELECT—
DENVER/CHERRY CREEK $$
455 South Colorado Boulevard
(303) 388-5561
www.ichotelsgroup.com

This hotel is within walking distance of the Cherry Creek Shopping Center (about a mile away). It was completely redecorated in 1997 and now houses 281 rooms, food service from The Front Range Grill, a martini bar, 13,464 square feet of meeting space, a fitness center, an attractive indoor pool and hot tub with skylights, and a poolside lounge.

HOTEL MONACO $$$
1717 Champa Street
(303) 296-1717, (800) 990-1303
www.monaco-denver.com

Offering guests a "world of hip, high style luxury," Hotel Monaco came on the scene in October 1998 in the renovated 1917 Railway Exchange and 1937 Moderne Title buildings. Like other urban Kimpton Hotel properties, Hotel Monaco offers 189 rooms and suites decked in plush interiors designed to create a residential feeling. Included are "tall rooms" with extra-long beds and heightened showerheads, in-room wellness programs that include the Yoga Channel and complimentary yoga accessories, bath menus, wired work stations, and CD players. Fourteen of the 32 suites contain whirlpool spas. On-site exercise facilities and the Renaissance Aveda Spa & Salon continue the pampering. Can't travel without your beloved pet? No problem. Or if you need a temporary pet, the hotel will provide a pet goldfish during your stay.

HOTEL TEATRO $$$

1100 14th Street
(303) 228-1100
www.hotelteatro.com

The boutique Hotel Teatro has made grandeur out of the historic downtown Tramway Tower, which was built in 1911. It now caters to the luxury business and upscale leisure markets from a prime downtown spot across from the Denver Center for the Performing Arts. It offers 111 well-appointed rooms that don't scrimp on anything. The hotel also houses Restaurant Kevin Taylor, a nationally known venue for elegant French cuisine, and Chef Taylor's more casual Italian room, Prima Ristorante. Meeting space is limited but does include an eighth-floor executive boardroom with a mountain view and fireplace. A fitness center and twenty-four-hour room service are available. Complimentary Cadillac Escalade service is available to guests traveling within a five-mile radius of the hotel. Valet parking is $26 a day. Pets stay free.

HOTEL VQ AT MILE HIGH $

1975 Mile High Stadium Circle
(303) 433-8331, (800) 388-5381
www.hotelvq.com

If you live and breathe football and consider yourself a Broncos fan, this is the hotel for you. It sits in the northeast corner of the INVESCO Field parking lot and provides close-up comfortable views of the stadium from many of the guest rooms. A 14-story circular tower holds 169 rooms and a penthouse restaurant called the Skybox Grill and Sports Bar, also providing great views of downtown Denver, located across I-25 from the hotel. Parking is abundant and free, as is transportation to downtown destinations. The VQ also has a seasonal outdoor pool, gift shop, and 2,000 square feet of meeting space.

✓ HYATT REGENCY DENVER AT COLORADO CONVENTION CENTER $$$

650 15th Street
(303) 436-1234
http://denverregency.hyatt.com

When it opened in 2006, this fancy 37-floor Hyatt was downtown Denver's first new high-rise in more than two decades. It also signified a new chapter in the life of the city's convention business, providing 1,100 hotel rooms and another 60,600 square feet of meeting and banquet space across the street from the Colorado Convention Center. It consists of two towers that sit side by side, with the Peaks Lounge topping the shortest of the two. Its 27th-floor windows provide one of the best panoramic views of the city, but the view doesn't come cheap. Expect to pay $10 to $12 apiece for cocktails. Guest rooms in the taller tower include 72 suites, several of which have 3,000 square feet of space and/or outside patio decks. Breakfast, lunch, and dinner are served at the Altitude restaurant, and the Strata Bar often has live entertainment. For snacks around the clock, visit Perks coffee bar and gift shop. Also on-site: a full-service health club, an outdoor lap pool, a spa, and a twenty-four-hour business lounge.

HYATT REGENCY TECH CENTER $$$

7800 East Tufts Avenue
(303) 779-1234
www.techcenter.hyatt.com

The Tech Center Hyatt is an outstanding visual landmark in this part of the Tech Center because it's surrounded by enough open space that you have great views of the Rockies even if you're standing in the parking lot. A majestic facility with 451 rooms, it's designed to give you the sense of being inside a large Colorado train station. Its grand ballroom, four banquet rooms, and 20 meeting rooms (totaling 30,000 square feet) make it a favorite meeting place for the business/convention crowd. For a scenic dining spot, visit the rooftop restaurant and lounge, or rejuvenate yourself in the indoor pool, dry sauna, sundeck, hot tub, and exercise room.

LA QUINTA INN—DENVER CENTRAL $

3500 Park Avenue West
(303) 458-1222
www.lq.com

Just north of downtown Denver, La Quinta Inn—Denver Central is a three-story, 106-room hotel with an outdoor swimming pool. A continental breakfast is offered. It's close to Coors Field and Elitch Gardens amusement park, and is also convenient to downtown, the west side, and the sports complexes of INVESCO Field at Mile High and the Pepsi Center.

LA QUINTA INN—
DENVER CHERRY CREEK $
1975 South Colorado Boulevard
(303) 758-8886
www.lq.com

It's nice to find an inexpensive but pleasant place to stay in the central business location of I-25 at South Colorado Boulevard, midway between downtown Denver and the Denver Tech Center. La Quinta Inn—Denver Cherry Creek is such a place, with the dependable La Quinta features of quiet, comfortable rooms, free high-speed Internet access, an outdoor heated pool, a continental breakfast, and a guest laundry facility. This particular area of Colorado Boulevard also has a lot of midrange and chain restaurants nearby.

LA QUINTA INN & SUITES—DIA $
6801 Tower Road
(303) 371-0888
www.lq.com

For those early-morning departures (or late-night arrivals), visitors and locals alike find this La Quinta a convenient place to stay. It has 169 rooms and a twenty-four-hour fitness center that includes an indoor pool. Guests receive a free continental breakfast.

LOEWS DENVER HOTEL $$$
4150 East Mississippi Avenue
(303) 782-9300
www.loewshotels.com

There's enough elegant Italian styling at this 11-story hotel to make your head swim. Custom furnishings, marble, murals, frescoes, and continental antiques fill the property, from lobby and library to the 5,000-square-foot meeting space. Well located near Cherry Creek, this exclusive hotel offers 183 guest rooms, including 17 suites. Those interested in exercise can take advantage of the aerobic center, which has equipment such

as exercise bikes and rowing machines. Meals are available at Tuscany Restaurant, an award-winning Italian room, and during happy hour at T-Bar lounge. Valet parking is complementary.

MAGNOLIA HOTEL $$$
818 17th Street
(303) 607-9000, (888) 915-1110
www.magnoliahoteldenver.com

One of downtown Denver's quaintest hotels, the Magnolia has 244 rooms, 117 of them suites, in a building that once housed the American National Bank. After a $20 million renovation, it opened in 1995. Guests have access to a health club, a free continental breakfast, and room service that is provided by a nearby restaurant. Other amenities include 10,000 square feet of meeting and event space, and the 3,000-square-foot Magnolia Club room, which is filled with wonderful couches, chairs and periodicals.

OXFORD HOTEL $$$
1600 17th Street
(303) 628-5400, (800) 228-5838
www.theoxfordhotel.com

The 80-room Oxford Hotel is in the heart of Lower Downtown, one of the city's liveliest urban neighborhoods, as it was when the hotel first opened in 1891. It was the Brown Palace Hotel and was designed by Frank Edbrooke, the leading architect of his day, and quickly became the preeminent lodging for travelers arriving in Denver by rail. Today its rooms are lush and modern, reflecting a thoughtful recent renovation. Reminders of its historic origins remain, including an extensive art collection, the piano of legendary gold rush queen Baby Doe Tabor, and the Cruise Room bar, which is an Art Deco jewel of a nightspot. McCormick's Fish House and Bar is located on the hotel's ground floor, although the Oxford's prime location leaves guests within walking distance of some of the city's best restaurants and nightclubs, as well as Union Station, Coors Field, the Pepsi Center, the University of Colorado at Denver, and Elitch Gardens. Amenities include 8,600 square feet of meeting space. Guests have access to The Oxford Club, a full-service health club located next door; complementary happy hour beverages in the lobby; Town Car service within a 2-mile radius; and the services of a dedicated bath butler. Pets are allowed, and valet parking is available.

QUALITY INN $
3975 Peoria Way
(303) 371-5640
www.choicehotels.com

This is one of the hotels that benefits from proximity to DIA. Located on I-70, west of the intersection with I-225, it's also convenient to the Denver Coliseum and the city of Aurora. It's a typical moderately priced business-traveler hotel. The 112 rooms are attractive but basic, with small work tables. Complimentary airport shuttle service is available, as is a free continental breakfast.

RADISSON HOTEL DENVER—
STAPLETON PLAZA $$
3333 Quebec Street
(303) 321-3500
www.radisson.com

The hotel's 300 guest rooms overlook a striking 11-story atrium lobby. Boardrooms are available on each floor, and the hotel has a 20,000-square-foot conference center, a business services center, a restaurant, and a lounge. The health club has fitness consultants, aerobics classes, racquetball courts, a year-round heated outdoor pool, a whirlpool, a steam room/sauna, and very nice exercise equipment.

RAMADA INN DOWNTOWN $$
1150 East Colfax Avenue
(303) 831-7700
www.ramadadenverdowntown.com

A few years ago urban archaeologists went looking for an underground tunnel that is said to have existed between Union Station and the Oxford Hotel. They didn't find the tunnel but, according to local legend, Teddy Roosevelt's aides once used it to whisk him from Union Station to the hotel when they decided he'd had too many spirits to be seen by the public.

East Colfax is not the most scenic street in Denver, but on this part of it you are still within the trendy urban Capitol Hill neighborhood Some fine restaurants are located within a few blocks, as are the Denver Botanic Gardens, City Park, the Denver Zoo, and the Denver Museum of Nature and Science. The Ramada has 143 rooms at very reasonable prices, with a heated outdoor pool and hot tub.

RAMADA LIMITED & SUITES DIA $
7020 Tower Road
(303) 373-1600
www.ramada.com

This Ramada is best known for its proximity to the airport. Each of its 102 rooms come with computer work stations. Other hotel amenities include, an indoor pool and spa, a business center, and a complimentary airport shuttle.

RED LION HOTEL—DENVER CENTRAL $
4040 Quebec Street
(303) 321-6666
www.redlion.com

The Red Lion is one of many hotels that serve the airport and the west side of Denver. It's located near the Stapleton neighborhood off I-70, which guarantees fast access to downtown Denver and points west. It boasts 297 guest rooms, two ballrooms, a restaurant and lounge, and 15,000 square feet of meeting space.

RENAISSANCE DENVER HOTEL $$$
3801 Quebec Street
(303) 399-7500
www.marriott.com

The Renaissance offers high-end accommodations to air travelers as well as people visiting the Stapleton neighborhood or doing business in the north and east sides of Metro Denver. Just south of I-70, it has 400 guest rooms, two Club Floors with enhanced facilities and service, a restaurant, a health club with spas, indoor and outdoor pools, and more than 25,500 square feet of meeting space. The airport shuttle is complimentary.

RESIDENCE INN BY MARRIOTT—DENVER DOWNTOWN $$$
2777 North Zuni Street
(303) 458-5318
www.marriott.com

Residence Inns are equipped as extended-stay accommodations, with per-night prices dropping substantially if you're there more than a week. Each of the 159 suites has a fully equipped kitchen and living room area. Either one-bed studio suites or two-bed, loft-style penthouse suites are available. This inn lies just off Speer Boulevard across the Central Platte Valley and I-25 from downtown Denver. It has a heated outdoor swimming pool, a hot tub, and an exercise room. It offers 900 square feet of meeting space, plus great access to Elitch Gardens and downtown.

RESIDENCE INN DENVER CITY CENTER $$-$$$
1725 Champa Street
(303) 296-3444
www.marriott.com

This new all-suite hotel opened in 2006, with 14 floors, 229 suites, and 760 square feet of meeting space. Suites range from studios to two-bedroom and come with full kitchens, flat-screen televisions, and wireless Internet. Amenities include a small fitness center, an eighth-floor patio with hot tub, and complimentary breakfast buffet and cocktails. The hotel's biggest selling point is its location—within walking distance of the 16th Street pedestrian mall, the 17th Street financial district, the State Capitol, Coors Field, and the Pepsi Center.

RITZ-CARLTON, DENVER $$$$
1881 Curtis Street
(303) 312-3800
www.ritzcarlton.com

This fine, big beauty of a hotel is Ritz-Carlton's first Denver property. It's a little more than two blocks from the 16th Street Mall and all its attractions, but is also close to the pubs, shops, and galleries of Lower Downtown, provided you can tear yourself away from the hotel's luxurious creature comforts. Each of the hotel's 202 guest rooms is more than 550 square feet. The hotel has 47 suites, 32 Club Level rooms, and one Ritz-Carlton suite. Elway's Downtown is the signature restaurant, named for retired Broncos quarterback John Elway. The property also includes 13,000 square feet of meeting space, a full-service spa, and free access to the nearby FORZA Fitness Club. Valet parking is available for $26 a day. Pets are allowed, but expect to pay a steep price for the privilege.

✓ SHERATON DENVER DOWNTOWN HOTEL $$
1550 Court Place
(303) 893-3333, (800) 444-2326
www.adamsmark.com

Formerly owned by the Adam's Mark chain, this downtown property is among the nation's largest with 1,225 rooms and 92 suites, the highest of which offer stunning panoramic views of the city. Every room is equipped with high-speed Internet service, and complimentary Wi-Fi is available in the lobby. The hotel has more than 133,000 square feet of meeting and exhibit space that can accommodate up to 3,700 people. It also houses a restaurant and Players Bar, a nightclub that often has live entertainment; a fitness center with sauna; an outdoor heated pool; and a sundeck. It's on the 16th Street Mall a block away from the Denver Civic Center, four blocks from the Colorado Convention Center, and a few blocks from the Denver Pavilions shopping center.

WARWICK HOTEL $$$
1776 Grant Street
(303) 861-2000
www.warwickdenver.com

The accommodations shine in this tony Uptown hotel, thanks to a $25 million renovation that includes leather mahogany desk chairs, 32-inch flat screen TVs, Serta Eurotop mattresses and Italian window treatments. Most of the 219 rooms have private balconies that overlook the hustle and bustle of downtown Denver. The open-air, rooftop pool is exceptional, as are the twenty-four-hour health club and Randolph's, the hotel's signature restaurant. The Warwick is known for its romantic and night-on-the-town weekend packages.

WESTIN TABOR CENTER $$$
1672 Lawrence Street
(303) 572-9100
www.starwoodhotels.com

Although the alphabet places this downtown hotel at the bottom of our list, it really deserves to be near the top. All downtown hotels can claim a central location, but the Westin is truly central to the best shopping, entertainment, and nightlife of downtown Denver. It's on the 16th Street Mall, at the Tabor Center shopping complex, a short walk away from the historic buildings, wonderful shops, and fine dining of Larimer Square and Lower Downtown. The hotel itself is palatial, with 430 rooms, a great restaurant (Augusta) and lounge, and enough ballroom and meeting space (more than 24,000 square feet, including a 200-seat auditorium) to make it one of the city's preferred gathering spots. The second-floor lobby lounge is a great place for people-watching. There's a health club, racquetball courts, an indoor/outdoor pool with a channel that allows you to swim between them, a sauna, and a nice hot tub on the western sundeck by the outdoor pool. The swanky ground-floor Palm Restaurant is the place to power lunch.

Adams County

COMFORT INN CENTRAL $$
401 East 58th Avenue, Denver
(303) 297-1717
www.choicehotels.com

This Comfort Inn is located along I-25, just north of I-70, which means it is well connected to Denver as well as being adjacent to the Merchandise Mart. It was recently renovated and has 161 rooms, a restaurant, a lounge, a balcony on every room above the second floor, an outdoor heated pool, a beauty/barber shop, and an exercise facility.

LA QUINTA INN—NORTHGLENN $
345 West 120th Avenue, Westminster
(303) 252-9800
www.laquinta.com

Northglenn is among the northernmost suburbs in Metro Denver, which makes this hotel attrac-tive to visitors arriving from the north or plan-ning trips that include visits to Rocky Mountain National Park, Loveland, or Fort Collins. The 130 rooms are basic but tidy, with the option of "King Plus" rooms that have a king-size bed, recliner chair, and two telephones. All the rooms offer free high-speed Internet access. This is the only La Quinta in Metro Denver with privileges at a nearby health club; it also has a heated outdoor pool, free continental breakfast, and guest laun-dry facility. Nearby restaurants include the Village Inn and Perkins.

RADISSON GRAYSTONE CASTLE $$
83 East 120th Avenue, Thornton
(303) 451-1002
www.radisson.com

You can't miss this place because it is, in fact, a gray stone castle. The medieval theme is carried out in some of the interior decoration, but it's a modern hotel with close to 9,000 square feet of meeting space and 133 rooms. Enjoy controlled access to the Concierge/Business Class level on the fifth floor, a restaurant, a pub lounge with extensive outdoor patio, an indoor heated swimming pool, a hot tub, a sauna, and an exercise room.

Arapahoe County

COURTYARD BY MARRIOTT— DENVER TECH CENTER $$
6565 South Boston Street
Greenwood Village
(303) 721-0300
www.marriott.com

The Courtyard by Marriott is in Greenwood Vil-lage's southeastern tip, near the intersection of I-25 and Arapahoe Road. It bills itself as "the hotel designed by business travelers," and that's appropriate for its setting in the Denver Tech Center area. The hotel has 143 large rooms, most with king-size or double beds, and suites with enclosed and living room areas. It also offers 1,304 square feet of meeting space, a mini gym, indoor pool and Jacuzzi, and the Courtyard cafe, and a lounge bar. Free shuttle rides are offered within a 5-mile radius.

DENVER MARRIOTT SOUTH $$

10345 Park Meadows Drive, Littleton
(303) 925-0004
www.marriott.com

This 279-room hotel is just 1 mile from Park Meadows Mall and is near such business hubs as the Park Ridge Corporate Center, the Meridian and Inverness office parks, and the Denver Tech Center. Its decor is inspired by the Arts and Crafts architecture popularized at the turn of the 20th century, and its main floor is anchored by a two-sided stone fireplace. Guests find themselves in what the hotel calls "rooms that work," three of which are suites. They come equipped for business with a desk, ergonomic chair, two-line phones with voice mail, and high-speed Internet access. The hotel also has 12,000 square feet of meeting space, an 8,230-square-foot ballroom, and a twenty-four-hour fitness center.

DOUBLETREE HOTEL DENVER
SOUTHEAST $$

13696 East Iliff Place, Aurora
(303) 337-2800
www.doubletree.com

This Doubletree Southeast is strategically situated alongside I-225, which translates into fast connections both south toward the Denver Tech Center and north to the airport. The hotel has 248 recently renovated rooms, each with two double beds or a king-size bed. All-day food service is provided by Fitzgerald's Restaurant.

EMBASSY SUITES DENVER
TECH CENTER $$$

10250 East Costilla Avenue, Centennial
(303) 792-0433
www.embassysuites.hilton.com

Close to the Denver Tech Center, Inverness Business Park, and I-25, this Embassy Suites has 246 two-room suites that provide a separate living room with sofa bed and table. Free transportation is provided within a 6-mile radius. The restaurant has Southwestern and traditional cuisine, and you can work your meal off at the fitness center, indoor pool, and whirlpool or at a nearby full-service health club.

HAMPTON INN DENVER/SOUTHEAST $

9231 East Arapahoe Road, Greenwood Village
(303) 792-9999
www.hamptoninn.hilton.com

Hampton Inn Denver/Southeast is one of several hotels clustered on the southeastern tip of Greenwood Village, adjacent to the intersection of Arapahoe Road and I-25. It has 150 rooms, an outdoor swimming pool, workout facilities, and a free continental buffet breakfast. It offers great access to stores in the Park Meadows shopping center.

THE INVERNESS HOTEL AND
CONFERENCE CENTER $$$

200 Inverness Drive West, Englewood
(303) 799-5800, (800) 832-9053
www.invernesshotel.com

Located west of Centennial Airport at the intersection of I-25 and County Line Road, the Inverness provides easy access to visitors traveling on to Castle Rock, Colorado Springs, and other southern destinations. Absolutely stunning from the outside, the hotel's high-tech, high-style exterior fits the state-of-the-art conference facilities inside, which host more than 750 meetings a year. They include 60,000 square feet of meeting space that has auditoriums, conference rooms, boardrooms, and breakout rooms with sophisticated audiovisual accommodations, all of which have earned certification from the International Association of Conference Centers. You don't have to attend a conference to enjoy the adjoining Inverness Golf Course, but you do have to be a hotel guest. The hotel also has a billiards room, three lighted tennis courts, indoor and outdoor pools, saunas, indoor and outdoor whirlpool baths, a full-service spa, and a health club with aerobics studio, exercise circuit, and exercise equipment. Guests in the 302 rooms can also enjoy four fine restaurants, including the award-winning, four-diamond Swan restaurant.

LA QUINTA INN—AURORA $

1011 South Abilene Street, Aurora
(303) 337-0206
www.lq.com

Aurora Regional Medical Center is right across

I-225 from this centrally located hotel, and I-225 provides quick access north to the airport and south to the Denver Tech Center and Douglas County. It has a heated outdoor pool and laundry facilities and includes a free continental breakfast and free cable TV. There are plenty of nearby restaurants. Its 121 rooms are basic but tidy and attractive, and you can opt for a "King Plus" room with a king-size bed, recliner chair, and two telephones, one of which is a dataport phone accessible to computer. Pets weighing 40 pounds or less are welcome.

RESIDENCE INN BY MARRIOTT— DENVER TECH CENTER $$$
6565 South Yosemite Street, Englewood
(303) 740-7177
www.marriott.com

Don't let the Englewood mailing address fool you. This 128-suite property is an extended-stay hotel that serves Greenwood Village and the Tech Center area. Even the "studio suites" include a fully equipped kitchen. Set in a neighborhood environment, the hotel has an outdoor swimming pool, heated spa, and complimentary passes to a nearby fitness club. There also is a fair amount of strip mall shopping, including coffee and bagel shops, nearby.

SHERATON DENVER TECH CENTER $$$
7007 South Clinton Street, Englewood
(303) 799-6200
www.starwoodhotels.com

Also boasting an Englewood mailing address, this Sheraton is situated at the far southeastern tip of Greenwood Village between the Denver Tech Center and Centennial Airport. It has great access to shopping at the Castle Rock Factory Outlet stores and Park Meadows shopping center. Guests can enjoy great views of the mountains, especially from the club levels on the 9th and 10th floors, which offer concierge service, complimentary breakfasts, and cocktails and hors d'oeuvres in the evening. Formerly a Radisson, the hotel has undergone a multimillion-dollar

renovation, including all 263 rooms. Other amenities include a 12,000-square-foot conference center, restaurant, lounge, exercise facility, outdoor heated pool, and whirlpool.

Jefferson County

DENVER DAYS INN & SUITES WEST $
15059 West Colfax Avenue, Golden
(303) 277-0200
www.daysinn.com

Another cost-conscious alternative on the west side, this Days Inn sits at a major node of the west side's transportation web. You can go straight west to Golden, hop on I-70 west or east, or jog south to catch US 6 for a fast no-stoplight run to downtown Denver. The hotel has 157 recently renovated rooms, a restaurant, heated outdoor swimming pool, hot tub, sauna, and exercise area.

DENVER MARRIOTT WEST $$
1717 Denver West Boulevard, Golden
(303) 279-9100
www.marriott.com

Denver Marriott West is set in the Denver West Office Park just off I-70 in Golden. Guests in its 305 rooms are 20 minutes from downtown Denver and 10 minutes from the foothills via I-70 west. It has indoor and outdoor pools, exercise equipment, saunas, restaurant, lounge, and 9,600 square feet of meeting space. Pets are welcome.

DENVER WEST INN $
7150 West Colfax Avenue, Lakewood
(303) 238-1251
www.denverwestinn.com

Denver West is an inexpensive choice for business and vacation travelers, with 122 rooms. It's well located near two major east-west thoroughfares (West Colfax Avenue and US 6) and less than 5 miles east of I-70, which provides easy access to both downtown Denver and the mountains. There's an on-site laundry, a seasonal outdoor pool, and free coffee 24 hours a day in the lobby.

DOUBLETREE HOTEL DENVER NORTH $
8773 Yates Drive, Westminster
(303) 427-4000
www.doubletreehilton.com

Visitors seeking ready access to Boulder County as well as Metro Denver will be well served by this Doubletree Hotel, located just north of US 36 in Westminster. It has 180 rooms, including "Jacuzzi suites," as well as 8,400 square feet of meeting space, a restaurant, a lounge, and a very nice whirlpool, sauna, indoor swimming pool, and exercise room.

HAMPTON INN DENVER—SOUTHWEST $
3605 South Wadsworth Boulevard, Lakewood
(303) 989-6900
www.hamptoninn.hilton.com

Convenient to the mountains, the city, and Jefferson County's largest businesses, the Hampton Inn has 150 rooms, an outdoor swimming pool, free continental breakfast, meeting rooms, neighborhood surroundings, and the Foothills Golf Course nearby.

HILLTOP INN GUEST HOUSE & SUITES $$
9009 Jeffco Airport Avenue, Broomfield
(303) 469-3900
www.guest-house.com

The Hilltop Inn could almost be listed in our Bed-and-Breakfast Inns section because of its quiet country-inn ambience, complimentary breakfast, and the comfortable great room with fireplace and books. Then again, it has amenities similar to those found in a hotel, such as satellite TV, Internet access, laundry room, conference and meeting rooms, and on-site catering and special-events coordinator. One might describe it as a "corporate B&B," although it's not just for the business crowd. The great room and patio are good places for wedding-related events as well as cocktail parties. Each suite has its own private entrance and fireplace, kitchenette, private bath, and king-size bed. Some have whirlpool baths and separate sitting rooms.

LA QUINTA INN—GOLDEN $
3301 Youngfield Service Road, Golden
(303) 279-5565
www.lq.com

Located near the Adolph Coors Co. brewery and the city of Golden, this hotel has 129 rooms on three floors and a heated outdoor pool. Pets are welcome.

LA QUINTA INN—WESTMINSTER MALL $
8701 Turnpike Drive, Westminster
(303) 425-9099
www.lq.com

This hotel is in an intermediate location between Denver and Boulder. It has 130 rooms, a heated outdoor pool, continental breakfast, and guest laundry facilities. Rooms are basic but tidy and attractive, and you can opt for a "King Plus" room with a king-size bed, recliner chair, and two telephones, one of which is a dataport phone, accessible to computer. Pets are welcome.

OMNI INTERLOCKEN RESORT $$$
500 Interlocken Boulevard, Broomfield
(303) 438-6600
www.omnihotels.com

This 390-room, four-diamond resort opened in 1999, providing luxury accommodations in a rather unlikely spot along the four-lane turnpike between Boulder and Denver. Over the years the surrounding area has grown up to meet it. Corporate neighbors now include the Broomfield Event Center, Corporate Express, Vail Resorts, and ConocoPhillips. The hotel boasts a 27-hole golf course, a full-service spa, an outdoor pavilion suitable for weddings and other large gatherings, a business center, a 9,000-square-foot ballroom, a conference concierge to oversee meetings and conferences, and free evening champagne in the lobby. High rollers who prefer to arrive in their own planes can land at nearby Jefferson County Airport and catch a shuttle to the Omni. The Tap Room offers microbrews, foosball, and pool tables. The Meritage restaurant is open for breakfast, lunch, and dinner.

SHERATON DENVER WEST HOTEL & CONFERENCE CENTER $$
360 Union Boulevard, Lakewood
(303) 987-2000
www.starwoodhotels.com

Aimed at the business traveler, with a full-service business center and more than 18,000 square feet of meeting space, this 242-room hotel is also one of the nicest places in Denver Metro's western quadrant. Right off US 6, it's a great staging point for trips to the mountains and business trips that involve the Denver Federal Center. It's surrounded by a thriving business and commercial area. The Sheraton has a restaurant and lounge, the full-service Aura Spa and Wellness Center, and a 10,000-square-foot health club with heated lap pool, hot tub, weight room and state-of-the-art cardio equipment. If you want to go whole hog, book a Sheraton Club room, which gives you access to the Club Lounge, and free breakfasts and afternoon hors d'oeuvres. Pets are allowed at no extra charge.

TABLE MOUNTAIN INN $$
1310 Washington Avenue, Golden
(303) 277-9898
www.tablemountaininn.com

Table Mountain is a very charming 74-room Santa Fe-style inn. Its main street location puts guests in the midst of the neighborly, small-town Golden atmosphere. It's within walking distance of the Coors Brewery and the Colorado School of Mines to boot. Its Southwestern-cuisine restaurant is not just a hotel restaurant but a west-side treasure that attracts destination diners from nearby cities.

WESTIN WESTMINSTER $$$
10600 Westminster Boulevard, Westminster
(303) 410-5000
www.starwoodhotels.com/westin

This four-diamond hotel has 369 guest rooms, 30,000 square feet of meeting space, and another 30,000 square feet of outdoor space that can be used for functions. Food service is available at O's, an elegant sit-down restaurant, and the adjacent O Room, a comfortable spot for an evening cocktail that also is known for its fresh oyster and seafood bar. An even bigger selling point is the Westin's location along the Boulder-Denver turnpike. It is situated across the boulevard from Westminster's western playground, the Promenade, so guests are within walking distance of a three-rink ice arena, a bowling alley, a dozen restaurants, a 24-screen theater, the unique Butterfly Pavilion, and the upscale Westminster Recreation Center.

BED-AND-BREAKFAST INNS

Some travelers prefer the charm, intimacy, and often historic surroundings of a bed-and-breakfast inn over the impersonal hotel/restaurant/gift shop experience. Metro Denver offers them a selection of inns that compare with the best anywhere.

In the use of our price-key symbols ($, $$, or $$$), representing double occupancy during the week, we've tried to represent the average price of accommodations for each bed-and-breakfast inn, but remember that the inns often have a limited number of rooms and have widely varying price ranges. All the inns in our listing are located in downtown Denver. All accept credit cards, and none accepts pets. None will turn away people with children, but in some cases, as indicated, children may be difficult to accommodate due to limits on room size and capacity.

CAPITOL HILL MANSION $$$
1207 Pennsylvania Street
(303) 839-5221, (800) 839-9329
www.capitolhillmansion.com

All the fineries you expect from a bed-and-breakfast inn can be found in this mansion of ruby sandstone, along with all the sense of place and history you expect in the historic inn experience. The mansion is on the National Register of Historic Places, having been built in 1891 as one of the last great mansions raised before the silver crash put a temporary damper on local development. It's in an area near the State Capitol and is surrounded by ornate historic structures built when Capitol Hill was known as "snob knob." The exterior is a turreted, balconied affair with a grand curved porch. The interior lives up to even the most aristocratic expectations, with crafted, patterned plaster and golden oak paneling opening to a dramatic sweeping staircase with stained-and-beveled-glass windows. The public parlors are inviting, and each room is individually decorated with such touches as brass beds, claw-foot tubs, private balconies, curved-glass windows, high ceilings, fireplaces, and oak floors. There is also a solarium and a hand-painted mural. Soothing music, soft lighting, and jetted tubs are among the other attractions. There are eight guest rooms, each with a private bath, some with whirlpools. Be sure to visit the Web site for photos of each.

CASTLE MARNE $$$
1572 Race Street
(303) 331-0621, (800) 926-2763
www.castlemarne.com
Victorian architecture with an eccentric flair is the charm of this bed-and-breakfast on Denver's near-east side, 20 blocks from downtown and an easier and more scenic walk from the Denver Zoo, the Denver Museum of Nature and Science, and the Denver Botanic Gardens. Built in 1889, Castle Marne really looks like a small castle. Its designer was the eclectic architect William Lang, who also designed Denver's famous "Unsinkable" Molly Brown House, now a major landmark and tourist attraction. Castle Marne is striking on the outside, stunning on the inside.

Some of the nine guest rooms have their own Jacuzzi tubs for two. Three of the rooms have private balconies with hot tubs for two. All have furnishings chosen to bring together authentic period antiques, family heirlooms, and exacting reproductions to create a mood of tranquil and elegant charm. You can find that same mood in the parlor, a serene retreat of high ceilings and glowing dark woods, and the cherry-paneled dining room. The castle's big visual treasure is what they call their Peacock Window, a circular stained-glass beauty partway up the grand staircase. The castle also has a gift shop, a game room, a Victorian garden, an airy veranda, and a guest office for the business traveler, including computer. Generally only well-behaved

children older than age 10 are allowed. Although that is the only restriction on children at Castle Marne, most rooms are subject to a maximum occupancy of two persons.

HOLIDAY CHALET $$
1820 East Colfax Avenue
(303) 437-8245, (800) 626-4497
www.holidaychalet.net
Though each of the 10 rooms has its own kitchen, Holiday Chalet serves a continental breakfast. This Victorian-charm hotel is a restored three-story brownstone mansion built in 1896 for a prominent Denver jeweler. The present owners represent the third generation of the same family that has served guests here. It's situated for easy walking to the Denver Zoo, the Denver Museum of Nature and Science, and the Denver Botanic Gardens. It's about 10 blocks from downtown.

LUMBER BARON INN & GARDENS $$$
2555 West 37th Avenue
(303) 477-8205
www.lumberbaron.com
One of Denver's newer bed-and-breakfast inns, the Lumber Baron was refurbished and opened for business in the summer of 1994, about a century after a Scottish immigrant named John Mouat built it to house his family. Mouat ran a major millwork and construction supply company, which explains the six kinds of wood used for his home's fancy woodwork. The first two floors have 12-foot ceilings and are divided among five suites, all with Jacuzzis large enough to hold two. The third floor has a 2,000-square-foot ballroom that is large enough for banquet and event rental. The entire house and grounds exemplify Victorian elegance. The inn is also known for the Murder Mystery Dinners it stages. A full breakfast is part of the package.

QUEEN ANNE BED & BREAKFAST INN $$
2147 Tremont Place
(303) 296-6666
www.queenannebnb.com
The Queen Anne Bed & Breakfast Inn is in the Clements Historic District, a restored area on the

edge of downtown that is Denver's oldest continuously occupied residential neighborhood. The inn itself consists of two adjacent Victorian buildings in the Queen Anne style of architecture, of 1879 and 1886 vintage, both of which are on the National Register of Historic Places. They boast elegantly restored interiors, period furnishings, eager service, and 14 quaintly homey rooms featuring individual baths, writing desks, piped-in chamber music, and fresh flowers. Westword, Denver's alternative newspaper, routinely rates this inn one of the city's best. Coors Field is 15 minutes away by foot.

HOSTELS

Hostels are for the truly cost-conscious traveler who is not looking for frills and is comfortable sharing a bathroom with other guests. In exchange, they provide opportunities for special camaraderie and locations that often are extremely convenient. We've listed only downtown Denver options, prices for which can be as low as $10 per night. All accept major credit cards but no personal checks. There are no age restrictions on occupants, except that people younger than age 18 cannot check in without a parent or guardian. You can get the full scoop on hostels in Metro Denver and throughout the United States by calling American Youth Hostels-Hostelling International at (202) 783-6161. For details about Rocky Mountain hostels, call this Boulder number: (303) 442-1166.

DENVER INTERNATIONAL HOSTEL $
630 East 16th Avenue
(303) 832-9996
The Denver International Hostel is just on the edge of downtown, just six blocks east of Broad-

way. All lodging is dormitory style, which means guests share bedrooms that are separated by gender. How many people share a room? It depends on the night. Bathrooms with showers are down the hall. The hostel has a communal kitchen a common room with a TV, library, and stereo, balconies, storage, and sports equipment. The office is open for check in from 8 a.m. to 10 a.m. and 5 p.m. to 10:30 p.m. There is no curfew; guests get keys to come and go as they please.

HOSTEL OF THE ROCKIES $
1717 Race Street
(303) 861-7777
www.innkeeperrockies.com
One of the newest facilities in the area, Hostel of the Rockies, can house 50 guests in dorms that hold 2 to 8 guests, as well as four private rooms. Each dorm-style room has its own bath and shower, with communal kitchen, patio area, TV and game areas. The location is central with easy bus access and dozens of restaurants within 1 mile.

MELBOURNE HOTEL & HOSTEL $
607 22nd Street
(303) 292-6386
This historic downtown hotel is located in Denver's Ballpark neighborhood, within easy walking distance of the Greyhound bus terminal, the Amtrak train station, and Lower Downtown. Rooms have sinks and beds. Bathrooms are off the hall. The 16 hostel rooms are dormitories, meaning you share a room with three to five people. Wine and beer are allowed, but no hard liquor. The Melbourne is Denver's most child-accommodating hostel. It has four family rooms, each of which has a double bed plus a set of bunk beds.

RESTAURANTS

Metro Denver residents love to dine out, and a host of innovative restaurateurs love to keep them fed. Lots of hot young chefs are busy in their kitchens creating menus that have their own distinctive Rocky Mountain charm. They emphasize game meats, trout, lamb, and other locally raised crops. (Colorado has the country's fourth-largest sheep population and is the country's largest processor of lamb.) Southwestern influences abound; many of the new chefs are liberal in their use of chilies, cilantro, tomatillos, and black beans. A number of restaurants also pride themselves on what they're able to do with buffalo meat, which is leaner than beef, and a few still hark back to Denver's frontier days by offering Rocky Mountain oysters— buffalo or cow testicles—that are sautéed or breaded and deep-fried. If a more traditional oyster is more to your tastes, they're readily available at a number of fresh seafood restaurants. Pacific Coast seafood and fish are flown in daily, and fresh sushi and sashimi are easy to find.

Reflecting the international appetites of its eating public, Metro Denver counts among its blessings several Ethiopian eateries as well as top-notch Vietnamese, Japanese, Korean, Mexican, Peruvian, and Brazilian restaurants. There are also plenty of California-influenced bistros, vegetarian specialists, and one-of-a-kind properties that reflect the talents of their chef/owners.

OVERVIEW

In this section we've left out chain restaurants such as Chili's and Pizza Hut, not because we have anything against them, but on the assumption that readers already know what to expect at these places. Locally owned chains that operate only within the Metro Denver area are included, as visitors couldn't be expected to know their fare. A national chain may have slipped into the listings here and there, either inadvertently or because omitting it would have left a particular geographic area underrepresented. In the case of exceptional merit, we've bent our rules on chains.

As you can imagine, no one book could ever describe all of Metro Denver's restaurants. We've picked out the best and the brightest, as is our mandate throughout this guide. Some are special-occasion places, others are neighborhood joints. Some are widely known local institutions, others much less so. We also tried to be clear about whether it's the food, the ambience, the crowd, the service, or all of the above that makes

a place worth a visit. Obviously we don't expect everyone to agree with all our choices, and restaurants are notoriously mutable creatures, apt to get better or worse or go out of business without warning. Hours and days of operation change, too, so we suggest you call before you go. Also, while some restaurants serve continuously, others close between lunch and dinner, so if you're looking for a mid afternoon bite, definitely call first.

For dining out with children, take a look at our Kidstuff chapter, where we have described restaurants that cater to kids or places where the entertainment is at least as memorable as the food. If you're looking to combine eating with music, or if you're more in the mood for a bar than a restaurant, check our Nightlife chapter.

We've listed restaurants alphabetically by category, based on our experience that Denverites, like most Westerners, are more inclined to drive to a destination than to pick a restaurant on the basis of what's within walking distance. At the end of each listing, however, we've given an indication of location. Downtown restaurants are all within walking (or free shuttle bus) distance of downtown hotels. Restaurants we've described as being central are usually more than a half-mile walk from downtown. Each restaurant is in Denver unless otherwise noted.

Listing by category has its own set of problems, of course. In Denver it seems that every third restaurant has at least a few Mexican-inspired items on the menu, and steak houses and seafood restaurants usually cross over into each other's territory.

Denver is very casual, and the suburbs even more so. It's possible to eat a $100 dinner in shorts and sandals and not feel out of place. But Denverites generally do dress up for a nice meal, especially at trendy bistros. In general, price is a good guide to how formal the clientele is dressed. Consider location, too. West Denver patrons are among the area's most casual, while those dining in Cherry Creek and Greenwood Village are among its dressiest.

Most of the restaurants listed in this chapter accept major credit cards; we have specified those that do not. Unless noted otherwise, all restaurants are open for lunch and dinner. Many downtown restaurants serve lunch on weekdays only.

Most Metro Denver restaurants accept local (but rarely out-of-state) checks. Occasionally a check-guarantee card is required, and, of course, there are some restaurants that don't take checks at all. Policies change, so call first if this is important to you.

Price Code

To give an idea of price, we've used the following symbols. These price codes are based on the average price of two entrees, excluding alcohol, dessert, tax, and tip.

$..................	less than $16
$$	$17 to $26
$$$	$27 to $34
$$$$	$35 and higher

AFRICAN

THE ETHIOPIAN RESTAURANT　　$-$$
2816 East Colfax Avenue
(303) 322-5939

The small, homey Ethiopian Restaurant has a warm pink dining room and serves lunch and dinner daily at reasonable prices, plus an exceptional Ethiopian honey wine. No credit cards. (Central/East)

MATAAM FEZ MOROCCAN
RESTAURANT　　$$$$
4609 East Colfax Avenue
(303) 399-9282
www.mataamfez.com

A meal at Mataam Fez is more than a meal, it's an experience. A five-course Moroccan feast is served in sumptuous tented surroundings with entertainment on the weekends. Patrons sit on the floor with their shoes off and eat with their fingers. This restaurant is open for dinner only. There also is a location in Boulder. (Central)

QUEEN OF SHEBA ETHIOPIAN
RESTAURANT　　$
7225 East Colfax Avenue at Quebec Street
(303) 399-9442

This is a small, casual spot that offers smiling service. Prices at Queen of Sheba are rock bottom. A favorite with meat eaters is the shish kebab. Beer and wine are the only alcohol served. Queen of Sheba serves lunch and dinner and is closed on Monday. (Central/East)

AMERICAN

ALTO RESTAURANT　　$$$
(303) 893-2586
www.altodenver.com

Opened in 2007 by Cherry Creek restaurateur Greg Goldfogel, this contemporary downtown bistro is off to a good start, thanks to elegant decor, refined service, and creative New American cuisine. The menu varies by season, but previous entrees included braised buffalo short ribs, thin-crust pizza, ahi tuna tartare, Colorado rack of lamb, and lemon olive oil cake. Vegetarian options are plentiful and just as innovative. The bar books live music Wednesday through Saturday, and weekend cabaret acts provide a change of pace. It's open daily for lunch and dinner. (Downtown)

AVENUE GRILL $$-$$$
630 East 17th Avenue
(303) 861-2820
www.avenuegrill.com
Denver's movers and shakers gather at the long bar here and do business at the banquettes with their cellular phones. This is not a place to hide out in a dark corner, as there are none. So what's to eat? Salads, sandwiches, burgers, a few Southwestern dishes, a tasty cioppino, and some killer desserts. It's a great people-watching spot on Denver's "restaurant row." Lunch and dinner are served daily, except Sunday when it's open for dinner only. (Central)

BANG! $$
3472 West 32nd Avenue
(303) 455-1117
www.bangdenver.com
This popular Highland spot seats about 30 inside and 16 outside on the patio. It can be noisy and crowded, but that's part of the charm. Downhome specialties include meat loaf and catfish, and there are less traditional offerings as well. Beer and wine are served. Lunch and dinner Tuesday through Saturday, brunch on Saturday, closed on Sunday. (Northwest)

BAYOU BOB'S $
1635 Glenarm Place
(303) 573-6828
www.bayoubobs.com
Itching for some jambalaya, red beans and rice, a po'boy sandwich, shrimp gumbo, or fried catfish? Bayou Bob's is one of the few places in town that serves authentic Louisiana Cajun food. Open for lunch and dinner daily, with slightly later hours Wednesday through Saturday. (Downtown)

THE BROKER $$$-$$$$
821 17th Street
(303) 292-5065
www.thebrokerrestaurant.com
The downtown Broker is situated in what was once a bank and seats some diners at tables in the old vault. It serves classic and contemporary American entrees and is known for its steaks, ice-cold peeled shrimp, good wine lists, and excellent desserts. This downtown restaurant is a popular place for a business lunch and is open for dinner seven days a week, and for lunch weekdays only. This is one of the rare Denver dining spots where the attire tends to be somewhat dressy, though it's not required. (Downtown)

CAFE STAR $$-$$$
3201 East Colfax Avenue
(303) 320-8635
www.cafestardenver.com
Chef Rebecca Weitzman has quickly turned this relatively new spot into the place to go for just about any reason—a fine meal, a quick cocktail, or shared appetizers. Our good friend Lisa recommends the pot pies, especially the ones with lobster in them. Cafe Star is open for lunch and dinner, with Sunday brunches, but is closed on Tuesday. (Central)

i Denver has always been a town whose inhabitants enjoy dining out. In fact restaurants are often filled all week long. If a restaurant takes reservations, make them. Otherwise count on long wait lists or plan to dine very early or late.

THE CHERRY CRICKET $-$$
2641 East 2nd Avenue
(303) 322-7666
www.cherrycricket.com
The Cherry Cricket is known for famously juicy burgers and an extensive roster of microbrews. The salads are substantial, fresh, and quite good. This is a loud neighborhood joint that goes crazy

on St. Patrick's Day. Once just a blue-collar dive, it has gained a substantial following among the monied shoppers and Cherry Creek residents who enjoy its comfortable simplicity. It's open for lunch and dinner daily. (Cherry Creek)

CROC'S MEXICAN GRILL $$
1630 Market Street
(303) 436-1144
www.crocsmexicangrill.com
A high-energy restaurant with brick walls, a big bar, and a 20-foot-long crocodile suspended from the ceiling, Croc's serves mainly Mexican food at reasonable prices. There are also burgers, seafood, and a wall-to-wall happy hour. Lunch and dinner are served daily in addition to a weekend brunch of Mexican omelets, huevos rancheros, and breakfast burritos. (Downtown)

DIXONS DOWNTOWN GRILL $-$$
1610 16th Street
(303) 573-6100
www.dixonsrestaurant.com
Dixons is the place to go when everyone is hungry for something different. You'll find steaks, seafood, a chili plate, Southwestern fare, pastas, burgers, and more. The atmosphere is relaxed, with large booths and an oak bar area. Popular items include the penne pasta with sausage, the peppercorn steak, and the herb-baked salmon. Dixons is owned by the same folks who own Racine's on Bannock. It's open daily for breakfast, brunch, lunch, and dinner. (Downtown)

EL RANCHO RESTAURANT & MOUNTAIN LODGE $$$
El Rancho exit 252 off I-70, El Rancho
(303) 526-0661
www.historicelrancho.com
A restaurant and lodge about 18 miles west of Denver near Genesee, El Rancho has a rustic log cabin atmosphere and seven fireplaces. The main dining room has a view of the Rocky Mountains and serves such regional specialties as buffalo, elk, and trout. The cinnamon rolls are locally famous. Open since 1948, El Rancho serves lunch, dinner, and a Sunday breakfast buffet. Live entertainment is offered on some weekend nights, and the rustic Trading Post gift shop is guaranteed to transport visitors back in time to the 1950s. The outdoor patio with its great views makes a meal special. The eight lodges are fun for a weekend getaway or for out-of-town visitors. (West suburbs)

GIGGLING GRIZZLY $-$$
1320 20th Street
(303) 297-8300
www.giggling-grizzly.com
You can tell from the big grizzly (yes, giggling) painted outside that this is a fun place to be. It's really more of a bar than a restaurant, but you can get burgers, sandwiches, and other comfort food snacks. The crowd tends to be young, with music best described as rockin' and on the loud side. Giggling Grizzly does a robust business, especially during Rockies games. It's a good place to sample LoDo fever and, well, drink lots of alcohol. The Grizzly serves dinner nightly. (Downtown)

GOVNR'S PARK $
672 Logan Street
(303) 831-8605
www.govnrspark.com
Named for its proximity to the governor's mansion across the street, this is a popular spot with the Friday-night crowd looking for the relaxed after-work scene. Once a dry cleaners, Govnr's Park has been a big, boisterous neighborhood restaurant and tavern since it opened in 1976, with a massive beer list and a menu full of sandwiches, burgers, and tavern dishes. The front patio, shaded by a large awning, is especially nice for an informal Sunday brunch. Lunch and dinner are served every day. Half of Govnr's is a pool room that draws a mainly twenty-something crowd. (Central)

GUNTHER TOODY'S $
4500 East Alameda Avenue, Glendale
(303) 399-1959

9220 East Arapahoe Road, Englewood
(303) 799-1958

7355 Ralston Road, Arvada
(303) 422-1954 8266

West Bowles Avenue, Littleton
(303) 932-1957

301 West 104th Street, Northglenn
(303) 453-1956
"Howdy Doody. . . . Gunther Toody's, this is San-dra Dee, what's shakin' bacon?" That's the way the phone gets answered when you call one of these local spots. You'll feel like you're in a scene in the movie *Grease* at this '50s-concept diner with gum-chewing waiters and waitresses. The food is classic American fare, and the milk shakes will bring out the kid in you. We highly recommend it for children. Breakfast, lunch, and dinner are served every day. (East, Southeast, West, and North suburbs)

JONESY'S EAT BAR $$
400 East 20th Avenue
(303) 863-7473
www.jeatbar.com
Located in a row of once-dilapidated storefronts, Jonesy's is a key player in the gentrification process of an urban area now known as Uptown. Its dining room is housed in the original soda fountain of a 1950s pharmacy, with a billiards room next door called The Horseshoe Lounge. Both are reminders that the neighborhood has history. Owners describe the food as gastropub fare, with beers and wines as prominent on the menu as salads, sliders, appetizers, and entrees such as shredded lamb and green onion gnocchi. Open daily for dinner and on Saturday and Sunday for brunch. Reservations are recommended. (Uptown)

LODO'S BAR & GRILL $$
1946 Market Street
(303) 293-8555
www.lodosbarandgrill.com

LODO'S HIGHLANDS RANCH
8545 South Quebec Street, Highlands Ranch
(303) 346-2930

LODO'S WESTMINSTER
3053 West 104th Avenue, Westminster
(303) 635-8025
The rooftop deck of the original downtown location near the home-plate entrance to Coors Field is legendary, letting you drink in the view while enjoying your meal. Meanwhile, the new Highlands Ranch south location offers a rooftop deck with stunning views of the Denver skyline and the mountains, including Pikes Peak. The newest location is perched on a bluff that overlooks the northern suburbs and has western views of Longs Peak. All three properties have big-screen TVs for watching sports, 24 beers on tap, and eats that include fish and chips, shrimp, fajitas, pasta, sandwiches, and salads. Lunch and dinner are served daily at both locations. (Downtown, South Central, North suburbs)

MARLOWE'S $$$
501 16th Street
(303) 595-3700
www.marlowesdenver.com
The epitome of Denver's singles scene in the 1980s, Marlowe's remains a popular gathering spot for lunch, dinner, or after work. The restaurant serves steaks, chops, seafood, salads, pasta, and fresh Maine lobster. Marlowe's features an extensive martini list as well as daily happy hour specials. Located across from Denver Pavilions, it boasts a nice patio on the 16th Street Mall with prime people-watching. Lunch and dinner are served daily. (Downtown)

MEL'S BAR & GRILL $$$$
235 Fillmore Street
(303) 333-3979
www.melsbarandgrill.com
New American fare and an upscale yet comfortable atmosphere are on the menu at Mel's. A prime Cherry Creek location, good wine list, and creative beef, chicken, and pasta choices make this a popular spot. The cozy bar draws folks in their 30s to 50s. Live jazz is performed most nights. It's open for lunch on weekdays and for dinner Monday through Saturday. (Cherry Creek)

MERCURY CAFE $-$$
2199 California Street
(303) 294-9281
www.mercurycafe.com
In addition to hosting one of the best and most eclectic performing arts scenes in town, the funky, friendly Mercury Cafe serves local, natural, or organic meals in its bohemian Ballpark space. It's open for breakfast and lunch on Saturday and Sunday, and for dinner Tuesday through Sunday. The menu is as varied as the entertainment lineup; a meal here might include vegetable, garlic, or bass linguine; marinated and breaded tofu; or grilled elk or chicken shish kabobs. Its owners are as green as they come, powering the place with wind and solar energy, and filling their gas tanks with recycled cooking oil. Closed Monday, and they do not accept credit cards. (Downtown/Central)

MUSTARD'S LAST STAND II $
2081 South University Boulevard
(303) 722-7936
You can't get more American than hot dogs, french fries, and root beer floats, all of which this plain little joint does to perfection. Its location near the University of Denver guarantees a steady clientele, but older folks sneak over for the Polish sausage, too. The original Mustard's Last Stand is at 1719 Broadway (at Arapahoe Avenue) in Boulder, (303) 444-5841. It's open daily; credit cards not accepted. (South Central)

MY BROTHER'S BAR $
2376 15th Street
(303) 455-9991
The entrance to this corner tavern looks less than inviting, but everyone is welcome behind the inauspicious doors. A mixed crowd gathers in this historic watering hole for burgers (a tasty vegetarian version is available) and beers. The pleasantly shaded patio out back is a hidden delight. It's a good place to keep in mind when you're hungry late at night, as they serve past midnight. It's closed on Sunday. (Downtown/Platte River area)

NINE 75 $$$
975 Lincoln Street
(303) 975-0975
This Golden Triangle hot spot is hard to forget, and not just because the name is actually the address and the phone number. It's located in a chichi high-rise across the street from Denver's premiere jazz club and attracts movers and shakers well into the evening. Those fans line up for big dishes to share with friends and small dishes to mix and match. Among my friend Lisa's favorites are the creamed spinach, baked mac and cheese, crabmeat California rolls (which look more like Napoleons) and, for dessert, a plateful of cotton candy. The owners call it comfort food with a twist. Open for lunch Monday through Friday and dinner Monday through Saturday. (Central)

PALACE ARMS $$$$
321 17th Avenue
at the Brown Palace Hotel
(303) 297-3111
www.brownpalace.com
The poshest of the Brown Palace's four restaurants, the Palace Arms is one of the very few places in Denver where gentlemen are urged, but not required, to wear jackets and ties. The setting and service are superb, holdovers from a more formal era. The room is decorated with antiques dating from the 18th century, including a pair of dueling pistols said to have belonged to Napoleon. The fare is contemporary regional cuisine, and the award-winning wine list features close to 1,000 varieties. Reservations are strongly recommended. Open daily for dinner. (Downtown)

THE PALM $$$$
1201 16th Street
(303) 825-7256
www.thepalm.com
This is the place for the gigantic-martini power lunch. The Westin at Tabor Center provides the backdrop for this top-notch restaurant, where Denver's business set devours thick slabs of dry-aged beef as heartily as talk of mergers and acquisitions. Lobsters are so big they once

needed their own apartment. Caricatures of Denver's noted and notorious hang on the wall. Everything is a la carte, so bring your American Express card. Lunch and dinner Monday through Friday; dinner only on weekends. Reservations are recommended. (Downtown)

PARAMOUNT CAFE $
519 16th Street
(303) 893-2000
www.paramountcafe.com

A favorite for people-watching, the Paramount's outdoor seating area extends into the 16th Street pedestrian mall. This casual lunch or dinner spot serves burgers, sandwiches, and Tex-Mex food at low prices in a setting reminiscent of a '50s diner. Happy hour after work is a lively scene. Lunch and dinner are served daily. (Downtown)

PEARL STREET GRILL $-$$
1477 South Pearl Street
(303) 778-6475
www.pearlstreetgrilldenver.com

A big friendly bar and restaurant with a particularly nice outdoor patio, the Pearl Street Grill has history. It's part of the commercial street that anchors an early-day neighborhood that sprung up south of downtown Denver and has been rediscovered by a new generation of young families and singles. The grill is best known as a casual spot for comfort foods such as pot roast and meatloaf, with a fair number of soups, salads, burgers, and beers to choose from. It serves lunch and dinner every day and offers brunch on Sunday. No reservations are taken. (South Central)

POTAGER RESTAURANT AND
WINE BAR $$$
1109 Ogden Street
(303) 832-5788
www.potagerrestaurant.com

Every so often you come across a restaurant you can't wait to tell your friends about. Potager is one of them. It's everything a great restaurant should be: intimate, friendly, and unpretentious, plus the food is sublime. Potager opened in 1997 in the

heart of Capitol Hill and draws raves from everyone who discovers its elegant yet cozy space. Chef Teri Rippeto is creative and bold in her choices. She specializes in fresh, local, seasonal food and changes the menu monthly. The decor is stark yet soft, with natural wood and nearly bare walls. Dinner is served Tuesday through Saturday. Checks are not accepted. (Central)

RACINE'S $-$$
650 Sherman Street
(303) 595-0418
www.racinesrestaurant.com

Racine's is a large, laid-back Capitol Hill landmark that is busy from breakfast through the last dinner, which on weekends is nearly 11 p.m. People love it for the urbane decor, the hip staff, and the powerbrokers who come to do business in corner booths. The menu has something for everyone, from sandwiches to pastas to a selection of Mexican entrees. An in-house bakery makes carrot cake, muffins, and Racine's locally famous brownies (in addition to the usual chocolate with or without nuts, flavors include white chocolate, peanut butter, and German chocolate)—all ready to be packaged up and taken home. (Central)

i In 1944 Louis Ballast dropped a slice of cheese onto a hamburger at his Denver drive-in restaurant and patented the invention as "the Cheeseburger." Other claimants can take up their case with the Denver Metro Convention & Visitors Bureau, which stands by this bit of trivia.

REIVER'S $$
1085 South Gaylord Street
(303) 733-8856
www.reiversbarandgrill.com

A popular watering hole in the Washington Park neighborhood, Reiver's is best known for its burgers and casual atmosphere. Among the house specialties are shepherd's pie, green chile and chicken fried steak, although the appetizer and salad menus are deep and varied. After your meal, stroll around the neighborhood and window-shop. Reservations are accepted, except on Friday evening. Lunch and dinner are served every day. It's also a great place for a casual Sunday brunch. Free valet parking is offered Thursdays, Fridays, and Saturdays. (South Central)

RIALTO CAFE $$$$
934 16th Street
(303) 893-2233
www.rialtocafe.com
Housed on the ground floor of a Courtyard by Marriott on Denver's busy 16th Street pedestrian mall, this great-looking restaurant features dark woods, a pressed-tin ceiling, and motifs from the '20s and '30s. The food is New American cuisine, served by a well-trained and attentive staff. Friday and Saturday evenings are good for martinis and people watching. Breakfast, lunch, and dinner served daily. (Downtown)

ROCKY MOUNTAIN DINER $-$$
800 18th Street, at Stout Street
(303) 293-8383
www.rockymountaindiner.com
A retro-Western diner with handsome green-leather booths, the Rocky Mountain Diner issues a down-home welcome on sign that says simply, GET IN HERE! Once inside, guests can choose from such things as buffalo meat loaf, chicken-fried chicken, and cowboy steak with mashed potatoes and vegetables. Save room for the white-chocolate black bottom banana-cream pie. Lunch and dinner are served daily. Brunch is served Saturday and Sunday. (Downtown)

SHIP TAVERN $$$
321 17th Street
at the Brown Palace Hotel
(303) 297-3111
www.brownpalace.com
In the Brown Palace Hotel (but accessible through its own entrance off Tremont Place), the Ship Tavern is modeled after a classic English pub and is crammed with replicas of actual ships from America's clipper period. The food is classic, too:

prime rib, Rocky Mountain trout, chicken, lamb, and sandwiches. Lunch and dinner are served daily; live entertainment is booked Wednesday through Saturday evenings. (Downtown)

STEUBEN'S $$$
523 East 17th Avenue
(303) 830-1001
www.steubens.com
Once a rundown auto shop, Steuben's is in one of the hottest areas of town. A trace of the old garage decor lingers in the renovated space, although there's nothing rundown about it now. Don't expect diner prices for dishes that mix nostalgia—tomato soup, deviled eggs, iceberg wedge with blue cheese dressing, milkshakes, grilled cheese, butterscotch pudding—with new takes on regional specialties—cayenne etouffe, Maine lobster roll, spicy pinto bean sloppy joe. Steuben's is the second Denver restaurant from Josh and Jen Wolkon and chef Matt Selby. Their first was Vesta Dipping Grill in LoDo. Open daily for lunch and, dinner, with Sunday brunch. Its kitchen stays open until 11:00 p.m. on Sundays and weekdays, and until midnight on weekends. (Uptown)

STRINGS $$$
1700 Humboldt Street
(303) 831-7310
www.stringsrestaurant.com
Diners rate this classy spot as one of Denver's best. They like its distinctively eclectic California-Italian menu of pasta, seafood, warm salads, and grilled dishes; appreciate the artistic presentation; enjoy its extensive wine list; and like its friendly owner, Noel Cunningham. The place is a perfect example of the vibrant spirit that typifies Denver, where the casual and the elegant mingle. It's open for lunch on weekdays, and daily for dinner. Reservations are recommended. (Uptown)

TRINITY GRILLE $$$
1801 Broadway
(303) 293-2288
www.trinitygrille.com

A popular spot for lunching lawyers and bankers, the Trinity Grille is brisk and shiny with polished wood, brass railings, and a black-and-white tile floor. Steaks, soups, sandwiches, fish, and homemade pasta dishes are the mainstay of the menu. The crab cakes, in particular, are highly recommended. It serves dinner Monday through Saturday and lunches on weekdays only. Closed Sunday. (Downtown)

VESTA DIPPING GRILL $$$-$$$$
1822 Blake Street
(303) 296-1970
www.vestagrill.com

Vesta was Josh and Jen Wolkon's first restaurant, providing Denver diners with relaxed yet upscale dining in a renovated warehouse with exposed brick walls, high-backed booths, and funky lighting. Its renovation was so stunning, in fact, that the American Institute of Architects singled it out among Colorado restaurants. Guests start off with a variety of appetizers, and move on to either skewered dinners or more traditional entrees, all served with a choice of three homemade sauces that give the meal spice, pizzazz, and variety. Sharing is encouraged. Dinner is served nightly, with the kitchen open until 10 p.m. Sunday through Thursday and 11 p.m. weekends. Reservations are recommended. (Lower Downtown)

WAZEE LOUNGE & SUPPER CLUB $
1600 15th Street
(303) 623-9518
www.wazeesupperclub.com

It's back to the '40s, or some other unspecified prior decade, at this laid-back pizza-and-burgers joint that has been open since the 1970s. A Lower Downtown favorite for years, it's hard to say just what makes this place so neat. The diverse crowd? The bohemian ambience? The pizza? Regardless, it remains popular year after year. Lunch and dinner served daily, with late-night until 1 a.m. Monday through Saturday. (Downtown)

ASIAN

BA LE SANDWICH $
1044 South Federal Boulevard
(303) 922-2129

Denver Post restaurant critics love Ba Le for a number of reasons. First, it's located in the heart of the city's largest Asian neighborhood, which means its diners know what they're looking for. Second, it specializes in the classic Banh Mi sandwich, a Southeast Asian staple made of French bread, pork pâté, carrots, cabbage, and chili. Third, prices are reasonable—just $2.50 for the sandwich, which is best when washed down with a sugarcane soda. (South Central)

BD'S MONGOLIAN BARBECUE $$$
1620 Wazee Street
(303) 571-1824
www.bdsmongolianbarbeque.com

Once you choose your meats, vegetables, and sauce, the cook stir-fries it while you watch. BD's is a no-frills way to dine when you're tired of all the upscale joints around town. Lunch and dinner daily. (Downtown)

DOMO RESTAURANT $$$
1365 Osage Street
(303) 595-3666
www.domorestaurant.com

No sushi. No upscale see-and-be-seen surroundings. Domo is all about an authentic Japanese country food experience. Teriyaki meats and fish, for example, are flavored like the real thing, not layered in gooey sauce. Lunch and dinner Thursday through Saturday. Reservations are strongly suggested, but are accepted only for parties of six or more. (Central)

IMPERIAL CHINESE RESTAURANT & LOUNGE $$
431 South Broadway
(303) 698-2800
www.imperialchinese.com

Imperial does indeed live up to its name, with opulent decor that resembles the set of *The Last*

Emperor. And better, the food matches the quality decor. The restaurant specializes in seafood, but don't pass up the sesame chicken or, if you're in the mood for the royal treatment, the fabulous Peking duck. Reservations are accepted for parties of four or more only. Lunch and dinner are served daily. (Central)

J'S NOODLES $
945-E South Federal Boulevard
(303) 922-5495
Many of Metro Denver's best and most authentic Asian restaurants are located along South Federal Boulevard. For many Thai aficionados, this plain storefront restaurant tops the list for its combination of outstanding food and low prices. Try a noodle bowl at lunch or a curry for dinner. J's Noodles is open Tuesday through Sunday. (Southwest)

LITTLE OLLIE'S ASIAN CAFE $$
2364 East 3rd Avenue
(303) 316-8888
www.littleolliescherrycreek.com
Little Ollie's puts a new twist on old favorites, with dishes such as stir-fried lobster and steamed sea bass. You might get a personal greeting at the door from owner Charlie Huang, and with a patio that's open year-round (heated in winter), you can always indulge in some sidewalk dining. Lunch and dinner are served daily, with daily lunch specials offered as well. (Cherry Creek)

NEW ORIENT $$
10203 East Iliff Avenue, Aurora
(303) 751-1288
A small, simply decorated restaurant, New Orient serves Vietnamese, Chinese, and "Amerasian" cuisine, updating traditional recipes with creative touches. This means that you can have roast-duck soup and pineapple-paprika shrimp for lunch with cappuccino mud torte for dessert. Seafood is a specialty at this nonsmoking restaurant. Reservations are recommended on the weekend. It's closed on Monday. (Southeast)

NEW SAIGON $$
630 South Federal Boulevard
(303) 936-4954
www.newsaigon.com
Yet another Federal Boulevard restaurant, New Saigon is a perennial winner in Westword's "Best Vietnamese Restaurant" category. One of Denver's first Vietnamese restaurants, it has been in business since 1987. Despite tons of competition, its loyal fans can't be lured away from the spicy beef and the acclaimed fish dishes. New Saigon offers great food in slightly more upscale surroundings than its Federal Boulevard counterparts. Lunch and dinner are served daily. (Southwest)

PARALLEL SEVENTEEN $$
1600 East 17th Avenue
(303) 399-0988
www.parallelseventeen.com
For small plates served in a small, cosmopolitan space, Parallel Seventeen is unparalleled. The food is fancy even though the prices aren't, and most cocktails on the large drink menu come with lychee fruit garnishes. Family recipes have been modernized, and the owners urge their guests to eat family style. Try the sticky Vietnamese barbecued ribs or the calamari fried with lemons and limes and served with mango on a bed of greens. Open for dinner daily and lunch on weekdays. (Uptown)

P.F. CHANG'S CHINA BISTRO $$
1415 15th Street
(303) 260-7222
www.pfchangs.com

8315 South Park Meadows Center Drive, Littleton
(303) 790-7744

1 West Flatlrons Circle, Broomfield
(720) 887-6200
Don't expect the usual sweet-and-sour chicken at Chang's. In fact, don't expect the usual Chinese fare at all; Chang's does it with a stylish twist. From crab wontons to mouth-melting flourless chocolate cake, P.F. Chang's serves flavorful

meals to the LoDo crowd. And the decor speaks LoDo's elegant language: exposed brick, polished woods, and ornate sculptures. Our only gripe: Entrees can be a bit sweet. Enlist the excellent wait staff to help ensure the best combination of items. Appetizers are a must. Our favorites: shrimp dumplings and lettuce cups stuffed with chicken. And don't forget the garlic snap peas, a P.F. Chang signature side dish. Lunch and dinner daily. Other P.F. Chang's restaurants operate in Park Meadows, Lakewood and Aurora. (Downtown, South, West, and Northwest suburbs)

SONODA'S $$$
1620 Market Street
(303) 595-9500
www.sonodassushi.com

550 Broadway
(303) 991-1000

Park Meadows Shopping Center, Littleton
(303) 708-8800

South Parker Road, Aurora
(303) 337-3800

550 Broadway
(303) 991-1000

Proprietor Kenny Sonoda calls his casual restaurants "Japanese seafood houses and sushi bars," and, indeed, the menu features changing seafood specials depending on what's fresh and available. His first one operated on Market Street in Lower Downtown for years before the second was opened, then two more restaurants followed quickly. All four locations get good reviews for freshness and flavor. Sonoda's restaurants serve lunch and dinner daily. (Downtown, Central, South, and Southeast)

SUSHI DEN $$$
1487 South Pearl Street
(303) 777-0826
www.sushiden.net

A chic, modern restaurant that just happens to be a sushi bar, Sushi Den does a superb job with cooked fish, too. The standout is the steamed

fresh fish in a bamboo basket. The sushi bar is a visual feast, and the dining room is modern with lots of black, granite, and concrete. Presentation here is artful, from decor to plate. It's open weekdays for lunch and daily for dinner, with service until midnight on weekends. (South Central)

THAI BISTRO $$
5924 South Kipling Street, Littleton
(720) 981-7700
www.thaibistro.net

Thai Bistro offers a wide array of menu choices that range from Pad Thai to curries to Thai tapioca, all excellent picks. The menus are user-friendly, and the servers will help guide you through the choices. Chef Noi Phromthong focuses on balancing sweet and sour, spicy and mild. Lunch and dinner are served Monday through Saturday. (Littleton)

T-WA INN $$
555 South Federal Boulevard
(303) 922-2378
www.twainn.com

The T-Wa Inn was Denver's first Vietnamese restaurant, opening in 1984. Its huge menu emphasizes seafood—a point driven home by the aquarium filled with giant silver arrow fish (for decoration only). The Asian decor is exotic without being overwhelming. Dinner dishes include a variety of vegetarian and meat choices. Should you desire Vietnamese coffee, it will be French-pressed for you at the table. Lunch and dinner served every day. (Southwest)

TOMMY'S THAI $
3410 East Colfax Avenue
(303) 377-4244
www.thommysthaidenver.com

Tommy's has been a staple on Capitol Hill since 1988, but its popularity has grown as seedy Colfax Avenue gentrifies. Once a narrow one-room joint, Tommy's has been expanded into a hip place for young and old. Although Chinese food is served, the best items on the menu are the Thai dishes. Those of note include the hot and creamy tom kha gai soup, fried tofu wedges, pork shumi dumplings, spring rolls, and, for the traditional Pad Thai with Thai iced coffee. (Central)

i Some of Denver's most unusual restaurants can be found in the small one-to-five-shop shopping centers in Denver's older neighborhoods.

YOISHO RESTAURANT $
7236 East Colfax Avenue
(303) 322-6265
A tiny Japanese restaurant with a devoted East Denver following, Yoisho has a simple menu with mostly fried Japanese dishes (no sushi here) and notable gyoza dumplings. There is no liquor license. Yoisho serves lunch and dinner daily. (East)

BAKERIES

DEVIL'S FOOD $
1024 South Gaylord Street
(303) 733-7448
www.devilsfoodbakery.com
Devil's Food started as a Washington Park bakery whose motto was "Open Bright and Surly." Then came the breakfast and lunch crowds The luscious homemade baked goods are present throughout the day, either over the counter for walk-ins or in the funky restaurant next door. Servers are as artistic as the atmosphere, and we've been told the owners are as mellow as their day is long. Open daily for breakfast and lunch. (East Denver)

OMONIA BAKERY $
2813 East Colfax Avenue
(303) 394-9333
This authentic Greek bakery will satisfy a craving for baklava, koularakia, kataifi, or galatatoboureko. A napoleon is available, too, and, of course, there's strong coffee to go with whatever sweet your heart desires. It's open daily until 9 p.m. and doesn't accept credit cards. (Central)

RHEINLANDER BAKERY $
5721 Olde Wadsworth Boulevard Arvada
(303) 467-1810
www.rheinlanderbakery.com
Authentic German rye bread tops the list at this charming family-run old-world bakery in Arvada's historic Olde Town district, which has been operating since 1963. Coffee cakes, Danish pastries, European-style tortes, and cookies are available, too. Bakers also do a wide range of special interest items with no gluten, no wheat, and no sugar. The Rheinlander is open seven days a week. (West suburbs)

ROSALES MEXICAN BAKERY $
2636 West 32nd Avenue
(303) 458-8420
This family-operated bakery carries 80 varieties of authentic Mexican pastries and bread baked fresh daily, as well as a selection of imported Mexican items. Neighbors know it as the place to go for Day of the Dead breads. Rosales also serves carnitas, tortas, and tamales, and is open daily from sunrise until bedtime. (West Denver)

BARBECUE

BROTHERS BBQ $
6499 Leetsdale Drive
(303) 322-3289
www.brothers-bbq.com

105 Wadsworth Boulevard, Unit E, Lakewood
(303) 232-3422

2589A South Lewis Way, Lakewood
(303) 989-9595

565 U.S. Highway 287, Broomfield
(303) 635-2424

9069 Arapahoe Road, Greenwood Village
(303) 799-9777

4645 West Colfax Avenue
(303) 534-2600

568 Washington Street
(720) 570-4227
Brothers BBQ dishes up award-winning slow-

smoked ribs either vinegary Memphis-style or sweet and smoky Kansas City-style at any of its seven Metro Denver locations. You might also try their smoky barbecued chicken or pulled-pork sandwich. Any choice is sure to be a good one. Most folks are amazed to discover that these American delicacies are being dished up by two Brits, the O'Brien brothers. Open for lunch and dinner daily, takeout is a good option as well. Call ahead for pickup. (North, Southeast, South Central, Central, Southwest)

M&D'S CAFE AND FISH PALACE $
2004 East 28th Avenue
(303) 296-1760
Owners Mack and Daisy Shead brought the family barbecue recipe with them when they migrated from Texas. Now their place in Denver' Five Points neighborhood is one of the few that appear regularly on all "Best of" lists. The decor is plain, but the sweet-hot BBQ is authentic, as are the cornmeal-battered and fried whiting and catfish. To round out a meal, add a side of collard greens, corn bread, and some sweet-potato pie. (Central)

SAM TAYLOR'S BAR-B-Q $
435 South Cherry Street, Glendale
(303) 388-9300
www.samtaylorsbbq.com
Is Sam Taylor's smoky-sweet and spicy barbecue the best in town? Lots of folks say it is. For years Taylor's restaurant was located on the links at City Park Golf Course, but, due to differences with the landlords, it moved to a new location. The atmosphere is still ultracasual family style, with picnic tables on the patio. The amazing melt-in-your-mouth barbecue is served daily for lunch and dinner. (Central/East)

WINSTON HILL'S RIBS & STUFF $
5090 East Arapahoe Road, Centennial
(303) 843-6475
For decades Daddy Bruce Randolph was the revered king of barbecue, but after his death in 1994, relatives have vied for the honor. Winston Hill is a cousin, and also a football player. He uses

---

Breakfast Burritos

Spend a few days in Denver and you should notice a fast food like none other, the hearty hold-in-one-hand breakfast burrito. Find it at vendors' stands throughout downtown and along major thoroughfares, or in neighborhood restaurants. The favorites of a *Denver Post* taste panel came from Little Anita's, 1050 West Colfax Avenue; Cafe Mexico, 3815 West 72nd Avenue, Westminster; The Burrito Co., 1290 South Santa Fe Drive; and Bow-Ree-Toe De-Lite, 5050 South Federal Boulevard.

Daddy's Arkansas-based recipes and serves them to the world's smallest crowd (about eight can squeeze into the restaurant at any one time). A larger audience comes to the "rib shack" for takeout. Closed Sunday. (Southeast)

WOLFE'S BARBEQUE $
333 East Colfax Avenue
(303) 831-1500
www.wolfesbbq.samsbiz.com
Here's hope for committed vegetarians: In addition to Wolfe's scrumptious traditional barbecued meats, you can get smoked, grilled tofu and vegetarian baked beans at this eatery a block from the State Capitol. For carnivores, the barbecue is first-rate. Wolfe's serves lunch and dinner Monday through Friday only. (Central)

BREAKFAST

BENNY'S RESTAURANT Y TEQUILA BAR $
301 East 7th Avenue
(303) 894-0788
www.bennysrestaurant.com
Benny's is actually a full-service Mexican joint with as much history as flavor in its food. But we've

listed it under breakfasts because it serves the best breakfast burrito known to humankind. Fat and filled with eggs, potatoes, and a choice of menudo, sausage, or meat, it's served smothered in green chili with tender chunks of pork. It's no diet plate, mind you, but great comfort food. And while you wait you can munch chips and salsa (also among the best in Denver). There are other breakfast items, all with Benny's Mexican flair. For lunch or dinner, choose from a variety of combos and a la carte items. If you go on the weekend, plan on slurping a few margaritas while you wait an hour for a table. Lunch and dinner served daily, breakfast is served Saturday and Sunday. (Central)

DELECTABLE EGG $

1642 Market Street
(303) 572-8146
www.delectableegg.com

1625 Court Place
(303) 892-5720

200 Quebec Street
(720) 859-9933

1005 West 120th Avenue, Westminster
(303) 451-7227

Traditional breakfast choices including omelets, eggs Benedict, waffles, French toast, and pancakes lure customers to this local spot. The original Delectable Egg is housed in an old warehouse in Lower Downtown, which makes it look a little like greasy-diner-gone-chic (although the food isn't unusually greasy). Other locations are spiffed up to match the good, standard breakfast dishes. Breakfast and lunch daily. (Downtown, Northeast, East)

DOZENS $

236 West 13th Avenue
(303) 572-0066
www.dozensrestaurant.com

Want a breakfast that will stay with you, but don't want to ingest too much grease? Dozens is the place. Located in a quaint renovated house on the outskirts of downtown, it serves a traditional American breakfast of wonderful omelets, griddle combinations, waffles, and pancakes.

Homemade baked goods are served, too. Dozens bustles weekdays with the business crowd and on weekends with the more relaxed coffee-drinking, paper-reading crowd. It serves breakfast and lunch daily. A second location has opened at 2180 South Havana Street in Aurora, (303) 337-6627. (Central, Southeastern suburbs)

ELLYNGTON'S $$$

321 17th Street
at the Brown Palace Hotel
(303) 297-3111
www.brownpalace.com

Best known for its lavish champagne brunch (with Dom Perignon, if you've got the bucks for it), the classy and urbane Ellyngton's also serves a tasteful breakfast and lunch, but no dinner. Sunday brunch is an extravagant buffet with impressive displays of food. (Downtown)

HOT CAKES DINER $

1400 East 18th Avenue
(303) 832-4351

If you're in the mood for pancakes (or any other home-cooked breakfast), head to Hot Cakes, a favorite of Uptown residents as well as employees from the surrounding hospitals. The cakes are so big that one is enough, and they come in a mind-boggling range of flavors. The lunch menu and environment are just as appealing as the flapjacks. The walls are filled with original works of art, and the wait staff is young, friendly, and appealingly funky. Open daily for breakfast and lunch. (Uptown)

LE PEEP RESTAURANT $

999 18th Street
(303) 244-0360
www.lepeep.com

1699 South Colorado Boulevard
(303) 759-3388

2456 South Parker Road
(303) 369-5404

1875 York Street
(303) 399-7320

Le Peep is a local chain with a dozen different properties throughout Colorado's Front Range, but it's best known as a Metro Denver breakfast legend. There's a small selection of sandwiches, but Le Peep is all about breakfast. Omelets, pancakes, French toast—you get the picture. There's nothing gourmet here, but it's tasty. Coffee drinkers will like the self-serve pot left on the table. Breakfast and lunch daily. We've listed locations in Denver proper, but others exist in Aurora, Boulder, Centennial, Englewood, Evergreen, Highlands Ranch, Lakewood, Littleton, Longmont, Northglenn, and Westminster. (Downtown, Cherry Creek, Southeast, East)

BREWPUBS

BRECKENRIDGE BREWERY $$-$$$
2220 Blake Street
(303) 297-3644
www.breckbrew.com

471 Kalamath Street
(303) 573-0431

The emphasis here is on the microbrewed beers and ales, but no one need go hungry with a menu that includes hearty pub fare—burgers, chicken sandwiches, salads, soups—for lunch and dinner daily. The original location is close to Coors Field, and is a great place for an after-game brew. The second is a few miles away in the Golden Triangle, on the eastern edge of downtown proper near the State Capitol and City Hall. (Downtown)

ROCK BOTTOM BREWERY $$
1001 16th Street
(303) 534-7616
www.rockbottom.com

A huge brewpub with outdoor seating on the 16th Street Mall, the Rock Bottom is related to the Walnut Brewery in Boulder. It's popular from lunchtime well into the evening, and the extensive menu includes salads, pastas, barbecued meats, and sandwiches. It's an all-around favorite with locals, whether the action is on the patio or

around the impressive bar. Open daily. New locations have opened in Westminster and Englewood, with details on the Web site. (Downtown)

SPORTS COLUMN $-$$
1930 Blake Street
(303) 296-1930
www.denversportscolumn.com

This traditional sports barhops during all Colorado Rockies, Colorado Avalanche, Denver Broncos, and Denver Nuggets games. The menu is fairly extensive and includes variations on burgers, sandwiches, pastas, salads, appetizers, and burritos that are sold daily until the kitchen closes at 1 a.m. Enjoy lunch, dinner or happy hour daily with good views of several big-screen televisions. A nice summertime feature is the rooftop deck with views of the city lights. (Downtown)

i The Seattle-style coffee shop is still popular in Denver, as in other big cities. Many of Denver's are great spots to take a break, experience a local neighborhood, and have a light meal. Most serve bagels, scones, desserts, and other treats as well as light sandwiches.

WYNKOOP BREWING COMPANY $-$$
1634 18th Street at Wynkoop Street
(303) 297-2700
www.wynkoop.com

Housed in the historic J. S. Brown Mercantile Building, the Wynkoop led the way in the resurgence of Lower Downtown. Before John Hickenlooper became mayor, he opened Denver's first brewpub in 1988. It still sizzles, serving a variety of handcrafted ales and pub fare, such as pot pies with quinoa crust, at reasonable prices for lunch and dinner. The main dining area is noisy, and crowded. Upstairs is a classic pool hall that hops with the 20 to 30 set. Reservations are accepted for large groups only. Lunch and dinner are served daily. (Downtown)

COFFEE

COMMON GROUNDS $
3484 West 32nd Avenue
(303) 458-5248
www.commongroundscoffeehouse.com

1601 17th Street
(303) 296-9248

A coffeehouse in the European tradition, Common Grounds doubles as a community center for the west Highlands neighborhood and has a second location in LoDo. Lots of free reading material, board games, and a piano for would-be Liberaces make this a place to stop and sit a spell. Pastries, cakes, muffins, and bagels are available. It's open seven days a week from sunrise until bedtime. (West Denver, Downtown)

PARIS ON THE PLATTE $
1553 Platte Street
(303) 455-2451
www.parisontheplattecafeandbar.com

Popular with neighborhood artists, some of whom exhibit their paintings here, Paris on the Platte is Denver's oldest coffeehouse, operating under several different names since 1972 and within a few buildings of the current site. The coffeehouse is now connected to a used bookstore and serves more than just coffee. Choose from sandwiches, salads, soups, pastries, and bagels. It's open daily, until the wee hours on Friday and Saturday. (Downtown/Platte River)

ST. MARK'S COFFEEHOUSE $
2019 East 17th Avenue
(303) 322-8384
www.stmarkscoffeehouse.com

The bohemian alternative to the much more crowded Market on Larimer Street, St. Mark's serves coffee, cappuccino, and baked goods daily from sunrise until bedtime. Patrons sit outside for people-watching or inside on folding chairs and former church pews. (Uptown)

STELLA'S COFFEEHAUS $
1476 South Pearl Street
(303) 777-1031
www.stellascoffee.com

Stella's is almost certainly the only Denver coffeehouse with a branch in Amsterdam—the owner's family runs a cafe by the same name in that European city. Stella's has lots of outdoor seating and scrumptious baked goods and desserts. It also serves a light lunch. The adjoining Amsterdam Room has live entertainment on weekends and can be booked for private meetings and parties. It's open seven days a week until midnight and until 11 p.m. on Sunday. (South Central)

CONTINENTAL

BRIARWOOD INN $$$$
1630 8th Street, Golden
(303) 279-3121
www.thebriarwoodinn.com

The Briarwood Inn isn't that far from downtown, but it's a world away from the hustle-bustle. A romantic getaway, the formal, old-fashioned Briarwood Inn is Victorian in its decor and continental in its cuisine. Dinner is served Saturday and Sunday, and lunch is served on weekdays. It's especially nice when it's decorated for the winter holidays. Reservations are required. (West suburbs)

THE BURNSLEY HOTEL $$$
1000 Grant Street
(303) 830-1000
www.burnsley.com

The intimate dining room at this small Capitol Hill hotel is extravagantly wallpapered and almost fussily furnished. This is the place to go when you don't want to run into everyone you know and would rather sink into a banquette and sip a martini. Live jazz bands play Friday and Saturday evenings. The food is Americanized continental, with lamb, chicken, seafood, and frequently changing specials. It serves breakfast, lunch, and dinner daily. (Central)

WELLSHIRE INN $$$-$$$$
3333 South Colorado Boulevard
(303) 759-3333
www.levyrestaurants.com

Housed in an English Tudor mansion on the grounds of the Wellshire Municipal Golf Course, the Wellshire Inn is richly decorated with 100+-year-old tapestries, stained glass, and handsome wood paneling. The Wellshire, opened in 1926, serves sophisticated continental fare, including rack of lamb and salmon. There are nightly specials. Lunch, dinner, and Sunday brunch are served. The eggs Benedict is the specialty, but the French toast with vanilla ice cream melted into the batter could tempt you away from the standard. (Southeast)

DELICATESSENS

ECONOMY GREEK FOODS $
717 Lipan Street
(303) 861-3001

A Denver institution since 1901, the Economy stocks hard-to-find varieties of imported feta cheese and olives as well as other Greek and Mediterranean specialties. It's open weekdays for breakfast and lunch, featuring gyros and other deli items. It's open Monday through Friday. (Central)

THE MARKET $
1445 Larimer Street
(303) 534-5140

Come to The Market for great food and desserts or just a cup of coffee and amazing people-watching. It's all here, from gourmet pasta to killer cakes, from black-leather-clad bikers to CEOs. You can make a meal out of the gourmet offerings, which include made-to-order deli sandwiches and a changing variety of soups and salads. It's not really a restaurant, so we've included it in this category. The baked goods, top-of-the-line chocolates, and shelves of imported food items make this as much a shopping destination as a dining spot, and the espresso bar is always busy. Bring a cup of cappuccino and a plate of biscotti out to a table on the sidewalk and watch the world go by. It's open seven days a week. (Downtown)

NEW YORK DELI NEWS $
7105 East Hampden Avenue
(303) 759-4741

New York Deli News serves breakfast, lunch, and dinner daily. You'll enjoy great pumpernickel bread, pastrami, bagels, corned beef (all flown in from New York), and—loosen your belt—genuine New York-style cheesecake. (Southeast)

THE SPICY PICKLE $
988 Lincoln Street
(303) 860-0730
www.spicypickle.com

745 South Colorado Boulevard
(303) 321-8353

This "upscale dive," as it's been called, serves up some of the freshest and most innovative sandwiches in town, with homemade mayo spreads and a choice of 19 toppings. The bread is Italian artisan style and is a great starting point for either sub or panini. The meats are all top quality, and every sandwich is accompanied by the spicy house-made pickle. Order at the counter, and your sandwich will be brought to your inside or outside table. Lunch and an early dinner are offered daily. Other locations are opening throughout Metro Denver. Details are available on the Web site. (Central)

ZAIDY'S DELI $$
121 Adams Street
(303) 333-5336
www.zaidysdeli.com

15th and Lawrence Streets
(303) 893-3600

Zaidy's may very well be the closest thing to an authentic New York Jewish deli that can be found in Metro Denver. This is a prime source for breakfast and lunches that range from potato latkes to smoked fish, and matzo ball soup just like your grandmother used to make. The Cherry Creek store is open daily from breakfast through the afternoon. The downtown store is open daily for breakfast and lunch. (Cherry Creek, Downtown)

FRENCH

LE CENTRAL $$

112 East 8th Avenue
(303) 863-8094
www.lecentral.com

Le Central styles itself as "the affordable French restaurant" and does a good job of living up to that claim without skimping on quality. The restaurant is a charming series of low-ceilinged rooms; the food is country French. Lunch and dinner are served daily in addition to brunch on Saturday and Sunday. (Central)

GREEK

YANNI'S $$

2223 South Monaco Parkway
(303) 692-0404

This is a classic Greek family-run tavern, with a blue-and-white interior and outdoor tables with umbrellas. The menu leans heavily on traditional, hearty dishes such as moussaka and pastitsio. Everything here is fresh, including the homemade bread. Knock back a shot of ouzo and let the feasting begin. Lunch is served Monday through Saturday, dinner nightly. (Southeast)

ICE CREAM

LIKS $

2039 East 13th Avenue
(303) 321-2370
www.liksicecream.com

Take a number and get in line for this well-known Denver spot. Formerly known as Lickety Split, this old-fashioned ice-cream parlor is the place to go for a fabulously indulgent sundae. The homemade ice creams come in such tempting flavors as Almond Roca and Cheesman Park (a strawberry-cheesecake concoction named for the park a few blocks away). Don't fret if they're out of your favorite flavor; they'll put it on the request list and call you when it's available. It's open seven days a week at noon and doesn't accept credit cards. (Central)

INDIAN

INDIA HOUSE $$$

1514 Blake Street
(303) 595-0680
www.indiahouse.us

Downtown's only Indian restaurant is refined in decor and in the wide range of tandoori dishes on its menu, which include two kinds of Cornish game hens and quail in addition to the more standard chicken. The lunch buffet is an especially good value, with a choice of entrees and as many as 22 items in all. Vegetarians will appreciate the many meatless dishes. Lunch and dinner are served daily. (Downtown)

INDIA'S $$-$$$

3333 South Tamarac Drive
(303) 755-4284

India's is a feast for the senses, with tantalizing aromas, colorful cloth hangings, and hypnotic Indian music. Located in a strip shopping mall just behind Tamarac Square, India's is Denver's oldest Indian restaurant and one of the finest you are ever likely to encounter. The curries are hot and spicy, and the tandoori dishes are very popular. Reservations are recommended. Dinner is served nightly, lunch Monday through Saturday. (Southeast)

JEWEL OF INDIA $$

10343 North Federal Boulevard, Westminster
(303) 469-7779
www.jewelofindia.com

Suburban Westminster may seem an unlikely place for one of the area's finest Indian restaurants, as may Jewel of India's location in a shopping center anchored by King Soopers. But once inside the narrow door, the truth becomes evident. Jujhar Singh has managed to transform the storefront into a little slice of India, complete with lamb, chicken, seafood, and vegetarian dishes, all of which come with homemade naan. If you're unfamiliar with the dishes, try the Thalis, which includes a little bit of everything to serve one or two people. Singh was raised in Punjab, India, and uses family recipes from the region. His Jewel of India serves lunch buffets and full-service dinners seven days a week. (Northwest suburbs)

ITALIAN

BAROLO GRILL $$$
3030 East 6th Avenue
(303) 393-1040
Since opening in 1992, Barolo has consistently ranked as one of the hottest of the city's hot spots. The food in this chic restaurant could be called "Cal-Ital," combining as it does northern Italian recipes with California ingredients. Barolo does several good fish dishes with great sauces. Wines are an especially good value. It serves dinner only, Tuesday through Saturday; with reservations strongly recommended. (Central)

BRAVO! RISTORANTE $$$
1550 Court Place
(303) 626-2581
www.adamsmark.com
It's not every day that diners are treated to show tunes and opera pieces by their wait staff. At Bravo! that's the norm. The staff are professional singers, so it's quite a treat. The dining room is large and spacious, and the cuisine is as memorable as the singing. The menu ranges from antipasto platter and bruschetta to ravioli, scaloppini piccata, and pizza. The room was closed for a major renovation through much of 2009, but will resume weekday lunch service and daily dinner service once the construction is completed. (Downtown)

CARMINE'S ON PENN $$
92 South Pennsylvania Street
(303) 777-6443
www.carminesonpenn.citysearch.com
Make a reservation; this place is way too popular to expect a table during the dinner hour without one. And for good reason. Piles of homemade pasta form the bed for spicy and flavorful sauces. The portions are enough to feed two, plus lunch the next day. The wine list is adequate, if not expansive. The atmosphere bustles with an eclec-

tic neighborhood scene. Carmine's is fast becoming a Denver institution. Dinner only, Tuesday through Sunday. (Central)

CHERRY TOMATO $$
4645 East 23rd Avenue
(303) 377-1914
The Cherry Tomato is another *Insiders'* favorite, best known as a neighborhood restaurant for Park Hill dwellers. Its Italian entrees are as filling as they are delicious, so come with an empty stomach. Among the specialties is Pasta Felese, made with chicken, artichoke hearts, and sun-dried tomatoes in a white-wine cream sauce. The place fills up fast and doesn't take reservations for parties of fewer than six. You can call ahead when you're leaving home to be put on the waiting list. Open for dinner only, Tuesday through Sunday; closed Monday. (East Denver)

CINZETTI'S ITALIAN MARKET $$$
281 West 104th Avenue, Northglenn
(303) 451-7300
www.cinzettis.com
Cinzetti's (pronounced Chin-ZEH-tees) is a "concept" restaurant that either works for you or it doesn't. It's designed around a central marketplace with food lines that resemble buffets, each serving something different—pastas, pizzas, fish and meats, and desserts, for example. All diners pay a flat rate at the door and can sample anything that strikes their fancies. The food is surprisingly tasty for mass-produced buffet fare, and wine and soft drinks are included in the price. Open daily for lunch and dinner. (North suburbs)

DINO'S $$
10040 West Colfax Avenue, Lakewood
(303) 238-7393
Denver Post restaurant critics rave about this landmark Italian restaurant in Lakewood, an early suburb west of downtown Denver. Homemade pasta, sausage, meatballs, lasagna, and spumoni are among the standouts on the menu. Lots of regulars come for the authentic Italian food; on Sunday they come right after church for a traditional family dinner. (Southwest)

IL FORNAIO $$$

8000 East Belleview Avenue,
Greenwood Village
(303) 221-8400
www.ilfornaio.com

A deliciously elegant dining option, Il Fornaio is a California-based restaurant whose specialty is its breads and baked goods (il fornaio means "the baker"). Meals can be quite good, too, though not always up to par with the prices and surroundings. Ask the server what's good and fresh to make the best selection. Lunch and dinner daily. (South suburbs)

i Both Mexican and Italian food are plentiful in Denver. One area of town where you're sure to find the best of both is northwest Denver, which was originally settled by Italian immigrants, welcomed a new wave of Hispanic immigrants and is still known today for its authentic cuisine.

LUCA D'ITALIA $$$

711 Grant Street
(303) 832-6600

Chef Frank Bonanno was a Denver legend before he opened this Tuscan place around the corner from his Mizuna restaurant. He quickly created buzz with the wild-boar ragu, the trio of rabbit (a confit of leg, tenderloin, and braised meat with leeks), and the classic Italian bread pudding (panzanella). It's open for dinner Tuesday through Saturday. (Central)

MAGGIANO'S LITTLE ITALY $$$$

510 16th Street, Denver Pavilions
(303) 260-7707
www.maggianos.com

7401 South Clinton Street,
Denver Tech Center
(303) 858-1405

Dark woods, brass, and red-checkered tablecloths give the feel of 1940s Little Italy at this family-style restaurant. Both places are friendly, and the large food portions are served with gusto. Salads are simple but fresh and crisp. Lunch and dinner daily. (Downtown, South)

PAGLIACCI'S $$$

1440 West 33rd Avenue
(303) 458-0530

Family-run for more than 50 years, Pagliacci's is another West Denver institution. The neon clown on the roof is famously visible from I-25 but not from the restaurant itself, which has a handsome, grottolike interior. If you can't stay for a meal, you can get the famous minestrone to go. Pagliacci's has fed generations of Denver families, and its red booths have been the scene of almost as many romantic dates. It serves dinner only and is closed Monday. (West Denver)

PANZANO $$$

909 17th Street
(303) 296-3525
www.panzano-denver.com

Housed in the Hotel Monaco Denver, Panzano is a trip into calming dark woods and earth tones. Chef Elise Wiggins is among Denver's finest, spending time in Central America and Puerto Rico before settling in Denver. Two open kitchens fill the air with scents of baked goods. Reservations, especially at the bustling noontime, are recommended. Breakfast, lunch, and dinner served weekdays, brunch and dinner served Saturday and Sunday. (Downtown)

LATIN

CAFE BRAZIL $$$

4408 Lowell Boulevard
(303) 480-1877

Cafe Brazil is a tiny, intimate restaurant in what used to be an old-world Italian neighborhood on Denver's west side. The colorful restaurant provides hot, tropical cuisine at its authentic best. Try the feijoada completa, Brazil's national dish. It combines black beans, meat, fruit, and rice in a most delicious way. Cafe Brazil is open for dinner only and is closed Sunday and Monday. Reservations are recommended. (West Denver)

CUBA CUBA $$
1173 Delaware Street
(303) 605-2822
www.cubacubacafe.com

Two tiny historic homes were joined together to make room for this Latin American restaurant in the Golden Triangle. You'll enter one and find yourself in the bar. Cross over into the other and you're in the dining room. The food is zesty and heavy on pork (Lechon Asado—or roasted pork, onions, and garlic—is its signature dish). Salads and coconut-lime rice make good vegetarian alternatives, and if cocktails are your thing, try the mojitos. They're among Denver's best. Open Monday through Saturday for dinner. (Central)

SABOR LATINO $-$$
4340 West 35th Avenue
(303) 455-8664
www.saborlatinorestaurant.com

A charming place in an interesting west Denver neighborhood, Sabor Latino serves South American and Mexican cuisine. The restaurant recently went upscale, at least in its new, expanded digs. But the food is still the same, and still good. Specialties of the house include Colombian tamales and South American empanadas, baked or fried. A nice selection of Chilean wines is available. It serves dinner Tuesday through Friday. Takeout is available, but reservations are not accepted. (West Denver)

SAMBA ROOM $$$$
1460 Larimer Street
(720) 956-1701
www.sambaroom.net

Situated in LoDo, the Samba Room anchors historic Larimer Square and does it to a hip Latin beat. The after-work crowd favors its comfy bar, and lunch and dinner guests enjoy entrees with Latin American influences. House specialties range from mango barbecued ribs to fried yucca, and afterward, the banana split comes with a fried banana. Reservations are accepted. Samba Room is open daily for lunch and dinner. (Downtown)

MEXICAN/SOUTHWESTERN

THE BLUE BONNET CAFE & LOUNGE $
457 South Broadway
(303) 778-0147
www.bluebonnetrestaurant.com

This Mexican joint was "discovered" by Denver yuppies in the 1980s and remains popular—prepare to wait a while for a table. There's nothing fancy here, but they serve lots of it with great big margaritas to wash everything down. The refried beans are a standout. Lunch and dinner are served daily. (Central)

EL NOA NOA $
722 Santa Fe Drive
(303) 623-9968

Santa Fe Drive anchors one of Denver's earliest Mexican-American neighborhoods, hence the authentic restaurants that line its streets. El Noa Noa is an elder statesman, with a series of small dining rooms inside and an exceptional outdoor patio, complete with fountain and wrought-iron chairs. They're prime seats for watching the Cinco de Mayo parade, listening to roving Mariachi bands or just enjoying the weather. The food is typical Tex-Mex with some home-style Mexican favorites thrown in for good measure, but El Noa Noa likely is best known for the tasty enchiladas, burritos, tacos, and rellenos it dishes out. Lunch and dinner are served daily. (Central)

EL TACO DE MEXICO $
714 Santa Fe Drive
(303) 623-3926

This simple restaurant holds its own, despite stiff competition from larger and better-known El Noa Noa next door. It's more like a diner than an evening dinner destination, with ultracasual meals served at the bar or at a few tables. It's open daily for breakfast, lunch, and dinner. Credit cards not accepted. (Central)

JACK-N-GRILL $-$$
2524 Federal Boulevard
(303) 964-9544
www.jackngrill.com

New Mexican dishes have made this cement hole-in-the-wall's reputation. Located on Denver's west side in a predominantly Hispanic neighborhood, Jack-n-Grill serves a mean green chili, vaquero tacos moistened with barbecue sauce, and seven-pound burritos so big the servers will take your picture if you finish one. The Martinez family left Albuquerque in 1994 to open a small chile shop in Denver, and grew it into this well-respected restaurant. (West)

JULIA BLACKBIRD'S NEW MEXICAN CAFE $$
3434 West 32nd Avenue
(303) 433-2688

This little jewel in the charming Highland neighborhood is quickly gaining in reputation, and the weekend lines prove it. The menu is true to its New Mexican roots with blue-corn tortillas, hearty posole, light and delicious sopapillas, and pine nut chocolate cake. Lunch and dinner are served Tuesday through Sunday, with lunch only on Monday. (West)

LA ESTRELLITA $
7617 West 88th Avenue, Arvada
(303) 422-3700
www.salsalaest.com

The Montoya family operates three casual La Estrellita locations, including this one in Arvada, one in Brighton, and one in Boulder. Their award-winning green chili is available hot, medium, mild, or vegetarian. Buy it by the quart for takeout or spoon it over anything on the menu. Breakfast, lunch, and dinner are served daily. (West suburbs)

LA LOMA RESTAURANT $-$$
2527 West 26th Avenue
(303) 433-8300
www.lalomarestaurant.com

In the up-and-coming Diamond Hill neighborhood just west of I-25 at Speer Boulevard, La Loma is rather incongruously housed in an 1887 Victorian home that has been renovated into a series of sprawling dining rooms. The restaurant is known for its big margaritas and authentic food. Lunch and dinner are served daily. (West Denver)

LAS DELICIAS $-$$
439 East 19th Avenue
(303) 839-5675
http://lasdelicias.net

7610 Conifer Road
(303) 430-0422

This family-run restaurant has five locations, and loyal customers still can't get enough of their Michoacán-style food. We've listed the two original Denver locations, but they've been joined by spots in Littleton, Parker, and Glendale. (Look for details on the Web site.) House specialties include carnitas and fajitas, carne adobada, taquitos, carne asada, and steak ranchero, as well as hearty Mexican breakfasts. Open daily for breakfast, lunch, and dinner. (North, Uptown, West, and Southern suburbs)

MEXICO CITY LOUNGE & CAFE $
2115 Larimer Street
(303) 296-0563

Denverites make a big fuss about authenticity when discussing the comparative merits of restaurants, but there's no argument here. This is the real thing, served inside a well-worn building in a neglected inner city neighborhood that only recently has begun to gentrify. The green chile and burritos are favorites, and breakfast is a real eye-opener. If you're a fan of menudo, this is the place to go. It's closed Monday, but serves breakfast and lunch on the other days. No credit cards. (Downtown)

MORRISON INN $-$$
301 Bear Creek Avenue, Morrison
(303) 697-6650

This is a fun, Americanized restaurant in an 1885 building smack in the heart of the foothills town of Morrison. It's known for custom-made (not premixed) margaritas and for its designation as a beginning—or ending—spot for motorcycle riders, mountain bikers, and hikers. The fare is standard Mexican served for lunch and dinner daily. (West suburbs)

PLAYA DE ORO $

3551 West 38th Avenue
(303) 433-5777

Playa de Oro is known for its crispy, golden brown chile rellenos—poblano chiles stuffed with Monterey Jack. They also serve a wide array of other Mexican dishes for breakfast, lunch, and dinner Monday through Saturday, and breakfast and lunch on Sunday. Prices are incredibly low to very reasonable. (West)

ROSA LINDA'S MEXICAN CAFE $

2005 West 33rd Avenue
(303) 455-0608
www.rosalindasmexicancafe.com

You say you want a neighborhood restaurant? Check out this one. Run by the Aquirre family since 1985, Rosa Linda's is a small, plain place with great burritos, enchiladas, and soft chile rellenos. It wins awards for its shredded beef burritos, chile rellenos, and other specialties. There are a few tables on the sidewalk. Open Monday through Friday for lunch and dinner. (West)

TABLE MOUNTAIN GRILL &
CANTINA $$-$$$

1310 Washington Avenue, Golden
(303) 277-9898
www.tablemountaininn.com

Enter the restaurant at modern adobe-style Table Mountain Inn for Southwestern dishes that range from prime rib of buffalo to cowboy chops and grilled salmon. For lunch, choose among buffalo burgers, chicken, salads, and daily specials—all spiced and prepared with Southwest flair. Breakfast, lunch, and dinner served daily. Brunch is available Saturday and Sunday. (West suburbs)

TAQUERIA PATZCUARO $

2616 West 32nd Avenue
(303) 455-4389
www.patzcuaros.com

An ultracasual restaurant in a Spanish-speaking pocket of the Highland area, Taqueria Patzcuaro draws fans from all over the city with traditional Michoacán dishes as well as its green chile and soft tacos. The neighborhood around Taqueria is alive with Mexican music. Lunch and dinner are served daily. There's no alcohol, and credit cards are not accepted. (West)

MIDDLE EASTERN

JERUSALEM RESTAURANT $

1890 East Evans Avenue
(303) 777-8828
www.jerusalemrestaurant.com

A tiny eight-table restaurant that does a bustling take-out business, Jerusalem is popular with students from the University of Denver campus nearby. Everything is good here, including the kebabs, hummus, baba ghanouj, and phyllo pastries. Students cramming for an exam no doubt also appreciate the fact that Jerusalem is 24 hours a day on Friday and Saturday, as well as for breakfast and lunch Sunday through Thursday. The space crunch is eased during summer months by the outdoor patio. Alcohol is not served. (South Central)

PITA JUNGLE $-$$

2017 South University Boulevard
(720) 570-1900

Also serving the University of Denver campus, Pita Jungle makes its own pita bread, which serves as a deserving base for outstanding hummus and shawarma. Lunch and dinner are served daily. (South Central)

PIZZA

BEAU JO'S PIZZA $-$$

2710 South Colorado Boulevard
(303) 758-1519
www.beaujos.com

7805 Wadsworth Boulevard, Arvada
(303) 420-8376

The original Beau Jo's is still in Idaho Springs, a beloved stopping point for Denverites on their way home from skiing who crave thick-crusted pizza. While diners wait for it to cook (good things take time), they can draw on napkins and pin them on the wall along with the thousands of others. Beau Jo's has these two branches in southeast Denver and Arvada, as well as six more that stretch from Evergreen to Fort Collins, and from Durango to Glenwood Springs. They are open daily for lunch and dinner. (Southeast, West suburbs)

BONNIE BRAE TAVERN $-$$
740 South University Boulevard
(303) 777-2262
www.bonniebraetavern.com
The crowds! The noise! The pizza! This astoundingly popular neighborhood pizza joint was founded in 1934 and is always busy, busy, busy. It's a fun place, but don't come here if you're in a hurry. Bonnie Brae serves lunch and dinner daily except Monday. Takeout is available. (South Central)

CAFE COLORE $-$$
1512 Larimer Street
(303) 534-6844
www.cafecoloredenver.com
Cafe Colore has a menu that's built around a clever gimmick: Pizzas come with sauces of red, green, or white, the three colors of the Italian flag. Other Italian entrees, plus calzones, are available. Smoking is allowed on the patio, which is where you'll want to be anyway in good weather. It's open seven days for lunch and dinner. (Downtown)

PARISI $
4401 Tennyson Street
(303) 561-0234
Parisi is a combination grocery, Italian deli, and pizza place—and it excels in all areas. Simone Parisi, who grew up in Florence, makes pizza in the true Italian tradition, meaning you order a rustica or Margherita, not pepperoni and mushroom. The crust is medium-thick, the tomato sauce chunky, and the mozzarella fresh. Sandwiches and pastas are equally fresh and delicious. Enjoy your meal in the recently renovated building or have your feast packed to go. You can also find authentic Italian groceries on the shelves in the shop. Open Monday through Saturday for lunch and dinner. (West)

PASQUINI'S PIZZERIA $
1310 South Broadway
(303) 744-0917
www.pasquinis.com

1336 East 17th Avenue
(303) 863-8252

2400 West 32nd Avenue
(303) 477-4900
A nifty little pizzeria with an artsy interior and mosaic-topped tables, Pasquini's serves New York-style thin crust, sauce-less bianca, and thick-crust Sicilian-style pizzas and individual pizzettas with interesting toppings. Also on the menu are calzones and subs. The original Pasquini's is nestled amid the antiques stores on South Broadway at Louisiana Avenue. The latest is a hipster style neighborhood joint in the Highland neighborhood, with an Art Deco bar and music menu next door, called Zio Romolo's Alley Bar. Lunch and dinner are served daily except Sunday, which is dinner only. Takeout and delivery are available. (South Central, Uptown, West)

PROTO'S PIZZERIA NAPOLETANA $-$$
2401 15th Street
(720) 855-9400
www.protospizza.com
Owners Pam Proto and Rayme Rossello developed their pizza tastes while on an extended trip to Italy. They then came back to their home in Longmont and started selling the thin-crusted pies layered with fresh ingredients. They now own six restaurants, including this one in Denver's Central Platte Valley. (The others are in Longmont; Lafayette; and Boulder, Broomfield, and Boise, Idaho.) Their places are hip and on the expensive side, but legions of fans say they're the best in town. (Central)

SEAFOOD

240 UNION $$-$$$
240 Union Boulevard at 6th Avenue, Lakewood
(303) 989-3562
www.240union.com

The menu changes seasonally at this creative restaurant on Denver's western flanks. It specializes in seafood, but pastas and pizzas round out the offerings. A nice enclosed patio and wall-to-wall open grill complement the wooden half walls designed to represent "the city meeting the foothills." 240 Union serves dinner nightly and lunch on weekdays. (West suburbs)

FRESH FISH COMPANY $$$
7800 East Hampden Avenue
(303) 740-9556
www.thefreshfishco.com

The aquatic theme extends to the decor at this big restaurant, which consists of walls of beautiful tropical aquariums. Mesquite grilling is a specialty here, and the Sunday brunch, with all-you-can-eat crab legs and shrimp, is very popular. On Sunday night there's a lobster bake, with discounts on the lobster. Lunch is served Monday through Friday, dinner nightly. (Southeast)

JAX FISH HOUSE $$-$$$
1539 17th Street
(303) 292-5767
www.jaxfishhousedenver.com

Jax won't slip a skimpy slice of fish on your plate. Here you'll get a hearty slab of fresh fish, well seasoned and served with a nice variety of side dishes. The raw oysters, stone crab claws, and crawfish are all delicious and succulent. Non-fish eaters can opt for a burger or steak, but fish is truly the dish. The place is hopping, too, so don't expect to be seated right away. Just take your time and enjoy the buildup. Jax serves dinner only, every night. (Downtown)

MCCORMICK'S FISH HOUSE & BAR $$$
1659 Wazee Street
(303) 825-1107
www.mccormickandschmicks.com

In this elegant dining room can be found some of the freshest fish in Denver. If oysters are in season, you'll find them here, on the ground floor of the venerable Oxford Hotel. You'll also find steaks, poultry, and pasta dishes. Private dining rooms

are available. It's open daily for breakfast, lunch, and dinner, with late night service until 1 a.m. on weekends. (Downtown)

STEAKS

AURORA SUMMIT $$$$
2700 South Havana Street, Aurora
(303) 751-2112
www.aurorasummit.com

A classic steak house with a dark, woodsy, masculine ambience, Aurora Summit serves USDA prime, aged, corn-fed beef. In the tradition of steak houses, the menu also includes seafood entrees. In the large front lounge, there's a small dance floor and piano bar that light up Monday through Saturday nights. Aurora Summit serves dinner daily. Reservations are preferred. (Southeast)

THE BUCKHORN EXCHANGE $$$$
1000 Osage Street
(303) 534-9505
www.buckhorn.com

The Buckhorn Exchange is an institution, proudly reminding patrons that it was Denver's original steakhouse (founded in 1893 by "Shorty Scout" Zietz) and is located in the city's oldest neighborhood, which is served by light-rail. It's famous for Shorty Scout's stuffed bird and animal collection, with more than 500 trophies that include moose, elk, buffalo, and bear. More than 500 of them are on display throughout the building. It's also famous for the traditional Western fare on its menu, with exotic options tucked in amongst the steaks and baby-back ribs. Try alligator tail, rattlesnake, quail, game hen, or the house specialty, Rocky Mountain Oysters. If you're vegetarian, call ahead to order a vegetarian plate made to order just for you. Dinner reservations are recommended. The Buckhorn is open for dinner daily, and for lunch on weekdays only. (Central)

THE DENVER CHOPHOUSE & BREWERY $$$
1735 19th Street
(303) 296-0800
www.chophouse.com

The Denver ChopHouse is housed in the old

Union Pacific Railroad warehouse, a block away from Coors Field. Its biggest asset is the outdoor barbecue area, with a patio and rolling roof, But the interior is also inviting, with rich, dark wood and high booths. The food is inventive; try the portobello mushrooms dipped in Worcestershire and garlic, then grilled. Lunch and dinner are served daily. Reservations are suggested for weekends. (Downtown)

ELWAY'S $$$
2500 East 1st Avenue
(303) 399-5353
www.elways.com

Bronco quarterback John Elway is a Denver legend, and after a few short years in business, so is his restaurant. In addition to good steaks and sides, cold martinis, and a great location alongside the tony Cherry Creek Shopping Center, Elway's often serves up celebrities who got hungry while shopping at Neiman Marcus and decided to drop in for a meal. It's open daily for lunch and dinner, with service until 11 p.m. on weekends. (Cherry Creek)

THE FORT $$$$
19192 Highway 8, Morrison
(303) 697-4771
www.thefort.com

The Fort is one of a kind, combining Wild West flair with classy fare; where else do waiters dressed in leather vests and beads open bottles of champagne with a tomahawk? Located in the foothills, with a panoramic view of the plains below, the restaurant is a full-size adobe replica of Bent's Fort, Colorado's first fur-trading post. Owners Sam Arnold and Holly Arnold Kinney were among the first restaurateurs to feature buffalo meat on the menu; other unusual entrees include elk, quail, rattlesnake, and Rocky Mountain oysters (rolled in seasoned flour and deep-fried). More traditional preparations of trout and steak are available, and for those who wish to sample a little bit of everything, there's a game plate. Reservations are recommended. The Fort serves dinner nightly. (West suburbs)

MORTON'S STEAKHOUSE $$$$
1710 Wynkoop Street
(303) 825-3353
www.mortons.com

Denver Crescent Town Center
8480 East Belleview Avenue,
Greenwood Village
(303) 409-1177

With locations in Lower Downtown across from Union Station and at the Denver Tech Center, Morton's is a classic, classy steak house. It is always mentioned when people talk about where to get great steaks. Only USDA prime served here. If surf and turf is what you're after, Morton's flies live lobster in from Maine daily. It serves dinner nightly; reservations are recommended. (Downtown, South)

RUTH'S CHRIS STEAK HOUSE $$$-$$$$
1445 Market Street
(303) 446-2233
www.ruthschris.com

Ruth's Chris is a steak-lover's steak house (only prime served here). The atmosphere is relaxed with plenty of dark wood, and the booths are big and private. The 20-ounce T-bone is the biggest; the 8-ounce filet the smallest. Also available are lobster, veal, chicken, and halibut. Dinner is served nightly, and reservations are recommended. (Downtown)

SULLIVAN'S STEAKHOUSE $$$$
1745 Wazee Street
(303) 295-2664
www.sullivansteakhouse.com

The interior of this LoDo favorite is as dark and rich as a medium-well steak. Live music from the bar drifts throughout as diners enjoy one of Denver's best steak dinners with all the trimmings. Open daily for dinner; reservations recommended; valet parking available. (Downtown)

NIGHTLIFE

Visitors who stroll Denver streets in the evening will notice something remarkable about them: The city hops until the wee hours, but in different ways and with different types of people. Artists and young bohemians are drawn to gallery openings along Santa Fe Drive, Tennyson Street, Navajo Street, and the River North district. Glitterati tend to congregate in Cherry Creek, Uptown, and certain Downtown landmarks. The party-hearty group heads for Capitol Hill's funky urban clubs or to Lower Downtown, where the streets are so full of well-dressed singles on weekends that cars and limos can barely move. Bars, restaurants, dance clubs, and movie theaters all over town rock on weekends and lots of weeknights when warm weather draws people out for a leisurely walk, a bite to eat, and a little live music.

OVERVIEW

In this chapter we survey Denver's nightlife, stopping in at a few of our favorite bars, brewpubs, live music venues, comedy clubs, and movie houses. This isn't meant to be a comprehensive listing; for that kind of inclusiveness, the best place to turn is *Westword*, Denver's free weekly paper. The Friday edition of the *Denver Post* carries weekend entertainment listings, as does the *Daily Camera* with Boulder's happenings. The newspaper *Out Front Colorado* is a good source of information about gay and lesbian nightlife. The paper is free and widely distributed in most coffee and sandwich shops.

Because people interpret "nightlife" so broadly—it includes everything from a wine bar with live poetry readings to an outdoor rock concert at a stadium—there is some inevitable overlap with other chapters. A brewpub such as the Wynkoop serves dinner but also draws a late-night billiards crowd. Theater and dance performances and concerts, such as those at the Denver Performing Arts Complex, are covered in our Arts chapter. We also direct your attention to such popular in-town music venues as the Paramount Theatre, the Ogden Theatre, and the Swallow Hill Music Association.

Unlike concert halls, where advance ticketing is recommended, most of the live music venues

described in this chapter serve food and drink and can be visited on a drop-in basis, although this is no hard-and-fast rule. Finally you can also find family attractions such as Elitch Gardens that don't shut down at dusk. They're described in our Tours and Attractions chapter.

Keep in mind, too, that today's hot spot could be tomorrow's Siberia. No guidebook could ever hope to keep up with the strange twists of taste that make one place worth lining up for and another worth taking pains to avoid. And, of course, music and dance clubs change their format and hours frequently. Some clubs rotate nightly, offering, for example, hip-hop on Monday, electronic music on Tuesday, karaoke on Wednesday, and DJs on Thursday. If you're looking for a specific kind of music, it's always best to call ahead.

The drinking age for any kind of alcoholic beverage is 21. Closing time at bars and nightclubs is generally 2 a.m., but most restaurants stop serving food earlier. The few that keep their kitchens open until midnight are noted in the Restaurants chapter.

Colorado is not a state that takes drunk driving lightly. Penalties are severe for driving under the influence or while impaired. If you've had too much to drink, any restaurant or bar will call a taxi for you. If you're headed into the mountain towns of Central City and Black Hawk for an evening of gambling (see the end of this chapter), consider taking one of the shuttle services rather than driving your own car.

BARS AND OTHER GATHERING SPOTS

BANNOCK STREET GARAGE
1015 Bannock Street
(303) 246-8275

This Golden Triangle watering hole is out of the way and sparkling, but its patrons still think of it as a dive bar. That may be because the walls are filled with motorcycle parts and logos, and the regulars tend to ride—and/or love—fast bikes. Owners took advantage of the building's roots as an auto garage when they did the renovation.

i If a listing in this chapter has an asterisk (*) after its name, that means it's described in further detail in our Restaurants chapter.

BROWN PALACE
321 17th Street
(303) 297-3111
www.brownpalace.com

The grande dame of Denver hotels, the Brown Palace has three dining rooms, including Ellyngton's* and the formal Palace Arms*, where gentlemen diners are encouraged to wear jackets and ties. The Ship Tavern* is the most casual, which makes a good place to stop for a drink or a bite to eat. It's more restaurant than bar, but with dark wood and nautical decor, it has the feel of an English pub. Churchill Bar is tucked unobtrusively into a corner of the hotel lobby, which makes it an excellent place to slip away for a snifter of cognac, a cigar, or a quiet conversation. Its menu includes more than 60 cigars, single-malt scotches, small-batch bourbons, and other temptations. Thanks to a fancy ventilation system, even nonsmokers can enjoy the ambience. Lunch and hors d'oeuvres can also be ordered.

THE BUCKHORN EXCHANGE*
1000 Osage Street
(303) 534-9505
www.buckhorn.com

The upstairs saloon at the Buckhorn Exchange has been a Denver institution for more than 100 years—Colorado's first liquor license is posted on the wall. The hand-carved, white-oak bar dates from 1857 and was brought over from Germany. Expect a daily happy hour and live country and folk music Wednesday through Saturday.

CRUISE ROOM
1600 17th Street
(303) 628-5400

The restored Oxford Hotel, a block away from Union Station, boasts a restaurant and bar complex that's among the city's best. The intimately sized Cruise Room was modeled after a lounge on the Queen Mary and has a wonderful art deco interior that dates from the lifting of Prohibition in 1933. A favorite with visiting authors, the Cruise Room is a great place for a late-night drink, especially if your taste runs to martinis. The bar doesn't have live music, but the jukebox is well stocked with jazz and Big Band music. Be forewarned: It can be tough to get a seat on the weekend unless you arrive early and stake out your spot. Also anchoring the ground floor of the Oxford Hotel is McCormick's Fish House and Bar*, with a roomy corner bar that attracts a big evening crowd for Guinness Stout on tap and other libations. Check out the well-priced happy hour appetizers after work or for a late night snack.

FADÓ IRISH PUB
1735 19th Street
(303) 297-0066
www.fadoirishpub.com

A welcome departure from the LoDo brewpub scene, Fadó brings Ireland to Denver. Most of this authentic Irish pub really is authentic—built in Ireland and brought to Denver piece by piece. Relax in one of nearly a dozen cozy nooks, or be in the middle of the crowd that surrounds the large central bar. There's a full Irish menu, too, with appetizers served until midnight. On Monday and Wednesday nights, Irish bands provide the entertainment.

GABOR'S
1223 East 13th Avenue
(303) 832-3108
Capitol Hill residents know Gabor's as a comfortable neighborhood bar with cheap beer and funky jukebox music. It attracts the young and artistic, serves a killer hamburger, and spices things up with daily drink specials.

PARIS WINE BAR
1553 Platte Street
(303) 217-5805
www.pariscafeandbar.com
The Central Platte Valley is filling with brownstones and pricey apartments, so what better place for the locals to relax than a warm, narrow womb of a bar? Wine lovers have a wide variety to choose from, and those in need of a light snack can order desserts or bread and cheese platters. DJs and live bands often shoehorn themselves into a corner of the bar, transforming what can be a quiet retreat into a rocking venue.

> **i** If you like the nightlife but aren't into the skimpy miniskirt crowd, try Fadó Irish Pub at 19th and Wynkoop. You'll find cozy spots for conversation and enjoy the authentic decor, much of which was shipped over from Ireland.

SANCHO'S BROKEN ARROW
741 East Colfax Avenue
(303) 832-5288
www.quixotes.com/sancho.htm
Sancho's is best described as a dive bar, but it's a very hip one devoted to the Grateful Dead and its fans. The decor, the music, the bands, and the crowd are as tie-dyed as they come. Sancho's is located across the street from the Fillmore Auditorium and on Monday night books jam bands.

It's one of three clubs owned by nightlife entrepreneurs Jay, Philip, and Aric-Dante Bianchi.

LIVE MUSIC

BENDER'S 13TH AVENUE TAVERN
314 East 13th Avenue
(303) 861-7070
www.benderstavern.com
The building at this location has been lots of things, but none of the businesses have been as successful as Bender's. It's known for the mural that covers its eastern exterior, and also for the odd assortment of bands that climb onto its stage. Offerings include rock, punk, rockabilly, and alt country. Or, as one regular described it, "everything but jazz."

BLUEBIRD THEATER
3317 East Colfax Avenue
(303) 322-2308
www.bluebirdtheater.net
For a diverse range of musical acts in a gritty neighborhood, try the Bluebird. Located on Denver's infamous East Colfax Avenue, the Bluebird opened as a movie house in 1913 and has since had several incarnations (including a stint as a porn house). Local bands as well as up-and-coming acts share the marquee. There's a balcony for the under-21 set, 550 seats on the main level, and several tables arranged to accommodate the evening's musical attraction (arrive early to secure a table). A dance floor sometimes serves as a mosh pit, depending on the act. Hours and ticket prices vary depending on who's playing.

DAZZLE
930 Lincoln Street
(303) 839-5100
www.dazzlejazz.com
Dazzle has become one of Denver's most respected jazz venues. Its location, along Lincoln Street in the Golden Triangle neighborhood, appeals to locals who are tired of fighting for parking in trendy LoDo. The stage appeals to mature jazz musicians who make their living

seeking out the fans who, in turn, work hard to seek out the music they love. The crowd is mature, too—in their 30s to 50s—and the restaurant and bar menus reflect their tastes. Expect martinis and smooth sounds here.

DULCINEA'S 100TH MONKEY
717 East Colfax Avenue
(303) 832-3601
www.quixotes.com

Care for a dive bar with jazz? While Dulcinea's skimps on the atmosphere, it more than makes up for it with the music. The owners book wonderful jazz and funk bands Tuesday through Saturday, and on Sunday Dulcinea's features a reggae DJ. It's located next door to Sancho's Broken Arrow, another of the Bianchi brothers' ventures, and is a block away from the Fillmore Auditorium.

EL CHAPULTEPEC
1962 Market Street
(303) 295-9126

Once on the edge of gentrified Denver, El Chapultepec used to be a slightly dangerous place to drink beer, eat a burrito, and listen to jazz. It now finds itself in the rising shadow of Coors Field, encroached upon by brewpubs, art galleries, and designer tile shops. So far, the essential attraction—sizzling jazz—has remained the same. The "'Pec" is a landmark that often attracts touring musicians, who jam with other jazz greats on its tiny bandstand after leaving the stage at larger venues. El Chapultepec is open every night; there's no cover charge, and they don't take reservations.

FUNKY BUDDHA
776 Lincoln Street
(303) 832-5075
www.funkybuddhalounge.com

Denver Post critic Ricardo Baca calls Funky Buddha "a happy-hour favorite," with cheap drinks and an hors d'oeuvres menu that includes stuffed mushrooms, hummus, red pepper dip, and lamb skewers. Denvercitysearch.com describes it as "La La Land without all the famous folk." With

no dancing but DJ music on the weekends, this chic urban bar is a hip place to meet and greet, located just south of downtown in the Golden Triangle neighborhood.

JAZZ@JACK'S
500 16th Street
(303) 433-1000
www.jazzatjacks.com

Since 1984 Stephen and Dave Watts have been playing their own blend of smooth and fusion jazz in a band called Dotsero. For many of those years, they played at their own club in the Central Platte Valley. In 2006 they moved their Jazz@ Jack's venue to the heart of Denver's downtown, on the third floor of the Denver Pavilions complex. Dotsero shares the stage with a broad range of guest artists and comedians. The room with a view can also be rented for private occasions.

LANNIE'S CLOCKTOWER CABARET
1601 Arapahoe Street, lower level
(303) 293-0075
www.lannies.com

This is an old-style nightclub but with the hippest acts in town. Singer Lannie Garrett spent several decades performing at other people's clubs before starting her own in downtown's historic Daniels & Fisher tower, and everything about the place is special. The underground room is intimate and romantic. When Lannie is on stage, expect anything from swing to torch songs, Hollywood tunes, disco hits, and the over-ripe country and western routine of her alter ego, Patsy DeCline. On other nights she fills the stage with burlesque, drag, R&B, soul, and traveling artists of all types. The kitchen is open until midnight, serving appetizers and desserts.

OGDEN THEATRE
935 East Colfax Avenue
(303) 830-2525
www.ogdentheater.net

Another of Denver's famed former movie houses, the Ogden attracts a wide range of acts, from Offspring to the more sedate Stephen Stills. The Ogden often has the best ticket in town, aside from major concert venues. Hours and ticket prices vary.

PURPLE MARTINI

1020 15th Street, Tabor Center
(303) 993-9383,
www.purplemartin.com

Belleview Promenade Center,
I-25 and Belleview,
Greenwood Village
(720) 234-1155

In the mood for an exotic martini? The Purple Martini offers 80 different kinds as well as live jazz Wednesday, Thursday, and Saturday. Acid jazz is played the other nights (although not live). Look for a 20- to 30-something crowd dressed in "business casual."

SING SING

1735 19th Street
(303) 291-0880
www.singsing.com

Located beneath the ChopHouse, Sing Sing offers dueling pianos in a sometimes-wild late-night setting and a chance to sing your heart out. This is definitely a more mainstream crowd that enjoys the likes of Billy Joel tunes. It's also not for the frail, as the improvisational songs can lean toward the raunchy. Food includes Old Chicago pizza and calzones. Sing Sing is open Tuesday through Saturday. Arrive early for best seating.

TRIOS ENOTECA

1730 Wynkoop Street
(303) 293-2887
www.triosenoteca.com

The popularity of Trios Enoteca waxes and wanes with the whims of trendy bar life, but it's still a great (if pricey) place to order from more than 300 wines or 25 different martinis. The cigar room draws the 30- and 40-something crowds. Live music is performed five nights a week, usually jazz and always loud. The decor is elegant, light woods with comfortable couches and high-backed chairs. A light menu is served. Closed Sunday and Monday.

DANCING

THE CHURCH

1160 Lincoln Street
(303) 832-3528

Take an old cathedral and transform it into a dance club, complete with stained-glass windows and an elevated altar area, and you've got one of Denver's hottest clubs. The Church attracts dancers of all ages (of course, the weekends tend toward the younger set) mainly because it is large enough to offer a variety of music styles; we recommend it for ages 18 to 25. The weekends offer different music in different rooms. There is a sushi bar, a wine bar, and a cigar bar. Thursday is 18+ night, and there's no cover before 10 p.m. Friday and Saturday.

THE HI-DIVE

7 South Broadway
(720) 570-4500
www.hi-dive.com

For live music, try the hi-dive for hip new bands, record-release parties, and DJs. It's well positioned in a string of small dives just a stone's throw from the galleries that line South Santa Drive. It seats 285 and has a killer sound system. Plan on occasional cover charges.

JACKSON'S LODO

1520 20th Street
(303) 298-7625
www.jacksonsdenver.com

A great place to drink while you listen to Top 40, hip-hop, and alternative music, Jackson's Hole attracts a youngish crowd—ages 21 to 30. It's open daily until the wee hours.

i While locals and visitors still flock to LoDo nightclubs, hipsters prefer these grittier scenes: the warehouse district, on Larimer Street but centered around 27th and 29th Streets; upper downtown, between 20th and 22nd Streets on California, Welton, Stout, and Champa Streets; and Broadway and Lincoln Streets as they intersect 11th Street.

LA RUMBA 99

West 9th Avenue
(303) 572-8006
www.larumba-denver.com

Catch the Latin, salsa, and swing craze at this neighborhood spot, which is open Thursday through Saturday. The 14-piece salsa band is popular, as are the salsa and swing lessons that begin at 9:30 p.m. Thursday and Saturday evenings. The decor is fun with comfy couches for resting between steps. The dress is classy. Cover is $5 to $7.

ZIGGIES SALOON

4923 West 38th Avenue
(303) 455-9930
www.ziggieslivemusic.com

Denver's oldest blues club, Ziggies offers live music nightly in its Berkeley Heights barroom and a dance floor for those who rock. On Sunday afternoon there's a no-cover-charge open-stage acoustic jam 4 to 8 p.m., followed by a blues jam 8:30 p.m. to 12:30 a.m.

ROADHOUSES

BUFFALO ROSE SALOON

1119 Washington Street, Golden
(303) 278-6800
www.buffalorose.net

Established in 1851, the Buffalo Rose is still going strong in its downtown Golden location. Three nights a week it presents musical acts that range from well-known rock groups to folk singers, with cover charges that start at around $3.

HERMAN'S HIDEAWAY

1578 South Broadway
(303) 777-5840
www.hermanshideaway.com

Herman's Hideaway is a live-music showcase with a large dance floor. The entertainment can vary from rock to Cajun. As you might expect of a funky South Broadway roadhouse, the decor is casual and the atmosphere laid-back. The crowd is 20s to 40s. Advance ticketing is advisable for special bookings of nationally known acts.

i A few restaurants that are equally good spots for a pre-dinner or late-night drink and a nosh are Marlowe's* at 16th Street and Glenarm Place, (303) 595-3700; Paramount Cafe*, next door to Marlowe's at 519 16th Street, (303) 893-2000; and Avenue Grill*, 630 East 17th Avenue, (303) 861-2820, the choice of Denver's uptown movers and shakers.

LITTLE BEAR

28075 Highway 74
(Main Street), Evergreen
(303) 674-9991
http://littlebearsaloon.com

Even folks from the plains brave the narrow mountain roads to make the scene at Little Bear. Neither the route nor the rollicking roadhouse atmosphere is for the timid, but it's a fine place to listen to national and local rock, folk, and blues musicians. It's open daily, with live entertainment six days a week and a small cover charge on the weekends. Pizza and burgers are served daily from 11 a.m.

COUNTRY-AND-WESTERN NIGHTCLUBS

GRIZZLY ROSE SALOON & DANCE EMPORIUM

5450 North Valley Highway
(303) 295-2353
www.grizzlyrose.com

Grizzly Rose has been voted the nation's No. 1 country music dance hall by the Country Music Association, and it's where the big names come to play when they're in town. With a 5,000-square-foot dance floor and headliners such as Willie Nelson, Merle Haggard, and Toby Keith, it's not hard to see why Grizzly Rose is the undisputed favorite in the live-music C&W category. Advance ticketing is recommended for national acts; call Grizzly Rose or Ticketmaster, (303) 830-TIXS. When no concert is scheduled, Tuesday and Wednesday are no-cover nights. Sunday night is family night, when all ages are welcome.

STAMPEDE MESQUITE GRILL & STEAKHOUSE
2430 South Havana Street, Aurora
(303) 696-7686
www.stampedeclub.com

Stampede Mesquite also bills itself as Denver's premiere Country bar and dance club, which tells you it all boils down to preference. The Stampede has a giant racetrack dance floor, line dancing and lessons, a yuppie clientele, and an antique bar. Call ahead for reservations at the restaurant, which is on a second-floor balcony overlooking the nightclub and offers well-priced dinner specials.

TEDDY'S RESTAURANT AND LOUNGE
4849 Bannock Street
(303) 292-9500

Teddy's Restaurant and Lounge, located in the Denver North Holiday Inn near the intersection of I-70 and I-25, has a different musical format every nigh, but we love it best on Country night. Genres vary from merengue, cumbia, and Latin rock, to country, disco, oldies, and Top 40. Happy hour comes with free hors d'oeuvres; meals are available at the hotel's full-service restaurant.

BREWPUBS, SPORTS BARS, AND POOL HALLS

BLAKE STREET TAVERN
2401 Blake Street
(303) 675-0505
www.blakestreettavern.com

One of the first brewpubs in the Rocky Mountain region, Flying Dog Brewery was born in Aspen in 1991. When demand outgrew capacity three years later, operations were moved to Denver, where Flying Dog currently produces and ships more than 400,000 cases of seven different brews. The tavern in front of the brewery now serves microbrews as well as a menu of salads, pizzas, calzones, and sandwiches plus pool tables and music. Just two blocks north of Coors Field, it's a good choice for Rockies fans.

BRECKENRIDGE BLAKE STREET PUB*
2220 Blake Street
(303) 297-3644
www.breckbrew.com

The Blake Street Pub, which opened in 1992, makes the same beers and ales as the original Breckenridge Brewery & Pub, its Summit County cousin. Both have beer drinking and billiards late into the evening (and early into the morning), with food available for those who need more. Tuesday evenings are set aside for a blues jam, and there's live music on weekends on the patio, weather permitting. There is no cover charge.

ROCK BOTTOM RESTAURANT & BREWERY*
1001 16th Street
(303) 534-7616
www.rockbottom.com

Yet another brewpub and pool hall, the huge, sunny Rock Bottom Brewery is popular with the young lawyers and bankers who work on 17th Street. Try the Red Rocks Red Ale, and drink it on the patio for some of the best people-watching on the 16th Street Mall. The food's pretty good, too. And, of course, you can shop at the in-house boutique for T-shirts and the like.

SPORTS COLUMN*
1930 Blake Street
(303) 296-1930
www.denversportscolumn.com

Billing itself as "major league excitement," Sports Column joins the ranks of Lower Downtown sports bars with picturesque rooftop patios. It has the requisite pool tables, foosball, and food. It also features five big-screen TVs, plenty of video games, and a kitchen that stays open late.

WYNKOOP BREWING COMPANY*
1634 18th Street
(303) 297-2700
www.wynkoop.com

After 5 p.m. is a busy time for the Wynkoop Brewing Company, Denver's first brewpub. Opened in 1988 by John Hickenlooper, now Denver's mayor, the Wynkoop offers comedy downstairs, dining on the first floor, and pool upstairs, all in the historic circa 1899 J. S. Brown Mercantile Building. Regulars like the Railyard Ale, but teetotalers swear by the house-brewed root beer. The billiards room has 22 pool tables, dart lanes, and two private pool rooms, as well as a full-service bar. Cue rentals and lessons are available; call for more information. Comedy is offered in the basement at the Impulse Theater. Details are provided in the Comedy Clubs section below.

ALL-AGES NIGHTLIFE

MERCURY CAFE*
2199 California Street
(303) 294-9281
www.mercurycafe.com
The reincarnation of a legendary Denver nightclub of the '70s and early '80s, Mercury Cafe offers everything from swing dancing and Big Band music to performance art, comedy, theater, and lectures. Mercury also serves dinner Tuesday through Sunday and brunch on weekends. Credit cards are not accepted.

COMEDY CLUBS

COMEDY WORKS
1226 15th Street
(303) 595-3637
www.comedyworks.com
Roseanne (formerly Barr and Arnold) is among the many comics who made appearances at Comedy Works early in their careers. Tuesday night is new talent night; Wednesday through Sunday nights are for established performers. Ticket prices vary, but $18 is about the upper limit unless a headliner is on the bill, which could cost up to $40. Reservations are recommended, and it's for ages 21 and older only.

IMPULSE THEATER
1634 18th Street
(302) 297-2111
www.impulsetheater.com

This show opened in 1987 and is billed as Denver's longest-running comedy show. It occupies the lower level of the Wynkoop Brewing Company, with performances Thursday, Friday, and Saturday. Don't expect stand-up. This place does skits, scenes, and ensemble comedy similar to *Saturday Night Live*. And customers feel like they're attending a sporting event since they decide which "team" is funniest. Reservations are recommended.

WITS END COMEDY CLUB
6080 West 92nd Avenue, Westminster
(303) 430-4242
www.witsendcomedyclub.com
Wits End Comedy Club offers the comic hijinks of local, national, and international jokemeisters. The humor tends toward the clean side, but you still have to be age 21 or older to attend. Comedians are booked Wednesday through Sunday.

MOVIES

Denver offers an extensive array of neighborhood theaters, most like those in any other town. The theaters listed below will give you a more unusual experience.

FILM ON THE ROCKS
Red Rocks Amphitheatre
I-70 West to Morrison exit, Morrison
(866) 464-2626
www.redrocksonline.com
This summer series pairs performances by local bands with screenings of great movies such as Willy Wonka and the Chocolate Factory, with opening act The Flobots and headliner Buckner Funken Jazz. The outdoor setting makes it a magical movie experience. Bring something soft to sit on and rain gear, just in case.

LANDMARK MAYAN
1st Avenue and Broadway
(303) 352-1992
www.landmarktheaters.com
Denver's finest art-movie house is the Mayan. This 1930s-era theater is decorated on every inch of

its wall and ceiling surface with wonderful Mayan figures and other designs. Everything is classy here: the decor, the audience, the films, even the espresso and pastries served in the second-floor cafe. There's one large screen on the main level and two smaller ones above. The Landmark Chez Artiste Cinema at 2800 South Colorado Boulevard, the Esquire Theater at 590 Downing Street, and the Landmark Theatre Greenwood Village at 5415 Landmark Place, are owned by the same company. Discounted multiple admission tickets are available and can be used at all four locations. Be sure to buy popcorn at any of these theaters: They use real butter!

STARZ FILMCENTER
900 Auraria Parkway
(303) 820-3456
www.starzfilmcenter.com
The Starz FilmCenter is home to the Denver Film Society and the University of Colorado at Denver and Health Sciences Center's College of Arts & Media film education program, in addition to offering a broad selection of films that appeal to viewers with discretion. It also is host to the Starz Denver Film Festival. The center books indie films as well as classics, foreign films as well as wide-release films that slip in and out of commercial theaters too quickly. The Starz FilmCenter is located in the old Tivoli Brewery building, which was saved during the construction of UC-D's Auraria campus. The theater is newer than most art houses, which means the seats are more comfortable and the sound system is stronger.

GAMBLING

Since gambling was legalized in 1991, casinos have replaced nearly every retail shop, restaurant, snack shop, and business in the historic mining towns of Central City and Black Hawk, a little more than 30 miles from downtown Denver.

To get there, take US 6 west through Clear Creek Canyon to Highway 119 and follow the signs, or take I-70 westbound to the Central City exit 243 and head north. Parking is at a premium and difficult to find close in, but the good news

is that it's validated as long as you gamble. Better yet, let someone else do the driving. If you're just visiting, ask at your hotel about transportation, or check the yellow pages under "Buses—Charter and Rental" for the names of companies that offer round-trip bus and shuttle service to Central City and Black Hawk. A few shuttle services you might look into are the Coach U.S.A./Ace Express (303) 421-2780, and the People's Choice (303) 289-2222.

Once you get there, most of the casinos are fairly similar. The biggest decision is whether to stay in Black Hawk, which is right on Highway 119, or turn on the spur road and travel 1 mile farther to Central City. Shuttle buses connect the two, but if you're only up for the evening, you probably won't want to spend your time going back and forth. If you'd like to mix your gambling with a little history, head into Central City. It's been tarted-up a lot since its mining days, but you can still get a sense of what it used to be like.

Limited-stakes gambling is the rule here, with $5 being the maximum bet. Only poker, blackjack, and lots of one-armed bandits are allowed at the nearly 40 parlors that operate between 8 a.m. and 2 a.m.

For a complete listing of casinos and accommodations, visit www.blackhawkcolorado.com and www.centralcitycolorado.com. The *Colorado Gambler*, a free newspaper, is also a good guide. It's widely available in the gambling towns and often in Denver, especially at hotels.

AMERISTAR BLACK HAWK
111 Richman Street, Black Hawk
(303) 946-4000
www.ameristar.com/blackhawk
National powerhouse Ameristar bought this casino in 2004 and promptly remodeled until it was the state's largest gambling complex. It boasts 15 blackjack and 10 poker tables, as well as slot machines, live entertainment, and one of the area's best casino buffets. Other food options include a steak house, a grill, a pizza joint, and a coffee shop. A 536-room hotel and spa were projected to open in fall 2009.

CANYON CASINO

131 Main Street, Black Hawk
(303) 777-1111
www.canyoncasino.com

Canyon Casino is more of a Las Vegas-style casino, but don't expect Vegas-style entertainment. It is well supplied with video poker and slot machines, with a grill to ease your hunger pains, but if you're looking for music or a show, keep on moving.

COLORADO CENTRAL STATION CASINO AND HOTEL

401 Main Street, Black Hawk
(303) 998-7777
http://isleofcapricasino.com

The Grand Central Station has a high profile in Black Hawk, with 238 rooms and minisuites, two restaurants and two grills, and live entertainment. Gambling options run the gamut from slots and video poker to black jack and poker.

FORTUNE VALLEY HOTEL AND CASINO

321 Gregory Street, Central City
(303) 327-2200, (800) 924-6646
www.fortunevalleycasino.com

This is one of Colorado's lushest combination hotel-casinos, with 118 rooms. Look for live entertainment, live casino action, slots, and a restaurant that serves barbecue.

THE GILPIN CASINO

111 Main Street, Black Hawk
(303) 582-1133
www.thegilpincasino.com

The Gilpin Hotel has poker tables, something not all the casinos can claim. Its Mineshaft Bar long predates gambling—it has been a local hangout for more than 100 years.

SHOPPING

In this chapter we focus on three major shopping areas that have a great concentration and variety of stores: Cherry Creek North; Downtown, LoDo, and Larimer Square; and South Broadway. The Cherry Creek and Larimer Square areas are small enough to view by foot, and that's how we've written those sections, with directions from one place to the next. South Broadway is more spread out—we survey the shops from north to south, but you'll want to travel by car or bus rather than walk the whole span.

To finish off your introduction to Denver shopping, we've included a roundup of where to go for arts and crafts, books, clothes, food and gourmet cooking supplies, furniture, gifts, and outlet and bargain stores.

Most stores are open daily and accept credit cards, but call ahead to be sure.

But first, the basics—department and grocery stores. Major department stores with more than one location in Greater Denver include Macy's, Dillard's, Sears, and JCPenney. For Western wear, Rockmont, Miller Stockman, and Sheplers have locations throughout the metro area. Sports Authority, Recreational Equipment Inc. (REI), Eastern Mountain Sports (EMS), Dick's, BassPro Shops, and Cabela's stores supply Denverites with gear for camping, hiking, biking, rafting, and other outdoor activities.

A top source for consumer electronics, including stereos, televisions, VCRs, and cellular phones, is Ultimate Electronics. There are several stores throughout the metro area. You'll find the Denver location at 1370 South Colorado Boulevard.

The big supermarket chains include King Soopers and Safeway. For natural foods, visit any of the Whole Foods, Sunflower, or Vitamin Cottage markets.

MAJOR SHOPPING AREAS

Cherry Creek North

The neighborhood directly to the north of the mall, Cherry Creek North, is a delightful mélange of interesting shops, galleries, clothing designers, cafes, and restaurants.

At the corner of Detroit Street and 2nd Avenue is **Room and Board,** a contemporary furniture store that consistently ranks high in local "Best of" polls. Just across the street at 221 Detroit Street is **DjUNA**, a locally owned vintage-inspired furniture store. If you're looking for something to hang above the sofa, **Saks Galleries,** 3019 East 2nd Avenue, specializes in 19th- and 20th-century representational art.

Pismo Contemporary Art Glass, 2770 East 2nd Avenue, stocks an unmatched selection of art glass by Coloradans Brian Maytum, Kit Karbler, and internationally known glass artist Dale Chihuly in its luxurious gallery. More art glass can be found at **International Villa,** 239 Detroit Street, named one of America's Top 100 Galleries. A great source for funky clothing and inexpensive jewelry for men and women is **Eccentricity,** 290 Fillmore Street.

Gallery M, 2830 East 3rd Avenue, features contemporary fine art, photography, and sculpture by both national and international artists. **Show of Hands,** 210 Clayton Street, on the other hand, showcases American crafts in clay, metal, wood, and fiber as well as stocking wall art and paintings.

Among the designer labels carried at **Lawrence Covell,** 225 Steele Street, are Yohji Yamamoto, Kiton, and Luciano Barbera. This upscale men's and women's store is known for its first-class service.

Kids' stuff can be found at **The Wizard's Chest,** 230 Fillmore Street, which in addition to children's toys carries grown-up games and an attic full of costumes and masks. **Kazoo & Company,** 2930 East 2nd Avenue, has educational games and toys.

Gardeners will love the **Smith & Hawken** store at 268 Detroit Street. Shop here for high-quality gardening tools, workwear, containers, plants, and garden furniture.

Hermitage Antiquarian Bookshop, 290 Fillmore Street, is a pleasant spot with neat library stacks of first editions and other rare and/or old books.

Downtown, LoDo, and Larimer Square

Downtown Denver's main shopping thoroughfare, 16th Street, was transformed into a tree-lined pedestrian mall in 1980 and now boasts 25,000 flowers in the summer. Free shuttle buses run the length of the mall as often as every 90 seconds, connecting Lower Downtown with the Civic Center area. Many of the stores along 16th Street are touristy, but it's worth strolling the mile-long stretch to see what's here. With **TJMaxx** and **Ross,** the corner of 16th and California Streets has become a mini off-price mecca in downtown. Restaurants along the mall often have outdoor seating—great for people-watching—and there are shaded benches for those who've brought their own lunch or their laptops. The entire mall offers free Wi-Fi service to all outdoor visitors. If you haven't planned ahead, buy a to-go lunch from a street vendor or fast-food restaurant.

More traditional shopping takes place at the glass-enclosed **Tabor Center,** which extends along 16th Street from Arapahoe to Larimer. The center once was a shining star in the downtown shopping scene, but it has struggled in recent years. It is undergoing a renovation that is expected to reenergize the center. Among the goals of the renovation is a desire to simplify navigation into and through the shopping center.

The heart of Larimer Square is Larimer Street between 15th and 14th Streets. From Tabor Center, walk 1 block south through the cluster of stores and restaurants called **Writer Square,** and on the other side you'll find yourself standing on the spot where Denver got its start in 1858. Denver's first bank, bookstore, photographer, and dry-goods store were located on this block. The original buildings were made of wood and were destroyed in a fire in 1863; the brick structures that now line the street were erected for the most part in the 1870s to 1890s, and the entire area was renovated in the mid-1970s. Interested visitors can pick up a walking-tour brochure and information on the individual buildings at the kiosk on the east side of the street.

Larimer Square has a nice mix of shops and restaurants, including **Cry Baby Ranch,** which has Western furnishings and pricey trinkets. **The Market** has an exhaustive selection of gourmet goodies as well as coffee, deli, and bakery items to take out or eat on the premises. **Z Gallerie,** on the corner of 15th and Larimer Streets, has contemporary home furnishings and accessories. Also on the block: **John Atencio** jewelry; Scarpaletto shoes; Eve women's clothing; and **Ted Turner's Montana Grill.** At this point you're just a few blocks from the **Tattered Cover Book Store** at 16th and Wynkoop Streets.

As you move into LoDo, check out **Bouquets,** 1525 15th Street, for the most unusual flowers and flower arrangements in town. It was voted Denver's top florist in 2003 by *5280* magazine.

Stop at **Rockmont Ranch Wear,** at 1626 Wazee Street, for a look back in time as well as an opportunity to buy authentic Western clothing. Rockmont founders invented the snap-front Western shirt, and for more than 60 years have been generating duds for rodeo cowboys, Hollywood stars, and city slickers alike. The building, open Monday through Saturday, includes a museum and a retail store.

The 1700 block of Wazee Street was once the heart of Denver's contemporary art district, and it still is, in a sense, although closures and additions have shifted the emphasis away from the avant-garde. We write more about that in our The Arts chapter.

A bit farther uptown, collectors of Native-American crafts head for the **Mudhead Gallery** in the Hyatt Regency Hotel, 555 17th Street, www.mudheadgallery.net.

The **Native American Trading Company,** a fine source for pots, textiles, and Edward S. Curtis photogravures, is across from the **Denver Art Museum** at 1301 Bannock Street, www.nativeamericantradingco.com.

On the upper, southern edge of downtown is one of Denver's most venerable stores. **Sports Authority** is at 10th Avenue and Broadway, in a wildly extravagant building known as the Sports Castle. This seven-level store, originally built as a car dealership, stocks everything, including tents, cameras, bicycles, and tennis shoes. Originally known as Gart Sports, it now has dozens of other locations throughout the state (find them at www.sportsauthority.com) but none is as architecturally distinctive as this one.

South Broadway Belmar

South Broadway is an antiques lover's paradise. In fact, the area between Arizona and Iowa Streets is dubbed "Antiques Row." There are a few furniture stores tucked in as well. Your best bet is to just make your way south on Broadway (it's one way north of the I-25 interchange). Many of the shops are listed in our Antiques category.

SHOPPING MALLS

ASPEN GROVE LIFESTYLE CENTER
7301 South Santa Fe Drive, Littleton
(303) 794-0640
www.shopaspengrove.com
Built in 2001, Aspen Grove was one of metro Denver's first "lifestyle centers," or outdoor shopping centers that allow for more than just mall shopping. It draws clients from throughout the area, but its primary customers come from Littleton and southwest Denver. Its stores include Chico's,

Talbot's, Children's Place, Pier 1, and Williams-Sonoma. Dining choices include Buca di Beppo, Noodles & Co., Ted's Montana Grill, and Panera Bread Co.

BELMAR
408 South Teller Street, Lakewood
(303) 742-1520
www.belmarcolorado.com
The Belmar shopping area creates a new downtown for the first-tier Denver suburb of Lakewood. The new Belmar is still coming into its own, but fans already know it for the summer farmers' market, fall Italian festival, and winter holiday celebrations. They also know it as home to the area's newest Whole Foods Market, as well as chain stores and local restaurants strewn out along a network of new streets. Condos, row houses, and detached homes are being built on the site and will bring with them new residents who will amble down to the movie theater or Lucky Strike bowling alley. Until then, shoppers from throughout the metro area drive in to taste the development that has gained national attention for its scope, creativity, and future potential. In addition to national chains that are represented in most malls, Belmar boasts a Coldwater Creek that has a full-service spa, two dentists, five electronics and wireless phone stores, banks, bars and restaurants that serve American, Asian, Italian, and Mexican food.

CHERRY CREEK SHOPPING CENTER
3000 East 1st Avenue
(303) 388-3900
www.cherrycreekmall.com
Anchored by Saks Fifth Avenue, Neiman Marcus, and Macy's, the Cherry Creek Shopping Center also has high-end specialty stores such as Louis Vuitton, Abercrombie & Fitch, Banana Republic, and Ann Taylor. Even the restroom is above average: Clad in marble, with automatic fixtures, it was written up in *Time* magazine! There is a dining area with quick food and several upscale restaurants, such as Kona Grill. Retail tenants include Tiffany & Co., Williams-Sonoma, Tommy Bahama, and Anthropologie.

Another attraction is an elaborate play area for kids, with seating for adults, near the mall entrance to Macy's. The area features super-size, colorful breakfast-food items for the kids to crawl on. Kids can't resist sliding down the bacon into an egg yolk. The attraction is so popular that mini playgroups have formed for regular visits.

COLORADO MILLS

14500 West Colfax Avenue, Lakewood
(303) 384-3000
www.coloradomills.com
Colorado Mills is one of the newest malls in the metro area. The stores in this snazzy center are all one-of-a-kind outlets, offering reduced prices on merchandise from such retailers as Ann Taylor, Neiman Marcus Last Call, Tommy Hilfiger, Off 5th Saks Fifth Avenue, Borders Books and Music Cafe, Bath & Body Works, SKECHERS, Levi's, Kenneth Cole, Eddie Bauer, Chico's, and Nine West. Off Broadway Shoe Warehouse is big enough to satisfy any shoe lover, carrying designs that range from sane to gotta-have-it crazy.

Located off I-70 on the west side of the metro area, Colorado Mills is a convenient stop for travelers on their way to and from the mountains, and residents from all parts of town find it worth the drive for the unique selection and bargain prices. The mall has a standard food court and a 16-screen theater complex.

DENVER PAVILIONS

On the 16th Street Mall between Tremont
and Welton Streets
(303) 260-6000
www.denverpavilions.com
The Pavilions doesn't fit into traditional mall or shopping area categories because it offers more than retail. Pavilions bills itself as the new wave of retail, restaurant, and entertainment. You can browse Banana Republic, indulge in something decadent at the Corner Bakery, then take in a flick at the United Artists theater (all high-backed stadium seating).

Denver Pavilions boasts several large attractions, including Maggiano's Little Italy, Coyote Ugly Saloon, Lucky Strike Lanes, Jazz@Jack's, Hard Rock Cafe, Virgin Records Megastore, along with more familiar shops such as Barnes & Noble, Bath and Body Works, Gap, Victoria's Secret, and 30,000-square-foot NikeTown (one of only 15 in the United States). Mall crawlers used to the confines of suburban malls will be surprised at the Pavilions' open-air setting. But with a yearly average of 300 days of sunshine, outdoor shopping is rarely a problem in Denver.

FLATIRON CROSSING

US 36 at Interlocken
or FlatIron Circle exits
(720) 887-9900
www.flatironcrossing.com
FlatIron Crossing is an indoor-outdoor center with 1.5 million square feet of shopping anchored by Nordstrom, Macy's, and Dillard's. Its 170 specialty retailers include well-known names like Gap and Ann Taylor as well as lesser-known shops in the Village. The center is located amid 30 acres of green space and parklike settings and offers access to local trails.

NORTHFIELD STAPLETON

8340 East 49th Avenue
(303) 375-5464
www.northfieldstapleton.com
Northfield is one of Denver's newest outdoor-lifestyles centers, opening in 2006 with Harkins Theatre, Colorado's only Bass Pro Shop, SuperTarget, and Macy's as anchors. Another 50 tenants fill out the Main Street segment, with 25 more to follow. Restaurants include Bar Louie, La Sandia, and Ling & Louie's Asian Bar and Grill. In addition to providing one of the region's roomiest parking lots, the center is located at what may be the best crossroad for out-of-state visitors. I-70 (which runs from Kansas to Utah) and I-270 (which veers north to Nebraska) intersect near the center's southwest corner.

PARK MEADOWS

8401 Park Meadows Center Drive
Lone Tree
(303) 792-2999
www.parkmeadows.com
Park Meadows is anchored by Nordstrom, Dillard's,

Close-up

Indoor-outdoor FlatIron Crossing

FlatIron Crossing opened with a splash in August 2000 and continues to attract both stores and shoppers. Touted as reflecting the outdoor lifestyle of Coloradans, the center combines a 1.2-million-square-foot interior mall with a 240,000-square-foot outdoor, streetscaped shopping area. A 14-screen AMC theater anchors the southwestern corner.

The idea was to create more than just another shopping experience. According to Westcor Partners, the center's developer, the goal was to create a place that people think of as both a community showplace and a great place to spend a Saturday afternoon. With its 30 acres of green space and parks, access to local trail systems, and two parklike areas with lush landscapes and streams and fountains, FlatIron Crossing may do just that.

Inside the mall, natural materials and abundant sunlight were essential design elements. The interior makes generous use of wood beams, iron, patterned stone, and Colorado limestone. Some windows allow high-morning sun, while others are set to capture the glow of late afternoons.

The center's largest tenants are Nordstrom, Macy's, and Dillard's. The interior stores tend to be highly recognizable national chains like Eddie Bauer, Banana Republic, Fossil, and Pottery Barn, while smaller and, in some cases, local stores populate the Village. All told, there are more than 200 specialty retailers and restaurants located throughout the mall's far-flung properties. In an effort to bring more people out of the mall and into the Village, the center hosts farmers' markets and Thursday-evening street fairs.

FlatIron Crossing launched the FlatIron Crossing Music & Art Foundation to help restore endangered music and arts programs in Colorado schools and communities. Guided by board members from the local arts and education communities, the foundation will benefit from many activities at FlatIron Crossing over the years as well as raise funds through community, business, and government sources.

Located off US 36, the center is conveniently situated along the growing Denver-Boulder corridor and draws residents of both cities.

and Macy's. The dining hall is huge, and the restaurants are on the swanky side. Park Meadows grows ever-larger each year with the addition of retail around its perimeter. It's a great mix of low-, mid-, and high-end retail.

SOUTHWEST PLAZA
Wadsworth Boulevard and West Bowles
Avenue, Littleton
(303) 973-5300
www.southwestplaza.com
Once Denver's largest mall, Southwest Plaza serves Jefferson County's booming population. Anchored by Dillard's, Macy's, JCPenney, and Sears, it has almost every type of clothing, food, music, and shoe store, as well as a movie theater and a SuperTarget.

THE STREETS OF SOUTHGLENN
South University Boulevard and East
Arapahoe Road, Centennial
Like many other aging indoor shopping malls, the old Southglenn Mall is in being reinvented as an outdoor lifestyle center. The original mall was demolished in June 2006, although anchor tenants Sears and Macy's remained open during the transformation. Once it is completed, city officials and tenants hope the 70-acre site will become a focal point for community events and festivals as well as providing destination shopping. Retail tenants will include Whole Foods, a 16-screen movie theater, Barnes & Noble, a health club, restaurants, and clothing stores.

Close-up

Park Meadows Draws Shoppers from Afar

When Park Meadows opened in August 1996, it was hailed as a shopping center unlike any ever built. In fact, it was described as a retail "resort." We're not sure whether shoppers feel like they're on vacation, but they are certainly attracted to Park Meadows as if it were a vacation spot. About thirteen million people came the first year to check out Greater Denver's largest shopping center—all 1.5 million square feet of it.

With three top-drawer anchors—Colorado's first Nordstrom, Denver's first Dillard's, and Colorado's largest Macy's—Park Meadows attracts visitors from a seven-state region and is fast becoming one of the area's must-see places.

While most malls are conglomerates of individual stores, Park Meadows was designed to feel like a mountain ski lodge (a very, very busy one!). Massive natural wood-beam cathedral ceilings soar above the second level, the shopping center is bathed in natural light, and large stone fireplaces are located throughout. Shoppers can rest in overstuffed leather chairs and couches. Hahn Company, the developer of Park Meadows, also commissioned eight Colorado artists to create $2 million worth of artwork.

The shopping center is home to 160 stores, many of which were new to Colorado when they opened, including Crate and Barrel, Restoration Hardware, and Nordstrom. While the obligatory dining area is located near the center, Park Meadows also houses "better" restaurants, including California Cafe, Red Robin, and P.F. Chang's China Bistro. Even the movie theater here is a little bigger and a little glitzier. In addition to the multiscreen movie theater, there are four virtual-reality experiences, including "Virtual Hanglider."

THORNTON TOWN CENTER MALL
10001 Grant Street (off I-25 at 104th Avenue East), Thornton

This fairly small outdoor mall (25 stores) is anchored by a Super Wal-Mart, a Home Depot, and a theater complex.

TOWN CENTER AT AURORA
off I-225 at East Alameda Avenue and Sable Street, Aurora
(303) 344-4120
www.simon.com

This center has the look and feel of a fairly typical suburban mall. Anchored by Macy's and JCPenney, it offers recognizable stores like the Disney Store and Old Navy, as well as 125 smaller, more boutique-type shops.

WESTMINSTER MALL
Sheridan Boulevard and 88th Avenue Westminster
(303) 428-5634
www.shopwestminstermall.com

Westminster Mall has four anchor stores, Dillard's, Macy's, JCPenney, and Sears. Like many aging indoor malls, Westminster is beginning to show its age, but it continues to serve shoppers from North Metro counties.

ANTIQUES

The South Broadway area has the greatest concentration of antiques stores in the Metro Denver area. In addition to the stores we mention by name below, you're sure to find more, especially continuing farther south on Broadway. And if you're willing to travel out of Denver 30 to 40 minutes, you might want to check out the town of Niwot and its 2-block main street filled with antiques shops. Auctions are sometimes held on Sunday. To get to Niwot, take I-25 north to Highway 52 west to connect with Highway 119. Niwot is about 1 mile north of the intersection of Highways 52 and 119.

The town of Lyons, which lies at the mouth of St. Vrain Canyon on the way to Estes Park, about 45 minutes from downtown Denver, is another great antiques lover's mecca. Antiques stores dot both sides of the old-fashioned Main Street. You'll find a few that specialize in Western memorabilia. To get there from central Denver, take I-25 north to the Highway 66 exit, then go west about 17 miles.

Closer to town, check out the following shop.

DECADE
56 South Broadway
(303) 733-2288
Voted "Best Store Anywhere on Broadway" in 2001 by the readers and editors of *Westword*, this little shop mixes vintage and new. They have a constantly changing array of furniture that spans the decades and a good selection of home accessories as well. They also have a small clothing boutique in the back that offers mostly new men's and women's clothing, jewelry, and such. The shop tends to carry more vintage options in the fall than earlier in the year.

ARTS AND CRAFTS

For arts and crafts, make Cherry Creek North your first stop (see Major Shopping Areas at the beginning of this chapter). Additional sources include the following.

AKENTE EXPRESS
919 Park Avenue West
(303) 297-8817
Akente Express is an African-American heritage shop that stocks original fabrics from Africa, handmade clothing, jewelry, artwork, sculpture, and all-natural, alcohol-free essential oils.

OLD SANTA FE POTTERY
2485 South Santa Fe Drive
(303) 871-9434
www.oldsantafepottery.com
Old Santa Fe Pottery houses two rows of shops filled with Oaxacan wood carvings, painted Talavera ceramics, furniture, rugs, and all sorts of pottery. You'll enjoy a pretty central courtyard reminiscent of a Mexican village.

BARGAIN SHOPPING

Denver has its share of off-price retailers, including Loehmann's, 9555 East County Line Road, (303) 708-9966, which sells primarily name-brand women's clothing at low prices. Beyond that, there are several great consignment and near-new stores, such as the following.

GUMBALLS
5787 South Gallup Street, Littleton
(303) 795-6557
Tired of paying top dollar for kids' blue jeans? Gumballs often has a rack of them priced around a dollar. But that's not all; go here to find a lot of gently used children's clothing.

THE SNOB SHOP
2804 East 6th Avenue
(303) 355-6939
www.thesnobshopdenver.com
This one's been around for a while and is known for its discriminating selection of clothing for men, women, and children plus shoes and accessories. Check it out for anything from casual to dressy.

TWICE AS HAUTE
600 Downing Street
(303) 753-6003
www.twiceashaute.com
This consignment shop deals only in women's clothing. As its name implies, it features labels such as Carole Little, Donna Karan, Armani, and the like. It has a broad selection of dresses for special occasions.

BOOKS

The behemoth Tattered Cover Book Store dominates Metro Denver's literary scene, but Denver's readers are avid enough to support more than one general-interest bookstore. Large chains such as Borders and Barnes & Noble Booksellers have branches in many regional shopping malls. Another good all around bookstore is the **Book Rack,** 2382 South Colorado Boulevard in Denver, 303-756-9891.

Specialty Bookstores

THE BOOKIES
4315 East Mississippi Avenue, Glendale
(303) 759-1117
Though The Bookies is primarily known for its great children's selection, it also carries most best-seller titles, too. Better yet, every book is sold at a discount of at least 15 percent off. (The discount does not apply to educational and teacher resource books.)

CULTURAL LEGACY BOOKSELLERS
3633 West 32nd Avenue
(303) 964-9049
www.culturallegacy.com
Cultural Legacy Bookstore is the only bookstore in Colorado to specialize in Chicano and Latino literature, with Spanish, English, and bilingual books and magazines for children and adults. Ask about book signings and other special events.

GALLAGHER BOOKS
1498 South Broadway
(303) 756-5821
www.gallagherbooks.com
Located on Denver's famed antiques row, Gallagher Collection is a member of the Rocky Mountain Antiquarian Booksellers Association. The shop features rare and out-of-print books, books and posters on WWI and WWII, fine binding, and other specialty items.

MURDER BY THE BOOK
1574 South Pearl Street
(303) 871-9401
www.murderbythebook.com
Murder by the Book, a cozy store in a former home, specializes in new and used mystery novels and crime fiction. If your kids love mysteries, check out the children's selections.

NEIGHBORHOOD BOOKSTORE
5661 South Curtis Street, Littleton
(303) 730-3682
The Neighborhood Bookstore is your basic general-use bookstore. You'll find mostly modern, currently popular titles in just about every genre. About 20 percent of the titles are new; the rest are used books. Ask about their trade-in system for used books.

TATTERED COVER (THREE LOCATIONS)
www.tatteredcover.com

TATTERED COVER CHERRY CREEK
2526 East Colfax Avenue
(303) 322-7727

TATTERED COVER LODO
1628 16th Street
(303) 436-1070

TATTERED COVER HIGHLANDS RANCH
9315 Dorchester Street, Highlands Ranch
(303) 470-7050
The Tattered Cover is truly one of the country's finest independent bookstores—and for book lovers, one of Denver's finest attractions. Built on the philosophy of comfort and personal service, the store provides readers and browsers a place to while away an afternoon (or full day) amid shelf after shelf of books, cozy corners, and overstuffed chairs and couches. Opened more than 35 years ago, the original Cherry Creek store expanded a number of times before moving into the renovated Lowenstein Theater, on the corner of Colfax Avenue and Elizabeth Street, in 2006. A second location followed in historic LoDo, just blocks

from Coors Field. In 2004 a third location sprang up in suburban Highlands Ranch, a 21,754-square-foot addition to the suburban neighborhood. Tattered Cover now houses more than half a million books—150,000 titles—in its three locations. In addition to this expansive book selection, all locations offer a coffee shop, newsstand, and extensive calendar of signings and literary events. You can sign up for the online mailing list to receive an online newsletter and announcements of special events and promotions.

CLOTHING

See our Major Shopping Areas section earlier in this chapter for a good overall roundup of clothing stores. Here are some more options to consider.

5 GREEN BOXES
1596 South Pearl Street
(303) 777-2331
www.5greenboxes.com
Yoga mamas and citizens of the world beat a path to 5 Green Boxes in the Old South Pearl district. It stocks hard-to-find trinkets like Chinese paper wallets and patterned Hot Sox, along with queen of the rodeo belt buckles and an ever changing collection of handmade, natural fiber blouses, skirts, and drawstring pants. A furniture store by the same name has been added a block away at 1705 South Pearl Street, carrying equally funky household accessories.

ANDRISEN MORTON CO.
210 and 270 St. Paul Street
(303) 321-0404,
www.andrisenmorton.com
Between its men's and women's stores, Andrisen Morton covers nearly one full block in Cherry Creek North. It specializes in designer brands and individualized service, attracting a crowd that likes everything from high fashion jeans to business suits to evening wear. Brands vary by season, but expect to see the likes of Armani, Escada, Dolce and Gabbana, and YSL.

BARBARA & COMPANY
7777 East Hampden Avenue
(303) 751-2618
This powerhouse store keeps southeast Denver's Tamarac Square alive, but you'd never know it from the street. Inside this aging suburban mall, Barbara & Company hums with the energy of women on a high-fashion mission. Lines are trendy and international, with items in every shade of the rainbow lining the walls of this 3,000-square-foot store. They're sized for trophy wives; larger sizes do exist, but you'll have to dig through racks of size 0s and 2s to find them.

TOO GOOD TO MISS

Like any city, Denver has a few unique places that don't fit into other categories but are worth checking out just for the novelty. We've included a few below.

BOYER'S COFFEE COMPANY
7295 North Washington Street
(303) 289-3345, (800) 452-5282
www.boyerscoffee.com
Boyer's, a Denver-based coffee roaster and packager, offers its coffee and related items at lower-than-supermarket prices. Its warehouse store is open to the public weekdays only.

EUROPEAN MART
5225 Leetsdale Drive
(303) 321-7144
When you're in the mood for Hungarian salami or hearty sausage, the European Mart is the place to stop. Filled with eastern European delicacies—meats, fish, candies, cookies—this shop is the real thing. The Russian owners are helpful and eager to please, and the food is great.

STEPHANY'S CHOCOLATES
6770 West 52nd Avenue, Arvada
(303) 421-7229
Stephany's Chocolates are a Colorado tradition and a popular gift for visitors to take home. The Denver Mints—get it?—are a big seller. Stephany's has only one store, at its Arvada production facility.

KACEY FINE FURNITURE
1201 Auraria Parkway
(303) 571-5123
www.kacey.com

311 East County Line Road, Littleton
(720) 283-0900

11000 South Parker Road, Parker
(720) 214-6700

11305 West 6th Avenue, Lakewood
(303) 233-8888

Although Kacey Fine Furniture is in several locations (there's even one in Frisco), the main store on Auraria Parkway is the largest, with floor after floor of everything from leather couches to traditional bedroom sets to funky coffee tables. Kacey has a great selection and reasonable prices. Better yet, every year on the owner's birthday, she offers a discount equal to her age. She's currently in her early 50s.

FOR HEAVEN'S SAKE
4383 Tennyson Street
(303) 964-9339
www.forheavensake.com

This New Age gift and book shop in the Berkeley neighborhood area offers a wide array of products such as candles, crystals, books, music, and the increasingly popular "lucky bamboo." The store also sponsors in-house events and classes, including a monthly Psychic Fair, which features palm and tarot readings among other events.

OUTLETS

THE OUTLETS AT CASTLE ROCK
Exit 184, Meadow Parkway
(off I-25 South), Castle Rock
(303) 688-4494
www.outletsatcastlerock.com

The largest outlet mall in the Front Range, Castle Rock has 110 stores—everything from designer clothes to electronics. Open seven days a week, the outlet has an easy and convenient layout and a central food court with the usual fast-food offerings.

THE OUTLETS AT LOVELAND
I-25 North to exit 257B, Loveland
(970) 663-1717
www.outletsatloveland.com

With 82 stores, The Outlets at Loveland include the standard offering of clothes and kitchenware. Though there is no food court on-site, several restaurants are within walking distance.

TOURS AND ATTRACTIONS

In this chapter we've rounded up our favorite museums, gardens, and historic houses. What Metro Denver has to offer in this category may surprise newcomers: The Museum of Nature and Science is the fifth largest of its kind in the country, and the newly expanded Denver Art Museum is the largest such institution between Kansas City and the West Coast. Denver's Zoo and its Botanic Gardens are both highly respected, and the city is full of special-interest museums devoted to such diverse subjects as firefighters, railroads, African Americans in the West, dolls, and the English painter J. M. W. Turner. Among the most popular tourist attractions in the area are the tours at the United States Mint in Denver and Coors Brewery in Golden.

We've organized this chapter by category: museums, historic houses and other historic sites, parks and gardens, and tours. Readers with a particular interest in the arts may also want to check our The Arts chapter, as community art centers and galleries are listed there. At the end of the chapter, we suggest ways to combine visits to different sites that are near each other or that tie in thematically (for example, if you want to spend a day immersing yourself in Western history).

Because hours and admission prices are subject to change, we have included only the basics, with phone numbers and Web site addresses for you to check once you're ready to visit.

MUSEUMS

THE BLACK AMERICAN WEST
Museum and Heritage Center
3091 California Street
(303) 482-2242
www.blackamericanwestmuseum.com

The Black American West Museum is a small but fascinating place that sets a lot of records straight and provides a long-buried picture of the role played by black Americans on the frontier. For example, few people know that the first black mayor of a major American city was Francisco Reyes, owner of the San Fernando Valley until he sold it in the 1790s and became the mayor of Los Angeles. The 1950 Van Heflin movie *Tomahawk* featured white actor Jack Okie playing explorer Jim Beckwourth, who discovered Beckwourth Pass through the Sierras. The movie's only problem: Beckwourth was black, as were up to one-third of all cowboys in the early West. The museum is housed in the former home of Dr. Justina L. Ford, Colorado's first licensed African-American female doctor. It is closed Sunday and Monday.

BUFFALO BILL GRAVE AND MUSEUM
987½ Lookout Mountain Road, Golden
(303) 526-0744
www.buffalobill.org

Dramatically located on top of Lookout Mountain, this fascinating museum is filled with memorabilia honoring the famous frontier scout, showman, and Pony Express rider William F. Cody, colloquially known as Buffalo Bill. Included are gun collections, costumes, and posters from the Wild West show and a collection of dime novels. The grave site affords an expansive view of the plains to the east and mountains to the west. A kids' corral offers young visitors interactive opportunities. The museum is open daily from May through October; Tuesday through Sunday the rest of the year.

COLORADO HISTORY MUSEUM
1300 Broadway
(303) 866-3682
www.coloradohistory.org

The Colorado History Museum offers permanent and changing exhibitions about state history. Special exhibits have included everything from the story of Colorado's Hispano residents to the tale of Cheyenne Dog Soldiers who fought at the historic Sand Creek massacre. As part of what is called the Civic Center Cultural Complex, the history museum, the library, and the art museum collaborate on programs and share resources. The museum has an outstanding collection of William Henry Jackson photos and a comprehensive research library that is free and open to the public Tuesday through Saturday. The museum is open daily.

COLORADO RAILROAD MUSEUM
17155 West 44th Avenue, Golden
(303) 279-4591, (800) 365-6263
www.crrm.org

One of our personal favorites, this museum houses more than 70 historic locomotives and cars as well as additional exhibits in a 15-acre outdoor setting. Don't miss the D&RG Engine No. 346, the oldest operating locomotive in Colorado. The museum is open daily. To get to the museum, take exit 265 off I-70 West and follow the signs.

THE DENVER ART MUSEUM
100 West 14th Avenue Parkway
(720) 865-5000 (recorded information)
www.denverartmuseum.org

The Denver Art Museum is the largest art museum between Kansas City and the West Coast and is especially noted for its superb collections of Native American, pre-Columbian, and Spanish colonial art. Its seven floors also house impressive displays of American, Asian, and contemporary art and galleries devoted to design, graphics, and architecture. See our The Arts chapter for more details.

DENVER FIREFIGHTERS MUSEUM
1326 Tremont Place
(303) 892-1436
www.denverfirefightersmuseum.org

Housed in old Station No. 1, which was built in 1909, the museum has a collection of original hand-drawn firefighting equipment, two engines from the 1920s, and various antique firefighting memorabilia, including helmets, uniforms, and trophies. The museum is open Monday through Saturday.

DENVER MUSEUM OF MINIATURES DOLLS AND TOYS
Pearce-McAllister Cottage
1880 Gaylord Street
(303) 322-1053
www.dmmdt.org

The two-story Pearce-McAllister Cottage, built in 1899, is of interest for its architecture, original decor, and changing displays of vintage dolls, dollhouses, toys, and miniatures. The museum offers year-round workshops for adults and kids on doll-making, toys, and arts and crafts in miniature. There are three free days in the summer sponsored by the Scientific and Cultural Facilities District; call to find out when. A small gift shop sells toys, dolls, and dollhouse furniture. The museum is open Tuesday through Sunday (closed major holidays).

THE DENVER MUSEUM OF NATURE AND SCIENCE
2001 Colorado Boulevard (in City Park, at Colorado Boulevard and Montview)
(303) 322-7009, (800) 925-2250
(303) 370-8257 (hearing-impaired TDD)
www.dmns.org

The Denver Museum of Nature and Science is the largest cultural attraction in the Rocky Mountain region, with an average of 1.5 million visitors annually. In addition to more than 90 dioramas depicting animals from around the world, the museum's permanent exhibitions include a Hall of Life devoted to studying the human body and a fine gem and mineral collection that includes examples of Colorado gold and the largest rhodo-chrosite gem in the world. Other highlights include the Hall of Ancient Peoples, which deals with early man and early civilizations. Don't forget to take a look at the redesigned Egyptian Mummies exhibit. The museum also houses an award-winning dino-saur exhibit, the $7.7 million Prehistoric Journey. It includes walk-through "enviroramas" complete with controlled lighting and temperatures, sounds, vegetation, and even bugs!

The museum's $50 million, 24,000-square-foot Space Odyssey provides an immersion experience in the wonders of space with inter-active opportunities to learn about areas of the cosmos. Visitors can feel what it's like to dock a space shuttle, fly into deep space, and walk on the surface of Mars. The completely digital Gates Planetarium enables visitors to leave Earth's sur-face and fly through the solar system. It's one of the country's first all-digital planetariums and is equipped with surround sound. Although Space Odyssey is free to those who buy admission to the museum, the planetarium shows and some special exhibits cost extra. Watch for special exhi-bitions, which in the past have included artistic and archaeological blockbusters such as *Ramses II* and *Body Worlds 2*, and entertaining fare such as *Star Trek: Federation Science*.

The museum is open daily and has a cafete-ria-style restaurant and the T-Rex cafeteria.

DOWNTOWN AQUARIUM
700 Water Street (in the Platte River
Valley just west of downtown)
(303) 561-4450, (888) 561-4450
www.aquariumrestaurants.com
Denver's most unusual attraction isn't exactly a museum, but it fits well under the category of other top-notch local and tourist spots in this chapter. Opened in the summer of 1999, this long-awaited addition to the Central Platte Valley was originally called Colorado Ocean Journey because it showcased water as it made its ways on two journeys from the Continental Divide to the Sea of Cortez and from an Indonesian rain

forest to the depths of the Pacif
complex was purchased in 2003 k
taurants and reopened in 2005 as an entertain-ment and dining complex. Downtown is open daily. Parking is extra, as are meals.

FORNEY TRANSPORTATION MUSEUM
4303 Brighton Boulevard
(303) 297-1113
www.forneymuseum.com
This longtime Denver favorite displays all kinds of old vehicles, including a number of one-of-a-kinds. Of special interest are the world's largest steam locomotive, Prince Aly Khan's Rolls Royce Phantom I, and an original McCormick reaper. The museum is open Monday through Saturday, but is closed on Christmas, Thanksgiving, and New Year's Day.

FORT VASQUEZ
13412 U.S. Highway 85, Platteville
(970) 785-2832
www.coloradohistory.org
Forty miles downstream from Denver on the South Platte River lies Fort Vasquez, a reconstructed 1830s fur-trading post operated as a museum by the Colorado Historical Society. The museum fea-tures exhibits and dioramas depicting the trading era. In summer "mountain men" entertain visitors with reenactments of Old West trading days. A buffalo tepee will interest youngsters. Admission is free; it is open daily year-round.

MIZEL MUSEUM
400 South Kearney Street
(303) 394-9993
www.mizelmuseum.org
The Rocky Mountain region's only museum of Judaica was established in 1982. Special pro-grams, workshops, speakers, seminars, and films are designed to complement the museum's changing exhibitions, whether drawn from its own collection or borrowed from such presti-gious institutions as the Israel Museum and the Smithsonian Institution. In 2001 it merged with the Mizel Family Cultural Arts Center and moved

to the campus of the Jewish Community Center. Call for details about programs, hours, and fees.

MUSEO DE LAS AMERICAS
861 Santa Fe Drive
(303) 571-4401
www.museo.org

The Rocky Mountain region's first museum dedicated to Latin-American art, history, and culture, the Museo de las Americas showcases art from all the Americas, including the Caribbean, in changing exhibitions. (See our The Arts chapter for more information.)

ROCKY MOUNTAIN QUILT MUSEUM
1111 Washington Avenue, Golden
(303) 277-0377
www.rmqm.org

The tiny Rocky Mountain Quilt Museum is as much a resource center for quilters as a museum, with more than 300 old and new quilts in its collection. Exhibits change five times a year. Quilts and other needlework are offered for sale at the museum, which also conducts classes and outreach programs. The museum is open Monday through Saturday.

UNITED STATES MINT
320 West Colfax Avenue
(303) 405-4761
www.usmint.gov

One of Denver's most popular tourist attractions, the Mint produces fifteen billion coins each year. Free tours are conducted weekdays Reservations are required for the 15-minute tours, and the Mint strongly suggests that you make them online, since walk-up reservations are first-come, first-served and may not always be available. Go to the Web site listed above, click on "Make A Reservation," and follow the instructions. The tours leave every 15 to 20 minutes from the Cherokee Street entrance. Expect a long line during the summer. Children younger than age 14 must be accompanied by an adult. Wheelchairs are OK but cameras are not. No photos can be taken inside the building. Hours for coin sales are the same as tour hours. The Mint is closed on all legal holidays and for one week in summer, usually in late June, for inventory.

WILDLIFE EXPERIENCE
10035 South Peoria Street, Parker
(720) 488-3300
www.wildlifeexperience.org

The $50 million Wildlife Experience opened in 2002 about 10 miles south of downtown Denver and 1 mile east of I-25. It's the brainchild of RE/MAX cofounders Dave and Gail Liniger, in which art and natural history are combined. They describe the museum as "where art and education lead to greater appreciation of animals in their natural habitats." The 101,000-square-foot facility has space for oil paintings, metal sculptures, traveling exhibits, art and photo galleries, and a 315-seat IWERKS theater for wildlife movies. The museum also contains a cafe, a gift shop, and both indoor and outdoor facilities big enough for special parties and meetings. It's open Tuesday through Sunday, closed Thanksgiving and Christmas. To reach Wildlife Experience, travel south on I-25, take E-470 east, then exit at Peoria and follow it south to Lincoln Avenue.

WINGS OVER THE ROCKIES AIR AND SPACE MUSEUM
7711 East Academy Boulevard
(303) 360-5360
www.wingsmuseum.org

Perhaps the last remnant of Lowry Air Force Base in east Denver, this air and space museum on the site of the decommissioned base houses a wide range of aircraft and space memorabilia. Its permanent collection includes a B-18 Bolo, an RF-84K Thundercraft parasite, a B-1A Lancer, and an Apollo control module. It's open daily.

HISTORIC HOUSES AND OTHER HISTORIC SITES

BYERS-EVANS HOUSE
1310 Bannock Street
(303) 620-4933
www.coloradohistory.org

John Evans was Colorado's second territorial governor. William Byers founded the *Rocky Mountain News*. Both men and their families were prominent during Denver's early years, and their names appear on avenues and mountain peaks. This house, built by Byers in 1883 and sold to Evans's son in 1889, has been restored to the 1912–24 period. The house is open Tuesday through Sunday. Combination tickets including entrance to the Colorado History Museum (a block and a half away) are available.

COLORADO GOVERNOR'S MANSION
400 East 8th Avenue
(303) 837-8350
(303) 866-3682 (tours)
www.colorado.gov
Completed in 1907, the governor's mansion was originally the private residence of the Walter Scott Cheesman family. In 1927 the house was sold to the Boettcher family, and in 1960 the Boettcher Foundation gave the property to the state to use as the governor's mansion. The colonial revival structure contains artwork from all around the world and a Waterford chandelier that once hung in the White House. The mansion can be visited on Tuesday afternoon between June and August. Tours leave every 10 minutes. The mansion is open to the public for a week during December, when it's decorated for Christmas. Call for dates, as they vary every year.

COLORADO STATE CAPITOL
Broadway and Colfax Avenue
www.colorado.gov
The Colorado State Capitol stands exactly 1 mile above sea level. On the 13th step there's a carving stating the elevation as 5,280 feet, but a small brass plaque on the 18th step corrects the carving and proclaims itself the true mile-high marker. Inside the capitol building, free tours lasting about 45 minutes are given Monday through Friday. Due to heightened security, there is no public access to the gold-plated dome. Although the gold on the outside of the dome tends to receive more attention from the casual passersby, the real precious mineral is on the inside of the

building, where rose-colored Colorado onyx was used as wainscoting. The onyx came from a small quarry in Beulah, Colorado, and has never been mined elsewhere.

CUSSLER MUSEUM
14959 West 69th Avenue, Arvada
(303) 420-2795
www.cusslermuseum.com
Author Clive Cussler lived in metro Denver during his early years and, as his popularity grew, he diverted some of his financial proceeds into an extensive vintage automobile collection. Among the rarest are the foreign cars—a 1929 Isotta Fraschini and a 1936 Avions Voisins, for example. Cussler found ways to write many of the vehicles into his Dirk Pitt novels, and he often posed with them for the book jacket photos. Today the collection is tended by his daughter, and it's open to the public Mondays and Tuesdays during the summer months.

FAIRMOUNT CEMETERY
430 South Quebec Street
(303) 399-0692
This 320-acre privately owned cemetery dates from 1890 and is the final resting place for many former mayors, socialites, gunfighters, madams, and Civil War veterans. An infamous "resident" is Colonel John M. Chivington, responsible for the massacre of defenseless Indians at Sand Creek in 1864. The grounds contain more than 50 types of trees, and tours are given periodically by the Denver Botanic Gardens for those interested in this aspect of the cemetery. Self-guided tours are possible anytime (a guidebook can be purchased at the site), and free guided tours are available.

FOUR MILE HISTORIC PARK
715 South Forest Street
(720) 865-0800
www.fourmilehistoricpark.org
Designated a Denver Landmark in 1968, Four Mile Historic Park commemorates the site of a former stage stop and contains the oldest home still standing in Denver. In addition to the 1859 log home, visitors can tour the living-history

farmstead and, on nice days, have a picnic here. Special-events days are held about six times a year and include horse-drawn wagon rides and demonstrations of blacksmithing, butter churning, and other chores. There are reenactments of Civil War events during the spring and summer as well as a heritage program and evening concerts. It's open Wednesday through Sunday.

LAKEWOOD HERITAGE CENTER
801 South Yarrow Street, Lakewood
(303) 987-7850
www.lakewood.org/comres/page.cfm?ID=17
&LakewoodsHeritageCenter
A historic site and museum with several structures, including an 1880s farmhouse and a 1920s schoolhouse, Lakewood Heritage Center also has a barn gallery with changing exhibits. The visitor center has a permanent exhibit on May Bonfils, daughter of one of the founders of the Denver Post, and exhibits of work by local artists that change monthly. The visitor center is staffed Tuesday through Saturday. Call to ask about special children's programs. Groups of five or more should make reservations.

LITTLETON HISTORICAL MUSEUM
6028 South Gallup Street, Littleton
(303) 795-3950
www.littletongov.org/museum
This living-history museum consists of a reconstructed 1860s homestead and a turn-of-the-20th-century farm that re-creates pioneer life. Among the original buildings on the 14-acre site are a 1910 ice house, a sheep and goat shelter originally built as a settler's cabin in the 1860s, an 1890s farmhouse, and the first schoolhouse in Littleton. The main museum underwent a three-year, $8.5 million expansion and reopened in 2006 with expanded galleries and workshops and a lecture hall and research center. Outdoors, costumed staff and volunteers care for the chickens and livestock and go about the business of tending a 19th-century farm. They're not too busy to stop and explain things to visitors. Admission is free (large groups are charged a small fee and

should call first). The museum is open Tuesday; it's closed on Monday and major holidays.

MOLLY BROWN HOUSE MUSEUM
1340 Pennsylvania Street
(303) 832-4092
www.mollybrown.org
Only Baby Doe Tabor can match Molly Brown for name recognition among turn-of-the-20th-century Denver women. Each has had her life memorialized in song: Baby Doe, in the opera The Ballad of Baby Doe, and Molly Brown, in the Broadway musical The Unsinkable Molly Brown. Molly was one of early Denver's more flamboyant characters and achieved true heroine status for her actions during the sinking of the Titanic, which she survived. Her Victorian home has been restored and furnished in period style with many personal mementos and possessions. Museum officials suggest arriving early as they do not take reservations. The museum is open Tuesday through Sunday, with the last tour starting daily at 3:30 p.m. A number of special dinners, teas, readings, and workshops are scheduled throughout the year; call for more information.

RIVERSIDE CEMETERY
5201 Brighton Boulevard Commerce City
(303) 293-2466
Denver's oldest cemetery, founded in 1876, contains the graves of three Civil War medal-of-honor winners; Augusta Tabor, the first wife of turn-of-the-20th-century silver baron Horace Tabor; and Colorado's first black ballplayer, Oliver E. Marcel. Visitors can pick up a booklet and map for $2 during office hours, weekdays from 8:30 a.m. to 4:30 p.m. The cemetery is on Brighton Boulevard about 2 miles north of I-70.

PARKS AND GARDENS

DENVER BOTANIC GARDENS
1005 York Street
(720) 865-3500
www.botanicgardens.org
One of Metro Denver's most lovely refuges, the

Botanic Gardens encompasses 23 acres and includes an herb garden and other specialty gardens. The one-acre rock alpine garden is considered one of the finest in the country. Our personal favorite is the lovely Japanese Shofu-en (Garden of Pine Wind) designed by America's foremost Japanese landscaper, Koichi Kawana. It is complete with an authentic teahouse. Local residents look to the water-saving xeriscape demonstration garden and the home demonstration garden for ideas they can put into use in their own yards. A tropical conservatory and pavilion houses orchids, bromeliads, and other warmth-loving species. Outdoor concerts are held here in the summer; come early and bring a picnic dinner. Schedules are available at the gate in early spring, but they sell out quickly. The Botanic Gardens are open daily.

THE DENVER ZOO CITY PARK
East 23rd Avenue and Steele Street
(303) 376-4800
www.denverzoo.org

Easily combined with a trip to the Museum of Nature and Science, the Denver Zoo has the usual complement of lions and tigers and (polar) bears as well as monkeys and birds, in a mix of enclosed and open habitat areas. Perhaps the most famous creatures to come from the Denver Zoo are Klondike and Snow, the adorable polar bear siblings who made national news while being nursed to health by zoo officials. Klondike and Snow have since moved on to another home. The $10 million Tropical Discovery exhibit is designed to re-create a rain forest habitat inside a glass-enclosed pyramid. More than 700 animal species live here, nearly double what the zoo had previously. There is a separate nursery area where new arrivals needing human help get their first taste of what it's like to be in the public eye. Primate Panorama, a five-acre, all-natural habitat, is always a crowd-pleaser. For those who can't or don't feel like walking the zoo, a fun train circles the major outdoor exhibits frequently throughout the day. The zoo unveiled a new exhibit, Predator Ridge, and a new main entrance complex. The zoo is open daily, including all holidays; Tropical Discovery and Bird World have slightly shortened hours.

ELITCH GARDENS
25 and Speer Boulevard (exit 212A)
(303) 595-4386
www.elitchgardens.com

For more than 100 years, Elitch Gardens was a west Denver tradition. Opened in May 1890 as Elitch Zoological Gardens by John and Mary Elitch, it boasted three thrilling roller coasters: the Wildcat, the wooden Twister, and the Sidewinder. In 1995 Elitch Gardens reopened in a larger, 68-acre location in the Central Platte River Valley just off the Speer Boulevard exit from I-25. (At night, all lit up, it's a beautiful and memorable sight for anyone driving through Denver on the interstate.) A rebuilt 100-foot-high Twister II is one of the top attractions. There are 49 major rides in all, including several added in the past few years: The Flying Coaster (billed as the cure for the common coaster), an indescribable face-down ride that feels like you're flying through the air; The Half-Pipe, a 100-foot-tall ride on a 40-footlong snowboard; and the new Edge ride at the Island Kingdom Water Park, a four-story near-vertical waterslide. For tamer pursuits there's a 300-foot-high observation tower with a panoramic view. The 1925 carousel made the move downtown. Elitch's is open daily roughly from Memorial Day through Labor Day.

LAKESIDE AMUSEMENT PARK
4601 Sheridan Boulevard (I-70 and Sheridan)
(303) 477-1621
www.lakesideamusementpark.com

An all-ages amusement park, Lakeside has a merry-go-round, a Ferris wheel, a roller coaster, and other exciting rides. One of the best things to do at Lakeside is to ride the train around the lake after dark. The park is open from May through Labor Day weekend. In May the park is open on weekends only. It is open seven days a week June through Labor Day.

Close-up

Elitch Gardens Thrills Downtown Visitors

Elitch's started in 1890 when John and Mary Elitch turned a small apple orchard into picnic areas and ball fields open to the public. It later boasted Denver's first zoo. In 1891 the Elitch Theatre opened its first season and for 96 years hosted such luminaries as Sarah Bernhardt, Cecil B. DeMille, Grace Kelly, and Edward G. Robinson. In 1925 the treasured carousel with 67 hand-carved horses and chariots was installed. The restored carousel is a focal point of the new park.

Over the years, Elitch's became known for its signature gardens, a sprawling collection of impressive flowers, trees, and shrubs. It will take many years before the "gardens" in the new Elitch Gardens come anywhere close to the impressive foliage tenderly raised at the old site. Meantime, efforts have been made to capture some of the nostalgia of the old Elitch's. A Victorian-style promenade with colorful storefronts and restaurants harkens to the old Elitch days. The Trocadero Theater, built in honor of Elitch's famed Trocadero Ballroom at the old park, seats 700 and features live shows. Although the park opens weekends in May, Memorial Day is the official launch of the season.

SUGGESTED OUTINGS

ONE-DAY FAMILY OUTING . . .

Visit the Denver Museum of Nature and Science and the Denver Zoo. Take in a show at the IMAX theater. Then, if you have time, the Denver Museum of Miniatures, Dolls and Toys isn't far away.

WITHIN WALKING DISTANCE DOWNTOWN . . .

The Denver Art Museum, the Museum of Western Art, the Colorado History Museum, the U.S. Mint, the Colorado State Capitol, the Molly Brown House, the Firefighters Museum, and the Byers-Evans House are all within walking distance of one another downtown. Don't try to see all these sights in one day, but pick the ones that interest you most; plot a route and save the rest for another afternoon.

FOR ART LOVERS . . .

The Denver Art Museum and the Western Art Museum can be visited in one day if you don't try to see the whole art museum. If you're at the Denver Art Museum at lunchtime, eat in its cafe.

TRAINS AND AUTOMOBILES . . .

Metro Denver has three museums of special interest in this category: the Forney Transportation Museum, the Colorado Railroad Museum, and the Denver Firefighters Museum. With a car, all could be visited in one day.

ONE-DAY OUTING IN GOLDEN . . .

Start with a drive up to the Buffalo Bill Grave and Museum and the nearby Mother Cabrini Shrine, which honors the first American saint (see our Worship chapter for more information). For lunch take a picnic to Red Rocks Park if the weather's nice, or pick a spot in downtown Golden. In the afternoon visit the Colorado Railroad Museum or the Rocky Mountain Quilt Museum.

HISTORY BUFFS . . .

Don't miss the Black American West Museum. A visit there combines well with a visit to the Colorado History Museum.

ETHNIC HERITAGE TOUR (HALF-DAY) . . .

Divide your time between the Black American West Museum and the Museo de las Americas.

Afterward stop for lunch at one of the authentic Mexican restaurants along Santa Fe Drive. Try El Noa Noa or El Taco de Mexico (see our Restaurants chapter for full descriptions of these eateries).

ART AND GARDEN TOUR . . .

Spend half the day at the Denver Art Museum, the rest at the Denver Botanic Gardens.

FAUNA AND FLORA . . .

Spend half the day at the Denver Zoo, the rest at the Denver Botanic Gardens.

WALKING TOURS . . .

A booklet of six downtown walking tours collectively called the Mile High Trail is available at the Denver Metro Chamber of Commerce, 1445 Market Street, (303) 534-8500, or log on to www .denverchamber.org. The information booth at Larimer Square can provide historical and architectural information about buildings in the 1400 block of Larimer Street. The city of Denver home page on the Web offers several walking and driving tours that you can download and print, including tours of the downtown Civic Center area and Fairmount Cemetery (the oldest cemetery in the city). Go to www.denvergov.org/ aboutdenver/today_walking_civiccenter.asp.

PUBLIC ART TOUR . . .

A brochure identifying public art throughout the city is available at the Denver Visitors Information Center, 918 16th Street, (303) 892-1112. The brochure contains a suggested walking tour and driving tour. Don't miss the outdoor murals on the 15th Street viaduct and Barbara Jo Revelle's vast tile mural of photographic images of people from Colorado's history.

KIDSTUFF

We think of Denver as kids' country. Metro Denver offers a multitude of activities for the younger set—but we admit we like the outings, too. Best of all, Denver's laid-back attitude says kids are welcome just about anywhere—assuming they aren't totally unrestrained, of course.

One of the first places guests to Metro Denver should look for fun is outdoors: Take them out to play with Mother Nature. It doesn't matter what trail or mountainside you take them to; short hikes or climbs for smaller kids are found in the same places where adults and older kids go to get serious. There's an abundance of trails and natural beauty close to Denver. When hiking, make sure to protect yourself and your kids by using sunscreen and taking water bottles.

Mother Nature is only one of the kid-friendly attractions around Metro Denver. Check the other chapters of this book for ideas, especially Tours and Attractions, Spectator Sports, Annual Events and Festivals, Parks and Recreation, and Day Trips.

What follows is limited to a reasonable number of unique attractions aimed at the younger set, but there are others too numerous to mention. Take the kids fishing at any of the many reservoirs and rivers along the Front Range and in the nearby mountains. Go horseback riding at any of the stables around Metro Denver. Walk or ride bicycles on trails, usually along creeks, rivers, canals, and lakeshores that thread the greenbelts of the metro area.

Call nearby public libraries about story hours and other child-oriented activities. Call city and county departments of parks and recreation in your area to see about kid activities ranging from soccer and baseball to art classes. Local recreation centers are listed in our Parks and Recreation chapter.

One of your best local resources to kid activities is *Colorado Parent* magazine, (303) 320-1000, http://colorado.parenthood.com, a free monthly publication that can be found at 800 locations ranging from bookstores and libraries to doctors' offices and day-care centers.

WET 'N' WILD

There are swimming pools all over metro Denver, and some of them go the extra mile to be kid-friendly.

CARPENTER RECREATION CENTER
11151 Colorado Boulevard, Thornton
(303) 255-7800
The Carpenter Recreation Center is a fantastic indoor 15,000-square-foot aquatics center, which includes artificially generated waves, lap swimming, a raindrop play area with waterfall and Jacuzzi, a lazy river, and a waterslide.

THE GOLDEN COMMUNITY CENTER
1470 10th Street, Golden
(303) 384-8100
The Golden Community Center has an indoor pool that kids will love, with a raindrop play area, waterslide, and hot tub as well as a lap pool and leisure pool.

WATER WORLD
88th Avenue and Pecos Street
Federal Heights
(303) 427-7873
www.waterworldcolorado.com
Metro Denver's biggest outdoor water park, Water

World offers more than 64 acres of aquatic fun. Float down a circular series of chutes and pools on an inner tube. Ride a huge rubber raft down a torrent. Sit on a plastic sled that plunges almost straight down and builds up enough speed to aquaplane across the pool at the bottom. Or try the newest attraction, the Zoomerang. Water World has it all. The park also added a Journey to the Center of the Earth ride, in which you cruise through caves where moving dinosaurs menace you. Water World is open from late May to the end of summer. If you're age 60 and older or age three and younger, it's free. Check the Web site for promotional discounts.

WESTMINSTER CITY PARK RECREATION CENTER
10455 Sheridan Boulevard, Westminster
(303) 460-9690
This indoor facility has a large children's pool with a tile beach sloping gently at one end, a fountain, and a slide just for kids. The main pool for lap swimmers bulges out at one side under a waterfall. You can go behind the waterfall and look through windows to get an underwater view of the next pool, one floor above and dedicated entirely to swinging out on and dropping from a rope fastened at the ceiling three stories up. Above the rope-swing pool is the beginning of a waterslide that ends with a splash in the main pool.

EATING OUT

Kids are welcome at just about any restaurant in town. Still, we've listed those that have true kid appeal.

CASA BONITA
6715 West Colfax Avenue, Lakewood
(303) 232-5115
www.casabonitadenver.com
Rising from the JCRS Shopping Center in Lakewood, the distinctive steeple of Casa Bonita has become a Metro Denver landmark. Although this is a perfectly good Mexican restaurant with

American dishes, too, people come here more for the play than for the food. It's like eating in a cave with huge chambers and a complex labyrinth of tunnels and hidden nooks. Strolling mariachis and cliff divers entertain while you eat. Kids love Black Bart's cave, a series of creepy scares in tunnels sized for kids. There's a video arcade and other entertainment. The crowning glory is the 30-foot waterfall, where divers plunge into a pool below while performances at the top of the waterfall involve cowboy gunfights and explorers tangling with a gorilla. Every performance ends with somebody falling 30 feet into the pool. It's a popular place for kid birthday parties and for parents who want to kick back while their kids run wild.

GUNTHER TOODY'S
4500 East Alameda Avenue, Glendale
(303) 399-1959

9220 East Arapahoe Road, Englewood
(303) 799-1958

7355 Ralston Road, Arvada
(303) 422-1954

8266 West Bowles, Littleton
(303) 932-1957

301 West 104th Avenue, Northglenn
(303) 453-1956
The staff at Gunther Toody's dress like characters from *Grease* at this 1950s concept restaurant, and they usually do such a good job of acting their sassy, gum-chewing parts that there must be a Gunther Toody's acting school somewhere. The only games are a few classic pinball machines, and it's not exclusively a kid restaurant. But that's why we're mentioning it here, because it deserves wider recognition as a great, non-arcade dining place for kids and their families.

TRAIL DUST STEAK HOUSE
7101 South Clinton Street, Englewood
(303) 790-2420
Kids love the two-story slide that empties onto the hardwood dance floor at the Trail Dust Steak

House, and they'll howl when a waitperson cuts off someone's tie. The steaks are good, as are all the fixin's. Once the band begins to play, Mom and Dad can enjoy a little country dancing.

PLANES, TRAINS, AND BOATS

COLORADO RAILROAD MUSEUM
17155 West 44th Avenue, Golden
(303) 279-4591
www.crrm.org

A lot of Western city parks used to have trains that kids could climb around on, but now they're mostly surrounded by fences to keep the kids out. None of that nonsense here! The Colorado Railroad Museum is described in our Tours and Attractions chapter, but at 12.5 acres, with more than 50 pieces of "rolling stock," it's so fantastic for kids that it bears repeating. Kids can climb up and walk through the antique railway cars, climb into the cupolas of the cabooses to look out the windows, and climb up on the big engine right outside the museum building and pull the rope and ring the awesome bell. You have to be a bit older to appreciate most of the two floors of memorabilia inside the museum building, but kids love the enormous model train set up in the basement, which you can run by plugging in a quarter. Several times a year the museum fires up and runs the state's oldest railway engine.

PIKES PEAK COG RAILWAY
US 24 West from Colorado
Springs to the Manitou exit, west on
Manitou Avenue, and left onto Ruxton
Avenue, Colorado Springs
(719) 685-5401
cograilway.com

Adults become kids again when riding the world's highest cog train. We include more details about the 3½-hour trip to the top of Pikes Peak in our Day Trips chapter, but here we'll mention just one thing. Kids who most enjoy the experience are those of an age and temperament to tolerate a long ride. Reservations are required.

PLATTE VALLEY TROLLEY
2785 North Speer Boulevard
(303) 458-6255
www.denvertrolley.org

This turn-of-the-20th-century streetcar tour is for all ages, but small tykes may recognize its near-exact resemblance to the streetcar on the *Mister Rogers' Neighborhood* TV show. You'll enjoy a narrated tour along the Platte River, with bits of history and expositions on present and future features of this area such as INVESCO Field at Mile High and Golda Meir's former residence. The hour tour goes up Lakewood Gulch, along the tracks where the interurban trolley used to run from Denver to Golden. Children 6 or younger may prefer the half-hour tour. The trolley closes during winter months, operating between April and October. To get to the trolley, park at the Children's Museum of Denver (see our listing in this chapter) and walk east to the Platte River.

VENICE ON THE CREEK
Creek Front Plaza, at Larimer Street and
Speer Boulevard
(303) 893-0750
www.veniceonthecreek.org

One of Denver's newest attractions, Venice on the Creek is a great way to see Lower Downtown from the vantage point of a boat—or punt, in this case. A punt is a flat-bottomed boat, similar to a gondola. You can take a 10-block ride downstream and back up while hearing the history of Cherry Creek and the history of punts. Reservations are strongly recommended since the boats sometimes sell out their seats as much as two weeks in advance. Take a few steps down to the pedestrian path and follow it 1 block to Market Street where you'll embark. The punts operate between June and August.

WINGS OVER THE ROCKIES AIR AND SPACE MUSEUM
7711 East Academy Parkway
(303) 360-5360
www.wingsmuseum.org

Wings Over the Rockies does for aviation what the Colorado Railroad Museum does for the railroads, putting the biggest and best of the historic hardware on very impressive display for the public. With the exception of the Space Station Module, you can't actually go inside the displays, but up-close and gargantuan, they have a tremendous, visceral impact. Among the three dozen aircraft on display in the museum are big bombers, racy fighter jets, and helicopters—a scan of aviation history. You've got civilian and military aircraft, models, simulations, photographs, and space-related objects so visitors can experience scientific discovery. It's all contained in the vast interior of Lowry's Hangar 1. Since it's all indoors, it's particularly nice on a winter day when outside activities are curtailed. This excepts the B-52 bomber on display outside. There are also a variety of historic aviation artifacts and a museum store. Wings Over the Rockies is open daily. From I-225 take 6th Avenue west to Lowry Boulevard, turn left at the dead end, and proceed until you see the hangars. It's the first one to the west. Or you can take Alameda Street west to Fairmount Cemetery and turn right onto Fairmount Drive. Straight ahead you'll see the two hangars, and it's the first one to the east.

NIGHTLIFE FOR THE YOUNGER CROWD

CLUB 22
Northglenn Recreation Center
11801 Community Center Drive, Northglenn
(303) 450-8800
www.northglenn.org
Club 22 stands for "2 old for a sitter and 2 young to drive." This is a safe and supervised nightspot for adolescents of middle-school age. Parents check their kids in, and the kids don't leave until the parents check them out. In between, there's music and dancing, swimming, and other activities, such as volleyball and wallyball in the Rec Center's athletic facilities. There are contests, food and beverage concessions, and always some sort of special event, such as a movie or an entertainer or demonstrator. Club 22 takes place on the first and third Saturday of each month.

REC AND ROCK
Goodson Recreation Center
6315 South University Boulevard, Littleton
(303) 798-2476
The Rec and Rock and Kids Night Out program features safe and supervised weekend nightlife for adolescents age 10 to 14. They've turned out to be popular programs and take place during the school year. You'll typically find games, dancing, and music with a live DJ; activities such as basketball, dodgeball, wallyball, and volleyball; concessions for pizza and soft drinks; movies, contests, and special guests. There is one adult counselor for every 25 kids, a uniformed policeman on hand at all times, and parental check-in and checkout. Call the rec center for admission fees.

THE PLANT AND ANIMAL KINGDOMS

BUTTERFLY PAVILION & INSECT CENTER
6252 West 104th Avenue, Westminster
(303) 469-5441
www.butterflies.org
If your child loves butterflies, this place is a perfect destination. More than 1,200 butterflies live in a 7,200-square-foot tropical forest. At the emergence viewing area, you can watch the last two stages of metamorphosis as butterflies emerge from their chrysalides. Outside is a butterfly garden, with flowers designed to attract butterflies. The Pavilion is open daily, but closes on Thanksgiving and Christmas Day.

DENVER BOTANIC GARDENS
1005 York Street
(720) 865-3500
www.botanicgardens.org
Kids of all ages enjoy these lovely gardens and the tropical conservatory. We've described the gardens in detail in our Tours and Attractions chapter, but chances are good that children will be more interested in the changing menu of year-round kid activities, such as the Pumpkin Fest and the summer evening concerts listed in

A Day in the Park

Thanks to the vision of Mayor Robert Speer (after whom Speer Boulevard is named), Denver has a system of parks and greenways that ranks among the nation's largest.

Speer was inspired to adorn Denver while visiting the 1893 Chicago Exposition, and formulated a "City Beautiful Plan" after he was elected mayor in 1904. It platted tree-lined parkways and central Denver parks that form the framework for the city's open space (Civic Center Park, Washington Park, City Park, and Alamo Placita Park). Denver's first new park, Mestizo-Curtis Park, opened in 1968 at 31st and Curtis Streets and it is still a vital part of this north Denver neighborhood.

More than a century after Speer was elected, the city and county of Denver now has 281 urban parks, 125 miles of hiking and biking paths, 100 miles of parkways, and 20,000 acres of mountain parks. Go to the suburbs and you'll find many more.

Though all the parks are soothing oases, the following are particularly beloved by kids.

Belleview Park
5001 South Inca Street, Englewood
Belleview is simply one of the region's most entertaining family parks. Often called Airplane Park, it has two playgrounds filled with space-related jungle gyms, slides, and swings. It also has a miniature train that takes visitors around the park and a petting zoo with cows, pigs, goats, and rabbits. If that's not quite enough, a clear shallow stream running through the park is perfect for wading.

Cheesman Park
East 12th Avenue and Humboldt Street
Cheesman Park has some terrific playground equipment (not to mention a pretty spectacular view of the mountains). Kids love the castle structure for climbing and hiding, and the jungle gym is one of the best around. Most striking is the Cheesman Park Pavilion, a Parthenonlike structure perfect for running around or watching the sunset.

City Park
17th Avenue and Colorado Boulevard
This park just east of downtown is full of

our Annual Events and Festivals chapter. It's also a pretty place to run around, with a couple of grassy knolls that small kids love to climb on and roll down. It's a nice place for a picnic. The gardens are open daily, with reduced winter hours.

ℹ The Tattered Cover Book Stores devote lots of shelf space to children's books. They also have kid-sized tables and chairs where kids can read or look at pictures.

THE DENVER MUSEUM OF NATURE AND SCIENCE
2001 Colorado Boulevard
(in City Park, at Colorado Boulevard and Montview Street)
(303) 322-7009
www.dmns.org
See our Tours and Attractions chapter for more details on this museum, but don't forget it's one of the greatest places around for kids. When you walk under the claws of the huge Tyrannosaurus rex skeleton as you enter the front door, you

possibilities, not the least of which are visits to the Denver Zoo and the Denver Museum of Natural History. A lake in the middle offers paddle boating. A rose garden close to the museum provides a great picnic site. Need more activity? The park has a public golf course and tennis courts. And in the summer, it's easy to find a free concert in the bandshell near the lake.

Cushing Park
795 West Eastman Street, Englewood
This is the site of one of Metro Denver's first gold discoveries. Not surprisingly, its playground is reminiscent of the Old West, with a stagecoach, a tepee, a jail, and a horse and buggy—all of which keep active buckaroos busy while their parents lounge under a tree and relax. Cushing also has an area specifically for skateboarders.

Genesee Park
I-70 West to the Genesee exit, Genesee
How many cities boast a buffalo herd? The best reason to head to Genesee Park is to see the gentle giants roaming right off the highway. Once you see them, you won't care that all the other fancy trappings of city parks are lacking.

Ruby Hill Park
South Platte River Drive and West Florida Avenue
Denver Parks and Recreation folks have launched a major renovation of this West Denver park that will play out over several years. The first stages will include a walking trail, a new playground and a pavilion on the hill overlooking Denver. The park is already home to the city's Urban Rail Yard, a ski and snowboard hill that opens only in the winter.

Washington Park
Louisiana Avenue and Downing Street
This is one of Denver's most popular park destinations. Originally a prairie, it has two lakes that allow fishing (don't forget your license) and a lawn bowling/croquet green. Best of all, most of the streets are closed to vehicular traffic, so your family can in-line skate, bike, or walk without fear of being mowed down.

know you've entered a place of wonder. The museum has some great children's educational programs, but they fill up frighteningly fast once their scheduling becomes public knowledge. The museum is open daily.

THE DENVER ZOO
City Park, East 23rd Avenue and Steele Street (near the Denver Museum of Nature and Science)
(303) 376-4800
www.denverzoo.org
You can't miss with a zoo, and the Denver Zoo

may well be Metro Denver's most popular kid place of all. It's open daily, with some wonderful special events centered around the seasons (See our Tours and Attractions and Annual Events and Festivals chapters for details.

ROCKY MOUNTAIN ARSENAL NATIONAL WILDLIFE REFUGE
72nd and Quebec Streets
Commerce City
(303) 289-0232
www.fws.gov/rockymountainarsenal
Take a two-hour bus tour of one of the country's

former toxic waste sites, now overrun with all kinds of wildlife. On this tour you hear the history of the area as well as its environmental cleanup. If you're lucky you'll also see eagles, hawks, mule deer, and prairie dogs. If the wildlife is out romping, this will be one of those "WOW!" experiences. Call for current schedule. Though the tour is traditionally free, reservations have always been a must.

MUSEUMS

CHILDREN'S MUSEUM OF DENVER
2121 Children's Museum Drive
(303) 433-7444
www.cmdenver.org

There are dozens of things to do here, all of them aimed specifically at kids and all educationally oriented. There's a miniature grocery store, where kids can shop or be the checkout person, and a Denver Nuggets exhibit, where kids can compare their sizes to basketball players' sizes. There are laboratories where kids can work with earth sciences and natural phenomena and play educational games on computers. You'll find a light room and sound room, plant and animal exhibits, woodworking, and a traveling exhibit that changes every three months. Play Partners is a special toddler play area set up like the Three Bears' house.

It's a great museum, but a very busy one. The museum is open daily, but recommends coming between 2 and 5 p.m. on weekdays, when it's least crowded. Worthy of note is the museum's annual Halloween party, Trick-or-Treat Street, which runs for nearly a week, including Halloween. This is Denver's non-scary trick-or-treat alternative. Multitudes of kids show up in costumes to pass through the many exhibits and receive candy. The event includes pumpkin carving, performances, and other activities. New to the museum is the Parent Resource Center and the Center for the Young Child, a developmentally age-appropriate area for newborns to 4-year-olds. The museum can be a little tricky to reach, so here are some directions: It's right

off 23rd Avenue and I-25. If you exit from I-25, go east on 23rd and take the first right onto 7th Street and then an immediate right onto Children's Museum Drive.

MAKING MONEY

YOUNG AMERICANS CENTER FOR FINANCIAL EDUCATION
311 Steele Street, and
401 South Pierce Street, Lakewood
(303) 321-2954
www.yacenter.org/

This foundation was launched in the late 1980s by Bill Daniels, a cable TV pioneer. Until his death, Daniels was chairman of Daniels Communications Inc., a broker/dealer of major national cable systems. He started the foundation to give kids an early grounding in the business culture. Most widely known is the Young Americans Bank, a real FDIC-insured bank of which the foundation is the nonprofit holding company. Designed for ages 21 and younger, it's the only bank in the world exclusively for kids. They can have their own savings and checking accounts, ATM and credit cards, and mutual funds. It emphasizes individual attention to children, with small teller booths designed with steps so kids can look the teller in the eye, and tellers who teach the kids one-on-one about deposit slips, interest, and so on. The foundation also has hands-on programs designed to teach children the skills they will need to prosper in the free enterprise system.

AMUSEMENT PARKS (INDOORS AND OUT)

MR. BIGGS
9670 West Coal Mine Avenue, Littleton
(303) 972-4344
www.becooldoright.com

This is a 3½-acre indoor fun center for all ages. Activities include bowling, Grand Prix racing, laser tag, an 18-hole miniature golf course, and a video arcade. It's open daily year-round.

FUNTASTIC FUN

3085 South Broadway, Englewood
(303) 761-8700
www.funtasticfun.com

Kids on Metro Denver's south side have enjoyed this indoor play station for decades. Attractions include a Ferris wheel, a carousel, a train, swings, an air castle, a room filled with plastic balls, and a special room for younger kids so the squirts don't get roughhoused by the bigger kids. It's open daily during summer months, and Thursday through Sunday the rest of the year

HERITAGE SQUARE

18301 West Colfax Avenue, Golden
(303) 279-2789

Heritage Square appears to be a small Western town wedged into the foothills, with porticoed boardwalks along the front of retail stores, restaurants, and entertainment options lining its streets. They include an alpine slide on the hillside, an operating train, amusement rides, miniature golf, and a variety of vendors. The Heritage Square Music Hall offers melodramas, dinner theater and children's theater. Rides operate weekends in the spring and fall, and daily during the summer months.

ELITCH GARDENS

I-25 and Speer Boulevard (exit 212A)
(303) 595-4386
www.elitchgardens.com

Elitch Gardens is Denver's oldest fun park, dating from 1890 when it began as a botanical and zoological garden and had no mechanical rides. Since then it has become Denver's flashiest amusement park. Now it's even bigger, expanding in 1995 on 68 acres along the South Platte River. More details are available in our Tours and Attractions chapter. Getting to Elitch Gardens is no problem, since it has its own exit from the Speer Boulevard viaduct. There also is downtown access from 15th Street.

LAKESIDE AMUSEMENT PARK

4601 Sheridan Avenue
Just south of I-70, Lakeside
(303) 477-1621
www.lakesideamusementpark.com

Lakeside is an old-fashioned park that has changed little since the 1940s. Little trains that run around the lake are sentimental favorites of past generations. The extensive kiddieland has 15 rides sized for the tots. For cold-weather fun, take the kids tubing down a ski slope at Keystone. You'll get a gondola ride to the tubing spot and rope-tow rides back to the top. See our Ski Country chapter or call Adventure Point at (970) 496-4386. It opens weekends in May, goes full-time in June, and closes after Labor Day weekend.

SOMETHING DIFFERENT

COLORADO RENAISSANCE FESTIVAL

I-25 about 25 minutes south from Denver to Larkspur (exit 173), then follow the signs
(303) 688-6010

See our Annual Events and Festivals chapter for more on the Renaissance Festival, but it's such a kid-pleaser that it cannot be omitted from this section. It's a dizzying fantasy world full of battling knights, cavorting jesters, and associated monsters and grotesques, where hundreds of food vendors, craftspersons, and performers dress, act, and speak appropriately to their setting in this re-created 16th-century village. It's an event rather than a place, however, so remember it's only around for eight weekends in June and July. Discount tickets are available at King Soopers supermarkets.

DENVER PUPPET THEATRE

3156 West 38th Avenue
(303) 458-6446
www.denverpuppettheater.com

The Denver Puppet Theatre is a delightful experience for kids age three and older. With six different plays performed each year—classics, world stories, new plays—kids can come back every two months for a new show. Marionettes and shadow puppets make up the characters, and visitors can see all the puppets after each performance. (No autographs, however.) Performances are on Thursday, Friday, and Saturday.

TINY TOWN
6249 South Turkey Creek Road Morrison
(303) 697-6829
www.tinytownrailroad.com

Hidden away in a mountain canyon southeast of Metro Denver, this is a curious and charming town of 110 miniature buildings constructed at one-sixth scale on six acres. Kids can actually go inside some of the buildings, but it's a place where families enjoy just walking around. You can ride a miniature train pulled by a real—but tiny—steam engine over a mile-long course. They have a snack bar, a gift shop, and puppet shows on weekends. Part of the magic of this place is that it looks rather ancient, and it is. It's the oldest miniature town in the United States.

George Turner was the owner of a Denver moving and storage business just after the turn of the 20th century, and this was his mountain property. His granddaughter was chronically ill, so he built a few miniature houses in the pasture for her to play in, then kept adding to the tiny town. Turkey Creek Road was dirt then, and people would stop their cars and delight their kids with the magical little town. By the 1920s and 1930s, it was one of Colorado's major tourist attractions. After World War II it went through several decades of decline, including a flood and a number of failed attempts to make it a profitable tourist business. Now it's operated by the Tiny Town Foundation, which donates 30 percent of the profits to charities and uses a lot of volunteers. Admission is low. It's open weekends only in May, September, and October and daily Memorial Day through Labor Day. Take C-470 to US 285, travel about 4 miles southwest on US 285, turn left onto Turkey Creek Road, and go about 0.25 mile. You'll see Tiny Town on the right.

ANNUAL EVENTS AND FESTIVALS

Love a lively parade or jumpin' jazz fest? Denver and its surrounding communities offer enough parades, concerts, rodeos, art shows, and ethnic celebrations—pick a reason, we've got a festival—to keep your calendar full year-round. And we've included as many as possible, from those with instantaneous name recognition, like the Cherry Creek Arts Festival, which draws more than a quarter-million people every July Fourth weekend, to the lesser-known ones like the Olde Golden Christmas, held in December in downtown Golden.

Our listings include events that happen every year. Some, such as the Bolder Boulder 10K run, are one-shot deals. Others, such as the World's Largest Christmas Lighting Display at the Denver City and County Building, may stretch out over weeks. For the most part these entries are confined to the Metro Denver area, but you'll notice that we've also covered events during the year at nearby ski areas and mountain communities. This list goes far afield: Cheyenne, Wyoming; Estes Park; and Colorado Springs—all easy day trips.

Our list should be viewed as a practical guide to those festivals and events with a designated date and location, but a few words of warning: Dates can change from year to year, so an event listed in September, for example, may actually turn out to be in October. The best source of last-minute information about special outdoor events is the calendar of events at www.denvergov.org. From the home page, click on attractions and events. Also check the Friday weekend sections of the *Denver Post* and Boulder's *Daily Camera*, where the goings-on are listed in considerable detail, as well as *Westword*, Denver's leading weekly newspaper.

JANUARY

DENVER BOAT SHOW
Colorado Convention Center
700 14th Street
www.boatcolorado.org
This is boathead heaven in early January. The year's biggest boat show usually lasts four days, spanning a weekend and jammed with aquatic craft, rubber rafts, and gear and accessories fore and aft. It's great fun to ogle at the huge luxury boats.

CHEF'S CUP RACE AND BENEFIT DINNER DANCE
West Portal Station, Winter Park Resort
Winter Park
(970) 726-1590
www.skiwinterpark.com
During this early-January event, Fraser Valley chefs compete on the slopes and in the kitchen to benefit the Winter Park Competition Center. The day begins with a trip down the racecourse, after which the chefs head to the kitchen to prepare a specialty dish. The results are served at a benefit dinner, during which guests can sample the fare, bid on items in a silent auction, and dance to live music. Guests can watch the race for free from the resort's base. Tickets to the evening events can be purchased from the Competition Center at the number listed above.

ULLR FEST
Locations throughout Breckenridge
(970) 453-5579, (800) 936-5573
www.gobreck.com
Helmets with horns on them are the height of fashion at this free weeklong festival in honor of Ullr (pronounced "ooler"), the Norse god of snow. If you don't have a horned helmet, you will most

certainly be able to find someone willing to sell you one. (They are also handed out free at the parade.) Ullr Fest starts on a Friday and runs for a week in early January. It includes a parade, kids' activities, and a variety of different events daily. Other activities include a version of the Dating Game, an ice-skating party, children's concert, and Ullympics competitions such as Broom Ball and volleyball with snowshoes.

CHINESE NEW YEAR
Various locations throughout
Metro Denver

Denver has a relatively small Chinese population, but come January they turn out in force to sponsor Chinese New Year celebrations. Events are publicized by the Denver Buddhist Cultural Society, 2530 West Alameda Avenue; Denver Chinese School at George Washington High School, 650 South Monaco Parkway, www.denver chineseschool.org; and at the Far East Shopping Center, on South Federal Boulevard between West Alameda and West Mississippi Avenues. Events usually include lion dances and religious celebrations.

COLORADO RV ADVENTURE TRAVEL SHOW
Colorado Convention Center
700 14th Street
(303) 892-6800
www.bigasalloutdoors.com

This is Metro Denver's version of hog heaven for the recreational vehicle enthusiast. Admire and wander through the 100–200 state-of-the-art recreational vehicles, see the latest in RV accessories, and meet exhibitors from lodges and resorts that cater to the RV crowd. This event is held in early January.

NATIONAL WESTERN STOCK SHOW & RODEO
National Western Complex
4655 Humboldt Street
(Brighton Boulevard exit off I-70)
(303) 297-1166
www.nationalwestern.com

Founded in 1906, the National Western is the largest annual event in Denver—and it's growing.

You'll be in the company of more than 600,000 people, but the event is spaced over two weeks in mid-January, so there's plenty of room and time to take in all the horses, sheep, cattle, chickens, and rabbits being exhibited by ranchers from miles around.

Rodeo events go on every day, with the nation's top horse and bull riders, calf ropers, you name it, competing for nearly $500,000 in prizes. Between the big events, you can see all kinds of oddball fun: rodeo clowns, Western battle recreations (cover the kids' ears if loud noises scare them), and a sheepdog herding sheep with a monkey in a cowboy suit riding on its back. Tickets to the Professional Bull Riders are the most expensive. The National Western begins with a colorful parade through downtown Denver.

Also check out what Denver calls the World's Largest Display of Christmas Lights at the City and County Building downtown. The lights are on from the first Thursday in December until January 1, but they're turned on at night during the stock show as well.

ANNUAL COLORADO COWBOY POETRY GATHERING
Arvada Center for the Arts and Humanities
6901 Wadsworth Boulevard Arvada
(720) 898-7272
www.arvadacenter.org

Tales grow tall under a wide-open sky, and nobody spends more time under a wider sky than cowboys and cowgirls. Once a year in mid-January, the poetic cream of the ranching and cowpunching community brings its Western oral tradition of tales and humor to Arvada from Colorado and beyond. Expect about 40 poets, balladeers, and yodelers from 14 states and Australia to perform during the four-day event. Guests can attend on-stage concerts as well as theme-poetry and western music sessions.

INTERNATIONAL SNOW SCULPTURE CHAMPIONSHIPS
Locations throughout Breckenridge
(970) 453-5579

In late January the city of Breckenridge lends its

front-end loaders to fill wooden forms with 20-ton blocks of snow. Four-person sculpting teams from around the world climb on top and tromp and stomp until the snow is packed tight. The forms are removed, and what happens to each big block of snow is up to the contestants, who use only hand tools. Sculptures run the gamut from geometric to free-form to recognizable shapes and scenes. The sculptures can last up to 10 days, depending on the weather. The event is free whether you participate or just watch.

INTERNATIONAL SPORTSMEN'S EXPOSITION
Colorado Convention Center
700 14th Street
(800) 545-6100
www.sportsexpos.com
This pure hunting and fishing show sometime in late January features products and services related to archery, firearms, and fishing. This is a how-to show with a lot of demonstrations designed to improve your hunting and fishing skills. You can sit in a U-shaped theater-seating section, for example, to watch a presenter on stage explain how he ties flies or wraps fishing rods. Video monitors allow you to see the small work. Top-name seminar speakers from magazines such as *Field and Stream* and *Outdoor Life* will be here. Expect around 350 exhibitors and crowds in the low 30,000s.

FEBRUARY

REGISTRATION FOR RIDE THE ROCKIES
(303) 954-6702
www.ridetherockies.com
See the June entry, Ride the Rockies, for more on the largest and longest public group bicycling tour of the year, but right now is when you need to register if you're interested in taking part. It's a lottery, and you need to get on the stick if you want in. The *Denver Post*, sponsor of the ride, usually makes applications available in the first week of February, and they're due by the last week of February.

WELLS FARGO CUP
Winter Park Resort, Lower Hughes
Ski Trail, Winter Park
(303) 293-5711, (303) 316-1540
www.nscd.org
The Wells Fargo Cup, the largest fund-raiser of the year for the National Sports Center for the Disabled (NSCD), brings together world-class disabled ski racers, Denver Broncos alumni, and amateur skiers of all abilities. Teams of amateur skiers take to the slopes in the pro-am race, and a timing run enables casual skiers to compete against more aggressive skiers with racing experience. The *Denver Post* Celebrity Challenge brings together local media personalities, political leaders, and the occasional former football star, who team up with two racers from the NSCD's Winter Park Disabled Ski Team. The highlight of the weekend, the World Disabled Invitational, is the only race in which disabled skiers compete head-to-head on parallel courses, a format used in professional racing events.

CHSAA STATE WRESTLING CHAMPIONSHIPS
The Pepsi Center
1000 Chopper Place
(303) 344-5050
www.chsaa.org
Don't expect to see bellowing mesomorphs in outlandish costumes. Do expect to see real mainstream wrestling, as the top high-school contenders square off for the state titles. At any one time you will be able to see simultaneous contests on 10 different mats. The competition starts in mid to late February and runs on a Thursday, Friday, and Saturday. Tickets can be purchased at the Pepsi Center.

BUFFALO BILL'S BIRTHDAY CELEBRATION
The Buffalo Bill Grave and Museum
987½ Lookout Mountain Road, Golden
(303) 526-0747
www.buffalobill.org
Each year, Colorado's most famous Wild West showman is celebrated on his birthday at the museum that bears his name. Buffalo Bill's remains

are also buried on the Lookout Mountain site. Past celebrations have included bluegrass music, free ice cream and cake, and a birthday ceremony. Buffalo Bill look-alikes lend atmosphere. This party is held on a weekend close to Bill's February 26 birthday. Take I-70 west to exit 256, where the sign says LOOKOUT MOUNTAIN AND BUFFALO BILL'S GRAVE, and follow the well-placed signs to the top of Lookout Mountain. The celebration is free.

i Buffalo Bill Cody died in January 1917. He lay in state in the Colorado State Capitol Building one weekend while 50,000 mourners and gawkers filed by. During the six months before he was buried, his body had to be embalmed six times. For his interment on June 3, next to what is now the Buffalo Bill Grave and Museum, 25,000 people walked or rode horses up the narrow Lookout Mountain Road. Bill had once said he wanted to be buried in Cody, Wyoming, a town he founded, and its residents thought that was a good idea. They threatened to steal the body, so Denver stationed a military tank at the grave. The plot was later covered with concrete, perhaps to seal Cody's final resting spot.

MARCH

CHSAA STATE BASKETBALL TOURNAMENT
Locations to be determined
(303) 344-5050
www.chsaa.org
See the final competitions of Colorado's high-school basketball season. A permanent venue for this event is still being sought.

ST. PATRICK'S DAY PARADE
Streets of downtown Denver
(303) 368-9861
www.denversaintpatricksdayparade.com
This is big, folks, the second-largest St. Patrick's Day parade in the country (New York City is first). The devil, you say. Yes, it's true. It never seems to end. Past parades have taken more than four hours for

250 floats, bands, and other colorful entrants to pass as clowns, leprechauns, and vendors ply the awesome crowds of spectators. There are ancillary events during the entire week, including the Running of the Green, a 5-kilometer race, and Irish entertainment at various pubs throughout town. Watch for complete details in the *Denver Post* or at www.denverpost.com.

DENVER MARCH POW-WOW
Denver Coliseum
4600 Humboldt Street (take the Brighton Boulevard exit off I-70)
(303) 934-8045
www.denvermarchpowwow.org
Don't miss this one in mid to late March. More than 1,000 Native Americans of tribes from most of the United States as well as Canada dance simultaneously in full costume. At the edges of the dancing, groups of men surround huge drums and make the whole coliseum vibrate. The big en masse dancing and the Grand Entry happen all three days, with other activities scattered throughout. You'll get plenty of opportunities to see the costumes close up: The seats around you will be filled with Native American families related to the dancers. Costumed competitors will be sitting next to you and walking past you.

There's a modest Native American market downstairs. Expect between 40 and 50 drum groups to be at the powwow, along with representatives of 60 to 70 tribes and a total three-day crowd in the neighborhood of 80,000 (not including children younger than age six and adults older than age 60, who get in free). If you plan to bring a video camera, you must purchase a permit.

DENVER HOME SHOW
National Western Complex
4655 Humboldt Street (take the Brighton Boulevard exit off I-70)
(303) 892-6800, (800) 457-2434
www.homeshowdenver.com
There's nothing like a nice trade show in late March to get you ready for spring. This one show-cases more than 500 experts willing to talk about home decor and home remodeling.

APRIL

DENVER AUTO SHOW
Colorado Convention Center
700 14th Street
(888) 704-4199
www.denverautoshow.com
Shop among, or just enjoy looking at, all the new cars under one roof. (No driving from lot to lot and being stalked by salespeople.) The show includes imports and domestics, sometimes exotics, futuristics, and prototypes. Attendance at this five-day affair in early April has exceeded 170,000.

EASTER SUNRISE SERVICE
Red Rocks Amphitheatre (north of Morrison on Hogback Road; take I-70 West to the Morrison exit, then go south), Morrison
www.redrocksonline.com
One of the most inspirational places you'll ever find for an Easter sunrise service is this gargantuan natural amphitheater of red sandstone facing east over the plains. The event is non-denominational, free, and open to the public, attracting upwards of 12,000 people. Gates open at 4:30 a.m., and music begins at 6 a.m. Dress warmly, because this is an outdoor service that has been cancelled only five times in six decades due to bad weather.

SPRING SPLASH/CLOSING DAY
Winter Park Resort, Lower Hughes Ski Trail, Winter Park
(970) 726-1564
www.skiwinterpark.com
This is one of those events that public relations people love because they get to use the word "zany." In most years the sun is out, everybody wears sunglasses, and ski-babes in bikinis and ski-bozos in goofy costumes come barreling down the hill trying to hydroplane across a puddle of ice water. Most belly flop at the bottom with a big splash. The event is always held on the closing Sunday of the season (typically mid-April). It has become one of the quintessential Colorado outdoor spectacles, with viewers jockeying for position on the balconies of the base lodge.

Spectating is free; participating will cost you a lift ticket plus an entry fee.

MAY

FURRY SCURRY
Washington Park, East Louisiana Avenue and Downing Street
(303) 696-4941, ext. 379
www.ddfl.org
This annual 2-mile walk/run for humans and their canines benefits the Denver Dumb Friends League. Participants register for a fee and collect pledges as well. Dogs on leashes are welcome if they are at least six months old, have been spayed or neutered, and have current ID and rabies tags. Treats are available for people and their pets along the route and at the finish line. The event is usually held the first weekend in May.

CINCO DE MAYO
Celebrate Culture Festival
Civic Center Park, between Colfax Avenue and 14th Street
(303) 534-8342
www.cincodemayodenver.com
This is Denver's celebration of its Hispanic heritage, the largest of its kind in the United States, attracting more than 400,000 participants over two days in early May. Many confuse this with Mexican Independence Day, which is on September 16. Cinco de Mayo is held in remembrance of la Batalla de Puebla, the Battle of Ciudad Puebla, which took place during the Mexican battle for independence from France. Mexicans, equipped with little more than farm implements, whipped one of the greatest armies on earth, although the French came back five days later and made up for it. Still, it's a spiritual moment for Mexico and has become a big holiday in Denver. It starts with the Celebrate Culture parade, intended to celebrate diversity, and a traditional Mariachi mass in the park's Greek Amphitheater. Past celebrations included 250 exhibitors, a carnival, arts and foods, entertainment on six stages, ethnic-fashionwear showings, and Latin, jazz, rap, and contemporary music. Activities are also provided for children. The event is free.

DENVER BOTANIC GARDENS PLANT AND BOOK SALE

Denver Botanic Gardens
1005 York Street
(720) 865-3500
www.botanicgardens.org

The Gardens' annual plant and book sale serves as the unofficial start of the gardening season for hundreds of Denver-area green thumbs. It's one of the facility's most popular fund-raisers, offering thousands of flowers, herbs, and vegetables that are especially suited to Colorado's climate. Among the most popular in recent drought years are the water-smart plants, although regulars plan their beds around the large stock of annuals, roses, water plants, and perennials. Crowds can be fierce, especially during the first few hours of the sale, and parking is limited. Shuttle buses run continuously between the Church in the City parking lot, at 1530 Josephine Street, and the Gardens. Members can preview the sale at 8:30 a.m. Friday, with the public welcome after 10 a.m. Admission is free.

BOULDER CREEK FESTIVAL

Central Park and the Library-Municipal Building Complex, Canyon Boulevard (along the Boulder Creek Path), Boulder
(303) 449-3137
www.bouldercreekevents.com

In 1984 a group of volunteers agreed to meet along the banks of Boulder Creek over Memorial Day weekend to pick up trash along the 5.5-mile corridor from Eben G. Fine Park to the intersection of Pearl and 55th Streets. Their reward was an after-party that became so popular it turned into the Boulder Creek Festival. Now the trash cleanup is held the Saturday before Memorial Day weekend and is followed by a three-day festival that attracts more than 400 exhibitors and 150,000 participants. Booths display arts and crafts, outdoor equipment and services, health alternatives, and technology. Performers dance and play music, and food and beverage vendors sell a wide range of edible treats. Admission and entertainment are free.

i Find specifics on festivals and events each week by looking at the Friday sections of the *Denver Post*, and Boulder's *Daily Camera*. Also check the events listings in Denver's weekly newspaper, *Westword*.

BOLDER BOULDER

30th and Iris Streets, Boulder
(303) 444-RACE
www.bolderboulder.com

Since 1979 the Bolder Boulder has been a Memorial Day tradition in this athletic college town. The 10K race that began with 2,700 participants has become one of the world's 10 largest road races. It now attracts more than 50,000 runners, walkers, and wheelchair racers, including professional racers who compete for the world's largest non-marathon prize purse. The largest group of entrants are the "citizens," who leave the starting line in 68 waves that take several hours to stage. Faster runners are assigned to the early waves and must qualify for them by proving they can run the course in 60 minutes or less. Slower participants, including walkers and walk/joggers, are assigned to the latter waves and tend to cover the 6.8-mile course at their own pace. The course winds its way through neighborhoods, around the downtown area, and into the University of Colorado's football stadium. Along the way, participants are cheered by more than 100,000 spectators who show their support by wearing costumes, belly dancing, spraying sweaty runners with a hose, and playing music of all types. (Don't be surprised to pass a formally dressed string quartet on one corner and a troupe of high-stepping grannies on the next.) The race starts at the north end of 30th Street near the First National Bank of Boulder and finishes in Folsom Field. Registration fees start at about $26 for adults who preregister and climb from there depending on how late you register and what kinds of race T-shirts or paraphernalia you'd like to include. Two things you should know: Baby strollers and Walkman-type music systems are not allowed, and local traffic slows to a standstill most of race day. On Memorial Day, study the race route and carefully plan any outings in Boulder that require you to drive.

JUNE

BRECKENRIDGE FESTIVAL OF FILM
Various locations in Breckenridge
(970) 453-6200
www.breckfilmfest.com
This four-day fest in mid-June includes premieres of documentaries, feature films, and children's features as well as parties in local clubs and bars. Past years have seen visits by James Earl Jones, Mary Steenburgen, Elliott Gould, and Angie Dickinson. The Peak Ten Pass costs $199 and includes admission to all the films and events, plus a festival T-shirt.

CAPITOL HILL PEOPLE'S FAIR
Civic Center Park
Between Colfax Avenue and 14th Street
(303) 830-1651
www.peoplesfair.com
Capitol Hill is one of Denver's most colorful and historic neighborhoods. The annual festival that raises money for its neighborhood organization has, for more than 30 years, been held on the first weekend in June. Organizers claim this event is Colorado's largest arts and crafts festival, with about 500 exhibitors as well as food, dance, and entertainment on six stages, and kids' activities such as putt-putt golf, face painting, and more. In past years it has attracted crowds of 275,000; admission is free.

ELEPHANT ROCK CYCLING FESTIVAL
Douglas County Fair Grounds
Castle Rock
(303) 282-9020
www.elephantrockride.com
With bike tours of various lengths—from the 8-mile family loop to the 25-mile fat-tire course to road bike routes of 32, 50, 65, and 100 miles—the Elephant Rock festival is a bicyclist's paradise. Held the first Sunday in June, the event begins and ends in the Douglas County Fair Grounds and sends participants down country roads and through roll-ing hills, across ranch lands, and through the Black Forest. The free Kids' Race is held on a special loop around the area. Entry fees vary by the length of the course. To reach the Fair Grounds, take I-25 south from Denver to exit 181 east.

ESTES PARK WOOL MARKET
Stanley Park Fair Grounds, Community
Drive off U.S. Highway 36, Estes Park
(970) 586-6104
www.estesnet.com/Events/woolmarket.htm
Sheep ranching is a big part of Colorado's history and economy. This event, held in mid-June, is dedicated to those who raise and shear them. You'll find spinning and weaving classes; dyeing classes; showings of sheep, llamas, and alpacas; spinning and weaving demonstrations and contests; spinning wheels for sale; and commercial exhibits related to the wool industry. All events are free, but you'll pay to park.

COLORADO RENAISSANCE FESTIVAL
Off I-25 South, Larkspur
(303) 688-6010
www.coloradorenaissance.com
Renaissance festivals are ripping good fun, and this is truly one of the best. Spread out across a huge site beneath the trees, the festival re-creates a 16th-century marketplace filled with costumed characters and ruled by King Henry and Queen Anne. More than 200 costumed crafters sell handmade goods. One of the main attractions is the battling, strutting, and jousting by knights on foot and horseback. You'll also enjoy strolling minstrels, jesters, jugglers, medieval food, rides, and games galore for eight weekends in June and July. From Metro Denver, take I-25 South to the Larkspur exit, then follow the signs to the festival.

BRECKENRIDGE MUSIC FESTIVAL
Riverwalk Performing Arts Center
Park Avenue and Four O'Clock Road
Breckenridge
(970) 453-9142
www.breckenridgemusicfestival.com
Nearly every day from mid-June to mid-August,

visitors can enjoy performances by the National Repertory Orchestra, the Breckenridge Music Festival Orchestra, and nationally know performers, such as the Glenn Miller Orchestra. More than 45 concerts showcase classical, jazz, show tunes, and children's music.

SUMMER CONCERT SERIES
Arvada Center for the Arts and Humanities
6901 Wadsworth Boulevard, Arvada
(720) 898-7200 (box office)
www.arvadacenter.org
For a mixture of country, Big Band, jazz, and Cajun music, come to the Arvada Center's outdoor amphitheater. You can picnic on the grounds before the shows and browse the art gallery. If you'd like, you may bring your picnic inside for the concert. The center also stages a musical every summer.

RIDE THE ROCKIES
Statewide, a different route every year
(303) 954-6702
www.ridetherockies.com
If you have thighs like a Tyrannosaurus Rex, Ride the Rockies is for you. At the very least, participants should be experienced bike riders who are comfortable covering at least 50 miles a day. To enjoy the event, they also should be accustomed to riding at high altitudes and climbing mountain passes that leave small cars choking for air. This event lasts six to seven days, during which time a stream of about 2,000 bicyclists push their pedals for more than 400 miles. Past trips have taken them through such resort towns as Steamboat Springs, Telluride, Copper Mountain, and Vail and more "everyday" towns such as Walsenberg, Durango, Cortez, and Granby. At night they camp on high-school sports fields or in their gyms. Communities provide nightly low-cost meals and various forms of entertainment. Not everyone can take part. The event's title sponsor, the *Denver Post*, holds a lottery in February. If you win, you're in. The registration fee includes camping space, restrooms and showers, transportation of one suitcase, a jersey, aid stations, and medical support.

SUMMER CONCERTS
Denver Botanic Gardens
1005 York Street
(720) 865-3500 (information)
(866) 468-7624 (tickets)
www.botanicgardens.org
Sitting on the grass in the midst of the Denver Botanic Gardens on a summer evening is a great way to listen to world-class artists. Past performers have included Shawn Colvin, Arlo Guthrie, k.d. lang, Los Lobos, and Keb Mo. This series of outdoor concerts is aimed at families in an informal setting. Bring an elegant picnic and a blanket and you're set for a fun evening. Tickets go early, so buy them in the spring if you intend to go.

SCANDINAVIAN MIDSUMMER FESTIVAL
Bond Park
Virginia Street and Elkhorn Avenue
downtown Estes Park
www.estesmidsummer.com
June 24 is midsummer in the Scandinavian countries, which prompts their biggest celebration next to Christmas. Estes Park's version of the big, traditional Scandinavian festival features arts and crafts, ethnic foods, educational mini-seminars and demonstrations, and the raising of the maypole with appropriate Scandinavian folk dancers every hour. At least one dance group usually comes from Scandinavia. There's also a bonfire, which is how Norwegians celebrate midsummer. Not surprisingly, this free festival is held the Friday and Saturday closest to June 24. There's no phone number; so use the Web site listed for more information.

GREEK FESTIVAL
Assumption Greek Orthodox Cathedral
4610 East Alameda Avenue
(303) 388-9314
www.assumptioncathedral.org
Assumption Greek Orthodox Cathedral, with its gold dome, is a familiar landmark. Denver's Greeks and Grecophiles convene on the church grounds each year in mid-June for "wonderful

food prepared by the ladies of our church," live music, and Greek dance shows done by groups ranging in age from children to adults. Calamari, Aegean beer, wine, and beverages are served, and there is usually a gift shop and a small carnival area for kids. All proceeds benefit the church and its charitable partners.

YELLOW ROSE BALL: OPENING NIGHT
Central City Opera House
124 Eureka Street, Central City
(303) 292-6500
www.centralcityopera.org
In late June or early July, the Central City Opera's season begins, usually with the annual presentation of debutantes called the Central City Flower Girls, followed by a dinner at the Teller House and a performance.

FAT TIRE CLASSIC
Locations throughout Winter Park and Fraser Valley
(303) 293-5711, (303) 316-1540
www.nscd.org
This two-day mountain-bike pledge ride is held the last weekend in June to benefit the National Sports Center for the Disabled and the American Red Cross Mile High Chapter. It's not a race; it's just a tour, with events for all levels of riders. You should be in shape, though. Even the beginner's ride is a 15-mile off-road event. You'll find gourmet food, live musical entertainment on Saturday night, prizes for different categories of riders, and a raffle. Riders can pay the entire registration themselves or raise money from pledges. Prizes are awarded for raising pledges of $300 or more.

CHERRY BLOSSOM FESTIVAL
Sakura Square, Lawrence Street
(between 19th and 20th Streets)
(303) 380-8972
www.tsdbt.org/cherryblossom
This celebration of Japanese culture is held at Sakura Square, the heart of Denver's Japanese community. If you love Japanese food, check

out the food made by volunteers in the adjacent Denver Buddhist Temple. Also watch martial arts displays, bonsai demonstrations, taiko drumming, poetry singing, and traditional folk dancing. The festival, held in late June or early July, is free and open to the public. Food and beverages may be purchased.

JULY

Also see June entries for:
Breckenridge Music Festival
Colorado Renaissance Festival
Summer Concert Series, Arvada Center for the
    Arts and Humanities
Summer Concerts, Denver Botanic Gardens

RACE TO THE CLOUDS
Pikes Peak, outside Colorado Springs
(719) 685-4400
www.ppihc.com
You can enjoy this famous annual Pikes Peak hill climb even if you're not one of the top race-car drivers who come here to test their skills on one of Colorado's 14,000-foot peaks. But you do need tickets ($35) ahead of time to drive up, park, and watch the race from designated areas on the mountain. In preceding weeks other smaller races lead up to this big race, held the last week of June or first week of July.

CHERRY CREEK ARTS FESTIVAL
Cherry Creek North (on 2nd and 3rd Avenues between Clayton and Steele Streets)
(303) 355-2787
www.cherryarts.org
Pulling some 300,000 visitors for this event, Denver's upscale retail shopping area hosts a sidewalk festival during Fourth of July weekend that features fine arts and crafts. About 200 artists from around the nation and Mexico come for the juried show. National and international performers provide entertainment. Local chefs cook up their best for a block-long culinary-arts extravaganza. Browsing is free, but prepare to pay top dollar for the artworks.

INDEPENDENCE DAY CELEBRATION
Four Mile Historic Park
715 South Forest Street
(303) 399-1859
www.fourmilepark.org

Four Mile Historic Park, Denver's living-history park, throws a good old-fashioned, family-style Fourth of July party each year. This is a day of patriotic music, games, food, and costumed actors who do historical reenactments. Past events also included historic and craft demonstrations such as blacksmithing, quilting, weaving, lace making, and butter churning.

DRUMS ALONG THE ROCKIES
INVESCO Field at Mile High Stadium
(303) 424-6396
datr.bknights.org

This booming good time in mid to late July is the annual regional drum and bugle corps championships. About ten of the best drum and bugle corps from the western United States and Canada compete in the Drum Corps Regional Championships, usually including four or five of the top-ranked corps in the world.

NHRA MOPAR MILE-HIGH NATIONALS
Bandimere Speedway
3051 South Rooney Road, Morrison
(303) 697-6001
www.bandimere.com

This is motorhead heaven. Between 600 and 700 cars and the nation's top racers gather for three days of competition in pro-stock dragsters, top fuel cars, and nitro funny cars in mid-July. All seats are reserved.

BUFFALO BILL DAYS
Locations throughout Golden
(303) 384-0003
www.buffalobilldays.com

The city of Golden hosts this Western celebration, which started in Buffalo Bill's honor, on the last weekend of July. In past years it has included a parade and other activities on Main Street and in Parfet Park, 10th Street and Washington Avenue, and Clear Creek Living History Park. There has been musical entertainment, a golf tournament, country and western dance contests, living-history reenactments, a talent contest, 6K and 10K races, a burro race, and the Golden Derby for Young Racers. Admission is free.

CHEYENNE FRONTIER DAYS
Frontier Park, Cheyenne, WY
(800) 227-6336
www.cfdrodeo.com

This is a nine-day Western extravaganza centered around rodeo events, but it also includes a carnival, evening shows by some of the biggest names in country western music (in past years Toby Keith, Willie Nelson, Alan Jackson, and Chris LeDoux), parades, free pancake breakfasts, a chili cook-off, a performance by the Air Force Thunderbirds team, and a free entertainment area with music and other acts. Cheyenne is only 100 miles from Denver, so it makes an easy day trip. About 300,000 people show up during Frontier Days, but parking is generally no problem in the gravel lots around the stadium. The event starts on a Friday and runs through the last weekend in July. To get to Frontier Park, take I-25 North to Central Avenue (exit 12). Go east on 8th Avenue and turn right. After 0.25 mile, turn right onto Carey Avenue. The park is on your left.

ROOFTOP RODEO
Estes Park Fairgrounds
Community Drive off U.S. Highway 36,
Estes Park
(970) 586-6104
www.estesnet.com

A rodeo plain and simple, this six-day event in mid-July offers a rodeo parade and six Professional Rodeo Cowboy Association rodeos. On Western Heritage Day, these are joined by a mountain-man rendezvous, an Indian village, gold panning, and Western entertainment. Other past attractions include cowboy cartoonists and poets, a dirt dance, and concerts. The rodeo parade is free; admission is charged for the rodeo.

WELD COUNTY FAIR

Island Grove Regional Park
425 North 15th Avenue, Greeley
(970) 356-4000, ext. 2085
www.co.weld.co.us/WeldCountyFair

Weld County, north of Adams County, brings in the nation's fourth-largest amount of agricultural revenue, contains the world's two largest feedlots, and accounts for about a quarter of Colorado's agriculture. Its county fair, therefore, is the real thing. It doesn't have a carnival midway, but it does have a lot of animal showings and competitions, including about 1,400 4-H and FFA kids, with an animal-catching contest, food booths, a fun fair, a concert night, a dance, and a livestock auction. The fair is free to the public.

AUGUST

Also see June entries for:

Breckenridge Music Festival
Summer Concert Series, Arvada Center for the Arts and Humanities
Summer Concerts, Denver Botanic Gardens

ADAMS COUNTY FAIR AND RODEO

Adams County Fairgrounds
9755 Henderson Road, Brighton
(303) 637-8000
www.adamscountyfair.com

Adams County claims the largest county fair in Colorado, and it has included such attractions as rodeos, tractor pulls, more than 150 exhibits and livestock shows, 4-H events, a children's pavilion, petting zoo, multicultural village, artisans bazaar, free entertainment, and top-name concerts. Past entertainers include Alan Jackson and Mel Tillis. There's also a Mexican Cultural Day at the fair. Look for this event the first weekend in August. Admission to the fair is free; parking costs $5. To reach the fairgrounds, take I-76 north from Denver to US 85 (exit 12) and follow it north to Henderson Road. Turn left there.

COLORADO SCOTTISH FESTIVAL AND HIGHLAND GAMES

Highlands Heritage Park
9651 South Quebec Street, Highlands Ranch
(303) 238-6524
www.scottishgames.org

Wake up and smell the heather on the first weekend in August. Enjoy the competitions: bagpiping and drumming, highland athletic events, and highland dancing. You'll also find vendors selling merchandise from the British Isles, exhibitions of highland cattle and dogs, and Scottish food and beverages. Take C-470 east to Quebec Street and go south to the intersection with Lincoln Avenue. The park is on the southwest.

GENUINE JAZZ & WINE FESTIVAL

Maggie Pond at the base of Peak 9
and Main Street Station, Breckenridge
(866) 464-2626 (ticket sales)
www.genuinejazz.com

Breckenridge's three-day jazz festival in mid-August features Colorado artists as well as a national headliner such as Stanley Jordan. Evening sessions take place at local bars. Free daytime performances occur at Main Street Station and at Maggie Pond, where a stage is built over the water and spectators sit on the shore.

SCULPTURE IN THE PARK

Benson Sculpture Garden
29th and Taft Streets, Loveland
(970) 663-2940
www.sculptureinthepark.org

Loveland bills this as one of the largest outdoor juried exhibitions of sculpture in the United States. The Benson Sculpture Garden ordinarily is home to about 40 pieces, but on this day during the second weekend in August, it attracts about 180 artists from around the United States and Canada who show and sell their work. The event features entertainment, demonstrations by artists, a silent auction, and speed-sculpting (artists who sculpt while you watch). Proceeds from this event buy new art for the Sculpture Garden.

DOUGLAS COUNTY FAIR

Douglas County Fairgrounds
410 Fairgrounds Road, Castle Rock
(720) 733-6900
www.douglas.co.us/eventscenter

This is an old-fashioned August shindig with a rodeo, carnival, and all the accoutrements. Simultaneously with the county fair, Castle Rock holds a community fair that includes a parade to celebrate the 4-H winners, with more than 100 parade entries and a barbecue in the Courthouse Square.

WESTERN WELCOME WEEK

Various locations in Littleton
(303) 794-4870
www.westernwelcomeweek.com

This is Littleton's big yearly celebration, which runs for 10 days beginning the second Thursday in August. You'll find arts and crafts and continuous entertainment on Littleton's Main Street, with a circus, a parade, concerts, fireworks, a barbecue, pancake breakfasts, and used-book sales. Most events are free.

KAISER PERMANENTE MOONLIGHT CLASSIC

State Capitol Broadway and Colfax Street
(303) 282-9020
www.moonlight-classic.com

Imagine cycling through the deserted streets of downtown Denver with the glow of the moon defining the course for you. Imagine doing so alongside thousands of other riders. The Moonlight Classic begins and ends at the State Capitol. The 10-mile course passes through the business district, LoDo, and by landmarks such as Coors Field and the Cherry Creek shopping district. The event benefits Seniors, Inc., and is followed by the Lunar Breakfast, a breakfast with music and prizes. The first wave of cyclists leave at 10:30 p.m. and all must have helmets and front and back lights and reflectors.

CARNATION FESTIVAL

Albert E. Anderson Park
44th and Field Streets, Wheat Ridge
www.wheatridgecarnationfestival.org

Wheat Ridge was founded by farmers who supplied Denver with wheat, produce, and, in the 1940s, carnations. The Carnation Festival celebrates that heritage with a jolly small-town parade along 38th Street from Harlan to Upham Streets on the third weekend in August. Some floats are covered with carnations, but most just carry bigwigs and their families. The carnival in the park has rides for children, and the carnival midway has food and arts and crafts. There's also a fireworks display on Friday night. Admission is free.

ROCKY MOUNTAIN FOLKS FESTIVAL

U.S. Highway 36, Lyons (on the way to Estes Park)
(800) 624-2422
www.bluegrass.com

This festival in mid-August features folk-music performers, in the past including Warren Haynes, Indigo Girls, Norah Jones, and Rufus Wainwright. There is also the Song School, with workshops and activities geared toward future musicians, and a song seminar that includes sessions on songwriting, copyrighting, and bookkeeping. Campsites are available for an additional fee.

GILPIN COUNTY HISTORICAL SOCIETY'S ANNUAL CEMETERY CRAWL

Various historic cemeteries in Central City
(303) 582-5364
www.gilpinhistory.org

Lend an ear to the living dead at this entertaining and educational event portraying the life of Gilpin County 100 years ago. Members and friends of the Gilpin Historical Society transform into "spirits" of former residents, leaders, and movers and shakers of the period. The spirits share their stories as visitors walk through a different historic cemetery each year in mid-August.

KING OF THE ROCKIES MOUNTAIN BIKE FESTIVAL

Base of the Winter Park Ski Area, Winter Park
(970) 726-1590, (303) 316-1590
www.epicsingletrack.com

This festival in mid to late August features races and

guided tours for all levels of mountain bikers as well as a mountain-bike and summer-sports expo.

LAKEWOOD ON PARADE
Heritage Center at Belmar Park
Wadsworth Boulevard and Ohio Street
Lakewood
(303) 232-3389
www.lakewoodonparade.com
The city of Lakewood's community festival, this free event is held the weekend before Labor Day weekend. It typically combines food, games, entertainment, a parade, golf tournament, car show, and art show.

WINTER PARK FAMOUS FLAMETHROWERS HIGH ALTITUDE CHILI COOKOFF
The Village, Winter Park
(303) 316-1689
www.skiwinterpark.com
Held the last weekend in August, this two-day event is an opportunity to sample different types of chili and salsa produced especially for the cook-off. Costumed chili chefs vie for the Flame-thrower title. Guests can buy tickets to sample entries each day after they have been judged. The event benefits the National Sports Center for the Disabled.

COLORADO STATE FAIR
State Fairgrounds
1001 Beulah Avenue, Pueblo
(719) 561-8484, (800) 876-4567
www.coloradostatefair.com
The city of Pueblo is two hours south of Denver on I-25, but this is the state fair. It's one of the state's largest annual events and is well worth the drive. In addition to the full range of rodeo events, expect parades, art exhibitions, a Latin Fiesta Weekend, livestock sales, horse shows, cooking competitions, midway carnival rides, games, and lots of good food. Big-name entertainers in past years have included Pat Benatar, Tom Jones, Chicago, and Julio Iglesias. The fair runs for two weeks, late August to early September.

SEPTEMBER

AIDS WALK COLORADO
Cheesman Park, between 8th and
13th Avenues east of Lafayette Street
(303) 837-0166, (303) 861-WALK
www.coloradoaidsproject.org
Every year thousands of people converge on Cheesman Park in late August or early September to raise money for the Colorado AIDS Project and other AIDS organizations throughout the state. From there they follow a 10-kilometer walking route that brings them back to the park for an afternoon party.

THE FESTIVAL OF MOUNTAIN AND PLAIN: A TASTE OF COLORADO
Civic Center Park, between Colfax
Avenue and 14th Street
(303) 295-6330
www.atasteofcolorado.com
One of Denver's largest annual gatherings, A Taste of Colorado runs four days over the Labor Day weekend and attracts more than 400,000 people. Organizers usually even block off a street or two. You can sample culinary delights from more than 50 Metro Denver restaurants, so it's a good way to find new restaurants. In addition to the food, the festival offers entertainment on seven stages, kids' activities, cooking demonstrations, arts and crafts booths, a carnival midway, stages with live entertainment, and a kaleidoscope of buskers and vendors. Entertainment is free; food can be purchased with tickets.

COLORADO SPRINGS BALLOON CLASSIC
Memorial Park, Pikes Peak Avenue and
Union Boulevard, Colorado Springs
(719) 471-4833
www.balloonclassic.com
The Balloon Classic is a grand spectacle. Typically about 125 hot-air balloons from around the nation are invited to ascend en masse at 7 a.m. on Saturday, Sunday, and Monday of Labor Day weekend. They are preceded by the "dawn patrol," about five balloons going up at 5:30 a.m. and dangling strobe lights, just to let folks know

that the big event is coming. About 50 balloons light up Saturday and Sunday nights in the "Balloon Glo." (Albuquerque trademarked the name "Balloon Glow," so the folks in the Springs had to drop the "w.") The Kiwanis Country Breakfast is served in a big tent from 5:30 to 9:30 each morning. Other regular events include a hula-hoop contest, a photo contest, a scavenger hunt, and evening concerts on Saturday and Sunday. Admission is free.

LONGS PEAK SCOTTISH-IRISH HIGHLAND FESTIVAL
In the Stanley Park area; evening events at various locations in Estes Park
(970) 586-6308
www.scotfest.com
Held the weekend after Labor Day, the Highland Festival celebrates the Celtic tradition for four straight days—Thursday night through Sunday night—with performances and competitions by bagpipe bands, highland dancers, Irish step dancers, highland dogs herding sheep, and Scottish athletes throwing the hammer and the caber. There are parades, medieval reenactments and folk concerts, performances on the Celtic harp, and fiddle and tin-whistle contests. Each year organizers schedule a special seminar topic such as Scots and the military. Expect to pay a daily gate fee.

CASTLE ROCK ARTFEST
Old Courthouse Square
301 Wilcox Street, Castle Rock
(303) 688-4597
www.castlerockartfest.com
This arts festival is held in mid-September, with family entertainment, continuous musical performances, and food. It features more than 130 artists displaying, selling, and working in a full range of media.

SUMMERSET FESTIVAL
Clement Park, Bowles Avenue and
Pierce Street, Littleton
(303) 973-9155
www.summersetfest.com
This end-of-summer (second weekend after Labor Day) outdoor celebration generally draws more than 50,000 people. Events include hot-air balloons, a muscle car show, three stages of entertainment, a fishing derby, a pancake breakfast, a softball tournament, midway games, arts and crafts booths, and a skate festival. Admission is free.

AURORA'S FESTIVAL
International Fletcher Plaza
9898 East Colfax Avenue, Aurora
(303) 361-6169
www.aurorabusiness.org
In mid-September the city of Aurora likes to celebrate the end of summer by organizing a festival. It celebrates the music, dance, food, arts and crafts of more than 20 nationalities. The Saturday event includes special activities designed for children.

MINIATURES, DOLLS & TOYS FALL SHOW AND SALE
Doubletree Hotel Denver Tech Center
7801 East Orchard Road, Greenwood Village
(303) 922-0281
www.dmmdt.org
This is a benefit for the Denver Museum of Miniatures, Dolls & Toys, though the show and sale is never held at the tiny museum. It typically includes more than 100 national artists who specialize in making miniatures, dolls, teddy bears, and toys. They display and sell their wares during a two-day weekend in mid-September. The sale is preceded by three days of workshops that are open to the public but require preregistration.

OKTOBERFEST
Larimer Square, Larimer Street
(between 14th and 15th Streets)
(303) 534-2367
www.oktoberfestdenver.com
Denver's main bow to the famous harvest festival of Munich (and the nation's second-largest Oktoberfest celebration, according to sponsors) is filled with polka bands and beer-drinking and sausage-eating fun. You'll see plenty of jolly Germanic costumes. One of the highlights of Larimer Square's festival year, this event is free unless you

eat and drink. Oktoberfest includes Kinderplatz, a kids' area that has included Prince Ludwig's Castle, where kids can enjoy the Black Forest Maze and German storytellers, "the world's shortest parade," and more than 100 opportunities to do the Chicken Dance. The festival is usually held for six days in mid-September.

SPANISH MARKET AND 1840s RENDEZVOUS
The Fort Restaurant
19192 Colorado Highway 8, Morrison
(303) 697-4771
www.thefort.com
The last week in September, Morrison's unique Fort Restaurant opens its gates to a quintessentially Western event. Fine Spanish artists from Colorado and New Mexico gather on the grounds to display and sell their creations. They're joined by reenactors dressed as 1840s traders and interpreters for a weekend of entertainment, storytelling, competition, and dancing. A patron preview party is held on Friday night, followed by the market on Saturday and Sunday. To get to the Fort from downtown Denver, take I-70 west to C-470 (exit 260). Follow C-470 south to US 285 south (Fairplay exit), then go 1.5 miles to the Highway 8 Morrison exit. The Fort is on the right.

Nature's Annual Events

Nature puts on her own annual events: the changing of the aspen in the fall, which draws Denverites out of the city to high-country roads; the ritual of elk bugling from mid September to mid October at Rocky Mountain National Park; and the blooming of a sea of irises at Long's Gardens, 3240 Broadway, Boulder, in late May/early June, where you can gaze, photograph, or dig your own iris clumps for a reasonable price.

GREAT AMERICAN BEER FESTIVAL
Colorado Convention Center
700 14th Street
(303) 447-0816
www.beertown.org
This is America's biggest beer bash, usually held in late September or early October. Bring an ID that proves you are at least 21 and a designated driver because more than 1,600 beers will be available to taste, the product of some 300-plus American breweries, microbreweries, and brewpubs.

OCTOBER

ROCKY MOUNTAIN SNOWMOBILE EXPO
Denver Merchandise Mart, off I-25
at 58th Avenue exit
(303) 892-6800
www.bigasalloutdoors.com
Snowmobiles are one way of enjoying snow, so you may want to check out the latest in snowmobiles and accessories and snowmobile services and travel destinations.

GREAT PUMPKIN HARVEST FESTIVAL
Four Mile Historic Park
715 South Forest Street
(303) 399-1859
www.fourmilepark.org
Usually held in early October, this event takes place in the park's 12-acre historic farm. Activities include old-time music, dancing, hayrides, and scarecrow making. The event is free, and pumpkins are available for sale.

CIDER DAYS HARVEST FESTIVAL
Lakewood's Heritage Center
797 South Wadsworth Boulevard, Lakewood
(303) 987-7850
http://lakewood.org
In the early 20th century, apple trees were so common in Lakewood that the area was called Cider Hill. On the first weekend in October, the town celebrates its heritage with demonstrations of cider making, antique farm machinery, a vintage tractor-pull competition, food vendors, and live music.

PUMPKIN FESTIVAL AT CHATFIELD NATURE PRESERVE

8500 Deer Creek Canyon Road Littleton
(303) 973-3705
www.botanicgardens.org

Bring a wheelbarrow and pick your own pumpkin(s) from the pumpkin patch. From tennis-ball size to behemoth, the sale of these orange globes raises money for the arboretum. There are also hay-rack rides and crafts and food booths. This event is usually the second Saturday in. Take C-470 to the Wadsworth exit, then follow Wadsworth south to Deer Creek Canyon Road. Turn right; the entrance is 0.25 mile down on the left.

BOO AT THE ZOO

Denver Zoo in City Park
East 23rd Avenue and Steele Street
(303) 376-4800
www.denverzoo.org

Celebrate Halloween at the zoo on the last weekend in October. Trick-or-treat doors are set up throughout the zoo, and kids get a food or toy item at each door. There is also a medieval village offering storytelling and face painting. The event is free with paid admission to the zoo.

NOVEMBER

STARZ DENVER FILM FESTIVAL

Various Denver locations
(303) 595-3456
www.denverfilm.org

This 10-day festival showcases more than 175 top feature, documentary, and short films from around the world, screened at the Starz FilmCenter in the Tivoli Center, at the Buell Theatre at 14th and Curtis Streets, and at the King Center, on the Auraria Campus. They're all located downtown. Usually held the second week in November, it draws a host of actors, directors, and producers. Previous festivals have drawn celebrities such as Robert Altman, Geena Davis, Sean Penn, and Shirley MacLaine. After some film showings, enjoy a question-and-answer session with the director, producer, actors, or others involved in the film's genesis. Call for ticket information.

L'ESPRIT DE NOEL

Locations in Denver vary each year
(303) 292-6500
www.centralcityopera.org

Each year the Central City Opera Guild stages this fund-raiser to support the opera's education and community programs. Local florists donate their time to decorate upscale homes for the holiday season, then open the finished products for three days of tours. It's held the weekend before Thanksgiving, featuring homes in high-end developments. The event is kicked off with a patron preview party, then is opened to the public.

STARLIGHTING

Old Courthouse Square
301 Wilcox Street, Castle Rock
(303) 688-4597
www.castlerock.org

The annual lighting of the Christmas star on top of Castle Rock, the monolith that towers above the city of Castle Rock has been going on since 1936. It goes along with a ceremony in Courthouse Square that includes carolers, Santa, and hot chocolate. It is followed by a fire-department sponsored chili supper and dance (indoors), all on the Saturday before Thanksgiving. Everything is free except the chili, which will only set you back a couple of dollars.

WILD LIGHTS

The Denver Zoo in City Park
East 23rd Avenue and Steele Street
(303) 376-4800
www.denverzoo.org

This memorable family event begins the day after Thanksgiving and runs evenings through December Thousands of sparkling lights strung on trees create Christmas light sculptures of colored animals. There's nightly entertainment, storytelling, holiday refreshments, and an appearance by Santa Claus (until Christmas). Amid all the lights, it's fun to visit the animals and see what they do with their time on a winter night. Be aware that some of the animals are not out, but the seals and sea lions often make visitors laugh with their antics.

BOTANIC GARDENS HOLIDAY SALE

Denver Botanic Gardens
1005 York Street
(720) 865-3500
www.botanicgardens.org

Plants are for sale as well as herbs, oils, and vinegars that volunteers have been producing all yearlong. Ornaments are crafted and purchased. You'll also find books on gardening, tools, and other botany-related subjects. Held toward the end of November, the sale is free, as is admission to the gardens.

DECEMBER

WILD LIGHTS

See November entry.

HOLIDAY HIGH TEAS

Molly Brown House
1340 Pennsylvania Street
(303) 832-4092
www.mollybrown.org

Held on select dates throughout December and early January, the teas are traditional in their offerings of sandwiches, pastries, scones, and hot tea. Cost includes a tour of the home. Call for specific dates and reservations.

LODO HOLIDAY LIGHTING OF UNION STATION

17th and Wynkoop Streets
(303) 628-5428
www.lodo.org

Join as many as 3,500 people as they gather to watch the lighting of Union Station on the Wednesday after Thanksgiving. The LoDo district is seeking to expand coverage and promotion, making this a bigger event each year. Already it is a favorite among local residents.

WORLD'S LARGEST CHRISTMAS LIGHTING DISPLAY

City and County Building,
between Colfax Avenue and 14th Street
(across from Civic Center Park)
(720) 913-4900
www.denvergov.org

If light were music, the Denver City and County Building would be the world's largest pipe organ. About 30,000 floodlights turn this huge government building into one big neon sign. It has become a Denver holiday tradition to walk around and ogle on a frosty winter evening. Bundle up the kids. The display is up from the first Thursday in December until mid-January, after the National Western Stock Show has finished its run (see January entry).

OLDE GOLDEN CHRISTMAS

Throughout downtown Golden
(303) 279-3113
www.goldencochamber.org

Golden may be growing, but it's still one of the last Metro Denver communities with a real small-town feel about it. And here's an old-fashioned, small-town Christmas festival. Holiday festivities begin the first Friday in December with candlelight walks through downtown Golden. Everybody carries a candle and files down to Clear Creek to see the tree lights ignited. Santa Claus shows up. In the past the event has featured a clogging dance troupe and dancing kids. The first three Saturdays of the month are celebrated with Christmas carolers, sleigh rides, carriage rides, reindeer, and cookie decorating as well as hot chocolate, cookies, and candy. At the Clear Creek Living History Ranch, in restored cabins from the turn of the 20th century, folks serve up cowboy beans, doughnut holes, coffee, and great entertainment. At the Pioneer Museum, 923 10th Street, there's live musical entertainment, hot cider, cookies, and a big bonfire.

PARADE OF LIGHTS

Streets of downtown Denver
www.denverparadeoflights.com

This is truly one of the great public events of Denver's calendar: a night parade that lasts more than an hour and features floats, clowns, marching bands, and giant balloon figures, all lit up or festooned with lights. The whole event is one big Roman candle of multicolored holiday illumination. The crowds are big enough that special shuttles run into downtown from select bus stations. Check with RTD for schedules. You might consider bringing extra wraps, blankets, and a thermos of something hot and comforting. And as with all parades, if you want to position a folding chair for a front-row seat, get there an hour before the show. The parade is held the first Friday and Saturday night in December.

HANDEL'S *MESSIAH*
Boettcher Concert Hall
14th and Curtis Streets
(303) 893-4100
www.coloradosymphony.org
Holiday music lovers adore this one: classic Christmas music with the Colorado Symphony Orchestra and the Colorado Symphony Chorus performing Handel's *Messiah*. This is typically held the first or second weekend in December. Call for ticket prices.

CHRISTMAS WITH CODY
Buffalo Bill Grave and Museum
987½ Lookout Mountain Road, Golden
(303) 526-0747
www.buffalobill.org
This is the museum's free early-December Christmas event. Santa Cody rides in on his white horse to present gifts to all the good little cowpokes. Holiday music and crafts add to the festivities.

A COLORADO CHRISTMAS
Four Mile Historic Park
715 South Forest Street
(303) 399-1859
www.fourmilepark.org
Find an old-fashioned Christmas atmosphere at Four Mile Historic Park during this two-Saturday affair in mid-December. St. Nick, or Father Christmas, will be there; Christmas music will be per-

formed; and bobsled rides (if snow conditions permit) will be offered along with crafts, activities, food, and drink.

BLOSSOMS OF LIGHTS
Denver Botanic Gardens
1005 York Street
(720) 865-3500
www.botanicgardens.com
During the month of December, the Denver Botanic Gardens does for plants what the Denver Zoo does for animals (see November listing). There are giant flowers of Christmas lights and lights draped all over plants and other objects. There's nothing more invigorating than a stroll through a wonderland of lights on a frosty evening, and this event provides a different way of seeing Denver's beloved Botanic Gardens. Nightly entertainment is included, along with holiday refreshments.

A COLORADO CHRISTMAS
Boettcher Concert Hall
14th and Curtis Streets
(303) 893-4100
www.coloradosymphony.org
This is a benchmark in our year, a favorite way to celebrate the Christmas season. The concert, usually held in late December, features the Colorado Symphony Orchestra, the Colorado Symphony Chorus, and the Colorado Children's Chorale.

CHRISTMAS EVE TORCHLIGHT PARADE
Winter Park Resort, Winter Park
(970) 726-1564
www.skiwinterpark.com
On Christmas Eve guests begin by caroling around a bonfire at the base of the mountain. Santa Claus then leads a procession of torchbearers on skis as they make their way down Lower Hughes Trail. Their progress is punctuated with a fireworks display, followed by a nondenominational church service. Also on Christmas Eve, the mountaintop Lodge at Sunspot stays open for an elegant holiday dinner. Seating begins at 6 p.m., and reservations are required; call (970) 726-1446.

THE ARTS

Denver's arts scene has grown up over the past decade, in sync with the maturation of all the city's cultural attractions. A great deal of the credit goes to Mayor John Hickenlooper, who built his campaign around the notion that healthy cities are fueled by a thriving creative environment. During his tenure, artists of all types have felt the love, but business leaders also acknowledge that emerging neighborhoods attract artists, and artists attract the kind of attention that speeds their redevelopment. Core business leaders, members of the Downtown Denver Partnership, have worked hard to showcase the city's cultural attractions in a designated theater district, and city fathers support budding artists by funding studio and performances spaces.

Art lovers are the ultimate winners as galleries, theaters, concert halls, and literary cooperatives incubate throughout the city. In this chapter we've compiled a partial list of theaters and theater companies, art galleries, and art museums. Music venues, bars, movie houses, and restaurants with live entertainment can be found in our Nightlife chapter, and other kinds of museums are covered in the Tours and Attractions chapter. Given that one person's definition of culture may overlap with another person's idea of popular entertainment, expect to toggle between chapters to find the things that most appeal to your tastes. We begin by describing the Denver Performing Arts Complex, the historic hub of the city's cultural scene, then move through performing groups, theaters, theater companies, dinner theaters, popular music venues, art museums, community art centers, and art galleries. Finally, we detail the literary arts by describing the city's many writers' organizations.

PERFORMING ARTS

DENVER PERFORMING ARTS COMPLEX
Speer Boulevard and Arapahoe Street
(303) 893-4100, (800) 641-1222
www.denvercenter.org

The Denver Performing Arts Complex, a 4-block, 12-acre site, boasts more than 11,260 seats in nine performance venues and is the nation's largest in terms of the number and variety of performance spaces, the number and size of support facilities, and the variety of activities taking place. It is second only to New York's Lincoln Center in terms of seating capacity.

Performances are offered by many tenants, the largest of which is the **Denver Center for the Performing Arts** (DCPA). In addition to Broadway touring shows and the region's largest resident professional theater company, the complex

houses a state-of-the-art television, video, and recording production facility; offers the nation's only congressionally chartered graduate acting school; and conducts research with the world's only voice research laboratory associated with a performing arts center. Other tenants of the complex include the Colorado Symphony, Colorado Ballet, Colorado Children's Chorale, and Opera Colorado, all of which are described here. Tickets to all of the tenants' performances may be purchased by calling the numbers above.

The largest theater in the complex is the **Temple Hoyne Buell Theatre,** which opened in 1991 and has 2,830 seats. **Boettcher Concert Hall,** a unique 2,634-seat concert-hall-in-the-round, dates from 1978. The **Ellie Caulkins Opera House** is a grand old (1908) European-style theater with 2,268 seats. It was completely renovated in 2005.

The **Helen Bonfils Theatre Complex,** built in 1979, houses four smaller theaters. **The Stage** (770 seats) is a thrust stage; **The Space** is theater-in-the-round (well, it's actually more of a penta-gon) with 427 seats; the **Ricketson Theatre** is a 250-seat informal proscenium; and the **Jones Theatre,** with 200 seats, is an intimate experi-mental thrust stage. The **Donald R. Seawell Grand Ballroom,** named for DCPA's chairman of the board, opened in 1998. The 10,000-square-foot glass-and-steel ballroom has a maximum capacity of 1,029 people, and it can accommo-date a variety of functions with smaller configura-tions. Also in the complex is the **Garner Galleria Theatre,** which presents cabaret shows.

At intermission patrons spill out into the high, arched, glass-ceilinged galleria to stretch their legs and get some fresh air (or, conversely, to smoke a cigarette). The unique ceiling con-nects the diverse theaters.

DENVER CENTER ATTRACTIONS
Speer Boulevard and Arapahoe Street
(303) 893-4100, (800) 641-1222 (tickets)
(303) 893-4000 (information)
Broadway musical hits such as *Big River* and the pre-Broadway engagement of Disney's *Little Mer-maid* make Denver Center Attractions a preferred stop on the touring circuit. The division is also known for its own productions of cabaret musi-cals including *Forever Plaid* and Denver's longest-running production, *Always . . . Patsy Cline.*

DENVER CENTER THEATRE COMPANY
Speer Boulevard and Arapahoe Street
(303) 893-4100, (800) 641-1222 (tickets)
(303) 893-4000 (information)
The Denver Center Theatre Company, recipient of the 1998 Tony Award for Outstanding Regional Theatre, is the region's largest resident professional theater company and features an 11-play season, including traditional and contemporary drama and world premieres. Its shows are performed in the Stage, Space, Ricketson and Jones theaters, all part of the overall Performing Arts Complex.

i Don't let the names confuse you. The Denver Performing Arts Complex is the city-owned facility that is rented by various performance companies. The com-plex comprises nine performance theaters offering more than 10,000 seats. The Denver Center for the Performing Arts is an organi-zation that presents and produces Broadway touring shows and live theater through its two companies: Denver Center Attractions and the Denver Center Theatre Company.

Music

COLORADO CHILDREN'S CHORALE
2420 West 26th Avenue, Suite 350-D
(303) 892-5600
www.childrenschorale.org
The Colorado Children's Chorale, a 400-member chorus that tours nationally and internation-ally, celebrated its 35th anniversary in 2009. It started with 50 members and now involves 20,000 children each year through its outreach program. Each year the chorale joins the Colo-rado Symphony Orchestra for a very popular holiday concert.

COLORADO SYMPHONY ORCHESTRA
821 17th Street, Suite 700
(303) 623-7876
www.coloradosymphony.org
The Colorado Symphony Orchestra, with 80 members, plays classical music and popular classics in Boettcher Concert Hall during its sea-son, which lasts from September to May. Each season there are also several low-priced Sunday-afternoon concerts.

DENVER BRASS/ARIES BRASS QUINTET
2253 Downing Street
(303) 832-4676
www.denverbrass.org
Formed in 1981, the 12-member Denver Brass is one of very few symphonic brass ensembles in the country. Concerts feature something for

everyone, from splendid brass fanfares to Big Band music. Performances, including an annual Christmas concert, are held at the Newman Center for the Performing Arts at the University of Denver, and Bethany Lutheran Church, 4500 East Hampden Avenue.

Also under the same management is the Aries Brass Quintet. Founded in 1976, Aries has toured the United States, Europe, and South America; performed its fresh and vibrant renditions of chamber music live on National Public Radio; and recorded several albums. Aries is a resident company at the Lamont School of Music at the University of Denver.

DENVER YOUNG ARTISTS ORCHESTRA
2828 North Speer Boulevard, Suite 230
(303) 433-2420
www.dyao.org

The Denver Young Artists Orchestra was formed in 1977 as a means for Colorado's talented young musicians (ages 12 to 23) to rehearse and perform under professional standards. The orchestra plays three concerts each year in Boettcher Concert Hall and the Anschutz Family Theatre, 4000 East Quincy Avenue in Englewood.

OPERA COLORADO
695 South Colorado Boulevard, Suite 20
(303) 778-1500
www.operacolorado.org

Opera Colorado presents three grand operas each winter and spring, all performed at the Ellie Caulkins Opera House in downtown Denver. Performances are sung in the original language. Patrons are treated to seat-back titling at every seat in the house, in one of only three opera houses nationwide, nine worldwide, that provides such an amenity. Opera Colorado also performs at special holiday concerts and summer festivals throughout the state. The Opera Colorado for Children program includes children's opera workshops, matinee performances for students, and an in-school puppet opera.

Dance

CLEO PARKER ROBINSON DANCE
119 Park Avenue West
(303) 295-1759
www.cleoparkerdance.org

Cleo Parker Robinson Dance is a multicultural performing arts institution with a 12-person professional modern dance company and a dance school based in a historic African Methodist Episcopal Church. The ensemble performs regularly in Denver and extensively around the country and is one of the city's best-known exports in the arts field. Cleo Parker Robinson also sponsors a four-week artist-in-residence program called the International Summer Dance Institute.

COLORADO BALLET
1278 Lincoln Street
(303) 837-8888 (office)
www.coloradoballet.org

The Colorado Ballet was established as the Colorado Concert Ballet in 1961, and has been molding dancers ever since. The resident company of 32 dancers is under the artistic direction of Gil Boggs and is the only dance company in the state to perform with a live orchestra. Its repertoire includes full-length classical and one-act ballets. Performances are held in either the Buell Theatre or Ellie Caulkins Opera House from fall through spring.

DAVID TAYLOR DANCE THEATRE
1760 Glen Moor Drive Lakewood
(303) 789-2030
www.dtdt.org

David Taylor Dance Theatre is Denver's foremost professional contemporary ballet company. In addition, it's one of the region's major presenters of *The Nutcracker*, which is performed annually at the Lakewood Cultural Center and on tour throughout the state and the country. The main focus of the company, however, is original contemporary works. The *Rainforest Ballet* is one of its most popular productions. Although the company is headquartered in Lakewood, where it offers ballet classes for children and adults, it performs in different venues throughout Metro Denver from September through May.

KIM ROBARDS DANCE
1379 South Inca Street
(303) 825-4847
www.kimrobardsdance.org
Kim Robards Dance was established in 1987 as the Colorado Repertory Dance Company and is an important center for modern dance in Colorado. Its school and administrative offices are part of the emerging Platte River Drive South Cultural District, and include studio space that will evolve into a performance space. In the meantime, the company has a dynamic collection of works that include pieces by artistic director Kim Robards. The professional touring company has performed in New York and California, among other places. Locally the company presents a winter and spring season, a statewide educational outreach program, and classes for beginners aged 4 to adult and professionals at its school.

Theaters and Theater Companies

AURORA FOX ARTS CENTER
9900 East Colfax Avenue, Aurora
(303) 739-1970
www.aurorafox.org
From fall to spring, this historic landmark in the East End Arts District is home to the Aurora Fox Theatre Company and the Aurora Fox Children's Theatre Company. The adult theater company mounts five major productions each season, including musicals such as *A Christmas Carol* and dramatic classics such as *The Skin of Our Teeth*. The Little Foxes children's program offers classes and workshops, and produces several shows each summer.

THE BUG THEATRE
Performance and Media Arts Center
3654 Navajo Street
(303) 477-9984
www.bugtheatre.org
The buzz is good on the Bug Theatre, a renovated

movie house that's now an avant-garde showcase for emerging artists and their artwork, including poetry, music, film, and new media. Call the Bugline at (303) 477-5977 to find out what's coming.

DENVER CIVIC THEATRE
721 Santa Fe Drive
(303) 309-3773
www.denvercivic.com
The Denver Civic Theatre has been in its present location on Santa Fe Drive since 1991, producing well-known plays, Broadway musicals and original works year-round. The building was built in 1923 as a movie theater and over the years has been used for many different purposes—it was a meatpacking plant in the 1950s and 1960s and later a photographer's studio. Now it houses two theaters: a main stage proscenium with 285 seats and an intimate black-box theater that seats 104 and is often used for burlesque shows.

DENVER VICTORIAN PLAYHOUSE
4201 Hooker Street
(303) 433-4343
www.denvervic.com
The Denver Victorian Playhouse in northwest Denver is a restored and refurbished 1911 house with a 75-seat theater in the basement. A full range of comedies, dramas, and musicals are performed here year-round, with recent productions that include *Greater Tuna* and *The Fantasticks*.

EL CENTRO SU TEATRO
4725 High Street
(303) 296-0219
www.suteatro.org
El Centro Su Teatro was formed in 1971 by students at the University of Colorado at Denver as a forum for those interested in the Chicano civil rights movement. It has grown into a multidisciplinary cultural-arts center that sponsors concerts, drama, performance art, dance, festivals, film, poetry festivals, workshops, and art exhibitions. Theater performances emphasize original works by Chicano and Latino playwrights, including Rudolfo Anaya's classic, *Bless Me, Ultima*. El Centro Su Teatro is housed in a former elementary school.

FESTIVAL PLAYHOUSE

5665 Old Wadsworth Boulevard, Arvada
(303) 422-4090
www.festivalplayhouse.com

There's plenty of history behind the Festival Playhouse. The Denver Players Guild, formed in 1936, stages eight plays a year—primarily Broadway comedies—in this converted Grange building in Olde Town Arvada. The Players Guild believes it is the oldest community theater group in the country under the same family management, and the playhouse is even older. Built in 1874, it's the second-oldest standing Grange hall in Colorado and the oldest building in the city of Arvada.

GERMINAL STAGE DENVER

2450 West 44th Avenue
(303) 455-7108
www.germinalstage.com

Germinal Stage Denver was founded by four Denver actors in 1973, making it one of the longest-living small theaters in the region. Performances are held in an air-conditioned, 100-seat converted storefront, 5 blocks east of Federal Boulevard. The repertoire includes traditional works such as Tennessee Williams' *The Eccentricities of a Nightingale* to more arcane and experimental plays. The Germinal has an excellent reputation for producing quality theater.

THE PHYSICALLY HANDICAPPED ACTORS AND MUSICAL ARTISTS LEAGUE

P.O. Box 44216, Denver 80201
(303) 575-0005
www.phamaly.org

PHAMALY was formed in 1989, when a group of Boettcher School alumni decided to organize a theater company for people living with disabilities. This group stages one musical each summer at the Denver Performing Arts Complex, and a touring show that takes actors to businesses, senior centers, festivals, and schools. Performances are always wheelchair-accessible, and arrangements are made to provide assistance to hearing-impaired and visually impaired audience members. Recent performances include *Steel Magnolias* and *One Flew Over the Cuckoo's Nest*.

THE THEATRE OFF BROADWAY

13 South Broadway
(303) 777-3292
www.theatregroup.org

The Theatre Off Broadway presents Denver premieres of new Broadway and off-Broadway shows in a small black-box theater. The theater is one of two venues for the Theatre Group, which began in 1972 as the Lakewood Players. Artistic Director Steven Tangedahl joined it in 1979. The group also performs at the Phoenix Theatre at 1124 Santa Fe Drive. Past productions include *Torch Song Trilogy* and Howard Crabtreet's *When Pigs Fly*.

Dinner Theaters

HERITAGE SQUARE MUSIC HALL

18301 West Colfax Avenue
(U.S. Highway 40), Golden
(303) 279-7800
www.heritagesquare.info

Heritage Square Music Hall is a Victorian-style theater staging original comedies with melodramatic overtones and musical revues. A buffet dinner precedes the show, but it's possible to buy a ticket for the performance only. Performances are Wednesday through Saturday evenings, with Sunday matinees year-round.

> **i** Love the theater, but hate the high prices? The Denver Center Theatre Company offers one free performance per play—always a Saturday matinee. Tickets are distributed two hours before the performance at the box office at 14th and Curtis Streets. No reservations are accepted; it's first-come, first-served. Check the *Rocky Mountain News* or the *Denver Post* for notice.

Music Venues

Outdoor rock and other popular music concerts are held at Fiddler's Green Amphitheatre and Red Rocks Amphitheatre. Indoor venues include the Pepsi Center, the Fillmore Auditorium, the Ogden Theatre, and the Paramount Theatre. Tickets to all

Close-up

Germinal Stage Denver

Ed Baierlein played to perfection the buffoon role of Major Petkoff in George Bernard Shaw's comedy *Arms and the Man,* scowling and bellowing, gaping and grinning, and lolling his tongue, his face a writhing parade of expressions so foolish that the audience sometimes laughed loudest when he was saying nothing at all.

"That's some play you're running," a fan told him over the telephone one night an hour before the curtain went up. "You're quite a comedian."

"Well, thanks," Baierlein said. "We're doing pretty well. You wanted how many reservations now? Would that be Visa or MasterCard?"

More than a comedian, Baierlein is also one of the Denver area's most respected serious actors, but that doesn't mean he is above taking reservations, cleaning the theater, maintaining the mailing lists, and doing the books at the Germinal Stage Denver theater in northwest Denver.

Since its founding in 1973, Germinal Stage has built a faithful audience with more than 130 plays including everything from experimental, first-run productions to Ibsen, Shaw, and Shakespeare. Those plays have earned the theater a reputation and influence all out of proportion to its 100-seat facility in an old 5,000-square-foot building.

While the large theaters of the Denver Performing Arts Complex are a point of pride and a focus of entertainment on Denver's cultural landscape, Germinal Stage and the more than a dozen other smaller local theaters perhaps provide a truer measure of that landscape's cultural depth.

"In the smaller theaters the artists tend to be in primary control," Baierlein says. "They tend to be more eclectic, with a more specialized audience and repertoire. The problems today are fairly similar to what they were when we started out— on the one hand, maintaining the integrity of our repertoire, and on the other hand, being popular enough so that people will pay to see your next failure."

Baierlein and Sallie Diamond, his wife and partner in the nonprofit Germinal Stage and one of the area's most versatile and respected actresses, are among the many who came to Denver by chance and stayed by choice.

"I was in the Air Force and was shipped here in 1968 and spent most of my time in the service at Lowry Air Force Base," Baierlein said. "My wife and I decided this was the nicest place we had ever lived. My philosophy is, find a place where you like to live and then make the work happen there."

It was the city that attracted them, Baierlein said. The city is where they and their son, Thaddeus, who was born here in 1980, spend most of their time. From their home just a block away from the theater, they take periodic trips to Glenwood Springs, a three-hour drive to the west, to enjoy the world's largest outdoor hot pool.

"That's our favorite vacation, just to let the city seep out of us in the pools," Baierlein said. "We're not great outdoors people. We don't ski, and we don't camp."

Even so, Baierlein said they try to get to the mountains as much as possible, just to enjoy the beauty and solitude that is never far away from the lives and thoughts of even the most urbane of Metro Denverites.

"When you're away from here for any period of time, you really miss just the presence of the mountains," he said. "There's no other place I know where you can have the amenities of a big city and still, in a half hour, be absolutely isolated in a place where you feel nobody has ever been before."

venues can be purchased online or by phone, but a trip to the box office can generally (though not always) save you from paying a service charge.

THE BLUEBIRD THEATER
3317 East Colfax Avenue
(303) 377-1666
www.bluebirdtheater.net
The Bluebird Theater is one of three historic venues clustered along East Colfax that welcome music fans of all ilks to Denver's Capitol Hill neighborhood. Built in 1914 as a movie theater and originally used to show silent films, the Bluebird fell upon hard times and closed in the late 1980s. The restored theater reopened in fall 1994 as a performance hall for musicians of all kinds. Expect to see names such as Candlebox and Bonnie Prince Billy on the marquee.

FIDDLER'S GREEN AMPHITHEATRE
6350 Greenwood Plaza Boulevard, Englewood
(303) 220-7000
www.livenation.com
Fiddler's Green is a huge open air amphitheater that rocks during summer months. It holds 18,000 fans, which means only the performers who can draw a crowd are booked into this south Metro venue. Reserved seats are available, but you can also buy cheaper general admission tickets for the lawn area. In previous years, Fiddler's Green has hosted Rod Stewart, Def Leppard, Nine Inch Nails, and Bette Midler.

FILLMORE AUDITORIUM
1510 Clarkson Street
(303) 837-0360
www.livenation.com
This Capitol Hill landmark opened in 1907 as a skating rink but gradually fell into disrepair. It had a short but brilliant life at a concert hall called Mammoth Gardens in the late 1960s and early 1970s, hosting The Doors, The Who, and The Grateful Dead before closing its doors. New owners reopened it in 1999 and named it for Bill Graham's Fillmore Ballroom in San Francisco, which provided the original inspiration. It now holds

3,600 people (it seats a whole lot less than that), and has become one of Denver's premier venues for groups such as KORN, Thievery Corporation, and Sound Tribe Sector 9.

THE OGDEN THEATRE
935 East Colfax Street
(303) 830-2525
www.ogdentheater.net
A vaudeville-era theater that later became a movie house, the Ogden's newest incarnation is as a concert hall presenting a wide variety of local and national acts. It's located in the heart of Capitol Hill, along with the Bluebird Theater and the Fillmore. Some recent headliners included Brian Jonestown Massacre, Railroad Earth, and Lily Allen with Natalie Portman's Shaved Head.

PARAMOUNT THEATRE
1621 Glenarm Place
(303) 623-0106
www.paramountdenver.com
This historic Art Deco theater has more than once been on the verge of falling to the wrecker's ball. Built in 1930 by Temple Hoyne Buell, a prominent Denver architect, the theater is the epitome of art deco style and has one of only two Mighty Wurlitzer organs in the country (the other is at Radio City Music Hall in New York City). During the summer of 1994—under new management yet again—the Paramount underwent extensive remodeling. The Paramount seats 1,870 and presents a mixed bag of comedy, lectures, dance, film, and live music. Recent seasons have included jazz greats Chick Corea & John McLaughlin along with classic metal from Queensryche.

THE PEPSI CENTER
1000 Chopper Place
(303) 405-1111 (box office)
www.pepsicenter.com
Home to the Denver Nuggets and the Colorado Avalanche, the Pepsi Center also hosts big-name shows. The arena seats up to 16,000, with a killer sound system and jumbo TV screens so everyone in the house has good views of the stage. In

recent years, stars ranging from Eric Clapton and Steve Winwood to country greats Keith Urban and Sugarland have made tour stops here.

RED ROCKS AMPHITHEATRE INTERSTATE
I-70 West to the Morrison exit, Morrison
(720) 865-4220
www.redrocksonline.com
Red Rocks Amphitheatre is one of the most spectacular settings anywhere for a concert. About half the size of Fiddler's Green Amphitheatre, Red Rocks is a natural red sandstone amphitheater set deep into the foothills on Hogback Road near Morrison (take I-70 west to the Morrison exit and follow the signs). It was renovated in 2003 to include a $16 million visitor center. Leonard Cohen, REO Speedwagon, David Byrne, and the Mormon Tabernacle Choir are among the groups to have stopped here during recent tours.

SWALLOW HILL MUSIC ASSOCIATION
71 East Yale Avenue
(303) 777-1003
www.swallowhill.com
The well respected Swallow Hill Music Association is Denver's center for folk, roots, and traditional acoustic music. Concerts are held at two theaters, the largest of which seats 300. Swallow Hill also presents concerts elsewhere in the city, including summer concerts at Four Mile Historical Park.

VISUAL ARTS

Art Museums

THE DENVER ART MUSEUM
100 West 14th Avenue Parkway
(720) 865-5000
www.denverartmuseum.org
The Denver Art Museum is the largest art museum between Kansas City and the West Coast and is especially noted for its superb collections of Native American, pre-Columbian, and Spanish colonial art. Its seven floors also house impressive displays of American, Asian, African, and contemporary art and galleries devoted to design, graphics, and architecture.

The museum is nearly as well known for its buildings, the first of which was designed by Italian architect Gio Ponti in association with Denver architect James Sudler and the second of which was designed by architect Daniel Libeskind. The original building, completed in 1971 is a fortress-like seven-level structure with a 28-sided tiled exterior. The new 146,000-square-foot expansion was completed in 2006, almost doubling its size to house traveling exhibits and permanent modern, contemporary, African, Oceanic, and western American collections.

The museum is open Tuesday through Saturday, with extended hours on Wednesday evening. Family programs are held every Saturday, with free admission for Colorado residents. The museum has a shop and full-service restaurant.

KIRKLAND MUSEUM OF FINE AND DECORATIVE ART
1311 Pearl Street
(303) 832-8576
www.vancekirkland.org
Vance Kirkland may be Colorado's best-known painter. His work spans realism, surrealism, abstraction, abstract expressionism, and dot paintings, and his career stretched from 1926 to 1981. The museum showcases more than 600 of his paintings as well as housing a 2,000-object decorative arts collection and more than 300 works from Colorado artists. The building itself is worthy of note. Built in 1910-11, it's the second-oldest commercial art building in Colorado, designed in the Arts and Crafts style, and it served as Kirkland's studio. The museum is open Tuesday through Sunday. Children younger than age 13 are not admitted; children age 13 to 17 must be accompanied by an adult. Tours are offered daily.

MUSEO DE LAS AMERICAS
861 Santa Fe Drive
(303) 571-4401
www.museo.org
This museum is the only one in the Rocky Mountain region dedicated to Latin American art, history, and culture. Officially opened in July 1994,

the Museo de las Americas showcases art from all the Americas, including the Caribbean, in changing exhibitions. The museum supplements its temporary exhibitions with lectures, workshops, and other educational programs and has built a small permanent collection. It has twice shown an exhibition jointly with The Denver Art Museum, with some of the material at the art museum and some at the museo. The museum is open Tuesday through Sunday.

MUSEUM OF OUTDOOR ARTS
1000 Englewood Parkway, Englewood
(303) 806-0444
www.moaonline.org
Two large urban environments fall under this organizational umbrella—the former Cinderella City Shopping Center south of Denver that was redeveloped into City Center Englewood, and Greenwood Plaza, the Greenwood Village development that includes the 400-acre Greenwood Plaza. Many outdoor artworks are incorporated into the landscape and architecture of each site, creating museums without walls. Both are open to the public Monday through Friday during daylight hours. Details about their philosophy and art tours can be found online.

Community Art Centers
ARVADA CENTER FOR THE ARTS AND HUMANITIES
6901 Wadsworth Boulevard, Arvada
(720) 898-7200 (box office)
www.arvadacenter.org
The Arvada Center has two galleries, which display changing exhibits of contemporary art, folk art, design, and crafts. There's also a small historical museum. In addition, the center has both an indoor 500-seat auditorium and an outdoor amphitheater with 1,200 seats (600 covered, 600 on the lawn). It also maintains an impressive schedule of performing arts programming that includes children's and adult professional theater, dance, and music concerts. One resident company, the Arvada Center Chorale, calls the center home, but many groups perform here. It's

the site each winter of a cowboy-poetry gathering. A highly regarded deaf-access program makes many programs accessible to the hearing-impaired. After 24 years the Arvada Center became a full-equity professional theater in 2000. It's open daily; with free admission to the gallery and museum.

THE FOOTHILLS ART CENTER
809 15th Street, Golden
(303) 279-3922
www.foothillsartcenter.org
The Foothills Art Center is much smaller than the Arvada Center, but it is home to two prestigious national exhibitions—the biannual North American Sculpture Exhibition and Colorado Art Open and the annual Rocky Mountain National Watermedia Exhibition. It offers arts classes and hosts the statewide annual Colorado Clay exhibition. The center's schedule is composed of changing exhibits of national and regional arts and fine crafts.

Art Galleries

Downtown
Metro Denver's contemporary art galleries tend to be clustered the city's historic core, although they are sprinkled throughout most of its neighborhoods. Working on the assumption that there's strength in numbers, galleries in Lower Downtown, the Golden Triangle, Santa Fe Drive, Tennyson Street, and River North neighborhoods have banded together to coordinate openings and other special events, including First Friday events that are held the first Friday of each month. Especially in the summer, there's kind of a street festival atmosphere as patrons go from one gallery to the next, stopping to compare notes with friends on the sidewalk. Gallery openings are usually held on Friday and are, with rare exceptions, free and open to the public. Check *Westword* or the Friday edition of the *Denver Post* and the *Rocky Mountain News* for a list of openings and current exhibit information. Most galleries close on Monday, but this varies so call ahead to be sure.

Think of art galleries as a wonderful free smorgasbord of exciting things to see. Of course, the bottom line is that galleries must sell art to stay in business, but unlike art dealers in some cities, Denver's are notably low-key and happy to educate browsers without pressuring them to buy. Dealers know that the best way to develop customers is to make people feel comfortable, and high-pressure sales tactics aren't going to do that.

The heart of Denver's avant-garde arts district is the 1700 block of Wazee Street. You'll find several galleries in the surrounding district. Many others have chosen the areas adjacent to downtown for their affordability and Bohemian appeal.

CAMERA OBSCURA GALLERY
1309 Bannock Street
(303) 623-4059
www.cameraobscuragallery.com
Near the Denver Art Museum is Camera Obscura Gallery, devoted exclusively to photography. Owner Hal Gould is supremely knowledgeable. Spend a little time talking with him, and he'll show you the vintage treasures he keeps upstairs.

CENTER FOR VISUAL ART
Metropolitan State College of Denver
1734 Wazee Street
(303) 294-5207
www.mscd.edu/news/cva
Technically a college gallery, Metro seldom shows student work, but rather puts on some of the best and most provocative exhibitions in town. Traveling exhibits are booked years in advance for the purpose of art education. Past exhibitions have included contemporary Chinese painting, African-American quilts, and baseball paraphernalia from local collections.

DAVID COOK FINE ART
1637 Wazee Street
(303) 623-8181
www.davidcookfineart.com
David Cook offers a wide range of artists and styles, but its specialties are American regional art from the 19th and early 20th centuries, as well as historic American Indian art, from Navajo rugs

to Pueblo pottery, from beadwork to baskets. You can also find antique jewelry and paintings of the Rockies by early Colorado artists.

KNOX GALLERY
1512 Larimer Street
(303) 820-2324
www.knoxgalleries.com
Knox Gallery specializes in realistic bronze sculpture. Located in Writer's Square, the gallery represents local and regional painters and sculptors.

OLD MAP GALLERY
1550 Wynkoop Street
(303) 296-7725
www.oldmapgallery.com
If you're in the market for antique maps, this is the place. You'll find historic maps such as ones from the 16th century or maps of Louisiana before it was purchased. Maps range from $35 to several thousand dollars.

+GALLERY
2501 Larimer Street
(303) 296-0927
www.plusgallery.com
Since 2001 Ivar Zeile has been showcasing the works of emerging as well as nationally known talents from his Ballpark neighborhood gallery. In 2009 he moved to a spiffier space just five blocks north of LoDo. Shows rotate every six weeks and include sculpture, photography, painting, video, paper, and installation art. The gallery is open Wednesday through Saturday and by appointment at other times.

ROBISCHON GALLERY
1740 Wazee Street
(303) 298-7788
www.robischongallery.com
Robischon Gallery has been open in Denver since 1976, providing a space for regional, national, and international artists that include Robert Motherwell, Manuel Neri, Christo, and Jeanne-Claude. It specializes in contemporary art of all kinds, as well as emerging young artists.

THE SLOANE GALLERY OF ART
1612 17th Street
(303) 595-4230
www.sloangallery.net

The Sloane Gallery of Art, located next to the Oxford Hotel in LoDo, is devoted exclusively to contemporary Russian art. It exhibits oils, acrylics, drawings, pastels, and sculpture.

WILLIAM MATTHEWS GALLERY
1617 Wazee Street
(303) 534-1300
www.williammatthewsgallery.com

After a graphic arts career spend designing record album covers, William Matthews devoted himself to painting the working cowboys from America's great Western ranches. That body of work launched his career as a watercolorist with paintings included in the collections of the Denver Art Museum, the Buffalo Bill Historical Center, and the National Cowboy Hall of Fame. This gallery showcases his watercolors, as well as selling limited-edition prints, posters, and note cards. It is open Monday through Friday, and Saturday by appointment.

Greater Downtown
THE CHICANO HUMANITIES AND ARTS COUNCIL
772 Santa Fe Drive
(303) 571-0440
www.chacweb.org

CHAC, the Chicano Humanities and Arts Council, has a gallery that is open Wednesday through Saturday. It also sponsors a number of special events and programs throughout the city, including a Day of the Dead exhibition, the annual Chile Harvest Festival held at Four Mile Historic Park in August, and Las Posadas at the gallery during December. CHAC is a consortium of artists, individuals, and organizations dedicated to the preservation and promotion of Chicano/Latino cultures.

CORE NEW ART SPACE
900 Santa Fe Drive
(303) 297-8428
www.corenewartspace.com

Core New Art Space is a cutting-edge cooperative gallery that primarily features local artists who work in oil, photography, ceramics, and papermaking. It has two spaces, a main gallery, and an annex that can be rented for three-week runs.

PLATTE RIVER ART SERVICES
350 North Santa Fe Drive
(303) 571-1060
www.platteriverartservices.com

This premier frame shop is more of a conservation studio than an art gallery, but it is still the place to go when you want something unusual. The shop offers exquisite frames, including hand-carved, hand-gilded ones and restored antique frames.

i A funky collection of galleries in fast-changing northwest Denver is a fun and different way to spend a Friday or Saturday evening. Galleries such as Bug Theatre and Pirate are located in the 3600 block of Navajo Street. Have dinner at Patsy's Inn Italian Restaurant (3651 Navajo Street) and stroll through the galleries afterward.

RULE GALLERY
227 Broadway
(303) 777-9473
www.rulegallery.com

The peripatetic Rule Gallery opened in 1987 and was housed in several other places before landing on Broadway across from the Mayan Theater. This gallery specializes in modern and contemporary painting, sculpture, and photography by regional and national artists.

SPARK GALLERY
900 Santa Fe Drive
(720) 889-2200
www.sparkgallery.com

Spark Gallery is Denver's oldest artists' cooperative located in the vibrant Santa Fe Drive district. It features paintings, sculpture, and photographs sold directly by the artists, and is open year-round from Thursday through Saturday, and on Sunday between April and December.

WILLIAM HAVU GALLERY
1040 Cherokee Street
(303) 893-2360
www.williamhavugallery.com
William Havu is located in Denver's Golden Triangle, a core neighborhood that gentrified during
the 1990s and is now known for its high-rise lofts
and trendy restaurants. The gallery's contemporary art blends well into the upscale surroundings. Hours are Tuesday through Saturday, by
appointment Sunday and Monday.

Westside and River North Galleries
As LoDo has changed and rents have gone up,
many artists have moved their studios from
downtown to other transitional neighborhoods
to the north and west.

EDGE GALLERY
3658 Navajo Street
(303) 477-7173
www.edgeart.org
Open Friday through Sunday, EDGE is an independent exhibition space that is run cooperatively
by the artists who are shown there. It has nonprofit status, which means that it doesn't have
to depend on sales for its survival. As a result, the
contemporary art in the museum can be edgier
and more contemporary than that seen in more
traditional galleries. EDGE moved to its present
site in Denver's historic Little Italy in 1992.

PIRATE: CONTEMPORARY ART
3655 Navajo Street
(303) 458-6058
www.pirateart.org
Pirate has what are generally regarded as the hippest openings in town. It is one of the most experimental galleries in Denver, showcasing stunning
paintings and sculpture. Pirate is only open Friday
through Sunday, and shows change frequently.

River North Art District
NORTHEAST OF DOWNTOWN DENVER
www.rivernorthart.com
This emerging downtown arts district—roughly
bounded by I-25, and I-70, Park Avenue West, and
Lawrence Street—was once home to Denver's
early-day foundries, smelters, ironworks, and the
blue-collar families who made them run. For the
past decade it has drawn artists and real estate
investors priced out of nearby LoDo and the Coors
Field area. They banded together to form the informal River North Arts District, called RiNo for short,
and now sponsor district-wide studio tours and
individual events. The group's name comes from
its location along the northern edge of the South
Platte River. News is posted on the group's Web
site, as are details about each of its 41 members.

LITERARY ARTS
If you love the written word—or the company
of those who write—Denver has several writers'
organizations that appeal to both beginning and
advanced scribes as well as writers in a variety
of genres.

COLORADO AUTHORS' LEAGUE
P.O. Box 24905, Denver 80224
www.coloradoauthors.org
Founded in 1931, the Colorado Authors' League
is one of the oldest professional writers' organizations in the state. Counting such notables as
Clive Cussler, Clarissa Pinkola Estes, and Joanne
Greenberg among its ranks, this organization has
monthly meetings with speakers on topics from
spotting trends to writing with a collaborator.
Dues are $50 a year.

COLUMBINE POETS, INC.
8989 Yukon Street, Westminster
(303) 431-6774
Part of the National Federation of State Poetry
Societies, this organization promotes poetry
throughout the state by offering contests, workshops, and monthly critique groups. Call for
information about fee structures.

DENVER WOMAN'S PRESS CLUB
1325 Logan Street
(303) 839-1519
www.denverwomanspressclub.org
This club was formed in 1898 by 19 members

whose mission included "functioning as a stimulating gathering place for people in literary journalism and media endeavors." Today the club meets regularly for lunch and dinner programs, offers Saturday seminars for the community at large, and has afternoon teas featuring authors in town on book tours. Housed in a charming historic landmark, this organization of women writers is the oldest in the state. Dues run $75 a year.

MYSTERY WRITERS OF AMERICA
(Rocky Mountain Chapter)
(303) 665-3992
www.rmmwa.org

Monthly meetings and bimonthly programs keep the published and unpublished members of the regional chapter of Mystery Writers of America busy. Members get to attend all bimonthly programs for free. One of the highlights of each year is the annual meeting, where the featured speaker might be an FBI agent or a judge from a criminal court. National dues are $95, which allows membership locally.

ROCKY MOUNTAIN FICTION WRITERS
P.O. Box 545, Englewood 80151
(303) 331-2608
www.rmfw.org

This popular fiction-writing organization is geared to writers of commercial novels. Its 400 members are both published and unpublished and enjoy monthly meetings where speakers talk about anything related to writing and researching. Monthly newsletters offer market news, and critique groups are held all over Metro Denver. The annual conference in September is a much-awaited event; big-name writers, six or seven editors, and several New York agents attend. Dues are $45 a year.

WOMEN WRITING THE WEST
8547 East Arapahoe Road, Suite J-541
Greenwood Village 80112
(303) 773-8349
www.womenwritingthewest.org

This organization has 250 members from all over the United States, Canada, and Australia. The motto here is "We don't do meetings, and we don't do T-shirts." What they do is work on marketing themselves—all of whom are interested in writing about "a new view of the women's west." Members get a quarterly newsletter, displays at booksellers associations, and a major opportunity to network—all for $50.

PARKS AND RECREATION

Greater Denver is a recreational heaven. Where else is it possible to ski on Saturday and play golf on Sunday—all on a sunny March weekend? It doesn't stop there. We've got biking trails, hiking trails, climbing spots, and picnicking galore. You can boat, swim, fish, snow ski, water ski, or windsurf. You can hunt wildlife or simply admire it from afar. You name it, we've got it.

We have organizations, facilities, rental companies, and tour guides for bicycling, climbing, fishing, hunting, running, in-line skating, sailing, waterskiing, and horseback riding, to name a few. We even have ranges for skeet, trap, pistols, and rifles. Skiing, of course, is Colorado's most popular and famous form of winter recreation, which is why we've given it a chapter of its own called Ski Country.

Metro Denver's beautifully groomed urban parks are among its greatest assets, including those listed below. In general, Denver's parks are open from 5 a.m. until 11 p.m. and do not allow camping.

PARKS

Urban Parks

Metro Denver is laced with a network of city and county parks that provide everything from playing fields to playgrounds and trails for running, biking, and skating. In addition, Denver Parks and Recreation oversees the Denver Zoo, the city's golf courses, and 100 miles of foliated center strips on major streets.

Denver has about 250 parks, ranging from small triangles to enormous open spaces, as well as a trail system estimated at about 130 miles. Its Parks and Recreation department also oversees golf courses, the Denver Zoo, and 100 miles of foliated center strips along major streets. The city also boasts 14,000 acres of mountain parkland and parcels preserved as natural areas.

CHEESMAN PARK
Between 8th and 13th Avenues
East of Lafayette Street
This vast urban oasis just east of downtown features a great 1.5-mile walking/jogging path,

enormous trees, manicured flower gardens and, at the eastern edge, an impressive pavilion with a stunning mountain view. The compressed dirt jogging path is popular with nearby residents. The park was established in 1892 on the city's former first cemetery lot. It is adjacent to the Denver Botanic Gardens. To get there, take 14th Avenue east from downtown to Lafayette, then head south 1 block.

CITY PARK
17th Avenue Parkway and
Colorado Boulevard
The lake at City Park is ringed by acres of grass and mature trees that offer wonderful spots for picnicking. There also is an extensive path for biking, walking, and in-line skating. The historic City Park Pavilion has been restored, with a bandstand on the lake's west shore. During summer months, paddleboats can be rented for only $5 an hour. The Denver Zoo and the Museum of Nature and Science occupy the park's east end. To get there, take 17th Avenue east out of downtown to York Street. The park lies between York Street and Colorado Boulevard.

COMMONS PARK

Between 15th and 19th Streets on Little Raven Drive

Commons Park is Denver's most unusual urban park. It opened in 2001, reclaiming land that held Denver's earliest settlers from years of neglect. It was envisioned as the crown jewel in a string of riverfront parks that bisect the city. Forward-thinking city fathers (and mothers) spent more than two decades amassing the land, scraping away the rail yards and hobo shanties, and planning for redevelopment. First came the city park, a grassy knoll that offers people a place to stare at the eastern skyline and the mountains to the west or listen to a concert staged in the outdoor arena. Along one side, visitors can dabble their feet in the waters of the South Platte River. The pricey high-rises came next, attracting families and retirees, empty nesters, and urban professionals with their close proximity to Elitch Gardens amusement park, Coors Field, the Pepsi Center, and a free city-owned 50,000-square-foot skateboard park that attracts 200 to 300 skaters a day. Reach this rich cultural stew by riding the 16th Street shuttle west to its end point, then walking across the Millennium Bridge. By car, follow I-25 to Speer Boulevard, then exit south. Turn right at Elitch Circle, and keep turning right until you're on Little Raven Street. The park runs alongside Little Raven Street between 15th and 20th Streets.

DENVER BOTANIC GARDENS AT CHATFIELD

8500 Deer Creek Canyon Road, Littleton
(303) 973-3705
www.botanicgardens.org

This little gem offers historic sites, trails, and naturalist guides. It's a great place for a picnic, and the traditional playground next to the historic schoolhouse is fun for kids. Down the path along Deer Creek, you can see the foundation where the schoolhouse was before they moved it. Look for the piece of chain on one of the cottonwood branches above the path, the remnant of the swing where kids played more than 100 years ago. The nature preserve is just off Wadsworth Boulevard south of C-470 and is open daily from 9 a.m. to 5 p.m. Admission is charged.

ℹ The must-see view of Metro Denver and the Rocky Mountains is from the entrance to the Denver Museum of Nature and Science, in City Park at Colorado Boulevard and Montview Street. The sweeping vista of treetops, skyscrapers, and snow-capped peaks is the best in town.

RED ROCKS AMPHITHEATRE

Morrison
(303) 697-DINO (3466)
www.dinoridge.org

This unexpected park is a treasure of exposed dinosaur bones and tracks, along with plant and animal fossils. In 1877, some of the nation's best preserved dinosaur bones were found on the slope of this ridgeline, and highway construction exposed dinosaur tracks in 1930. Life and science teachers treat this geologic treasure as an outdoor classroom, introducing their students to the place where the mountains meet the prairie, and where plant and animal life of all kinds has been fossilized in rocks layers that have over time been uplifted until they pierced the ground.

A visitor center provides information about the discovery, but Dinosaur Ridge is essentially an outdoor experience. Reach it by traveling west on I-70 to the Morrison exit, then following Highway 26 south to West Alameda Parkway. Turn left and follow the road to the visitor center, which provides information about hours, tours and displays, and also contains a small gift shop. Guided tours of the wheelchair-accessible site are offered. Admission is free, but donations are accepted.

SLOAN LAKE PARK

17th Avenue and Sheridan Boulevard

Sloan Lake is a Westside landmark, with acres of landscape shoreline around a great boating lake. Dragon boat races are staged there each summer, joining a fleet of privately owned canoes and powerboats on the water. On dry land, children play in the large playground, joggers and strollers follow the trail that rings the lake, and others grab spots on the grass for picnics, Frisbee games, or summer naps. To get there, take Colfax

Avenue west to Sheridan Boulevard, then right to 17th Avenue.

WASHINGTON PARK
Louisiana Avenue and Downing Street

Also designed around water, Washington Park is popular with sports enthusiasts of all types. Its lakeside paths are often used for organized races, but they're just as fun for bicycling, walking/jogging, and in-line skating. Two lakes in the middle provide good fishing (especially for kids), and grassy lawns on all sides are used for impromptu soccer and volleyball games. The flower gardens along Downing Street are perfection, serving as the backdrop for many tourist photographs. But most of all, "Wash Park," as it's known, is a wonderful spot to relax and enjoy Denver's blue skies and sunny weather.

State Parks and Recreation Areas

County park and open-space systems extend the city's green space into Jefferson, Adams, Douglas, and Arapahoe counties. The Denver Mountain Parks system includes 14,000 acres of land scattered through four counties. Red Rocks Park is one of these, as is the Winter Park ski area (see our Ski Country chapter for details). Colorado also oversees four state parks and two state recreation areas within driving distance of Denver. Expect to pay use fees in most of these parks.

BARR LAKE STATE PARK
13401 Picadilly Road, Brighton
(303) 659-6005
http://parks.state.co.us/Parks/BarrLake

Barr Lake is a 2,700-acre state park surrounding a 1,900-acre prairie reservoir. Decades ago the reservoir used to be something of a sewage dump, and people would roll up their car windows when they drove past it on I-76. But that was long ago. Today it's a charming and tranquil place with more than 300 species of birds. It's the area's best place to watch eagles that hunt around the lake and nest in the trees at the lake's southern half, which is designated as a wildlife refuge (no pets allowed in this area). It's also the biggest lake in the Denver area, where you can canoe, kayak, or otherwise go boating without being buzzed by Jet Skis, powerboats, and water-skiers. The only boats allowed on the lake are sailboats, hand-propelled craft, and boats with electric trolling motors or gas engines of 10 horsepower or less. Hiking here is pleasant because the lakeshore is lined with cottonwoods. There are plenty of aquatic plants and marshes, where it's always interesting to watch the big carp rooting and sucking. On both the north and south ends of the lake, you can walk out on wooden boardwalks extending into the water and watch wildlife from the gazebo at the end. Bring binoculars. Camping is not allowed at Barr Lake, but the park is open 5 a.m. to 10 p.m. daily year-round. To get there, take I-76 northeast out of Denver about 20 miles to exit 22, Bromley Lane, east to Picadilly Road, and south to the park entrance. There's also a nature center with displays and information and a bookstore.

CHATFIELD STATE RECREATION AREA
11500 North Roxborough Park Road, Littleton
(303) 791-7275
http://parks.state.co.us/Parks/Chatfield

Here you'll find Metro Denver's widest range of outdoor experiences, from powerboating to appreciating nature in remote surroundings. Along the southern end of the park, where the South Platte River empties into Chatfield Reservoir, you'll find ample opportunities to enjoy heavily wooded areas that are tucked beneath a striking canopy of old-growth river bottom cottonwoods. People bike, hike, and ride horses along the river, stopping occasionally to cast a line into the stream. On the west side, between the river and US 75, you can walk along a wetlands area that contains ponds, waterfowl, animals, and flora. On the northern end, the reservoir is the star of the show. Its first-rate swimming beach is open Memorial Day through Labor Day. Boaters, water-skiers, and anglers share the water, with paddleboats, pontoon boats, water toys, and other vessels available to rent from the Chatfield Marina. Horseback rides are provided at Chatfield

Stables. (More details are available in the Horseback Riding, Boating and Windsurfing sections of this chapter). The campgrounds have more than 150 sites with all the amenities, but we suggest reservations, (303) 470-1144. Note that dogs are allowed in Chatfield if they are leashed or are in an off-leash exercise area on the north side of the dam. To reach Chatfield, take I-25 or I-70 to C-470, then C-470 to the Wadsworth Boulevard exit. The park entrance is on the left.

CHERRY CREEK STATE PARK
4201 South Parker Road, Aurora
(303) 690-1166
http://parks.state.co.us/Parks/CherryCreek
Because it is centrally located, Cherry Creek State Park attracts so many visitors it's often at capacity on summer weekends. Water lovers are drawn to the reservoir, which has 880 surface acres of water, while nature lovers find solace in the natural prairie environment that surrounds it. In addition to camping, picnicking, trail riding, and guided nature walks, Cherry Creek offers model airplane flying, a shooting range, and a riding stable. Along the trail systems you may see mule deer and white-tailed deer, owls, coyotes, and foxes. Plan to make camping reservations well ahead of time. (More information about the marina is provided in the Boating and Windsurfing section of this chapter.) The recreation area is 1 mile south of I-225 on Parker Road, and is open daily from 5 a.m. to 10 p.m.

GOLDEN GATE CANYON STATE PARK
92 Crawford Gulch Road, Golden
(303) 582-3707
http://parks.state.co.us/Parks/GoldenGate
Canyon
This is the most mountainous of the six state parks closest to Metro Denver. It covers 14,000 acres with altitudes that range from 7,600 to 10,400 feet; has 275 picnic sites, 35 miles of trails for foot and hoof, and more than 130 campsites, as well as 20 backcountry shelters and tent sites. Two yurts and fire cabins are a recent addition to camping choices. (Reservations are recom-

mended.) Stop at the visitor center on the park's lower east end (open 9 a.m. to 4 p.m. daily) to get your bearings, browse through the museum, and watch the trout in a nearby pool. A nature trail designed for the physically impaired begins just outside the center. To reach the park, turn west off Highway 93 onto Golden Gate Canyon Road and follow it for about 15 miles.

ROXBOROUGH STATE PARK
4751 North Roxborough Drive, Littleton
(303) 973-3959,
http://parks.state.co.us/Parks/Roxborough
Roxborough was Colorado's first state park to be designated both a Colorado Natural Area and a National Natural Landmark. There is only one building, the visitor center, which serves as the gateway to a number of lovely hikes through dramatic terrain. The hikes are gentle, but the geology is spectacular, especially the Dakota Hogback and the red-rock moonscape of the Fountain Formation. There are no picnic sites, nor are camping, rock climbing, and pets allowed. Reach Roxborough by following US 85 (Santa Fe Drive) south from Denver to Titan Road. Take a right onto Titan Road and go 3.5 miles. Follow Titan Road left onto Rampart Range Road. Go 3 miles and turn left onto Roxborough Park Road, then take an immediate right onto the park access road.

RECREATION

Bicycling

Cities in the Metro Denver area have put significant effort and money into building superb trails for bicycling, running, and skating. The City and County of Denver maintain good trail maps that can be downloaded or purchased (go to www.bikedenver.org/maps for details). I've listed a few of my favorites.

CHERRY CREEK BIKE PATH
Running east-west through Denver's urban core, the Cherry Creek Bike Path is one of a kind. It begins at Confluence Park, at the intersec-

tion of the South Platte River and Cherry Creek, and wanders through some of the ritziest areas of Cherry Creek before dumping riders out in Aurora. For much of the way, it follows the creek and is worlds away from the roadways above. Riders share the paved path with in-line skaters, joggers, and walkers, but in exchange they see everything from the Cherry Creek Country Club to beaver ponds.

EAST 7TH AVENUE BIKE ROUTE

This ride takes you through city streets, so watching for traffic is a must. But if you're more interested in sampling Denver's scenery and architecture than getting a real workout, this is a nice ride. Start just south of downtown at Broadway and East 7th Avenue, then head east on 7th and follow the bike route signs. You can take it for 4 miles before it dead-ends at Colorado Boulevard, through Denver's oldest neighborhoods, replete with mansions and stunning old trees.

THE HIGHLINE CANAL

This Denver-area highlight was built in the 1880s and is now lined by huge cottonwoods in what amounts to a river of ancient trees through the city. This favorite trail runs from Waterton Canyon in the west to Aurora's Environmental Park in the east. Depending on the time of year, the canal will either be swollen with spring runoff or bone dry. Watch for horses, as the dirt areas are popular with equestrians.

PLATTE RIVER GREENWAY TRAIL

This is a major bike trail in Metro Denver that runs from Chatfield Reservoir in the southwest to the city of Thornton in the upper north metro region. The trail passes through more than a dozen parks. Access points are legion; consult trail maps for details. Two popular access points are Confluence Park at 15th and Platte Streets near Lower Downtown and Ruby Hill Park near Evans Street and Broadway.

Resources

The State of Colorado has urban trail maps for four different areas of the state. One of those is for the metropolitan Denver area: Urban Trails in Colorado, Denver Metro Area. The state also has a very useful Colorado Trails Resource Guide. These references are available free if you stop by or write Trails Guides, 1313 Sherman Avenue, Room 618, Denver, CO 80203. Provide a self-addressed, stamped return envelope with six first-class stamps; the envelope should measure at least 6 by 9 inches. Some bike shops will have urban trail maps available as well.

Rentals

It's easy to rent a bike in Metro Denver. There are numerous rental shops in the area, but we've listed a few that have been around for a long time.

ADVENTURE CYCLING
4361 South Parker Road, Aurora
(303) 699-2514
http://adventurecycle.net
Adventure Cycling is convenient to those in the southeast part of Metro Denver.

THE BICYCLE DOCTOR
860 Broadway
(303) 831-7228
www.bicycledr.com
Located near downtown Denver, the Bicycle Doctor is a full-service shop that works on bicycles when it's not servicing skis. It also rents both.

SPORTS RENT
8761 Wadsworth Boulevard, Arvada
(303) 467-0200
This shop specializes in dirt bike, boat, Jet Ski, and ATV rentals.

TREADS BICYCLE OUTFITTERS
3546 South Logan, Lakewood
(303) 781-1162
www.treads.com

16701 East Iliff Avenue, Aurora
(303) 750-1671

10831 South Crossroads Drive, Parker
(303) 690-2900

This shop rents everything from trail bikes for pavement to high-performance mountain bikes and has maps and brochures for sale.

Mountain Biking

If any outdoor sport could be said to define Colorado, mountain biking would probably run a close second to skiing. Hikers are still the primary users of Colorado backcountry, but increasingly they are sharing their trails with bikers. Mountain bikes have fat nubby tires, super-light frames, and gearing low enough to ride up the steepest hills.

A lot of great mountain-biking trails are located in Jefferson County on Denver's immediate west side. These are wonderful places for their terrain, scenery, and/or technical aspects. All are accessible to anyone with reasonably fit lungs and legs.

DEER CREEK PARK TRAIL

This area is about 4 miles up Deer Creek Canyon from Wadsworth Boulevard, in Jefferson County Open Space. Its steep trails aren't for beginners or those who haven't been working out. Deer Creek Park has one hiker-only trail.

HAYDEN-GREEN MOUNTAIN PARK TRAILS

These intermediate trails also challenge riders. They wind through the park before climbing 1,200 feet to the Green Mountain summit. To get there, take 6th Avenue west to the Union Street exit, go south to Alameda Avenue, then right. The park is on the right side.

i The Sand Creek Regional Greenway Trail is a well-kept secret and will be until the 13-mile east-west walking and biking trail is completed. The mostly unpaved trail connects the Platte River Greenway in Commerce City with the High Line Canal in Aurora and completes a 50-mile loop through wetlands, along creek beds, and beneath an old airport runway.

MOUNT FALCON

Several bike loops for riders with moderate technical skills can be accessed from the pavilion at Walker's Dream Shelter. To reach it, take US 285 west past C-470 to the Morrison exit, then right. Follow the clearly marked signs. From the Morrison trailhead, you can head up the Castle Trail to the pavilion at Walker's Dream Shelter. Avoid the area's hiker-only trail.

WATERTON CANYON

There are lovely, gentle trails around the Chatfield Recreation area, but up Waterton Canyon it gets a little more dramatic. No dogs are allowed because the canyon is home to a herd of bighorn sheep. A 6-mile dirt road heads up past Cottonwood Gulch, Mill Gulch, and Stevens Gulch to the Colorado Trail. To reach it, take Wadsworth Boulevard south from its junction with C-470, 4 miles to the Waterton Canyon Recreation Area sign, and turn left to park.

References

One of the best overall references for these and other rides is *The Best of Colorado Biking Trails* (revised edition), published by Outdoor Books & Maps, Inc. of Denver and available in many local bookstores, bike shops, and outing stores. Another is *Mountain Biking Denver and Boulder* by Bob D'Antonio (Falcon).

Boating and Windsurfing

Boaters and windsurfers have a lot of lakes and reservoirs to choose from around Metro Denver, but if you're into powerboating, only a select few are large enough and allow enough horsepower to do more than putt from one fishing spot to the next. The most popular lakes for power-boating are the big boys: Cherry Creek and Chatfield Reservoir. Both are large reservoirs and, as part of state recreation areas, are nice environments in which to split the water. You can find more general descriptions of these areas in the State Parks and Recreation Areas section of this chapter, but boaters will be interested to know that both have extensive marinas offering a lot of rentals.

AURORA RESERVOIR MARINA
5800 South Powhaton Road, Aurora
(303) 690-1286
www.auroragov.org
This newer facility is 7 miles east of Quincy Reservoir in Arapahoe County. Powerboaters pay it little attention, since gas motors aren't allowed on the water, but the water is clean, and it's popular with sailors and windsurfers. There's a little marina with a general store, where you can rent electric motorboats, rowboats, sailboats, sailboards, paddleboats, and canoes. It also features a paved bike path that stretches about 8 miles around the lake. You'll find the reservoir by driving about 2 miles east of Gun Club Road on East Quincy Avenue and turning right at Powhaton Road. Hours vary depending on sunrise and sunset, but generally run from dawn to dusk, and visitors will be charged a daily vehicle pass fee.

BEAR CREEK LAKE PARK
15600 West Morrison Road, Morrison
(303) 697-6159
www.lakewood.org
There are three water areas here: Bear Creek Lake, Little Soda Lake, and Big Soda Lake. Bear Creek is mainly for fishing as it allows no motors greater than 10 horsepower. There also is some sailing. An admission fee is charged, and there are no rentals. The access point is easy to see off Morrison Road, once you exit C-470. Big Soda Lake is open to the public for nonmotorized boats and has its own Soda Lake Marina, (303) 697-1522, where you can rent paddleboats, kayaks, sailboards, and canoe. Big Soda also has a swim area. Little Soda Lake isn't open for public boating.

CHATFIELD MARINA
11500 North Roxborough Park Road, Littleton
(303) 791-5555
This marina for the Chatfield Reservoir includes a store with boating and fishing supplies, groceries, and take-out food. It's Denver's only on-the-water grill and deli restaurant with a patio and an observation deck. The season runs from April through October. Fishing boats, pontoon boats, and paddleboats can be rented by the hour or by the day. Call ahead for reservations.

THE CHERRY CREEK MARINA
4800 South Dayton, Greenwood Village
(303) 779-6144
(303) 699-2501 (yacht club)
www.cherrycreekmarina.com
The marina is on the west side of the Cherry Creek reservoir; just follow the signs after entering. It has slips and rents pontoon boats, fishing boats, mono-hull dinghy sailboats, Sunfish, paddleboats, kayaks, and canoes.

STANDLEY LAKE REGIONAL PARK
9805 West 88th Avenue, Westminster
(303) 425-1097
www.ci.westminster.co.us
Standley Lake, the big north Jefferson County lake bordered on the north and east by Westminster and on the south by Arvada, is a popular location for windsurfing, camping, fishing, bird watching, and ambling along the shore on trails. Motorboats are allowed there between May 1 and September 30, but you need a permit for boats with more than 20 horsepower, and the number of permits is limited. Call the number above for more information. There are no rental facilities at Standley.

Climbing

Climbing isn't a sport for beginners, but for anyone interested in getting the most from their workout, it can provide unparalleled challenges. Most of Colorado's best climbs are a drive away from the Denver area, but you can start by taking lessons and learning the ropes at local recreation centers with in-house climbing walls. Once you've mastered the basics, you can graduate to climbing areas just outside of Boulder, where the terrain is internationally known. Prefer to climb in groups? We've listed some that arrange excursions.

Public Recreation Centers and Programs

Public parks and recreation departments are your greatest resource for year-round exercise options. Public centers are prevalent throughout Metro Denver, most of which have indoor and outdoor swimming pools as well as fitness equipment, basketball courts, and other kinds of programming that can include youth team sports leagues. Because their offerings are too extensive to list here, we've just provided the contact numbers for you to call. Refer to other sections in this chapter for specifics about individual activities such as tennis or golf.

Denver
Denver Parks and Recreation Department
(720) 913-0696

Adams County
Adams County Parks and Community
Resource Aurora Parks and Open
Space Department
(303) 739-7160
Brighton Recreation Center
(303) 655-2200
Commerce City Parks and Recreation
Department (303) 289-3789
Hyland Hills Park and Recreation District
Federal Heights, (303) 428-7488
Northglenn Parks and Recreation
Department (303) 450-8800
Thornton Recreation Center
(303) 255-7800

Arapahoe County
Aurora Parks and Recreation Department
(303) 739-7160
Englewood Parks Department
(303) 762-2680
South Suburban Park and Recreation
District (303) 798-5131

Douglas County
Castle Rock Recreation Center
(303) 660-1036
Parker Recreation Center
(303) 841-4500

Jefferson County
Arvada Parks and Recreation District
(303) 424-2739
Broomfield Community Center
(303) 464-5500
Edgewater Recreation Center
(303) 274-6280
Foothills Park and Recreation District
(303) 409-2100
Golden Community Center
(303) 384-8100
Lakewood Recreation Department
(303) 987-7800
Westminster Parks and Recreation
Department (303) 460-9690
Wheat Ridge Recreation Center
(303) 231-1300

CITY PARK RECREATION CENTER
10455 Sheridan Boulevard, Westminster
(303) 460-9690
www.ci.westminster.co.us
City Park has its own climbing wall in the gymnasium, where people can practice or take climbing lessons while the basketballs bounce behind them. Classes are offered for beginner, intermediate, and advanced climbers. Or you can take a short orientation, then pay a low drop-in fee.

COLORADO MOUNTAIN CLUB
710 10th Street, No. 200, Golden
(303) 279-3080
www.cmc.org
Technical climbing instruction is available from the grandfather of Colorado mountaineering organizations, the Colorado Mountain Club, but classes are offered only once a year. Basic rock climbing is offered in May and June, and the intermediate class is usually in August or September. Membership is required, but reduced rates for Friends of Colorado Mountain Club memberships are available for out-of-staters.

ELDORADO CANYON STATE PARK
9 Kneale Road, Eldorado Springs
(303) 494-3943
http://parks.state.co.us/Parks/eldorado canyon
No discussion of mountain climbing can occur without mentioning Eldorado Canyon State Park. It's where athletes from around the world gather to practice their skills, swap stories, and train for the really big mountains. The park is day-use only and boasts 500 routes that rise as much as 1,500 feet above the canyon floor. The easiest are used for climbing lessons; the most challenging are reserved for the experts. Because the area is a state park, expect to pay a use fee and then relax at picnic tables or by biking or fishing in the stream.

PARADISE ROCK GYM
6260 North Washington Street, No. 5
(303) 286-8168
www.paradiserock.com
This is an indoor rock-climbing gym built around technical climbing, with 7,500 square feet of climbing wall and structure as well as lessons, a small amount of climbing accessory retail, and cross-training facilities such as weight machines, stationary bicycles, and stair machines. Beginners are welcome here for lessons. Call for information about lessons and the Stone Collective, a group of outdoor aficionados and industry experts who operate out of Paradise.

REI (RECREATIONAL EQUIPMENT, INC.)
1416 Platte Street
(303) 756-3100
www.rei.com
This gigantic store tempts visitors with its climbing wall at the entrance. REI offers a variety of classes for all levels. Kids climb free on Saturday, and free clinics are offered monthly. Call for details and times. REI's wall is designed for an introduction to climbing so it isn't equal to the rock gyms mentioned above. Beyond the wall, the store offers a full range of retail equipment for climbing and mountaineering. Walls and lessons also are available at REI stores at 1789 28th Street, Boulder, (303) 583-9970; 9637 East County Line Road, Englewood, (303) 858-1726; and 5375 South Wadsworth Boulevard, Lakewood, (303) 932-0600.

THRILLSEEKERS
1912 South Broadway
(303) 733-8810
www.thrillseekers.cc
This climbing gym offers more than 12,000 square feet of climbing space, including a 35-foot roof climb, 40 top ropes, five lead walls where climbers can get horizontal, and a separate "bouldering" area where you can free-climb. A complete lesson program is available for all levels, and a full retail section will fill your every climbing need. Lesson prices vary depending on level and number of people, so call ahead.

Fishing
One-third of the state's land area is open to public hunting and fishing, which is why Colorado is a national destination for these activities. People come from the Midwest and both coasts to cast a fly in rushing mountain streams.

Fishing in Colorado, of course, isn't just a matter of mountain trout streams. The state has flatland rivers, large lakes, and reservoirs aplenty. Colorado's 6,000-plus miles of streams and 2,000-plus lakes and reservoirs open to public fishing include high-country fishing for cutthroat, brook, brown, lake, and rainbow trout. There's also a lot of warm-water quarry such as walleye, largemouth and small-mouth bass, catfish, crappie, yellow perch, wiper, bluegill, and muskie. A lot of warm-water fishing is available right in Metro Denver. The state's record tiger muskie (40 pounds, 2 ounces) was caught in Quincy Reservoir, a half-mile east of Buckley Road on Quincy Avenue in Aurora.

The *Denver Post* publishes a weekly fishing and stocking report provided by the Colorado Division of Wildlife called "Colorado's Best Bets" that offers anglers up-to-the-minute scoops on hot fishing spots.

Recorded information about fishing (license fees, locations, limits, etc.) is available from the Division of Wildlife, (303) 291-7533; information on specific fishing conditions throughout the state is available from mid-April through Labor Day weekend at (303) 291-7534. You can also visit the Colorado Division of Wildlife's Web site at or www.wildlife.state.co.us/Fishing.

Licenses

Fishing licenses are required; you can get yours at most major sports and outdoors stores or online at www.wildlifelicense.com/co/. Cost is $26 per year for Colorado residents, $56 for nonresidents. A day license costs $9 for residents and nonresidents, and a five-day license is $21, nonresidents only. There are discounts for senior citizens and people with disabilities; children younger than age 16 do not need a license. Anglers receive a complete rules and regulations brochure when they purchase a license. Brochures are usually available where you buy your license. There are various size and quantity limits as well as rules on allowable bait, depending on the waters and type of fish.

Fishing Spots

Although Colorado has been suffering through drought conditions that have affected reservoir levels and stream flows, the state remains world-famous for its Gold Medal trout waters. These lakes and streams have a high-quality aquatic habitat, a high percentage of trout 14 inches or longer, and a high potential for trophy fish. The Colorado Division of Wildlife has a booklet on the state's Gold Medal waters and other hot spots; find it online at www.wildlife.state.co.us/fishing/wheretogo.

The South Platte River is one of the best rainbow and brown trout fisheries in the nation and is world-famous among fly fishers. This Gold Medal river is for the serious fishing enthusiast and has it all: proximity to Denver, lots of big fish, consistent insect hatches, and incredible scenery. The Cheesman Canyon section of the South Platte holds approximately 5,200 trout per mile that average 15 inches in length (although some locals will tell you it also seems to have at least that many fishermen).

The two best ways to reach Cheesman Canyon both involve traveling south to the Deckers area and then working your way back north along the river. Take US 285 west from Denver, then turn south onto County Road 126 at Pine Junction. Follow CR 126 for 20 miles toward Deckers; the Gill Trail parking lot is just off CR 126. The Gill trailhead is a 20-minute hike from the Gill Trail parking lot. If the hike to Gill Trail doesn't sound appealing, just continue on CR 126 into Deckers; parking and open fishing is plentiful right along the road north of town.

For those looking for an enjoyable but less rigorous fishing expedition, Denver-area reservoirs offer a wide range of opportunities.

Aurora Reservoir is home to some hefty rainbow and brown trout, with fish up to 17 inches not uncommon, and also contains many warm-water species such as largemouth bass, crappie, yellow perch, and walleye. The reservoir is open year-round from dawn until dusk. Take I-25 or I-225 to 6th Avenue and follow it until it turns south to become Gun Club Road. Quincy Avenue is about 2 miles past the BFI landfill. The reservoir is about a half-mile east at 5800 South Powhaton Road and charges a daily access fee.

Chatfield Reservoir is one of the Denver metro area's most popular recreation spots. The 1,100-acre reservoir is an impoundment of the South Platte River described earlier in this section and offers fishing access to the river both above and below the reservoir itself. A daily Colorado State Parks permit is required. From Denver, take

Wadsworth Boulevard (Highway 121) south past C-470, and turn left into the park at the Deer Creek entrance. As an alternate route, take Santa Fe Boulevard south to Titan Road and turn west. Go to Roxborough Park Road, and turn north to the Plum Creek entrance.

Golf

Metro Denver is a golfer's paradise, with more than 70 golf courses, 90 percent of them are public. And if you want to make a day of it, there are another 20 or so spectacular mountain-area courses within a one- to two-hour drive from downtown Denver.

As with many major metropolitan areas, Denver's city courses are typically smaller, older tracts, but they often have more character than the treeless suburban courses that tend to show up in housing developments. While these inner-city layouts might not attract tournament golf, they almost always present more of a challenge than you would expect, the price is usually easier on the wallet, and you can get to most of them by cab, avoiding the freeways around Denver.

On the other hand, there is nothing like teeing off in the Rocky Mountains at one of the nearby mountain courses. It's not unusual for a first-time player to return from a day of golf in Breckenridge or Winter Park only to find he can't remember how he played—he spent too much time looking around at the scenery!

Most courses require advance tee times but limit how far in advance you can call, usually not more than seven days. This is only a problem if you need a weekend tee time, when courses are most crowded, or if you have no flexibility in your schedule. Otherwise, local experience reports that many courses can fit you in with a same-day call, and sometimes you can even "walk-on" without a tee-time reservation. Resorts typically allow you to make tee times when booking your vacation.

There are several excellent publications and Web sites that you can use to get course information in the Denver area, plus we're going to highlight some of the more exceptional courses in this chapter.

Colorado AvidGolfer Magazine is available online at www.coloradoavidgolfer.com, by subscription at (720) 493-1729, or at local newsstands monthly.

Colorado Golf Magazine is available online at www.coloradogolf.com, or via quarterly subscription at (303) 688-5853.

GOLFViews Magazine, published in Littleton, is available online at www.golfviews.com, or phone (303) 797-8700.

ARROWHEAD GOLF CLUB
10850 West Sundown Trail, Littleton
(303) 973-9614
www.arrowheadcolorado.com
Designed by Robert Trent Jones Jr. in 1971, Arrowhead is a par 72, 18-hole course that winds 6,682 yards through a landscape of scrub oak and magnificent red sandstone rock formations. Arrowhead is regarded as one of the most beautiful and challenging courses in the state, and it regularly makes *Golf Digest*'s top 20 list of places to play in Colorado. Tee times can be made up to seven days in advance, with greens fees ranging from $129 weekdays up to $135 on weekends including the mandatory cart. No denim is allowed, and collared shirts are required. Take I-25 south to C-470 west, exit onto Santa Fe Drive, and go south 4 miles to Titan Parkway. Turn right onto Titan Parkway, follow it until it becomes Rampart Range Road, then follow the signs to Arrowhead.

BRECKENRIDGE GOLF CLUB
200 Clubhouse Drive, Breckenridge
(970) 453-9104
www.breckenridgegolfclub.com
Breckenridge Golf Club has the distinction of being the only municipally owned Jack Nicklaus-designed course in the world, and it is a masterpiece. Rated one of "America's Top 75 Upscale Golf Courses" by *Golf Digest*, Breckenridge features 27 holes that include some of the most beautiful valley vistas on any course anywhere. Like most mountain courses, the layout incorporates many of the surrounding area's natural settings, with tree-lined fairways, rock outcroppings, and haz-

ard areas filled with mountain bushes and flow-ers. Greens fees are typical for mountain courses, at $99 plus $16 for a cart; tee-time reservations can be made four days in advance. Breckenridge is about 90 miles west of Denver. Take I-70 west to exit 203, and turn south onto Highway 9. Go 7 miles to Tiger Road. Turn left onto Tiger Road and proceed to your first right turn. ·

FOX HOLLOW GOLF COURSE
13410 West Morrison Road, Lakewood
(303) 986-7888
www.lakewood.org
Fox Hollow is a 27-hole course you play by book-ing two of the three 9-hole venues, each of which offers a unique layout ranging from wide-open links to tree-lined river bottom to rugged canyon-lands. Call for tee times up to six days in advance, wear appropriate golf attire to the course, and think about adding a third 9 holes to your round for an extra $25. Take C-470 south to the Morrison Road exit, then go east on Morrison Road for 3.5 miles. The course, which is well signed, will be on your right.

LEGACY RIDGE
10801 Legacy Ridge Parkway
Westminster
(303) 438-8997
www.ci.westminster.co.us
Although parts of Legacy Ridge's 18-hole, par 72 course are laid out among housing develop-ments, the majority of the holes either wind through protected wetlands or traverse a ridge that offers spectacular views of the Front Range of the Rockies. Renowned Ohio architect Arthur Hills designed this course in 1994, and it regularly makes the top 10 in player polls. If you play late in the day, be sure to enjoy a classic Colorado sunset from the outdoor deck of the clubhouse bar and grill. From Denver take I-25 north to US 36 west, toward Boulder. Exit US 36 at the 104th Avenue exit, and head east on 104th Avenue to Legacy Ridge Parkway. Turn left and watch for the clubhouse on your left.

POLE CREEK GOLF CLUB
6827 County Road 51, Tabernash
(970) 887-9195, (800) 511-5076
www.polecreekgolf.com
When Pole Creek opened in 1985, it was named "Best New Public Course in the United States" by *Golf Digest*. Surrounded by 13,000-foot snow-capped peaks, at an elevation of 8,600 feet, Pole Creek is quintessential Colorado mountain golf. The original 18-hole layout, designed by Gary Player and Ron Kirby, has been expanded by Denis Griffiths to 27 holes that play up into the lodgepole pines, back down into the river-bottom meadows, and through some of the most beauti-ful scenery in the state. At this elevation golfers can expect an extra 15 percent distance on their shots, just one of the many benefits of making the drive up from Denver to play here. Tee times can be made five days in advance. Pole Creek is located 78 miles from Denver. Take I-70 west to exit 232, then follow US 40 to Winter Park. Pole Creek is 11 miles beyond the town of Winter Park. Turn left at the 220-mile marker and follow the signs to the course.

RED HAWK RIDGE
2156 Red Hawk Ridge Drive, Castle Rock
(720) 733-3500
www.redhawkridge.com
Red Hawk Ridge, south of Denver in Castle Rock, is a virtual cousin to nearby private Castle Pines, the country club famous for The International pro-golf tournament. Designed by Jim Engh and opened in 1999, the par 72, 6,942-yard Red Hawk Ridge received immediate rave reviews in national golf publications for its dramatic setting and design, including the 15th hole, a 528-yard, par 4 that shoots blind to a plateau, then down-hill into a valley where the green lies at the bot-tom. Tee times can be made up to seven days in advance. From I-25 take the Wolfensberger exit and turn west after approximately 0.5 miles. Turn right onto Red Hawk Drive and go about another 0.25 mile; the golf course is on the left.

RIVERDALE DUNES

13300 Riverdale Road, Brighton
(303) 659-6700
www.riverdalegolf.com

Riverdale Dunes is a true hidden gem. Designed by Pete and Perry Dye in 1985, this course garners national praise every year from leading golf magazines. Rated as one of the "Top 75 Public Courses" in the country by *Golf Digest,* and the "#1 Public Course in Colorado" by *Colorado Golfer Newspaper,* the Dunes is an 18-hole, par 72 course that plays 6,398 yards in a Scottish-style links layout. Though hard to find, this reasonably priced, immaculately maintained course is worth the effort. From Denver go north on I-25 to the 120th Avenue exit, then east to Colorado Boulevard and turn left. Follow Colorado Boulevard to 128th Avenue and turn right. 128th Avenue ends at Riverdale Road, and you will feel as though you're in the middle of nowhere, but turn left onto Riverdale Road and follow it about 1.5 miles to the enormous clubhouse, which you will see on your right.

Hiking

Hiking is the most common way of enjoying Colorado's backcountry. For information on hiking safety and our favorite places to hike, see our Great Outdoors chapter.

Horseback Riding

What's more quintessentially Western than an outing on the back of a horse, especially when you're trotting along on the prairies or foothills? Riding in the Denver suburbs may not compare with the more remote horse experiences in the high country and points west, but it beats a canter through Midwestern cornfields.

A lot of people on the outskirts of Denver have their own horses, but those who don't can book rides at a variety of fine local stables. Those located in the two state recreation areas on Metro Denver's south side are nice, if for no other reason than that they're located in large and carefully cultivated natural areas that are filled with nature trails on which to ride.

CHATFIELD STABLES

11500 North Roxborough Park Road
Littleton
(303) 933-3636
www.chatfieldstables.com

The stables at the Chatfield State Recreation Area provide a serene riding setting with great foothill views. Rides can be available as early as March or April, depending on how wet the spring is, but regular summer hours begin May 15 and last through September 15. Reservations are required, and a State Park pass must be purchased to enter the park. Hayrack rides and pony rides also are available. To get there from C-470, take the Wadsworth exit south and turn left at the third stoplight, into the park. From there, follow the signs.

PAINT HORSE STABLES

4201 South Parker Road, Aurora
(303) 690-8235
www.painthorsestables.net

With open meadows, natural grasslands, and wooded areas, Cherry Creek Reservoir State Recreation Area is a great spot for a ride. You need reservations to ride here, and a State Park pass must be purchased to enter the park. Paint Horse Stables also runs the Chatfield Stables; operating dates and programs are similar.

STOCKTON'S PLUM CREEK STABLES

7479 West Titan Road, Littleton
(303) 791-1966
www.stocktonsplumcreek.com

Stockton's has access to the 7,000 acres of Chatfield State Recreation Area via its own private entrance. The area is beautiful, with plenty of bird-watching opportunities on native prairie grasses. Find the stables by going about 4 miles south of C-470 on Santa Fe Drive and turning right on Titan Road. Call for information on hayrides and special events.

A WORTHY RANCH & STABLES

4241 West Parker Road, Parker
(303) 841-9405

On the south side of Metro Denver, A Worthy

Ranch & Stables offers lessons as well as riding along miles of trails. Guided rides are available by reservation only, with a two-hour minimum. Reach it by taking I-25 a little more than a mile south of its intersection with C-470, then traveling east about 2.5 miles on Lincoln Avenue (exit 193) before turning right on a little dirt road called West Parker Road. A Worthy Ranch & Stables is about 2 miles down West Parker Road on the left.

i If you want to hunt on private land, you have to ask the owner; it's legal in Colorado to hunt on private land with the owner's permission.

Hunting

Hunting and fishing pump $3 billion a year into Colorado's economy, second only to the ski industry in terms of economic impact. As vast as the numbers are, so are the locations and types of hunting that are available. It is legal on certain public lands as well as on private land with permission. The Colorado Division of Wlidlife's Web site, www.wildlife.state.co.us/Hunting/, is the best place for information about licensing, game types and limits, seasons, and permissible locations. You can also reach them at (303) 297-1192, or you can use the following recorded information lines: big-game hunting, (303) 291-7529; small game, (303) 291-7546; game birds, (303) 291-7547; and waterfowl, (303) 291-7548.

All hunting, including on public land, requires licenses that can be purchased at any major sports and outdoors stores. The cost varies depending on the game hunted. For example, a resident deer license costs around $31; nonresidents pay $326. Rare game such as moose will cost much more to hunt—$251 for residents and more than $1,800 for nonresidents. There are limits on the number of licenses issued, with more reserved for residents. A lottery is held for some big-game hunting where numbers are kept to a minimum. Brochures for the various types of

hunting are available from the DOW beginning in February and March, depending on the game, with yearly updates that spell out the rules and regulations. Most hunting is confined to specific seasons, whose dates vary from year to year.

Colorado is most famous for big game, including elk, mountain lion, black bear, mule deer, bighorn sheep, mountain goat, white-tailed deer, and pronghorn antelope. But 105 of the state's 113 species of sport game are small game, including ducks and geese, wild turkey, ring-necked pheasant, mourning dove, band-tailed pigeon, quail, grouse, rabbit, and coyote. During the winter, trappers hunt for beaver, muskrat, bobcat, weasel, marten, mink, badger, and fox.

Running

Runners are everywhere in Metro Denver: in the streets of downtown and the suburbs, in the city parks and greenbelts, and along the mountain paths. For those who prefer to run in parklike settings and on motorist-free trails, we will suggest a few popular locations.

Washington Park, between South Franklin and South Downing Streets just north of I-25, is one of the city's most popular running spots. That may be because it's one of Denver's biggest and most pleasant parks, or it may be because it's in an area with a lot of upscale empty-nesters who believe in exercise and don't have to get it by pushing their kids on the park's swings. Closer in, City Park, between Colorado Boulevard and York Street, 2 blocks north of East Colfax Avenue, is another popular running area where folks can get away from cars and run through some semblance of foliated quietude. Greenbelts, including the popular Highline Canal in Littleton, the Cherry Creek Bike Path, and the South Platte River trails at Chatfield Reservoir, are particularly nice because they have the same aesthetic. If you like running on natural terrain, you may want to try some of the mountain-biking trails outlined in our Mountain Biking section.

For those who enjoy the group experience, there are plenty of events and clubs. Greater Denver's largest annual running events include the 5-mile Cherry Creek Sneak in April, the Governor's Cup 5K in September, the Run for the Zoo 5K and 10K in October, the Race for the Cure 5K in October, and the 4-mile Turkey Trot on Thanksgiving morning.

Among the larger running clubs are the Colorado Masters, for the older-than-30 crowd, www.comastersrun.org, and the Rocky Mountain Road Runners, http://rmrr.org or (303) 871-8366. Don't forget that walkers have found increasing acceptance in the area's big running events. The Front Range Walkers, www.racewalk.com or (303) 377-0576, is perhaps the area's biggest walking club.

Some running stores also serve as information clearinghouses on running clubs, events, and race series and are places where you can sign up for races. This includes Runners Roost, 1685 South Colorado Boulevard, www.runnersroost.com or (303) 759-8455.

Skiing

You'd expect skiing to be the top entry in any guide to Metro Denver recreation, which is why we've given it its own Ski Country chapter. If you're a beginner, you may want to know about some ways to get into the sport.

Colorado Ski Country USA is a trade association for all the ski resorts in the state that publishes the *Colorado Ski Country Consumer Guide*. Within about 130 pages, it contains a lot of the information you may want to know about skiing in Colorado. Colorado Ski Country USA will mail it to you free if you give them a call at (303) 837-0793.

i One of the best bargains in fitness is the Denver Parks and Recreation membership. Depending on the recreation center and the offerings chosen, Denver residents can lift weights, play basketball, and swim for $150 a year. Nonresident fees are $200. Check with your nearest rec center for details or visit www.denvergov.org and search "recreation."

You may also want to know about Sniagrab (bargains spelled backward), and other big annual ski equipment and apparel sales staged every year by Metro Denver's largest sporting goods stores. They start on the Saturday before Labor Day and run through much of September.

Tennis

Metro Denver has plenty of tennis facilities, both private and public. You can find courts in just about any major city park. In Denver, try Washington Park, between South Franklin and South Downing Streets just north of I-25, and City Park, between Colorado Boulevard and York Street, two blocks north of East Colfax Avenue. Park play is free and usually runs on a first-come, first-served basis as long as there are no tournaments or lessons going on.

Beyond public courts, there are many organized centers and city recreation departments that offer players a chance to join group play, take lessons, and play in tournaments.

Metro Denver's central tennis resource is the Colorado Tennis Association (CTA), (303) 695-4116. If you're looking for courts or are interested in finding out how to get into organized tennis leagues or sanctioned tournaments, the CTA can help steer you to the right place. It also has copies of tournament schedules for adults and juniors as well as general information brochures. It's the local branch of the U.S. Tennis Association (USTA) as well, so you can get USTA memberships and publications through the CTA.

ARVADA TENNIS CENTER
Corner of 65th and Miller Streets, Arvada
(303) 420-1210
http://apexprd.org
This is a fine public facility with eight courts and sanctioned USTA play. If you want to take to the courts, we suggest making reservations in advance. It is open nightly and on Saturday and Sunday mornings.

AURORA PARKS AND RECREATION
Aurora-area parks
(303) 326-8700

Aurora has a good reputation for its public tennis program. Pros offer beginning, intermediate, and advanced lessons for one-week or two-week sessions as well as evening and Saturday lessons. Tournament play is available, too; check the summer brochure. Aurora maintains 72 courts on a first-come, first-served basis. Very few courts are lighted; one exception is Del Mar Park at 6th Avenue and Peoria Street.

DENVER PARKS AND RECREATION
Denver-area parks
(720) 913-0696

The city recreation district maintains a few dozen courts across the city for daytime play. There are junior programs and adult lesson programs throughout the Denver area. The USTA youth tournament program runs seven weeks of instruction in the summer and one week of tournaments beginning in early June. Adults age 18 and older can join the Congress Park (8th Avenue and York Street east of downtown) program or the Berkley Park (46th Avenue and Sheridan Boulevard northwest of town) program in June and July. Call for information on other programs.

GATES TENNIS CENTER
100 South Adams Street
(303) 355-4461
www.gatestenniscenter.com

This popular facility is just south of the Cherry Creek mall and consistently rated as one of the top public tennis facilities in the country. You don't need a membership, court times are reasonable, and lessons are competitively priced. It has one of the nation's largest tennis ladders, a challenge arrangement in which you sign up at a certain level and begin to play and move up and down the ladder. Gates has more than 1,000 people on its computerized ladder, enough to offer specialized ladders for singles, doubles, etc. There's even a coed ladder reputed to be a good place for singles to meet. It's a 20-court facility complete with clubhouse, locker room, and pro shop. Pros will teach you, and ball machines will test you.

HOLLY TENNIS CENTER
6651 South Krameria Way, Englewood
(303) 771-3654

Holly offers the most USTA-sanctioned tournaments in Colorado. It offers programs on a total of 40 courts, including use of courts in the South Suburban Recreation District. Six of Holly's courts are lighted. It also offers league play and group lessons.

KEN CARYL RANCH COMMUNITY CENTER
1 Club Drive, Littleton
(303) 979-2233

Ken Caryl has four indoor courts and six outdoor courts. You won't find prettier surroundings; the Ken Caryl Ranch community is in the red-rock moonscape of the valley hidden behind the Hogback Formation that runs north-south along C-470. The facility is actually owned by Jefferson County Open Space. Offered here are leagues, tournaments, and lessons for resident and nonresident youths and adults. You also can purchase a membership to the center. Cost varies depending on the program.

Wildlife Watching

While hunting wildlife is more traditional, a growing number of Colorado visitors and residents are interested in stalking wildlife either to photograph or just for the joy of getting an up-close look at the critters. There's something magical about watching a herd of elk feeding in a mountain field or catching a glimpse of a red fox as it darts amid trees. Colorado offers more than 100 places to view wildlife year-round. The best time to view is early morning and late evening (dawn and sunset).

As you travel Colorado's roads and highways, watch for signs that depict a pair of binoculars and say WILDLIFE VIEWING AREA, then follow the signs.

One such area is just outside Denver International Airport. Another is in the mountains along I-70 east of Georgetown (about an hour and a half from Denver). But there are dozens more. Contact the Division of Wildlife at (303) 297-1192 for a list, or pick up a wildlife viewing book at any major bookstore. The *Colorado Wildlife Viewing Guide* is available through the Colorado Wildlife Heritage Foundation for $12.95. Call (303) 291-7212 or visit online at www.wildlife.state.co.us/CWHF/shop/.

Wildlife viewing has its own etiquette that keeps everyone involved as safe and healthy as possible. Never chase or spook animals; it's illegal.

In recent years bird-watching has become an increasingly popular pastime. Reported as the nation's fastest-growing form of outdoor recreation, it attracts a well-educated and serious crowd in Colorado. Denver even boasts another kind of distinction—it's home to a best-selling Christine Goff, a mystery writer whose lead character is a bird-watcher. Among the sinister plots she has written about are meadowlarks being ousted from their habitat by vintners (*Murdered by Merlot*). Anyone interested in joining Denver-area bird-watchers should call the Audubon Society, (303) 973-9530.

THE GREAT OUTDOORS

Colorado's mountains offer unparalleled opportunity for adventure. You can venture deep into the Rockies for long trips or drive less than a half-hour and be surrounded by great exploring territory.

Camping, hiking, and biking abound in Colorado's great outdoors, so we've compiled a few tips on how to enjoy them.

More than one-third of Colorado's land area is owned by and is available to the public, including 8.3 million acres of Bureau of Land Management tracts and 14.3 million acres of national forest. There are 11 national forests in Colorado, covering major parts of the state. The national forests are basically undeveloped areas where you can hike, fish, hunt, ride, and camp just about anywhere. They are also where the vast majority of wilderness can be found, and if you want to hike to some remote and beautiful backcountry refuge anywhere in the United States, the likelihood is that you'll do it in a national forest.

NATIONAL FORESTS

While national forests are generally open to timber sales, mining, and other activities that purists might find at odds with the idea of a natural setting, national wilderness areas allow no permanent roads, structures, timber sales, or mining other than those that already exist. These areas are wild country, accessible only by trail and closed to anything but foot transport. No bikes are allowed, but horses are OK.

Three of Colorado's national forests are located immediately to the west, northwest, and southwest of Metro Denver: Pike National Forest, Arapaho National Forest, and Roosevelt National Forest. You can seek information on these from the USDA Forest Service's Rocky Mountain Regional Office, (303) 275-5350, or call each national forest office itself.

Arapaho and Roosevelt National Forests

Arapaho and Roosevelt National Forests, (970) 295-6600, are combined into a jurisdiction that spans the Continental Divide from the Wyoming border to just south of I-70, west of Denver. Roughly

speaking, the Roosevelt National Forest comprises that section east of the Continental Divide. The Arapaho National Forest lies west of the Continental Divide, although it comes east to cover the area south of I-70 to mid-Jefferson County.

Together they make up some 1.3 million acres in the Rocky Mountains and foothills, wrapping around Rocky Mountain National Park and including 47 national forest campgrounds and a number of wilderness areas such as the Rawah Wilderness on the Wyoming border, the Indian Peaks Wilderness west of Boulder, and the Cache La Poudre Wilderness around the Cache La Poudre River that flows through Roosevelt National Forest and down to Fort Collins.

Pike and San Isabel National Forests

Another jurisdiction combines the 2.3 million acres that comprise the Pike and San Isabel National Forests, (719) 553-1400. At its northern end, the San Isabel is about 100 miles of winding, two-lane US 285 away from Denver. At its southernmost end, it stretches almost to New Mexico. The 1.1 million-acre Pike National Forest is Metro Denver's southern neighbor, reaching southwest from I-70 and west from I-25 to Colorado Springs

(Pikes Peak is part of this national forest). It contains several converging sources of Metro Denver's South Platte River as well as that river's most scenic stretches before it reaches the Flatlands. It has a half-dozen of the state's tallest peaks, sharing Mount Evans with Arapaho National Forest. Its vegetation is drier than Arapaho and Roosevelt National Forests, with more juniper, oak brush, and bristlecone pine. Its major wilderness area is the Lost Creek Wilderness, 106,000 acres on which Pikes Peak granite has been eroded into domes, spires, turrets, and crests, with a lot of big-boulder slopes. Lost Creek is less popular than Indian Peaks and the other big wilderness areas to the north, and it's a good place to backpack and find a bit of solitude. One unique feature of the Pike is a designated motorcycling area near Sedalia that has 118 miles of trails.

HIKING

Hiking—with backpack, daypack, or no pack—is the most common way to enjoy the backcountry. You can hike just about anywhere on national forest land as long as it isn't posted as off-limits. Before we get into the details of where to hike in the Denver area, however, it's important to emphasize safety and preparedness. Even a short hike up a seemingly innocent, well-groomed trail just outside the city can turn into a nightmare if you underestimate the power of nature. Having said that, there are a number of common sense—and sometimes not so obvious—rules and guidelines. If you are careful to follow them, you will come away with memories of a wonderful, exhilarating experience.

The most important rule is to be prepared; even in the summer months, Rocky Mountain weather can be unpredictable and merciless. Wherever you hike, the scenery becomes more beautiful—and the necessity of preparedness more important—the higher you go. You will probably start out in the lower forests of aspen and ponderosa pines or in dark, moody groves of spruce and fir, but as you rise, the forest breaks open into the "krummholz," or crooked wood zone, where trees stunted by altitude and twisted by relentless winds make a border around the alpine meadows above. When you're above tree line, you're in the fragile alpine meadows, home to a stunningly beautiful landscape covered with wildflowers. You're also in the heights prone to drastic weather changes and a climate not unlike the arctic zones of the world.

Mountain-savvy folks dress in layers. When you start your hike during the warm months, you'll be inclined to wear T-shirts and shorts. But there are few things more miserable than reaching the high alpine meadows in them and watching a storm move it that drops temperatures into the 40s. Mountain storms also can bring high winds, cold rain or snow, and afternoon lightning. If you plan to hike in high altitudes, bring along a sizeable backpack with a long-sleeved wool or flannel shirt, a sweater or sweatshirt to put over that, and a windbreaker/raincoat to put over that. A hood is always nice, but you should at least have a knit cap and warm gloves. Bring trousers, or at least sweatpants, to put on over the shorts.

During colder months, including the spring and fall, make certain that none of these clothes is made of cotton, especially your socks. Instead, choose wool or synthetic fibers specifically designed to wick moisture away from the body and to dry quickly. Cotton clothing retains moisture and will not dry quickly when wet, presenting the very real possibility of hypothermia.

Carry plenty of fresh water with you, and never drink stream or lake water without boiling it for at least 10 minutes, using disinfectant pills, or first passing it through a portable disinfectant pump. Drinking untreated water can lead to a nasty case of giardia, and your vacation will come to an abrupt end. You will need to pack a sizeable water bottle, at least 32 ounces per person, and use the water disinfectant tablets or filtering pump as your backup for providing additional drinking water. Make sure you understand how to use the tablets or the disinfectant pump before leaving for the day.

As obvious as it might seem, don't forget your boots. Remember, you'll be on your feet most of the day, and good boots are a must. We don't recommend hiking in anything but hiking boots; sneakers, running shoes, and sandals might be attractive and look better with your shorts, but you'll be glad you left them behind if you encounter cold, wet weather, and your feet will thank you at the end of the day.

A good map is not only an essential emergency item, it adds to the enjoyment of planning your hike. Get a "quadrangle" map on a 1:24,000 scale, where 1 inch equals about 0.4 mile. You may need more than one to cover the area of your interest. Another great resource is the *Delorme Colorado Atlas & Gazetteer*, a road-atlas-size book that contains topographical maps of the entire state. Here the scale is more like 1 inch equals 2.5 miles, but you still get good detail, contour lines, and trail routes. You can find quadrangle maps and the *Delorme Colorado Atlas & Gazetteer* in well-stocked outdoor stores, bookstores, and even some gas stations. You can also get maps from the Bureau of Land Management in Lakewood, (303) 239-3600, or from the U.S. Geological Survey at the Denver Federal Center in Lakewood, Map and Book Sales, (303) 202-4700.

Altitude sickness is another major killjoy that can be avoided. It can affect anyone coming from a lower altitude to Colorado's mile-high regions. Most people in good health will experience nothing more than a slight headache, light-headedness, and shortness of breath. Usually these symptoms are not severe and can be treated with aspirin and rest. More serious symptoms can include dizziness, nausea, and impaired mental abilities. Severe altitude sickness, called high altitude pulmonary edema, can lead to seizures, hallucinations, coma, brain damage, and death.

To avoid altitude sickness, refrain from strenuous activities for your first few days at a new altitude while your body acclimates. While it actually takes a few weeks for your body to fully acclimate, each passing day spent at a higher elevation helps your body create the extra red blood cells it needs to capture the limited oxygen at higher altitudes. Take the time to get used to the altitude here before you charge off in pursuit of the high country. Getting off the plane from sea level one day and going on a 6-mile hike to 10,000 feet the next is asking for big trouble.

Mounting most of Colorado's peaks won't require technical mountain climbing skills or gear such as ropes, carabineers, or ice axes. If that's the kind of climbing you're interested in, look for a guide or instructor, and practice at any of the gyms and recreation centers that have their own climbing walls. (See our Parks and Recreation chapter for more details.)

Most people just want to climb the mountains on any of the hundreds of trails that range in difficulty from easy to extremely hard. Unless you are an experienced hiker and are acclimated to our high elevations, avoid the 500 or so Colorado peaks that rise higher than 12,000 feet. An elite group of climbers like to "bag the 14ers," or climb to the summits of all 56 peaks that are 14,000 feet or higher. Doing so can be dangerous if attempted by novices.

We've listed a range of moderate day hikes that are within easy driving range of Denver. Find more trails in books such as *Hiking Colorado* by Maryann Gaug (Falcon) and *Hiking Colorado's Front Range: Fort Collins to Colorado Springs* (Falcon). Four books by Tracy Salcedo focus more closely on the Denver area: *Best Easy Day Hikes Denver*, and *12 Short Hikes Denver Foothills North, Denver Foothills Central*, and *Denver Foothills South* (all Falcon). A good book for families is *Best Hikes with Children in Colorado* by Maureen Keilty (Mountaineers Books). And don't think just in terms of summertime hiking; the trails of summer become the snowshoe and cross-country ski trails of winter. Check out *Winter Trails Colorado: The Best Cross-Country Ski and Snowshoe Trails* by Andy and Tari Lightbody (Globe Pequot Press) or *Snowshoeing Colorado* by Claire Walter (Fulcrum Publishing).

GREEN MOUNTAIN TRAIL
About 4 miles north of Morrison
Jefferson County Open Space Department
(303) 271-5925
Map: Jefferson County Open Space map
for Hayden's Green Mountain Park
This easy trail in Denver's foothills wanders 3.5 miles one way (7.25 miles round-trip) and climbs 600 feet, from 6,200 to 6,800 feet. To reach it,

drive west from Denver on 6th Avenue past I-70 and turn left onto US 40. After a short distance, turn left onto Rooney Road and drive south to the parking area to the east. Walk across C-470 on the pedestrian bridge to join the Green Mountain and Lonesome Trails. Take the Green Mountain Trail for the best nature experience. From the top of the mountain, you'll have panoramic views, and along the way you may see mule deer, foxes, coyotes, rabbits, and up to 150 species of birds. If you'd like to do a round-trip loop, take the Lonesome Trail back, but be aware that it follows Alameda Parkway much of the way back to the parking area.

HIGHLINE CANAL
Near Chatfield Reservoir, between Waterton and the Rocky Mountain Arsenal
Denver Water Department, Office of Community Relations, (303) 628-6000
Map: USGS Front Range Corridor map, sheet 2
Another easy trail south of Denver, this one runs a total of 71 miles along the irrigation ditch completed in 1883 by Scotsman James Duff. Only 58 of those miles are hikeable, but they can be traveled in segments long or short enough to suit any appetite. Most of the trail is wheelchair and stroller accessible, and it's open year-round to walkers, hikers, joggers, horseback riders, bikers, and in-line skaters. It can be reached in Englewood on South Santa Fe Drive, County Line Road, or Hampden Avenue, and in Aurora on Havana Street or Colfax Avenue.

WHITE RANCH PARK
Northwest of Golden and southwest of Boulder
Jefferson County Open Space
(303) 271-5925
Maps: USGS Ralston Buttes quad or White Ranch Park map (available at the park)
Ute and Arapahoe tribes camped and hunted on this land before Welsh immigrants James and Mary Bond settled on it. Originally on their way to California, they decided to stop here after a young son fell beneath the wagon's wheels and was killed. The land is now open space owned by Jefferson County. It is crisscrossed by trails of varying difficulty that range from 0.3 to 4.5 miles. Several are good for children, and the relatively easy 1.6-mile Sawmill Trail leads to a campground (an advance permit is required to stay there, available from the Jefferson County Open Space office). To get to White Ranch Park, drive north from Golden on Highway 93 to Jefferson County Road 70 (Golden Gate Canyon Road). After 4.1 miles, turn right onto Jefferson County Road 57 (Crawford Gulch Road) and drive another 4.1 miles. Turn right to enter the park.

CAMPING

Finding a location to camp on national forest land is simple once you've determined whether you want to "car camp" or backpack into a more remote location. The main distinction is simple: Car camping usually means you won't have to hike in, and will likely be at a designated campground with amenities such as outhouses and running water. If you car camp, you'll likely be near others—anywhere from 50 feet to a few hundred feet depending on the campground—and have a designated fire pit. You'll also pay a small daily fee for your site. If you backcountry camp, you can go virtually anywhere on national forest land and camp for free, but you won't have any amenities.

The rules for backcountry camping are fairly simple, but important: You must pick a spot at least 100 feet from a roadway, trail, or stream and at least a half-mile from standing water. Unless fire danger is high, as it has been for several years, fires are allowed for cooking and warming but must be in a contained pit. You must restore the fire area when you leave. Your car can be as much as 300 feet off the road but not parked in a bog; if you have a catalytic converter, do not park over grass as it can start a fire.

Making a reservation for car camping in designated campgrounds is highly recommended and nearly imperative on holiday weekends (see our list of phone numbers). Backcountry camping does not require a reservation and can be done anywhere as long as the rules are followed.

If you car camp, you can get to a campground early and take your chances at cruising around looking for an empty space or finding people who look like they are about to leave. Usually you need to show up by 7 p.m. or your reserved spot could be taken. The rules are somewhat loose and depend on individual campgrounds. The national forests have a toll-free number, and in any part of Colorado, a certain percentage of the forest service campgrounds are part of that reservation system. You can call (877) 444-6777 or go to www.reserveusa.com. Make sure to have ready not only the name of the campground you want, but also a selection of other campgrounds in the vicinity. If the one you want is not open to reservations, you'll be able to ask for your second or third choice.

Following is a helpful list of national forest campgrounds in Colorado that are served by the centralized reservation system. Note that a road atlas or Colorado state map is likely to have a little tree symbol representing each campground but no name. The *Delorme Colorado Atlas & Gazetteer* often has the name of a lake or creek that coincides with the nearby tent symbol indicating a campground. One resource that names each campground on the map is the national forest visitor map, one for each national forest, produced by the USDA Forest Service itself and available from the USDA Forest Service's Denver Regional Office, (303) 275-5350, 740 Simms Street, Lakewood.

Campgrounds

Following are just a few of the national forest campgrounds; there are many more. The daily fees average about $15. For a full list you can call the USDA Forest Service's Rocky Mountain Region Office at (303) 275-5350. They'll mail you the free brochure, "Rocky Mountain Region Campgrounds," which lists all the campgrounds in Colorado, as well as in the national forest and national grasslands of Wyoming, Kansas, Nebraska, and South Dakota.

ARAPAHO/ROOSEVELT NATIONAL FOREST
(970) 295-6600

BOULDER RANGER DISTRICT BOULDER
(303) 444-6600
Fort Collins
(970) 498-2733
Clear Creek Ranger District, Idaho Springs
(303) 567-3000

PIKE NATIONAL FOREST
(719) 553-1400
Pikes Peak Ranger District
Colorado Springs
(719) 636-1602

SOUTH PARK RANGER DISTRICT, FAIRPLAY
(719) 836-2031

SOUTH PLATTE RANGER DISTRICT, MORRISON
(303) 275-5610

SULPHUR RANGER DISTRICT, GRANBY
(970) 887-4100

You can find a lot of books about camping, but a good basic reference is *Camping Colorado* by Melinda Crow (Falcon). For more information about recreation in other areas of Colorado, pick up copies of the *Insiders' Guide to Boulder and Rocky Mountain National Park* by Ann Alexander Leggett, and the *Insiders' Guide to Colorado's Mountains* by Linda Castrone (both from Globe Pequot Press).

Resources

There are umpteen books on how to enjoy Colorado's recreational, scenic, and natural opportunities. A pass through a major bookstore will load you down with more than you need. Following are a few other informational resources.

BUREAU OF LAND MANAGEMENT
www.co.blm.gov

THE COLORADO DIRECTORY
(303) 499-9343
www.coloradodirectory.com

COLORADO DIVISION OF WILDLIFE
Headquarters, Denver
(303) 297-1192
www.wildlife.state.co.us

COLORADO MOUNTAIN CLUB
(303) 279-3080
www.cmc.org

COLORADO STATE PARKS
(camping, boating, and recreation)
(303) 866-3437
www.parks.state.co.us

DENVER AUDUBON SOCIETY
(303) 973-9530
www.denveraudubon.org

DUDE RANCHERS ASSOCIATION
(serving all western states including
Colorado)
(866) 399-2339
http://duderanch.org

SKI COUNTRY

Although Denver is located on the plains, it's only about an hour away from some of the best skiing on the continent. Most ski areas are open from Thanksgiving to mid-April, but in good snow years (and with the help of snowmaking), the season can stretch from mid-October through June.

Colorado is home to 25 ski areas, ranging from down-home to world-famous, with seven major areas close enough to qualify as day trips from Denver. If downhill skiing isn't your thing, expect to find lots of things that can be done without skis. Ride the chairlift to Winter Park's Lodge at Sunspot, for example, just to have lunch and enjoy the view. Other options include ice skating, snowmobiling, snowshoeing, dog sledding, or riding in horse-drawn sleighs. Cross-country skiing and snowshoeing also are popular, with groomed tracks and trails available at most downhill areas. Most ski areas also offer adult and child lessons, child care, and specialized lessons.

The mountain fun doesn't stop when the snow melts. Colorado's ski areas are really year-round resorts that offer as many things to do in summer as in winter. Mountain biking? How about an easy lift up with your bike on the gondola and a wild ride down. Music festivals? Ski slopes make great outdoor amphitheaters in the summer. Boating? Try it on a mountain lake or reservoir ringed in jagged peaks. Drift over the Vail Valley in a hot-air balloon, golf at a high-altitude course, or bike along more than 50 miles of paved paths that extend from Breckenridge to Vail.

It's crucial to take altitude into consideration when traveling to the mountains. Even folks accustomed to Denver's 5,280 feet above sea level can get dizzy at 12,000 feet unless they guard against altitude sickness. Drink plenty of water, avoid alcohol, give yourself time to adjust, and slow down if you get a headache or feel nauseated. Also, no one should set out on back-country trails without sound knowledge of avalanche awareness, direction-finding skills, and adequate clothing, food, and water. Even people going on day trips should be prepared to spend a night outside, as weather conditions in the mountains change in seconds. Local bookstores are filled with trail guides that offer basic safety information. And always let someone know where you're going and when you expect to be back. If you want to enjoy the great outdoors when the snow is gone, see our The Great Outdoors chapter for hiking and climbing information.

We've listed and described a few ski areas that make feasible day trips from Denver, with information about winter and summer activities, dining, shopping, and accommodations, should you decide to stay longer. For more information about all the state's ski resorts, contact Colorado Ski Country USA, a trade association, at (303) 837-0793, www.coloradoski.com.

LOVELAND

Useful contact information:
(303) 569-3203, www.skiloveland.com

Loveland is the ski area closest to Denver, just 53 miles and an easy hour's drive west on I-70. It straddles the east face of the Eisenhower Tunnel but is accessed from exit 216, just before the east tunnel entrance. This area is strictly for skiing and snowboarding—Loveland offers no lodging, and its food service is limited to a traditional cafeteria serving deli fare, soups, baked goods, and specialty pizzas. A 5,000-square-foot retail area rents skis and snowboards, and sells clothing, gloves, and other outdoor essentials.

Loveland boasts the world's highest quad lift, at more than 12,600 feet above sea level, which serves 450 acres of expert terrain. With an average annual snowfall of 385 inches and prices that are lower than other close-in areas, there's plenty to pull you off the highway before you pass through the tunnel. One drawback: Loveland can get windy, especially on trails above tree line.

WINTER PARK

Useful contact information:

WINTER PARK RESORT
(970) 726-5514
(303) 892-0961, direct dial from Metro Denver
www.skiwinterpark.com

WINTER PARK/FRASER VALLEY
Chamber of Commerce
(970) 726-4118
This ski area is one of Denver's mountain parks, even though it is 70 miles away—hence the name. Winter Park is a favorite with Front Range skiers because of its excellent terrain and casual ambience. Its ski terrain consists of three interconnected mountains, a high alpine bowl, and Vasquez Cirque, all accessible with one lift ticket. Winter Park and Vasquez Ridge offer a mix of beginner, intermediate, and advanced cruising runs. Mogul enthusiasts like the Mary Jane runs, and the high-alpine Parsenn Bowl, at 12,060 feet, is best known for its gladed tree skiing and above-timberline vistas.

Get there from Denver by driving west on I-70, take the US 40 West exit to Empire and continue over Berthoud Pass. There are two entrances to the ski area. Expert skiers turn off at Mary Jane, while beginners and intermediates continue to the main Winter Park base. The town of Winter Park is a few miles farther down the road, and Fraser is another 5 miles away. Both

towns have grown up alongside the resort, and all remain casual. A free shuttle connects the ski resort with the towns of Winter Park and Fraser. Both have restaurants, shops, and places to stay, although Fraser is known as the place where locals also shop for necessities—it has a Safeway, for example.

If you balk at driving over a mountain pass, you can make the trip by train. On weekends the Ski Train departs Denver's Union Station on weekends at 7:15 a.m., dropping skiers within walking distance of the lifts, and leaves Winter Park at 4:15 p.m. just after the lifts close. The trip takes two hours each way and passes through the Moffat Tunnel. For information and reservations, call (303) 296-4754 or visit www.skitrain.com.

Winter Activities
Eight high-speed quad lifts carry skiers and snowboarders to 2,886 acres of terrain. Winter Park is also home to the **National Sports Center for the Disabled,** (970) 726-1540. Its 39 full-time staff members and more than 1,000 volunteers can handle the needs of people with more than 40 different disabilities.

Down-valley from the ski resort is a top-notch cross-country and snowshoeing center called **Devil's Thumb Ranch,** (970) 726-8231 or (800) 933-4339. Skate-skiers and snowshoers love the 125 kilometers of groomed trails that fan out into the forest from an expansive meadow. To get there, drive west from Winter Park to the town of Fraser and turn right onto County Road 83. Lessons and equipment rental are available. Devil's Thumb Ranch is open year-round, with gourmet dining in the Ranch House Restaurant & Saloon and private or bunkhouse-style accommodations available. Ask about moonlight sleigh rides in the winter and horseback riding, trout fishing, rafting, and kayaking in the summer.

Backcountry skiers like the trails on top of Berthoud Pass and the Jim Creek Trail that begins directly across from the Winter Park ski area. No one should set out on these trails without knowledge of avalanche awareness, adequate clothing, food, water, and a trail guide or maps.

Dogsled rides are expensive, but if you're an Iditarod fan, there's nothing like them. Call **Dog Sled Rides of Winter Park,** (970) 726-8326. If you'd rather be pulled by horses than dogs, go for a sleigh ride. Call **Grand Adventures,** (970) 726-9247. Ice skaters can try the **Fraser Ice Rink,** 601 Zerex Avenue, (970) 726-4708. The rink is free, but bring your own skates. It is outdoors and features bonfires at night.

Winter Park guides also offer Sno-Cat rides to the top of the ski mountain and snowshoe tours that start with a lift ride and conclude with a gentle descent through wooded terrain. Get information and reservations for both at (970) 726-1616.

Summer Fun

Every summer the green slopes of Winter Park are the site of acclaimed musical events. If you plan to go, bring a lawn chair and rain gear. Other summer activities include an alpine slide, mountainside minigolf, a human maze, a climbing wall, and bungee and gyroscope rides. Winter Park also is known as Mountain Bike Capital USA. More than 600 miles of marked, mapped, and maintained trails wind through the Fraser Valley. At the ski area itself, riders can take the easy way up via the Zephyr Express chairlift to connect with another 45 miles of steep, exciting trails. Pick up a trail map at local bike stores or the Chamber of Commerce Visitor Center on the east side of US 40 downtown. Bike rentals are available at any number of local stores.

The Fraser River Trail is paved and the easiest, most mellow ride for families; it's good for in-line skaters, too. Valley trails go up from there, to rides even locals find frightening. Helmets, of course, are highly recommended. An all-day park pass for all activities, including the Zephyr lift for mountain biking, is $49. A Zephyr ticket for mountain biking also is available.

Golfers will enjoy the beautiful 27-hole **Pole Creek Golf Club** about 10 miles northwest of Winter Park in the town of Tabernash. Pole Creek consistently rates as one of the top public courses in Colorado. Look for more details in our Parks and Recreation Chapter. There also is the **Grand Lake Golf Course,** about 40 miles farther west. It's not quite Pole Creek, but it's easier to get tee times.

Nongolfers can choose among fishing, hiking, horseback riding, Jeeping, and rafting. Much of the Fraser Valley that isn't privately owned falls within the boundaries of the Arapaho National Forest. The Winter Park/Fraser Valley Chamber of Commerce can provide more information.

Dining

Winter Park has traditionally been a day-use area for Denver families, but as it grows, so do the dining choices.

Gasthaus Eichler, in downtown Winter Park on US 40, is noted for its Austrian and German specialties. Reservations are suggested, (970) 726-5133. **Deno's Mountain Bistro,** (970) 726-5332, is also located in downtown Winter Park on US 40. Locals have been coming here since 1973 for steaks, pasta, pizza, and some of the best burgers in town. Its après-ski atmosphere is one of the town's mellowest. It's open for breakfast, lunch, and dinner.

Carvers Bakery & Cafe, (970) 726-8202, is a popular breakfast location. It can be hard to find, tucked behind Cooper Creek Square, but locals agree it's worth the search. Housed in a quaint log building, it's known for home-baked breads and pastries. Its lunches are just as good, featuring homemade soups, stews, and vegetarian dishes.

Lodge at Sunspot at the top of Winter Park mountain, is a great experience if you're looking for something a little more memorable. Reservations are suggested, (970) 726-1444. For more casual dining and nightlife—it can get wild at times—there's the **Crooked Creek Saloon & Eatery** at 401 Zerex Avenue off US 40 in Fraser, (970) 726-9250, which serves Mexican and American food and no small amount of beer.

Accommodations

Accommodations in Winter Park range from mountainside condos to bed-and-breakfasts in town. **Winter Park Central Reservations,** (800) 979-0332, can arrange lodging in more than 50 condominiums, motels, hotels, lodges, inns, and bed-and-breakfasts.

If full-service hotels are what you're after, check into the **Vintage Hotel,** (800) 472-7017 or www.vintagehotel.com. Its restaurant, Five Mountain Tavern, is a reasonably priced family place, featuring American home-style food, sandwiches, and pizzas. There's a pool on-site. **Arapahoe Ski Lodge,** (970) 726-8222, offers moderately priced lodging packages with breakfast and dinner or breakfast only.

Buy reduced-price lift tickets at Metro Denver locations including Safeway, and King Soopers supermarkets; Total gas stations; and Sports Authority, Christy's, and REI sporting goods stores.

The bulk of available lodgings are condominiums in larger complexes. **Beaver Village Resort,** (800) 666-0281, is well-run and centrally located, although not lavish. The **Viking Lodge,** (800) 421-4013, is great for small budgets, and it's clean and well maintained.

SUMMIT COUNTY

Summit County's four ski areas—Breckenridge, Keystone, Arapahoe Basin, and Copper Mountain—collectively attract more skiers than any other ski destination in North America. And why not? There offer tremendous variety, good shopping and restaurants, dependably fine snow, and easy access from Metro Denver.

Summit County is about 90 minutes west of Denver on I-70. We've treated each Summit County area separately, but things are close enough that it's possible to ski at Breckenridge, eat in Dillon, and stay overnight in Frisco. An excellent free public transportation system, the Summit Stage, makes it easy to get around without a car. Pick up a schedule at the visitor center in Frisco, 011 South Summit Boulevard, or in Dillon, on US 6 about 1 mile south of I-70 at the Dillon Dam Road. The visitor centers are open daily year-round.

BRECKENRIDGE

To reach Breckenridge, take the Frisco exit from I-70 and drive south on Highway 9 for 9 miles.

Useful contact information:

BRECKENRIDGE RESORT CHAMBER AND CENTRAL RESERVATIONS
(800) 221-1091

BRECKENRIDGE SKI RESORT
general information: (970) 453-5000
http://breckenridge.snow.com

BRECKENRIDGE WELCOME CENTER
(970) 453-5579

TOWN OF BRECKENRIDGE TROLLEY
Information: (970) 547-3140

Winter Activities

The oldest and largest of the Summit County communities, Breckenridge is a former mining town that got its start when gold was discovered nearby in 1859. Its Main Street is a National Historic District lined with handsome Victorian buildings that now house great shops, art galleries, and restaurants. Breckenridge has 27 lifts and more than 2,208 skiable acres spread across four distinct peaks. There's close-in pay parking near Beaver Run and the Peak 8 base, but most skiers park in one of the town's public lots and take the free shuttle to the slopes. Cross-country skiers and snowshoers can find what they're looking for at the Nordic skiing center adjacent to the ski area, (970) 453-6855. Other winter activities in Breckenridge include sleigh rides, snowmobiling, ice skating, and a variety of distinct winter festivals. Visit our Annual Events and Festivals chapter for more information. Ice-skating is available at the outdoor Maggie Pond, at the Village at Breckenridge, (800) 847-5445, and the indoor Breckenridge Ice Rink, (970) 547-9974.

Escape the ski resort crowds at the Frisco Nordic Center, alongside Dillon Reservoir about

5 miles north of Breckenridge. Snowshoers and cross-country skiers find serenity among snow-covered evergreens and sloping trails. Stop at the horse barn and have lunch on the seat of a sleigh. Rentals and maps are available at the center's outpost. Call (970) 668-0866.

Snowmobilers can book rides with Good Times Adventures at (970) 453-7604. Sno-Cat tours are operated out of Ski Cooper, a small local ski area near Leadville, (719) 486-2277. For disabled skiers, adaptive skiing with special seats and equipment is offered by the Breckenridge Outdoor Education Center, (970) 453-6422.

Summer Fun

In summer there's hiking in the Arapaho National Forest and outstanding golf at the Jack Nicklaus-designed municipal course, the **Breckenridge Golf Club,** (970) 453-9104. More information is included in our Parks and Recreation chapter.

The Pioneer Trail is an easy and popular trail for mountain bikers. Start at the top of the Colorado SuperChair and wind down the front side of Peak 8, through thick forests and wide-open ski runs. Breckenridge offers lift rides up for mountain bikers.

The **Breckenridge Recreation Center** at 880 Airport Road, (970) 453-1734, is open every day except Christmas and has indoor and outdoor tennis courts, a pool, racquetball courts, a steam room, a hot tub, and separate locker room facilities for men and women. Visitors can purchase a daily admission.

If you'd rather see the Ten Mile Range from the back of a horse, check out the gentle horses at **Breckenridge Stables,** (970) 453-4438. Two 90-minute rides are available, one of which is a breakfast ride.

The Blue River, which runs through Breckenridge, is a favorite fly-fishing locale. Fishing licenses are required and can be purchased at sporting goods stores where fishing equipment and bait are sold. A water activity in Breckenridge that's fun for the whole family is paddleboating on Maggie Pond in the Village at Breckenridge.

The **Breckenridge Outdoor Education Center,** (970) 453-6422, also offers disabled visitors summer recreation events such as kayaking and rope courses.

Dining

Breckenridge has superb dining options. Among my favorites are the **Briar Rose,** 109 Lincoln Avenue, (970) 453-9948; **Cafe Alpine,** 106 East Adams Avenue, (970) 453-8218, a dinner only room that is known for its tapas bar and wines by the glass; **Breckenridge Brewery,** 600 South Main Street, (970) 453-1550, which is one of the state's first brewpubs; the **Blue Moose Restaurant,** 540 South Main Street, (970) 453-4859, which has affordable natural food and a friendly atmosphere; and **Mi Casa Mexican Restaurant & Cantina,** 600 South Park Street, (970) 453-2071, which serves Mexican lunches and dinners (no reservations) with daily specials.

Shopping

Breckenridge's shopping also gets rave reviews. A few hours spent walking up and down Main Street will acquaint you with the very best the town has to offer. In addition to the usual array of T-shirt and souvenir shops, there are galleries to check out. Get a complete list of them at the **Breckenridge Welcome Center,** 309 North Main Street, (970) 453-6018.

You won't want to miss **The Twisted Pine,** 505 South Main Street, and 100 South Main Street. It features fur and leather apparel and mountain home decor. For a free catalog call (970) 453-6615. **Goods,** at 105 South Main Street, is the most popular basic clothing shop in town.

Accommodations

Accommodations in Breckenridge range from luxury condominiums to Victorian-style bed-and-breakfasts in historic homes. The Breckenridge Central Reservations, (877) 593-5260 can help with listings and reservations. **Barn on the River** bed-and-breakfast, 303 North Main Street, (970) 453-2975, is an especially well-appointed 19th-century trio of buildings with period furniture and antiques, but guests also enjoy the modern pleasures of whirlpool tubs for two, private balconies, and sumptuous breakfasts. The **Village at Breckenridge,** (970) 453-5192, is a huge complex with athletic facilities. **Pine Ridge Condominiums,** (800) 333-8833, has full kitchens and washer/dryers in the units. The complex has two common hot tubs and a pool. The **Lodge & Spa** at Breckenridge, (970) 453-9300, has the distinction of being the world's highest athletic club and spa. The fitness center features individualized training for all levels. The **River Mountain Lodge,** (970) 453-4711, offers the convenience of being in town and is of high quality. **Allaire Timbers Inn,** (970) 453-7530, is a high-end bed-and-breakfast with each room decorated individually. **Beaver Run Resort,** (800) 525-2253, is a ski-in/ski-out resort that's popular with visitors.

KEYSTONE

To get there, exit onto US 6 at the Dillon-Silverthorne exit 205, turning left at the traffic light. Keystone is 6 miles down the road.

Useful contact information:

KEYSTONE RESORT
General information and reservations:
(970) 496-2316
http://keystone.snow.com

SUMMIT CHAMBER OF COMMERCE
(970) 668-2051

Winter Activities

Keystone is known for its excellent beginner and intermediate slopes, as well as steep and bumpy terrain on North Peak, and powder-filled glades at Outback and the Outback Bowls. It excels at snowmaking, which often allows the ski runs to open earlier than its neighbors, and offers night skiing on some nights until 8:30 p.m. Keystone runs daily NASTAR races, including a self-timing system that allows skiers to improve with practice runs.

Keystone's Nordic Center, (970) 496-4275, is located in The River Course clubhouse on the west side of the resort. It has 16 kilometers of groomed trails and 57 kilometers of packed trails in the White River National Forest, and offers programs in cross-country skiing, snowshoeing, ski-skating, telemark skiing, and family tubing. If you'd rather strike out on your own, some of the best cross-country skiing in Summit County is found by continuing along the road to Montezuma past the Ski Tip Lodge. Peru Creek (for beginners) and St. Johns and Wild Irishman Mine (for intermediates) are favorite tours for Front Range skiers. Remember to take precautions: Don't go unless you are an experienced skier, and even then let someone know where you're going and when you expect to return.

As for other winter activities, Keystone is home to Keystone Lake, the largest maintained outdoor skating lake in the country. It's right in the center of the village, and skate rentals are available. Sleigh rides and snowmobiling can be arranged by calling the Keystone Activities Center.

Summer Fun

In summer Dillon Reservoir—locally known as Lake Dillon—provides landlocked Coloradans with one of the state's greatest recreational assets, a 3,000-acre reservoir ringed by mountains. The lake can accommodate sailboats, kayaks, and fishing boats; charters are available. Weather and water-level permitting, the marina is open from the end of May through the last weekend in October. Swimming is allowed but only recommended for the hearty, as this mountain reservoir is ice-cold even in August. For information call the Dillon Marina at (970) 468-5100.

There's golf at the **Keystone Ranch Golf Club,** (970) 496-4250, designed by Robert Trent Jones Jr.; the **River Course** at Keystone, (970) 496-4444; and the **Raven Golf Club** at Three Peaks, (970) 262-3636.

The main fishing artery in Summit County is the Blue River, where anglers aim for trout. For more information, contact a local fishing shop or the Colorado Division of Wildlife, (303) 291-7533.

Mountain bikers can sign up for the resort's **Dirt Camp** weekends, in which elite-level coaching and training techniques are taught by world-class professionals. Hikers may want to try a Llama Lunch Trek, where you have fun hiking while the llama carries your lunch.

Dining

The award-winning **Alpenglow Stube,** atop Keystone's North Peak, serves Bavarian-accented contemporary cuisine for lunch and dinner and is reached via enclosed gondola chairlift. It is closed during the spring and autumn shoulder seasons, when the gondola doesn't operate. The rustic **Keystone Ranch,** rated among Colorado's best restaurants by the Zagat Survey, is a restored ranch with six-course dinners. It's open year-round. To make a reservation at either restaurant (required), call Keystone's Dining & Activities center, (970) 496-4386.

Cook your own steaks on the grill at **The Mint in Silverthorne,** 347 Blue River Parkway, (970) 468-5247. In one of the county's oldest buildings, The Mint is a fun-for-the-whole-family dining spot. For a hearty pre-ski or pre-sail breakfast, take your appetite to the **Arapahoe Cafe & Pub,** 626 Lake Dillon Drive in Dillon, (970) 468-0873. **The Snake River Saloon,** 23074 US 6 in Keystone, (970) 468-2788, is locally famous for its spirited après-ski and late-night entertainment. **The Ski Tip Lodge,** (970) 496-4950, offers American regional cuisine, including several wild-game dishes, in a rustic atmosphere. This historic spot was Colorado's first skiers' lodge. Seating is limited so reservations are essential.

Keystone Resort has three fun options, all accessible at (970) 354-4386. **Der Fondue Chessel,** (970) 354-4386, entertains diners with Bavarian music while serving them a Swiss-style four-course fondue dinner. Dinner sleigh and wagon rides pull guests up to the **Soda Creek Homestead** and serve a Western-style meal while a cowboy performer leads the crowd in a sing-along. The **Bighorn Steakhouse** in Keystone's village is a good place to enjoy a western meal while overlooking the lake.

Shopping

The factory outlet stores in Silverthorne are reason enough to drive up from Denver. Clustered in three malls just off I-70 at exit 205 are bargain outlets for 80 well-known manufacturers, including **Bass Shoes, Eddie Bauer, Nike, OshKosh B'Gosh, Great Outdoor Clothing,** and **Wilson's Leather.** The stores are open seven days a week and claim a 40 percent average savings over retail. For information call (970) 468-5780.

Accommodations

Accommodations in Keystone are plentiful, with 1,600 lodging units available at the resort in seven neighborhoods. They include the luxurious Keystone Lodge and the truly deluxe Chateaux d'Mont. There are also condominiums of all sizes and private homes available for rent. Contact **Keystone Reservations,** (970) 496-4242. **Western Skies Bed and Breakfast,** (970) 468-9445, features a secluded 10,500-foot elevation and reasonable rates. **The Ski Tip Lodge,** (970) 496-4950, offers good access to cross-country trails in a funky historic Colorado building.

Simpler but charming and comfortable lodging can be found in Frisco, Dillon, and Silverthorne. The **Galena Street Mountain Inn,** (970) 668-3224 or (800) 248-9138, is a pretty, modern bed-and-breakfast in Frisco tucked a half-block back from Main Street and near the bike path. The **Best Western Ptarmigan Lodge,** (970) 468-2341, is on Lake Dillon at 652 Lake Dillon Drive (take exit 205 off I-70). The lodge has deluxe motel accommodations, kitchenettes, and condominiums with fireplaces. The **Best Western Lake Dillon Lodge** at 1202 North Summit Boulevard in Frisco, (970) 668-5094, has some family rooms with three double beds, as well as an indoor pool, hot tub, restaurant, lounge, and ski shop. The 217-room **Holiday Inn** at 1129 North Summit Boulevard in Frisco, (970) 668-5000, is more convenient than scenic. There's an indoor pool, sauna, hot tubs, restaurant, lounge, gift shop, and ski shop on the premises, and you are also within walking distance of Frisco shops and restaurants.

With ski traffic mounting every year, think about renting a condo for the weekend to avoid day-skiing hassles. On Saturday take a shuttle to the slopes. To avoid the heavy weekend traffic through Idaho Springs on Sunday, be the first on the slopes and the first to leave, or stay another night and drive down in the morning.

ARAPAHOE BASIN

To reach Arapahoe Basin, take I-70 to exit 205, Dillon/Silverthorne, and follow US 6 for 12 miles. Arapahoe Basin is 5 miles past Keystone.

Useful contact information:
(970) 468-0718, www.arapahoebasin.com

At a base altitude of 10,800 feet above sea level, Arapahoe Basin is where Insiders head for unbeatable spring skiing. On years when late snows replenish its base, Arapahoe has welcomed skiers through the first week of August, but that's not its only claim to fame. Arapahoe Basin offers the highest lift-served terrain on the North American continent, with a summit at 13,050 feet. It is characterized by tough terrain and tough weather conditions—but a good day here is a great day. Don't forget the sunscreen.

Arapahoe Basin is a full-service resort, if not glamorous. The most important thing you'll find here is great skiing (490 acres; 40 percent expert), backed by a cafeteria, bar, ski school, rental shop, and retail store.

COPPER MOUNTAIN

Useful contact information:

COPPER MOUNTAIN CHAMBER OF COMMERCE
(970) 968-6477

COPPER MOUNTAIN RESORT
General information, **(970) 968-2882**
www.coppercolorado.com

SUMMIT COUNTY CHAMBER OF COMMERCE
(970) 668-2051

Winter Activities

Copper Mountain was constructed in the early 1970s as a self-contained resort. It's still a very enticing place for experienced skiers, with 2,400 acres of skiable terrain and more than three-quarters of the trails ranked intermediate to expert.

Copper is Summit County's largest ski area. More than $500 million has been spent since 1998 to refurbish the base area. Among the additions were expanded base restaurants near the Super Bee lift, Commons, and Union Creek; additional snow-making capacity; and a Super Pipe Dragon for carving out a larger half-pipe.

Copper has also put a great deal of effort into its ski school program, so beginners will feel comfortable here as well. In the past, Copper has even offered free skiing on its easiest lifts, K and L, which access 53 acres of terrain and have an easy grade just right for the first-time skier or boarder. The mountain is naturally divided between harder and easier skiing.

The cross-country skiing tracks begin near the Union Creek base area and branch off into the rolling, wooded valleys of the Arapaho National Forest. Dinner sleigh rides are offered nightly in winter and in summer (on wheels) and include a gourmet meal mid-mountain. Call the Copper Mountain Stables at (970) 968-2232.

Summer Fun

The **Copper Creek Golf Club** is the highest-altitude championship golf course in America, at 9,650 feet, which means your ball will fly 15 percent farther than at sea level. Summer activities include an outdoor climbing wall, a quad-powered bungee jump and Go-Karts. Hikers, backpackers, and horseback riders enjoy challenging themselves on the Wheeler-Dillon Pack Trail, which begins across the highway from Copper Mountain and climbs rapidly into the rugged Gore Range in the Arapaho National Forest. The Colorado Trail, a 469-mile trail that extends from Denver to Durango, passes near Copper Mountain, too. You can also arrange a breakfast or dinner horseback ride out of Copper Mountain Stables.

From mid-June until about Labor Day you can ride the American Eagle lift free. Also free is the 18-hole Frisbee golf course through the base of the village. Mountain bikers can ride up the lift, for a fee, and ride down on either the mountain road or a twisty single-track. Bike rentals are easily found. Try Gravitee, (970) 968-0171. Intermediate riders might want to try the Ten Mile Canyon ride, which follows the old railroad grade along Ten Mile Creek.

Dining

Endo's Adrenaline Cafe, (970) 968-3070, is the place to chow down on huge sandwiches and specialty drinks. It's located in the Mountain Plaza Building. At **Double Diamond,** (970) 968-2880, in the Foxpine Inn, you'll find a selection of steaks, sandwiches, pizza, and burgers. **Tucker's Tavern,** (970) 968-2033, features burgers, top sirloin sandwiches, pizza and a full dinner menu. It is located in Snow-bridge Square.

Accommodations

Copper Mountain is about 75 miles west of Denver. To get there, take I-70 west to exit 195. Virtually all the overnight lodging at Copper Mountain is in condominiums. Call **Copper Mountain Resort** for rental information.

VAIL AND BEAVER CREEK

Vail is located on I-70 about 100 miles west of Denver; Beaver Creek is 11 miles farther west.

Useful contact information:

BEAVER CREEK RESORT
(970) 845-9090
www.beavercreek.com

VAIL/BEAVER CREEK RESERVATIONS
(970) 845-5745

VAIL RESORT
(970) 476-5601
http://vail.snow.com

VAIL VALLEY PARTNERSHIP
(970) 476-1000

Winter Activities

For as long as Vail has been a playground of plenty, Front Range residents have had a love-hate relationship with it. They love the skiing—acres and acres of varied, magnificently designed slopes—but hate the crowds, glitz, and high prices. Driving to Vail from Denver also means navigating Vail Pass, which can be treacherous in bad weather and an incentive to exit at Copper Mountain or sooner. Still, every self-respecting skier should try Vail at least once. It's the largest single ski-mountain complex in North America: three base areas, more high-speed quad chairlifts than any other ski area, and vast powder-filled back bowls that spread out across 5,200 acres of spectacular alpine terrain. China Bowl alone is as large as many ski areas. Intermediates especially can ski all day and never go down the same run twice. It attracts a diverse international crowd, so expect to hear a variety of foreign languages on the slopes and in the shops. The Eagle Bahn gondola is heated and lighted. The Adventure Ridge mountaintop activity center features an outdoor skating rink, snowmobile tours, and other winter activities. Chaos Canyon is for kids only, featuring an obstacle course and other kid-friendly attractions.

A ticket at Vail also is valid at Beaver Creek, Vail's little (but even richer and more exclusive) sister 11 miles farther west. First opened in 1980-81, elegant Beaver Creek attracts an international elite clientele as well as local skiers who praise the area for its spectacular natural beauty, lack of crowds, free parking, and intimate feel. About 65 percent of the runs at Beaver Creek are intermediate or advanced. Snowboarding is permitted at Vail and Beaver Creek.

Kids do not ski free here. There are, however, a total of 12 kids-only areas (in addition to the large Chaos Canyon) featuring historical Indian tepee villages, a mountain lion's den, ski-through mock gold mines, and a fort. Modeled after a Tyrolean village, Vail is a charming town that caters to pedestrians. Free buses link all the base areas and run from morning to late night. Vail is home to the **Colorado Ski Museum,** at the Vail Transportation Center, (970) 476-1876, and is the frequent site of World Cup ski races. Vail and Beaver Creek have Nordic centers that offer lessons as well as equipment rentals and tours. Vail's Nordic Center is located at the Vail Golf Course, (970) 476-8366, with backcountry access to Vail Mountain and the White River National Forest and the **Beaver Creek Nordic Sports Center,** (970) 754-5313, at the bottom of Strawberry Park lift (chair 12). At Beaver Creek skiers and snowshoers ride the lift up to McCoy Park, which is home to a system of groomed trails.

There are abundant opportunities for backcountry touring throughout the Vail Valley; the summit of Vail Pass itself is often the first ski tour of the year for many Denver backcountry enthusiasts, as it receives plentiful early snow. The town of Vail and Vail Pass are the starting or ending points for several overnight tours to huts that were built during World War II for soldiers from the 10th Mountain Division, including the (relatively) luxurious Shrine Mountain Inn. Reservations are essential; call the **10th Mountain Division Hut Association,** (970) 925-5775.

The bobsled run at Vail is a thrilling ride. Snowmobile and sleigh rides can be booked through local companies, and Vail's world-class **John A. Dobson Ice Arena** is open for public skating, (970) 479-2271.

The **Adventure Ridge** mountaintop activity center, (970) 476-9090, features an outdoor skating rink, tubing hill, snowmobile tours, thrill sledding, ski biking, laser tag, snowshoeing, orienteering, and a free nature center. It's open in winter only until 10 p.m. and has three restaurants.

Summer Fun

Summer is glorious in the Vail Valley. In fact, many Denverites who avoid Vail's winter glitz look forward to its more laid-back summer style. Hikers and backpackers can explore a large network of trails, either on foot or on horseback. Most of these trails are fairly steep, but the many lakes and waterfalls provide lots of resting and picnic spots. Much of the land around Vail is part of the White River National Forest. For suggested routes and maps, call or visit the **Holy Cross Ranger District Office,** (970) 827-5715, located in Minturn at 24747 US 24.

Four chairlifts on Vail and Beaver Creek mountains make it easy to reach new mountain-biking heights and nearly 100 miles of world-class trails. Rentals are easy to find at any number of shops in town or at the Wildwood Shelter on top of Vail's Wilderness Express lift.

The Vail Valley has several public and private golf courses, the most touted of which is the **Beaver Creek Golf Club,** (970) 845-5775, a Robert Trent Jones Jr. course. The **Cordillera Club,** (970) 569-6480, has four courses in four microclimates, from valley floor to mountain summit. A fun and more affordable option is the **Eagle-Vail Golf Club,** (970) 949-5267, located between Vail and Avon. **Vail Golf Club,** (970) 479-2260, is a par 71 public course with spectacular views of the Gore Range.

If you'd like to hike or ride a mountain bike in the Holy Cross Wilderness Area near Vail, Aspen, or Copper Mountain but aren't keen on sleeping in tents, the 10th Mountain Division Hut Association huts also are open in the summer from July 1 through September 30. Call (970) 925-5775 for more information or to make reservations.

If you're looking for Vail glamour, book a treatment at the **Sonnenalp Resort**'s spa, (970) 479-5404. For the musically inclined, the **Bravo! Vail Valley Music Festival,** (970) 827-5700, features an array of classical music and jazz.

Dining

Two of the state's finest restaurants are in Vail: **Sweet Basil,** 193 East Gore Creek Drive, (970) 476-0125, and **The Wildflower,** 174 East Gore Creek Drive in the Lodge at Vail, (970) 476-5011.

Both are expensive but well worth it for special occasions; reservations are recommended. Sweet Basil serves inventive American cuisine in a pretty spot by Gore Creek. The Wildflower offers up superbly creative American cuisine in an elegant setting. Less expensive is **Los Amigos,** (970) 476-5847, at the top of Bridge Street, which serves standard Mexican fare in a bustling atmosphere. Also more for the budget-minded, **Blu's,** 193 East Gore Creek Drive, (970) 476-3113, is a long-time favorite serving breakfast, lunch, and dinner. The food is eclectic American cuisine, including soups, salads, pizzas, great desserts, and coffee.

Dining in Beaver Creek is even more heavily tilted toward the expensive than Vail, and reservations are de rigueur. **Mirabelle,** located in a former home at 55 Village Road, (970) 949-7728, receives high praise for its romantic ambience, excellent service, and French cuisine with a twist. It's closed briefly during the spring and fall, between ski season and summer. Up on the slopes of Beaver Creek, **Beano's Cabin** offers more than just a meal. Reached by sleigh ride, this elegant log-and-glass lodge offers six-course gourmet meals as well as entertainment for adults and children. In the summer you can get there via horseback or horse-drawn wagon (about a one-hour trip) or by shuttle van (a 10-minute trip). Naturally, an experience like this does not come cheap. For reservations call (877) 354-0061. For a more casual meal, visit **Pazzo's Pizzeria,** 122 East Meadow Drive, (970) 476-9026, at the end of the Vail Village pedestrian mall.

Shopping

Vail and Beaver Creek are known for their fine selection of shops and galleries, but this is not bargain shopping. Sticker-shock is common, as are full-length furs, custom-designed jewelry, and designer labels. Vail and Beaver Creek offer resort-town shopping at its finest. **The Golden Bear,** 286 Bridge Street, has ladies' clothing and men's and ladies' jewelry, including earrings, pendants, bracelets, and other accessories featuring its trademark golden bear (available in sterling silver,

too). **Pepi Sports,** 231 Bridge Street, is another longtime source for outerwear and sportswear as well as ski, bike, and in-line skate rentals. There's also **True North,** 100 East Meadow Drive, which stocks an array of Canadian-designed outerwear, sweaters, pants, and boots. **Slifer Designs** specializes in interior design and is located in nearby Edwards. For colorful, contemporary regional art, visit Vail Village Arts, 100 East Meadow Drive.

Accommodations

A reasonably priced room can be hard to come by in the Vail Valley. When money is no object, grand lodges and luxury hotels are happy to oblige. Try **The Lodge at Vail,** (970) 476-5011; **Beaver Creek Lodge,** (800) 525-7280; and the truly special **Lodge & Spa at Cordillera,** (800) 877-3529. A bed-and-breakfast somewhat off the beaten path is the **Minturn Inn,** 422 Main Street in Minturn, (970) 827-9647, a completely refurbished 1915 hewn-log home. **The Roost,** (970) 476-5451, touts itself as the least expensive lodging in Vail and offers continental breakfast.

SKI COUNTRY RESOURCES

ARAPAHO NATIONAL FOREST
Dillon Ranger District,
680 Blue River Parkway, Silverthorne
(970) 468-5400
www.fs.fed.us

COLORADO CROSS COUNTRY SKI ASSOCIATION
Information on cross-country centers
www.colorado-xc.org

COLORADO DIVISION OF WILDLIFE
Fishing information, (303) 291-7533
www.wildlife.state.co.us/fishing

DAILY SKI CONDITIONS/REPORTS (STATEWIDE)
(303) 825-7669
www.coloradoski.com

NATIONAL WEATHER SERVICE
Denver and central mountains
(303) 494-4221
www.crh.noaa.gov/den/
Road conditions within two hours of Denver,
(303) 639-1111
http://cotrip.org

**10TH MOUNTAIN DIVISION HUT
ASSOCIATION**
Aspen
(970) 925-5775
www.huts.org

USDA FOREST SERVICE
Denver Regional Office
740 Simms Street, Lakewood
(303) 275-5350
www.fs.fed.us

U.S. GEOLOGICAL SURVEY
Topographical maps
(303) 202-4700
www.usgs.gov

WHITE RIVER NATIONAL FOREST OFFICE
900 Grand Avenue, Glenwood Springs
(970) 945-2521
www.fs.fed.us

SPECTATOR SPORTS

Spend a few days in Denver, and you're likely to think the term "sports town" was coined for the Mile-High City. This town is rabid about its teams.

Denver is one of only a few cities that boast five big-league sports teams: football's Denver Broncos, baseball's Colorado Rockies, hockey's Colorado Avalanche, basketball's Denver Nuggets, and soccer's Colorado Rapids. When baseball's National League was looking for expansion cities, a majority of metro Denver fans anted up with a tax hike to fund a stadium. "Build it and they will come" became the local mantra. We have Coors Field to show for our efforts.

The Pepsi Center opened as home to the Denver Nuggets and Colorado Avalanche in 1999. The 675,000-square-foot arena is also host to dozens of other events such as concerts, circuses, and ice shows. It is located in the Central Platte Valley on the edge of downtown and is connected by a pedestrian walkway to Elitch Gardens amusement park. Inside are 17 concession stands, a 236-seat club restaurant, 95 luxury suites, and fully upholstered cast-iron armchairs throughout the arena. The INVESCO Field at Mile High opened in fall 2001 to house the Denver Broncos. That year it hosted the first Monday-night game of the season when the Broncos met the New York Giants on September 10. The latest addition is Dick's Sporting Goods Park in Commerce City, the home field for the Rapids soccer team, which opened in 2007.

The National Western Complex and Coliseum in central Denver host periodic livestock events and rodeos, the largest of which is the National Western Stock Show & Rodeo in January. It's detailed in our Annual Events and Festivals chapter.

BASEBALL

COLORADO ROCKIES
Coors Field, 2001 Blake Street
(303) ROC-KIES (762-5437)
www.rockies.mlb.com

The Colorado Rockies was one of two expansion teams added to the National League in 1993. Despite a losing inaugural season, they won the hearts of Coloradans and received national media attention for the record-breaking attendance they attracted.

After two seasons playing in Mile High Stadium, the Rockies began their 1995 season in their new home, Coors Field, at Blake and 20th Streets. Designed by Hellmuth, Obata & Kassabaum, a Kansas City firm, the 50,249-seat all-baseball stadium is an updated version of a classic ballpark. Its exterior is built of two shades of red brick, and its seats provide views of the Rocky Mountains. The nation got a good look at Coors Field when Denver hosted the 1998 All-Star Game. The game was a weeklong celebration of baseball and Lower Downtown fun for thousands of local and visiting fans.

Such an intense focus on baseball in Colorado once made the best game seats hard to come by, but things have since eased up, and good seats are available for almost every game. During the season, tickets can be purchased at the stadium at Gate C between 20th and 21st Streets and Blake Street or at Rockies Dugout Stores and King Soopers supermarkets. Wheelchair-accessible seating is available. Day-of-game "Rockpile" seats go on sale at the stadium two hours prior to game time at discounted prices. Coors Field has two "family sections" where alcohol is not served. Ask for sections 141 and 342.

Close-up

Colorado Rockies Bring Baseball, Big Bucks, and Beer to LoDo

The time is the 1970s, the place is a small section of Denver—dirty, a little rough, and definitely seedy.

Brown bags and empty booze bottles litter the streets like bad reminders of the night before. Graffiti covers plywood, which covers shattered warehouse windows. The only signs of life are at night, and these aren't the signs of prosperity and possibility. If the place had a disclaimer, it would shout: "Danger: Go Away."

This is no place for America's favorite pastime.

Now fast-forward to the mid-1990s. Red brick surrounds gleaming windows in renovated warehouses. Litter is gone, replaced by bustling shops and streets and smiling pedestrians. Tourists lounge on the sunny patios of upscale joints and savor microbrewed beer. Above it all towers Coors Field, home of the Colorado Rockies.

This dramatic turnaround may sound like a scene from a developer's dream, but it's the reality of lower downtown Denver's revitalization. Much of the metamorphosis was prompted by the Colorado Rockies' new baseball stadium.

The Rockies have done wonders for Denver's economy and, specifically, the once-blighted area Insiders call "LoDo." An economic-impact study done in 1994 estimated the Rockies would bring nearly $200 million a year in new spending. That's a lot of beer and hot dogs.

Of course, there's more to LoDo than beer and dogs. In fact, unless the beer has a fancy name from one of 11 local brewpubs (Sagebrush Stout, anyone?) and the dogs are dressed up with freshly crushed green chile salsa and served in the center of a dazzling food display, it probably isn't in LoDo. Indeed, LoDo (sort of like SoHo, only not quite) is home of the hip, cool, and happening.

Development around the stadium in the past few years is remarkable. More than 40 new restaurants and brewpubs have sprung up in LoDo since Coors Field opened.

RTD (Regional Transportation District) provides special buses to and from Rockies games from 16 suburban park-and-rides. Regular service to and from Market Street Station also brings you within walking distance of the stadium but may not be as conveniently timed for evening games. Schedules and fare information are available at (303) 299-6000, www.rtd-denver.com, or TDD (303) 299-6089.

BASKETBALL

DENVER NUGGETS
The Pepsi Center, 1000 Chopper Place
(303) 405-1100
www.nba.com/nuggets
Under the guidance of head coach George Karl,

the Nuggets continue to pursue their playoff goals with a lineup mixture of seasoned veterans and top draft choices. Nuggets tickets are available by calling the number above or through Ticketmaster at (303) 830-TIXS. There are a number of special deals, such as family and youth nights and group discounts. Wheelchair seating is available on request. The Nuggets share the Pepsi Center, located in the Platte Valley next to Elitch Gardens, with the Colorado Avalanche.

FOOTBALL

DENVER BRONCOS
13655 Broncos Parkway, Englewood
(303) 649-9000
www.denverbroncos.com

High-rise residential buildings have also begun to rise around Coors Field. Now that the abandoned warehouses have been revived into posh lofts, many of which advertised "Coors Field access," a new Ballpark Neighborhood is emerging that is seen as an incubator for art studios, galleries, and other creative enterprises.

The city of Denver has done its part to build the area. Baseball-related infrastructure improvements include millions in road construction (at least $36 million for the city of Denver alone). Another $5 million has gone toward LoDo economic development projects and streetscaping.

In fairness to the LoDo area, much of the revival was launched pre-Rockies. But nearly everyone agrees the Rockies have stimulated business and interest in LoDo. The Rockies alone bring more than three million people to downtown during baseball season (of course, many of those are repeat customers). But the games lure people downtown who might not otherwise have made the trek—like suburbanites who in the '80s stayed away from the city. Those same people, having sampled the excitement and vibrancy of LoDo, return to eat, shop, and party. In a downtown Denver survey, 37 percent of metro respondents said baseball was the main reason they went downtown.

"It's turned LoDo into a year-round destination," says Ben Wright, chief economist for the Denver Metro Chamber of Commerce.

To some extent, the phenomenon happened out of luck—and lack of parking. A dearth of spaces near Coors Field (only 15,000 spaces for 50,000 fans) was once considered a drawback. But the paucity has forced fans to park in lots all over downtown and walk to the game—passing enticing restaurants and shops along the way.

A recent nationwide survey placed the Rockies and Coors Field 11th on the list of top tourist attractions. LoDo rose in popularity to seventh place. How does a neighborhood achieve that kind of success while balancing the quality-of-life issues that having a major-league team in your backyard brings?

If you're Coors Field and lower downtown Denver, you do it with a little luck and a lot of style.

After losing three Super Bowls (1986, 1987, and 1989), the Broncos finally granted fans their ultimate wish—the 1997 championship. And then they followed with the 1998 championship. Broncos fans were joined by legions of John Elway supporters across the country who wanted to see the long-time quarterback win a Super Bowl title. Although Elway has since retired, it's no surprise that virtually every home game is a sellout. If you want to attend, you'll have to call well in advance for tickets and information or show up at the game and take your chances that someone in the parking lot has a ticket to sell. The Broncos played their first regular-season game in their new stadium, INVESCO field at Mile High, in the fall of 2001. The new stadium comes compliments of metro-area voters, who in November 1998 approved partial public funding for the old Mile High Stadium to be demolished and replaced with a state-of-the-art facility. Tickets, if you can get them, are available from the Broncos at (720) 258-3333 or through Ticketmaster at (303) 830-TIXS.

i The hottest spot to meet for pre-Broncos game beers, burgers, and boasting is Zang Brewing Company, 2301 7th Street, visible from INVESCO Field at Mile High. If you don't have tickets but want to experience Bronco fever, stop by any number of sports bars, including Jackson's Hole at 6th and Kipling Streets, to cheer on the team via television.

RTD's BroncoRide services all home games from a number of locations in Metro Denver, with special shuttles available for fans catching the BroncoRide along Federal Boulevard and at the Auraria campus. Call RTD at (303) 299-6000 for schedules and current fare information.

i The Broncos have developed a well-deserved reputation for finding little-known college running backs who become phenomenons in the team's offensive system. Starting with Terrell Davis, Denver has introduced the NFL to Mike Anderson, Olandis Gary, and Clinton Portis.

HOCKEY

COLORADO AVALANCHE
The Pepsi Center, 1000 Chopper Place
(303) 405-1100
www.coloradoavalanche.com
In mid-1995 Denver boasted about having four major-league teams when it announced that the Quebec Nordiques were coming to town, renamed as the Colorado Avalanche. In 1996 the boasting continued when its new team won the Stanley Cup. They repeated that win in 2001 against the New Jersey Devils in Game 7 of the series. The Avs remain an annual playoff contender, and they boast a legion of devoted followers. Single-game tickets go on sale in early fall at the number above, or at Ticketmaster, (303) 830-TIXS. Ask about group discounts if you plan to bring a crowd.

RACETRACKS

ARAPAHOE PARK RACETRACK
26000 East Quincy Avenue, Aurora
(303) 690-2400
www.mihiracing.com
Pari-mutuel thoroughbred, quarter horse, and other races are held here from June through early August, and other races from throughout the country are simulcast from the park. Call for dates and event details.

BANDIMERE SPEEDWAY
3051 South Rooney Road, Morrison
(303) 697-6001
(303) 697-4870 (recording)
www.bandimere.com
Championship drag racing events are held from April to October at Bandimere Speedway in Morrison (off C-470 between Alameda Avenue and Morrison Road). Events aren't limited to drag racing; they include motorcycle and snowmobile events as well as such unusual shows as "most unique vehicle" and "stereo wars."

COLORADO NATIONAL SPEEDWAY
4281 Weld County Road 10, Erie
(303) 665-4173
www.coloradospeedway.com
Colorado National Speedway is in Erie, 20 minutes north of Denver, off I-25 at exit 232. It hosts NASCAR and a variety of other races on a paved ⅜-mile oval track on Saturdays from April through September.

MILE HIGH GREYHOUND PARK
6200 Dahlia Street, Commerce City
(303) 288-1591,
www.mihiracing.com
Live pari-mutuel races take place at Mile High Greyhound Park in Commerce City June through August and again in December and January. Matinee and evening races are scheduled throughout the week. During the off-season, horse races are simulcast at the park. General admission is free, as is parking.

SOCCER

COLORADO RAPIDS
Dick's Sporting Goods Park
6000 Victory Way, Commerce City
(303) 405-1100
www.coloradorapids.com
The Colorado Rapids kicked off their first home game in April 1996 and have been gaining momentum ever since. In 1997 the team captured the western conference championship.

Close-up

INVESCO Field at Mile High

Nearly three years and $400 million after the proposed design of the new Denver Broncos stadium was unveiled, INVESCO Field at Mile High opened on August 11, 2001, with a concert featuring the Eagles. A pyrotechnics extravaganza followed, rivaling the millennium festivities in downtown Denver.

Throughout the development process, efforts were made to retain ties to the history of Mile High Stadium while creating a first-class, state-of-the-art facility. To that end, the new stadium logo incorporated the recognizable standing horse silhouette. And "Bucky" the bronco was reconditioned and moved to a perch atop the new south scoreboard. The "Mile High" moniker was negotiated into the naming rights agreement.

The differences, however, are more striking than the similarities, particularly in terms of amenities. While the seating capacity has remained nearly identical, the stadium's total square footage was doubled from 850,000 square feet to 1.7 million square feet. Approximately 8,500 club seats have been included, as well as 762 pairs of Americans with Disabilities Act-compliant seating. All seats have expanded in both width and length. Each seat now has a cup holder—a change welcomed by most but decried by a few for taking up precious leg room. Televisions, escalators, and a greater number of elevators have been added. The number of restrooms has doubled, and the number of concession stands has more than quadrupled. Finally, video boards have been added to each end of the field and increased in size over the one video board present in Mile High Stadium.

The naming of the stadium proved to be an emotionally charged issue for fans who had filled every seat in Mile High Stadium for every regular season game since 1970. Torn between reducing the public's debt load and retaining the historic "Mile High" name, the Metropolitan Football Stadium District was able to negotiate a naming rights agreement that incorporated "Mile High." INVESCO, a company that has had ties in the community for more than 70 years, will no doubt be on the lookout to prevent shortening of the name to "Mile High," but in agreeing to retain those words in the stadium name, they satisfied at least part of the public's desire.

The September 10 game between the Broncos and the New York Giants kicked off the 2001 Monday-night football season, while simultaneously being the first regular-season game in the new stadium. In addition to the Broncos, INVESCO Field at Mile High hosts community events and festivities.

In 1998 four of its star players made the All-Star lineup: Marcelo Balboa, Chris Henderson, Paul Bravo, and Adrian Paz. Along with the 1997 title, the team also has the distinction of raising its win/loss record from "worst" in 1996 to "first" in 1997. Attendance averages 15,000 per game. The Rapids moved to their new home in 2007, Dick's Sporting Goods Park in Commerce City. Tickets can be purchased at the number above or from Ticketmaster, (303) 830-TIXS.

DAY TRIPS

Measure 100 miles from Denver in any direction and you'll have defined more than 3,000 square miles from which to plan day trips. We've recommended a few that will take you north and south along the Front Range as well as west into the mountains. That's not to say that the Great Plains to the east aren't worth visiting. Few landscapes are more tranquilizing than the endless rolling prairie, and few things are more magnificent than 180 degrees of sky, but the majority of Colorado's visitors come with mountain scenery in mind. Bear in mind that snowstorms can render high mountain roads treacherous, if not impassable, from September through May. Consider calling (303) 639-1111 for the Colorado State Highway Patrol's report on road conditions before taking off on a mountain jaunt during these months. If conditions are bad, Make sure your vehicle has good snow tires or carry chains. If the chain law is in effect at a particular pass, those without chains will be turned back, no matter how good their tires are. And sometimes the road will close to all traffic until the weather improves. It's really a pain to pull out of Vail heading east up I-70 and discover that they've swung the gates closed across the interstate.

BOULDER

There's so much to do in this college town that a day trip won't do it justice. That said, we've outlined a few of the best things about Boulder. When approaching it on US 36, watch for the Louisville/Superior exit and watch for a sign that says Scenic Overlook. From that turnoff you'll get a stunning view of the town and its mountainside setting. During the warmer months, the Boulder Convention and Visitors Bureau operates an information kiosk on Davidson Mesa, as this hill is known.

Boulder is contained within the scenic bowl of Boulder Valley by the foothills of the Rocky Mountains. The most identifiable rock formation is the Flatirons, enormous sandstone monoliths

i When opening carbonated beverages in the car during high-altitude drives, remember that they have been bottled at a lower altitude and pressure. When opened, they can squirt in your face and all over the interior of your vehicle.

that lean against the slopes like a row of fossilized aircraft carriers.

Detractors still call it "the people's republic of Boulder," a nickname from the Vietnam era protest days that stuck. Today Boulder is a national mecca for alternative medicine, natural foods, spirituality, and outdoor sports such as bicycle racing, mountain biking, and technical climbing.

Naropa University, a national center for Buddhist studies based in Boulder, is the only fully accredited, Buddhist-inspired institution of higher education in North America, offering bachelor's and master's degrees. Tours of its main campus are offered weekdays at 2 p.m. when school is in session. Tours of the Paramita and Nalanda campuses are by reservation only. Call (303) 444-0202 or visit www.naropa.edu for more information.

Celestial Seasonings Herbal Tea, 4600 Sleepytime Drive, was founded here and still manufactures teas at its Gunbarrel headquarters. Tour the facility for an up-close look (and sniff) of the fragrant herbs that find their way into the teabags. Call (303) 581-1202 or visit www

.celestialseasonings.com for more details. Boulder is filled with other examples of innovation that has led to national recognition. Many are spin-offs started by scientists originally affiliated with the University of Colorado and federal government laboratories such as the National Center for Atmospheric Research and the National Institute of Standards and Technologies. CU is nationally prominent in fields ranging from molecular biology to telecommunications and works closely with that community.

Start your visit on the **Pearl Street Mall,** which serves as the center of the city. Formerly Boulder's main street, it's now a pedestrian mall lined with unique shops, restaurants, art galleries, flower gardens, and street performers. It makes for a delightful stroll in any but the worst weather, except for the occasional panhandler. Next try **University Hill,** south on Broadway from Pearl Street and up the hill, where you can enjoy a walk around the graceful CU campus.

Go farther south on Broadway past the campus to Baseline Road, turn right onto Baseline, and go up a long hill. Just past 9th Street you'll find the entrance to **Chautauqua Park & Auditorium** on the left. Its auditorium is a lovely venue for a summer evening concert. For information, call the Chautauqua box office at (303) 440-7666. If possible, stay for breakfast, lunch, or dinner at the **Chautauqua Dining Hall,** built in 1898, where you can gaze out at the mountains as you eat; call (303) 440-3776.

Chautauqua serves as the gateway to **Boulder Mountain Parks,** some 8,000 acres of trails and rough climbing through terrain that includes Bear Peak, Green Mountain, Flagstaff Mountain, and, of course, the Flatirons.

Another entrance to the park, and an attraction in its own right, is the **National Center for Atmospheric Research,** commonly referred to around Boulder simply as NCAR (say it EN-car). The agency works with universities to study the atmosphere, but its building, designed by the renowned architect I. M. Pei, may be its best known asset. It perches like an Italian hill fortress on a mesa to the south of Chautauqua, provid-

i It's always cool in the mountains at night, even in the summer. Take a sweater.

ing views of the mountains and plains and the weather fronts that move across them. You find it by going still farther south on Broadway from Baseline to Table Mesa Drive. Turn right, and keep going until you run into the facility. You may see deer on the way. You can pick up a map in the lobby and take the self-guided tour daily, including holidays. Guided tours take place daily at noon. The Science Store stocks a great selection of books and activities for children. And best of all, admission is free. More information is available at www.ncar.ucar.edu or (303) 497-1174. Outside NCAR, you can hike on 400 acres of the mesa top on a nature trail that is wheelchair-accessible. Just west of the mesa, you can access Boulder Mountain Park trails.

Climbers scaling the Flatirons are a common sight, but the best place for close-up watching of technical climbers is **Eldorado Canyon.** Keep going south on Broadway from Table Mesa Drive until Broadway becomes Highway 93. Watch for the Eldorado Springs Drive turnoff on the right or Highway 170, just more than 5 miles south of Boulder. **Eldorado Springs** is about 8 miles down that road. Around the turn of the century this resort town was called "the Coney Island of Colorado" because of the people who flocked here for resort hotels and 76-degree hot springs. Pass through the town to reach **Eldorado Canyon State Park,** where you'll find a magnificent cut between high cliffs. The little smudges of white on the rocks are chalk from climbers' hands. In good weather you'll see people dangling from the canyon walls.

COLORADO SPRINGS

"The Springs," as locals call it, is 67 miles or an hour's drive south of Denver. It has the largest single cluster of tourist attractions within day trip range. **Pikes Peak** is the biggest show in town.

You can drive to the top by taking US 24 west to Cascade and turning left on the same road driven by international auto racers to the summit during the annual Pikes Peak Hill Climb. Or you can do the dizzying trip on the **Pikes Peak Cog Railway.** Reach its terminal by driving west from Colorado Springs on US 24 to the Manitou exit, west on Manitou Avenue, and left onto Ruxton Avenue. This is the highest cog railway in the world. Established in 1889, it's a historical as well as a sensory experience. During the three-and-a-half-hour round-trip, you get more panoramas than you can stuff into your brain, including Manitou Springs and the Garden of the Gods below. On a clear day you can see north to Denver and south to New Mexico. Take care not to exert yourself too much at the 14,115-foot summit: Oxygen is scarce up there, and altitude sickness is not a pleasant experience. Also on the summit are an information center, gewgaw shop, and concession area. The railway is open daily from April to October, and reservations are required. Information is available at www.cograilway.com or (719) 685-5401.

Garden of the Gods is another of Colorado Springs's most famous sights. A drive through the park reveals one of the most spectacular displays of dramatic red sandstone formations in Colorado. It's just northwest of downtown at 1805 North 30th Street, (719) 634-6666, www.gardenofgods.com. **Cave of the Winds,** in Manitou Springs on Highway 24 West, is the biggest commercial underground cave in Colorado, and well worth touring. More information is available at (719) 685-5444 or www.caveofthewinds.com.

If you want to go a bit beyond the 100-mile limit of our day trip definition, you will certainly enjoy the Cripple Creek & Victor Narrow Gauge Railroad, (719) 689-2640, www.cripple-creek.co.us. **Cripple Creek,** one of Colorado's most famous old mining towns and a National Historic District, is worth visiting too. Since limited-stakes gambling was legalized here in 1991, the town's ambience has changed, but it still provides a peek into the state's rough and tumble ancestry. About an hour's drive from Colorado Springs

on Highway 115 is the Royal Gorge, where you can drive or walk across the world's highest suspension bridge 1,178 feet above the Arkansas River. The accompanying theme park includes an aerial tram, a minitrain, a carousel, a wildlife park, and an incline railway, a cagelike ride that takes you down to the bottom of the canyon to the river's edge. Information is available at www.royalgorgebridge.com or (719) 275-7507.

Other things do in the Colorado Springs area include the Victorian town of **Manitou Springs** and its natural hot springs; the **Cliff Dwellings Museum** on US 24, (719) 685-5242; the historic **Broadmoor Hotel,** (719) 634-7711, and its spa and 18-hole golf courses; **Santa's Workshop at the North Pole,** (719) 684-9432, a funland open mid-May through Christmas Eve; and the **Pro-Rodeo Hall of Fame,** which shares space with the **Museum of the American Cowboy,** both at (719) 528-4764.

Of all Colorado Springs's attractions, the busiest is the **U.S. Air Force Academy.** Although it covers 18,000 acres, visitor access is limited for security reasons. You can stop at the visitor center from 9 a.m. to 5 p.m. daily, take a self-guided driving tour around the grounds daily between 8 a.m. and 6 p.m., or walk the one-third-mile nature trail to the cadet chapel, which is architecturally striking. Perhaps the best way to experience the academy is at a football game or by attending the spring graduation ceremony, where you can watch cadets tossing their caps in the air and enjoy a performance by the Thunderbirds, the Air Force's famed jet-acrobatics team. You do need advance tickets for commencement, which is always held on the first Wednesday after Memorial Day. Call the academy's visitor center at (719) 333-2025 for tickets and other information.

Directly across I-25 from the north gate of the Air Force Academy is the **Western Museum of Mining and Industry.** It's a nice place for a picnic, with 27 acres of rolling hills, trees, meadows, streams, beaver ponds, and picnic tables. The museum itself has more than 15,000 square feet of exhibits in four buildings, along with outdoor displays. It's a treat to watch employees fire up the 1895 Corliss steam engine, which drives a 17-tone flywheel. You can see mining and milling demonstrations and even pan for gold. The museum is open 9 a.m. to 4 p.m. Monday through Saturday year-round, and until 5 p.m. June through August. More information is available at www.wmmi.org or (719) 488-0880. To reach the museum get off I-25 at exit 156A, Gleneagle Drive.

FORT COLLINS

We go to Fort Collins when we need a small-town fix, although this college town (home of Colorado State University) has seen tremendous growth in the last few years. Reach it by driving about an hour north of Denver on I-25, then taking the Harmony Road exit. Go right for a quarter of a mile until you see a farm with 150 shiny sculptures. This is the **Swetsville Zoo,** a menagerie of dinosaurs and mythical creatures made by owner Bill Swets. This self-styled artist makes his creatures out of car parts and farm equipment. Open every day year-round, the zoo is free, though donations are appreciated.

Once you're ready to head into town, get back on I-25 and go north to the Mulberry Street exit. Follow it past downtown and to Roosevelt Street. Here you'll find City Park and the **Fort Collins Municipal Railway,** a fancy term for a restored trolley car that travels downtown along Mountain Avenue. Powered by 600 volts of electricity, the trolley runs on tracks that line the grassy median of one of the city's major thoroughfares. Don't be surprised if the conductor gets out when you reach downtown and smokes a pipe before returning to City Park. Remember, this is small-town living, not a New York subway. It operates weekend afternoons and holidays from May through September.

Fort Collins offers shopping that transcends the typical mall experience. **Historic Old Town Square** at College and Mountain Avenues is a trove of art galleries, shops, and outdoor cafes all housed in historic buildings. Like the Pearl Street Mall in Boulder, this is a pedestrian-only area with

places to sit and watch people when you're tired of shopping.

For beer drinkers, a visit to Fort Collins wouldn't be complete without a free tour of the **Anheuser Busch Brewery,** off of I-25 at exit 271. Opened in 1988, the world's largest brewery offers free tours daily. The 75-minute tour shows high-tech brewing processes as well as a chance to see the famous Clydesdale horses. Best of all, at the end, you can visit the Hospitality Center to taste a few brews. Information is available at www.budweisertours.com or (970) 490-4691.

To visit **Colorado State University** (CSU), stop at the visitor center just south of College Avenue and Laurel Street for a map of the campus and a current schedule of events.

GEORGETOWN

Georgetown is a historic mining town that has been lovingly maintained and restored, with a turn-of-the-20th-century style that makes it resemble the miniature towns that adorn model railroads. It's a National Historic District that nestles deep into a valley that is overshadowed by the steep slopes of several 12,000-foot mountains.

The biggest single attraction is the **Georgetown Loop,** an old Western railroad train that hauls tourists and train history buffs on a 3-mile loop between Georgetown and **Silver Plume.** The train ride includes passage over a 100-foot trestle known as Devils Gate Bridge. We can't recommend this trip highly enough, not just for the scenery or the fun of riding but for the historic element and the bits of cinder that fly from the engine stack and settle on the passengers behind. It's one of the few great antique train rides in Colorado, by far the closest one to

i Layering is the key for dressing in Colorado, especially in the mountains. Temperature changes often take visitors off-guard, but if you're prepared, it's not a problem. An inexpensive rain poncho for mountain showers can be a trip-saver.

Denver. For a special treat, do it in the fall when the aspens are at high color. The train operates from May through October, and reservations are suggested. For reservations and information call (888) 456-6777.

Georgetown was founded in 1859, but transformed itself into "the Silver Queen of the Rockies" by the 1870s. Now it's just a fun place to stroll past shops, restaurants, museums, galleries, and National Historic Register sites. The museums include the **Hotel de Paris,** the **Hamill House,** and the **Energy Museum,** which was renovated with help from the State Historic Fund. The Hamill House was built in the 1870s in the Gothic Revival style and has been restored to that period. The Hotel de Paris, owned by Louis Dupuy, included a fine dining room and is open for tours, as are all the museums. Reach Georgetown by taking I-70 exit 228, about 50 miles west of Denver. You can also drive south from Georgetown on the **Guanella Pass Scenic Byway,** which goes all the way to the town of Grant on US 285. The byway tops out at Guanella Pass, elevation 11,669 feet, where you have wonderful views that include Mount Bierstadt. The summit is a good place to get out of the car and look around, but don't stand up too fast in the thin air at this altitude. Find a big rock and have a picnic.

Georgetown has another neat little element. The State of Colorado chose a spot near the lake east of Georgetown for its first **Watchable Wildlife Viewing Station.** Stop and see if you can spot a herd of bighorn sheep on the mountainsides. Sometimes you can seem them while whizzing by on I-70. Georgetown visitor information is available at (800) 472-8230.

GRAND LAKE/GRANBY LOOP

We call this the Grand Lake/Granby loop drive because the sightseeing trip is anchored by those two towns on the western side of the Continental Divide. Reach it by driving from Denver to Estes Park and over Trail Ridge Road (closed in winter), through Rocky Mountain National Park and down to Granby. To return to Denver, take US 40 from Granby south through Winter Park, over Berthoud Pass through Empire to I-70 east. The loop is almost 200 miles and takes a full day to drive, especially if you stop along the way. If that's too much of a commitment, consider dividing it in two, with the Boulder, Estes Park, and Rocky Mountain National Park trip one day and the Denver to Grand Lake trip on another.

Grand Lake is the name of the city as well as the lake on which it perches. Lake Granby sits to the west of Grand Lake. You'll travel along their western edges, enjoying scenery reminiscent of Switzerland. The lakes are huge, clear, and deep blue in color, lined with small resorts and usually decorated with sailboats. Grand Lake is the state's largest glacier-fed lake; the town is a quaint historic village with boardwalks along the main street. Walk around and catch a bite to eat, or buy something and head out for a picnic at **Arapahoe Bay,** on the far southeastern end of Lake Granby. It's a favorite fishing spot in June, when the Mackinaw, or lake trout, are at their peak. Reach it by taking the first left turn off US 34 at the southwestern tip of Lake Granby. A long gravel road passes over Granby Dam and skirts the southern edge of the lake. At the end of the bay, you'll find campgrounds and some nice short hiking trails. You can follow the trail east past Monarch Lake and go as far as you want toward the Indian Peaks Wilderness. Return to civilization by heading out to meet US 40 just west of Granby. You may want to take an added excursion west, or right, on US 40 along the scenic highway toward Steamboat Springs. If not, return to Denver by taking a left onto US 40 and follow it through Granby, Tabernash, Fraser, Winter Park, Berthoud Pass, and Empire onto I-70.

Most people just hustle through **Empire,** but there are some nice places to stop for refreshments. Its most famous is **The Peck House,** Colorado's oldest operating hotel (303) 569-9870. You can see it from the highway to the east, a big white building with red trim. It's a moderately priced hotel with a nice restaurant.

HOT SULPHUR SPRINGS

This quaint town of about 375 residents came alive again when the Hot Sulphur Springs Resort was renovated in 1997. To reach this town located 90 miles northwest of Denver, take I-70 to US 40, heading west. Follow the road through Winter Park and Granby before heading west toward Kremmling. Once in town, you'll see the Riverside Hotel and Casa Milagro Bed-and-Breakfast on the close side of the Colorado River. Cross the river to get to the **Hot Sulphur Springs Resort & Spa,** which is nestled against 70 acres of sagebrush.

The Ute Indians once "took the waters" here to heal and relax. Today people come for the same reasons. You can soak in any of the 22 pools where 200,000 gallons of hot mineral waters flow at temperatures of 95 to 112 degrees F year-round. Too darn hot? Go to the kid's pool that runs around 85 degrees.

This casual resort has private pools, pools with views, and cavelike pools. And if you're feeling particularly luxurious, you can book a massage and facial. If you're feeling invigorated, you may want to hike and picnic in the beautiful surroundings. The pools are open year-round from 8 a.m. to 10 p.m. More information is available at (970) 725-3306 or www.hotsulphursprings.com.

The **Riverside Hotel,** across the bridge from the resort, is a blocky wooden structure that was built in 1903. It was spruced up in the 1980s, then was sold in 2007 to innkeepers intent on preserving its history. Its 16 rooms are elegantly decorated and named for past occupants. Dinner is served seven days a week in the white linen River Room Restaurant, with cocktails and appetizers available in the adjacent Jayhawk Bar. Information is accessible at (970) 725-3589 or www.riverside-hotel.com.

IDAHO SPRINGS

Idaho Springs, 32 miles west of Denver, is the first mining town you'll hit on your way west on I-70. Thanks to the yellow tailings piles that spill from holes dotting the mountainside, the town's historic roots are obvious. If you want a closer look at this phenomenon, take the "Oh My God Road" from Idaho Springs to Central City, a narrow and scary road with even more holes and tailings dotting the hillsides.

Prospector George Jackson launched Idaho Springs in early 1859 when he pulled out nearly $2,000 worth of gold in one week. Miners flocked in, and the town was off. Two of your best choices for a look into the town's mining past are the **Argo Gold Mill** and the **Phoenix Mine.** The Argo Gold Mill is the biggest structure on the north side of the valley, and the name is printed in large letters on its front. Where much of the local ore was processed is now a museum and National Historic Site that can be toured from May to October, (303) 567-2421. The Phoenix Mine, sunk in 1872, is once again a working mine, although it can be toured year-round, weather permitting, with an experienced miner as the guide. Learn about the history, geology, and art of gold mining; dig your own ore; and pan your own gold. Call (303) 567-0422 or visit www.phoenix goldmine.com.

Idaho Springs also has natural hot mineral springs. The **Indian Springs Resort and Spa,** a National Historic Site, offers hot baths and a covered mineral-water swimming pool. It's east of downtown at 302 Soda Creek Road. Call (303) 989-6666 or visit www.indianspringscalistoga .com for details. For more information on these and other attractions, call the Idaho Springs Visitor Center at (303) 567-4382.

MOUNT EVANS

If you love mountains, this is the fastest route to the region's greatest vistas. For out-of-town visitors with only a morning or afternoon to see the mountains, this is the best recommendation we can make. Highway 5 to the top of Mount Evans is the highest paved road in the world, providing the opportunity to visit of the summit of a Colorado "14er" without having to huff and puff up thousands of feet. You can park at about 14,260 feet, wander around, and look down and out 100 miles in every direction. The view is absolutely magnificent. To reach it from Denver, take I-70 west to Idaho Springs, a 30-minute drive. Get off at exit 240, and follow Highway 103 uphill to its intersection with Highway 5 at **Echo Lake.** This is where rangers will collect a daily visitors' fee. The lake is a nice place for a picnic and some fishing. Head uphill on Highway 5 for another 14-mile trip to the top. Acrophobics should be warned that this stretch may produce whiter knuckles than any paved road in Colorado. The road is very narrow, especially on the ride down. Looking out from the passenger seat, you can easily imagine the car slipping off the side and cartwheeling into the abyss.

Once at the parking lot, you can climb a short trail to the highest point and look down to the west on the Continental Divide, east over Denver and the Great Plains, north over the Roosevelt National Forest, and south over the Pike National Forest. Bring along a state map; it's fun to identify some of the major peaks. If you like boulder fields, there are plenty to scramble around on. If you're a flatlander who hasn't been in Denver for at least three days, bear in mind that there's only about half as much oxygen up here as there is at sea level. Altitude sickness can hit you right away, or it can hammer you after you've been back in Denver for hours. Take it easy, drink lots of water, and you should do fine. The road to Mount Evans is open only in the warmer months, and even then, weather can turn bad. To check on road conditions or ask other questions, call the Clear Creek Ranger District of Arapaho National Forest at (303) 567-3000.

THE PEAK-TO-PEAK

The Peak-to-Peak Highway is so called because it follows the eastern slopes of more peaks than you can shake a stick at. It's basically the road that follows the Continental Divide between the tourist mecca of Estes Park on the north to the historic towns and gambling meccas of Black Hawk and Central City on the south. Along the way there are plenty of westerly turnoffs that will get you

closer to Longs Peak, Mount Meeker, Chiefs Head Peak, Isolation Peak, Ouzel Peak, Mount Alice, Mount Orton, Mahana Peak, and Copeland Mountain—and those are just some of the peaks along the first 10 miles. The highway is about 60 miles long and actually consists of Highway 7, Highway 72, and Highway 119.

Take the Peak-to-Peak in either direction. The entire route is a winding road of beautiful vistas and lovely mountainsides. It's a worthwhile tour anytime but an especially great place to take in the views of autumn's golden aspens, generally in September. Ten miles south of Estes Park, you find the well-traveled turnoff for the Longs Peak trailhead. This may be the most popular ascent of a Colorado "14er," but it's rigorous. Don't try it without consulting an expert for tips about how to prepare.

Another 4 miles or so along, you'll find on the right the turnoff for the **Ouzel Falls Trail at Wild Basin.** If you want to get out of your car for a pleasant walk to a gem-like waterfall in the cool forest, this is the opportunity. The falls are only about 3 miles up the trail.

All along the Peak-to-Peak, turnoffs to the west lead to scenic areas and other attractions, while turnoffs to the east take you back to the flatlands in case you decide to bail out midway. At one of these points, the historic mining town of Ward, you can head downhill via **Lefthand Canyon** or head west up to **Brainard Lake.** This crystalline, high-mountain lake is a beautiful place to absorb spectacular views without walking more than a few steps from your car.

Pass on south to Nederland and Rollinsville. A drive west from here on a gravel road will bring you to the Moffat Tunnel, which connects Denver by railroad with points west. A trail to the east of the tunnel makes a nice hike and is popular in winter with cross-country skiers.

The biggest tourist attractions await you in **Black Hawk** and **Central City,** where it has been legal to gamble since 1991. For more information about them, see our Nightlife chapter. Black Hawk was one of the first mining camps near Gregory Gulch, where gold was discovered

Special Summer Events

Denverites don't mind the 45-minute trip to Central City or Boulder for the following summer performing arts events.

The **Central City Opera,** (303) 292-6700, is a favorite summer tradition. Begun in 1932, the opera holds its performances in the historic Opera House, which was built in 1878 and ceased operations in 1927. The Central City Opera Association took over the building in 1932, and began restoration and performances. Such notables as Edwin Booth, Mae West, Helen Hayes, and Beverly Sills have performed here. Three operas are staged each summer.

The summer concerts at Boulder's **Chautauqua Auditorium** are another reason to head west. Boulder's Chautauqua dates from 1898, when a national movement brought the arts to numerous Chautauqua summer camps throughout the country. Before the evening concerts in the wonderful wooden auditorium, concertgoers can enjoy a picnic dinner under the big shady trees at the base of the foothills or a sit-down dinner at the Chautauqua Dining Hall, (303) 440-3776. Chautauqua concerts include both a popular music series, (303) 440-7666 (box office), and the Colorado Music Festival, (303) 449-1397 or www.coloradomusicfest.org, (303) 449-2413 (summer ticketing), which emphasizes classical music.

The **Colorado Shakespeare Festival** (www.coloradoshakes.org or (303) 492-0554) is another summer-only event in Boulder that draws audiences from Denver and beyond. Held at the outdoor Mary Rippon Theatre and indoor University Theatre on the University of Colorado-Boulder campus, the annual event features both traditional and modern renditions of Shakespeare's plays and non-Shakespearean classics.

Falstaff's Fare, a box dinner, can be ordered and eaten on the lawn before the show begins. There are evening and matinee performances.

---

in 1859. Nearby Central City, in the middle of Gregory Gulch, became the prominent population center because of its location, which claims the "richest square mile on Earth." It is a great old mining town, but some feel that its historic authenticity has been obliterated by the casinos. The **Central City Opera House** is still one of Colorado's reigning opera performance centers during its summer season. In 1878 it was built on the site of the Montana Theatre, which had burned to the ground in 1874. Closed when the silver boom ended, it has been operating again since 1932. Call the Denver business office at (303) 292-6700 for opera information.

The **Teller House,** next to the opera, is Central City's historic hotel, perhaps best known for the "Face on the Barroom Floor." Although painted in 1932, the faded image of a woman has intrigued visitors with its mysterious expression. The **Gilpin County Historical Museum** has preserved the history on this gold and silver town, (303) 582-5283.

Your Peak-to-Peak Highway tour is likely to run into heavy gambler traffic here, bumper-to-bumper on busy gambling nights. Also be warned that this area is well patrolled by police. A short ride down the road will take you to I-70, if you're in a rush to get back home. But if you're here for the scenic route, you're well-advised to take a left on US 6 down scenic Clear Creek Canyon to Golden.

ROCKY MOUNTAIN NATIONAL PARK

With the possible exception of Yellowstone in Wyoming, Rocky Mountain National Park, (970) 586-1206, is the nation's most famous. It provides the full spectrum of Rocky Mountain nature in one gulp. You can roam from the darkest sub-alpine forests below to the sun-sprinkled meadows and granite grandeur of the continent's roof—265,000 acres of which are well connected by roads and trails.

The best way to do the park by auto is on Trail Ridge Road, 48 miles of US 34 that vault over the park from Estes Park on the east to Grand Lake on the west. The drive over the top is one of the nation's great scenic routes, although its two lanes are jammed in the summer season. The opening of Trail Ridge Road by snowplow some time around Memorial Day is an annual Colorado event. The road closes again in late October, but you can access the park year-round. The east side has plenty of lovely drives and hiking opportunities. To reach the west side in winter, take I-70 west from Denver to US 40 at Empire, then US 40 north to Granby, where you go right on US 34 to the park. Autumn and spring visits are particularly enjoyable. We love to visit on late-summer or early-autumn evenings when the elk are bugling, particularly in the Kawuneeche Valley on the western side.

RELOCATION

Colorado has always been a popular place to live, and population experts predict it will continue to be, regardless of the financial vagaries of its major industries. Starting with 19th century gold mining, then continuing through the oil boom of the 1970s and the telecommunications explosion of the 1990s, Colorado has always attracted newcomers looking to make a fortune. These boom cycles are always followed by a bust, but they do little to stop the state's rampant growth. In 2000 the U.S. Census found Colorado to be the country's third-fastest growing state, adding new residents at a rate of 2.2 percent per year, while the U.S. average was just 1.2 percent. After the dot-com bust of 2001, however, growth cooled. By 2004 migration had flattened considerably, and the net population gain was nearly zero.

The same things attract newcomers today as attracted them in the 1880s—breathtaking mountains, blue skies, sunny days, and the opportunity to live the kind of outdoor lifestyle so many Americans crave. Some Colorado transplants were hooked during college, coming to the University of Colorado or Colorado State University and falling in love with the state's beauty. Others were among the 26.2 million tourists who come here on vacation each year and leave with an appreciation of Denver's charm. It also appeals to entrepreneurs looking to locate in beautiful surroundings without compromising their business edge. Denver is the largest city between San Francisco and St. Louis, which makes it an excellent place to headquarter businesses serving the western half of the country. And Denver International Airport makes it easy for globally oriented businesses to connect with transportation hubs on the East Coast and in Europe.

Housing prices are among the nation's highest, however, which can be discouraging for transplants from cities other than urban hubs like Boston and San Francisco. Bargains can be found, but it takes some research and legwork to find them. The Neighborhoods and Real Estate Resources sections in this chapter have information about housing prices and the region's largest real estate firms, respectively.

Public schools in metro Denver are among the nation's best, and private-school options abound, from those with religious connections to those specializing in college preparatory programs. Colleges also abound. Colorado's state-financed junior college and university system offers a wide range of program and location options.

Metro Denver also has one of the nation's highest percentages of baby boomers (not to be confused with retirees), which may explain

the broad support for public recreation centers, parks and open-space areas, arts and entertainment complexes, shopping centers, and fine restaurants. Younger families can also find the amenities they are looking for, from parks to child-friendly destinations (see our Kidstuff chapter for some places to get started) to good, dependable child care.

Like other cities, Denver has plenty of day-care homes and centers but lacks enough infant care. If you find yourself in the market for child care, we suggest several good places to get started. One good resource is *Colorado School Guides™* by Margerie Hicks (www.coloradoschool guides.com). Metro Denver Child Care Resource and Referral Partners, (303) 561-2244, can refer callers to child-care providers in their neighborhoods. The Colorado Office of Resource and Referral Agencies, (303) 290-9088, is an umbrella organization that can refer callers to other sources of child-care information in their area.

If you'd like to check the background of a day-care provider before hiring him or her, you can do so at the Colorado Division of Child Care, 1575 Sherman Street, Denver, (303) 866-5958. With the correct name and/or street address of the provider, this office can tell you if the person's license is current. If you want to know about complaints that may have been filed against your candidate, ask to speak to a counselor who can help you view the case file (72-hour advance notice is required).

Colorado does have its growing pains. The number of students in its public and private schools grew by 29 percent from 1990 to 2000, according to the state's Department of Education. And traffic problems have kept pace with the population. The *Denver Post* reported a 22 percent increase in traffic along one section of interstate during the same decade. Major thoroughfares are being widened and light-rail routes are being expanded as quickly as possible, but that means construction projects will inconvenience drivers in the meantime.

Newcomers to metro Denver needn't feel like they're alone, however. More than one in four residents has arrived within the past decade, and many remember what it feels like. Two groups are designed to help transplants settle in. The Newcomers Club, www.newcomersclub.com/co.html, arranges social events for people throughout the metro area. After the Boxes Are Unpacked faith-based workshops are offered in Highlands Ranch, Englewood, Castle Rock, and Colorado Springs; visit www.justmoved.org for details.

A line charting Denver home sales over the years looks like a wave—up, down, up, down, up, down. Denver's housing market historically mirrors the state's "boom/bust" economy. Even so, while housing values fell as much as 35 percent in some states in the wake of the mortgage meltdown, Colorado's homes on average lost only about 5 percent.

For a cursory look at Denver's real estate market, turn to the Internet, where you can find information on prices, neighborhoods, agents, and photos of properties. It's an easy way to scan listings. If what you seek is the offbeat, then "cohousing" might be for you. Specially planned communities that house residents in individual homes but bring them together in jointly owned kitchens, greenhouses, nursery schools, gardens, and workshops can be found in at least eight Colorado locations. Closest to the city are two near Boulder and one in Golden. Some of Denver's neighborhoods are hotter and more expensive than others. Cherry Creek North, in the shadow of Denver's No. 1 tourist attraction, Cherry Creek Shopping Center, is booming. Tiny crackerbox houses once occupied by working-class families are being bought, demolished, and replaced with expensive townhomes and row houses fashioned in the old, East Coast style. Price tags easily climb as high as $1.2 million. (Walking distance to Saks Fifth Avenue has its price.)

Loft living is another hotter-than-hot trend. In the late 1980s developers began transforming rundown warehouses into empty, but very stylish, loft shells for a reasonable price. You supply the walls, kitchen, etc. Today's urban palaces can cost more than $1 million, but most are much less.

New-home sales have cooled a bit. The vast majority of that market is in the suburbs, where land is plentiful and opposition to development is minimal. New development inside Denver's city limits tends to be small, exclusive infill projects on vacant lots. Two major redevelopment projects are the exception: at the former site of Stapleton Airport, which was replaced by Denver International Airport, and at Lowry Air Force Base, which was closed by the federal government. Both have been redeveloped to include a "new urbanism" mix of residential homes, parks, open spaces, and retail. The 1999 redevelopment of the historic Elitch Gardens site in northwest Denver also incorporated new urbanism concepts.

A full picture of Denver's residential scene would require a book much larger than our entire guide, since Denver alone has more than 70 officially designated neighborhoods, and hundreds more are contained in surrounding counties.

Nonetheless, we've scanned several to give you an idea of Metro Denver's residential fabric.

The most important factor to remember is that prices within neighborhoods can vary greatly. In Capitol Hill, for instance, a lovely Victorian condo can be a mere 3 blocks from a mansion that commands ten times as much. Because no centralized data exists about housing prices, we've resisted the urge to speculate. If that's what interests you, turn to the Internet for a little comparison shopping. Online listings can provide you with the latest data about specific neighborhoods that attract you.

NEIGHBORHOODS

Denver

As Metro Denver's urban center, the city and county of Denver covers the widest range of neighborhood types and home prices, from humble to haughty. Downtown includes the Union Station area on the north, the Auraria neighborhood to the west, and the Civic Center area on the southwest. It reaches east to Broadway, where it borders the North Capitol Hill and Capitol Hill neighborhoods. This is where you live if you like the downtown lifestyle, and here you almost certainly live in a condo.

Lower Downtown, the redbrick historic area between the central business district, Union Station, and the Central Platte Valley, is particularly popular of late. LoDo has been hot since Coors Field was built, and stays hot because so much revitalization is in progress.

Downtown Denver is just as chic, but is an anomaly as far as residential opportunities. Condo prices are high, and single-family homes are virtually nonexistent.

After an exodus of families from Denver to the suburbs in the 1980s, the inner city is experiencing a resurgence of popularity. The Denver Public Schools have done their part to improve test scores and the overall quality of education. In fact, in 1998 voters approved a bond to upgrade and build new schools in the core city to accommodate growth.

The **Uptown** neighborhood, just east of downtown and centered around 17th Avenue, is experiencing a revival that includes several new infill projects. Most notable here are three-story, statuesque row houses, mixed with grand mansions that have been turned into law offices, graphic arts studios, and single-family homes. The feel is urban elegance. Prices haven't skyrocketed because of the neighborhood's proximity to East Colfax Avenue, known for sleaze and crime.

Just east of downtown Denver, you'll find historic neighborhoods untouched by the revitalization boom shaking Lower Downtown. **North Capitol Hill** and **Capitol Hill,** bounded roughly by 20th and 6th Avenues, Clarkson Street, and Broadway, were among the first of Denver's housing developments in the 1800s. While those in the working class were making their homes down by the river and in other outlying sections, the aristocrats were populating this area east and upslope from the business district. Here you find most of the historic mansions and a stretch of Grant Street once known as "Millionaires' Row." In recent years people have come to appreciate the historic charm of the area and its accessibility to downtown. Many of Capitol Hill's mansions have been converted to condominiums, offices, and bed-and-breakfast inns, and there are a lot of cultural and fine-dining opportunities close by. Because of Capitol Hill's reputation for crime, many prefer to live farther east in the Cheesman Park or City Park West neighborhoods. The **Cheesman Park** neighborhood, bounded by University Boulevard, Clarkson Street, and Colfax and 6th Avenues, surrounds one of Denver's finer parks, Cheesman Park, and borders one of the city's finest amenities, the Denver Botanic Gardens. The Cheesman Park neighborhood contains two historic districts and has a feel of urban gentility with lots of pedestrians, coffee shops, and neighborhood gathering spots.

Things start to get more expensive as you move south of Cheesman. Still relatively reasonable, however, is **City Park West,** an urban treasure trove of historic homes going back to Denver's silver boom of 1880-93. Bounded by

Clarkson Street, University Boulevard, and Colfax and 23rd Avenues, it's located between North Capitol Hill and City Park, Denver's largest central park, containing the Denver Zoo and the Denver Museum of Nature and Science. It's a moderate walk to the Botanic Gardens and a reasonable walk to downtown, and it has a hospital complex on its northern edge. The 17th Avenue strip of fine restaurants and entertainment runs right through it.

Washington Park is Denver's other big, well-known public green space, and the Washington Park neighborhood is one of Denver's most popular living areas. It has a lot of homes built in the early to mid-1900s. It's convenient to transportation, bordering on I-25 to the south and Colorado Boulevard to the east. The Denver Country Club is just north of it, where home prices climb to more than $1 million.

Just east of the Denver Country Club is fashionable **Cherry Creek.** Bounded by University Avenue, Colorado Boulevard, and 6th and Alameda Avenues, it's an area of large- to moderate-size homes, expensive condos, and shopping nirvana. It's Metro Denver's premier retail and arts area. It has a gracious ambience, one reason its residences are highly sought after.

Directly east of Cherry Creek is **Hilltop,** another prestigious living area of well-cared-for streets adjacent to the major north-south corridor of Colorado Boulevard. **Park Hill,** to the north and just west of City Park, is an area of handsome old homes and large mature trees. Prices climb the farther south you go.

One area that has become particularly interesting of late is the area known as **Far Northeast Denver.** These neighborhoods stand out not only geographically but also as a focus of growth expected as a result of the new airport. **Montbello** and **Green Valley Ranch** are established, quiet neighborhoods, although some complaints about noise have been filed since Denver International Airport opened. The oldest homes in Montbello were built in the 1970s, while the oldest in Green Valley Ranch were built in the 1990s. These are low-crime areas with panoramic views of the mountains, room for another 9,400 dwellings, and a lot of open space. They're still the extreme edge of Denver's urban fabric, places where residents can take a walk and see a deer or an eagle in flight and maybe even hear coyotes howling at night.

Gateway, between Montbello and Green Valley Ranch and directly bordering the airport on the north, is where Denver planners envision big-time development. Already launched are the beginning stages of a planned $1 billion Denver International Business Center just a few miles from the terminal. The local media has referred to Gateway as "our first 21st Century neighborhood" and represented it as a future community of 65,000 people with strong economic links to the airport. Although it was annexed by Denver to link the city with the airport, it's not yet officially a neighborhood. Denver planners envision it as a new employment area on the level of the Denver Tech Center, which is only one-sixth the size of Gateway.

Southeast Denver is a popular area with a variety of housing options. In general, houses tend to be more expensive and newer than their northwest counterparts. However, that doesn't necessarily mean homes are bigger. Southeast Denver offers anything from tiny frame two-bedroom homes on up. Neighborhoods such as Southmoor Park offer quiet residential living with plenty of trees and nearby parks. There also are plenty of upscale apartment, condo, and townhome choices.

We've given a lot of mention here to the central and eastern parts of Denver, perhaps more than is fair. But this is where the oldest neighborhoods, the big-name neighborhoods, and the well-known neighborhoods are. A lot of people, however, prefer the west side of the city. It's the smaller part, is closer to the mountains, and generally has a feeling of being near to its country roots.

Northwestern Denver is the city's smallest quadrant, bounded by West Colfax Avenue on the south, 52nd Avenue on the north, Sheridan Boulevard on the west, and the South Platte River on the east. The **Highland** and **Jefferson Park** neighborhoods, stretching west from the high ground above the South Platte, were where Denver put its first residential neighborhoods west of the South Platte. Around the turn of the 20th century, there was a large Italian neighborhood here. Descendants of truck farmers in what are now the western suburbs still tell of taking their produce downtown for delivery to Italian produce salesmen who would sell their wares in the streets. These neighborhoods now have a rich ethnic mix and some fine restaurants, including Latin American and Vietnamese establishments. Here, as elsewhere, prices are on the rise.

Sloan Lake, West Highland, Berkeley, and **Regis** are some of the neighborhoods to the west that are pleasantly equipped with quiet streets and the greenery of lawns and parks around small lakes. These northwestern neighborhoods are as old as a lot of east Denver neighborhoods between downtown and Colorado Boulevard, but they're across the river, up the hill, and over the ridge from the central city. The feeling here is apart from the urban bustle.

Southwest Denver is larger, more extensive, and more dynamic than the west side of the city. Certainly it has its older neighborhoods close in, such as **Val Verde** and **Sun Valley.** Val Verde, Spanish for "green valley," was a separate town established in 1873 and annexed into Denver in 1902. Bordered by 6th and Alameda Avenues, the South Platte River, and Federal Boulevard, it is today an ethnically diverse neighborhood with a large industrial and warehousing base. As you move southwest toward southern Lakewood, however, you get a sensation of increasingly newer urban landscape. Not that there haven't been homes in this area since the 1800s, of course, but the neighborhood wasn't developed as early and extensively as the northwest.

One of Denver's few areas where major new development is taking place is the **Marston** neighborhood that juts down into unincorporated Jefferson County on Denver's farthest southwestern point. Near Marston Reservoir you'll find particularly high-quality residential living. Generally,

however, southwest Denver vies with northwest Denver for the city's lowest overall housing prices, and a much larger percentage of its population consists of married couples and families.

Adams County

Adams County is often viewed as the area's most blue-collar, working-class county, and that has a lot to do with the heavy industry and warehousing around Commerce City, northeastern Denver, and the I-76 corridor leading northeast. **Commerce City,** Adams County's industrial-warehousing heartland, where twice as many people work as live, certainly has some of the county's lowest housing prices.

One of the first things you may notice in driving north on I-25 to Thornton, Westminster, and Northglenn is a sensation of climbing to higher ground. **Federal Heights,** a community between Westminster and Thornton, is well named. From here you're actually looking down at the tops of downtown Denver's highest buildings. Much of this northern area seems to be on high ground, and since there is little in the way of high-rise buildings, Denver's northern suburbs have some of the grandest views of the Rockies.

Westminster is the northside suburb that is closest to the mountains. Westminster spreads all over the place, so it isn't easily categorized. It's roughly centered around the Westminster Mall off US 36 at 88th Avenue, but the newest parts of the city stretch north to 120th Avenue. To the west, 88th Avenue contains extensive shopping complexes. To the north there are attractive housing developments clustered and scattered through a lot of open country with big-sky views. Another arm of Westminster protrudes west and wraps around two sides of Standley Lake, one of Metro Denver's best water recreation resources. Westminster has lots of upscale town-homes and middle-class neighborhoods as well as established areas with mature trees and big lots.

Westminster's eastern half, near **Northglenn** and **Thornton,** is where you'll find the most building, with the newest developments ringing the well-respected Legacy Ridge Golf Course.

Movies Filmed in Denver

Even if you've never been to Denver, you may have seen it in the movies. The hit movie *Die Harder*, starring Bruce Willis, had major scenes filmed at the old Stapleton Airport. Portions of Woody Allen's 1973 film *Sleeper* were shot in Denver and vicinity, including the exterior of the National Center for Atmospheric Research in Boulder and a modernist home visible from I-70 near Genesee that's known locally as the Sleeper House.

Between July 1996 and June 1997, 188 film productions took place in Denver, including eight feature films, according to the Mayor's Office of Art, Culture and Film, which keeps tabs on such things. All this production activity tucked $32.8 million into Denver's coffers.

Among the movies shot in Denver in past years were Warner Brothers' *Under Siege II: In Dark Territory*, with Steven Seagal, and Boat Drink Productions' *Things to Do in Denver When You're Dead*, starring Andy Garcia. *Under Siege II* has scenes in Lower Downtown, including around Union Station and Coors Field. *Things to Do* was shot largely in the Five Points neighborhood at 26th and Welton Streets, including the historic Rossonian Hotel. For some key scenes the Rossonian's bar was transformed into a malt shop. *Elephant Man* (also known as Nickel and Dime), with Bill Murray, was filmed in Denver and elsewhere in Colorado. John Sayles's 2003 *Silver City* was filmed in downtown Denver.

The made-for-TV film *Asteroids* was filmed in downtown Denver and prominently displayed the campus of East High School, one of Denver's beautiful, old schools. The remake of *The Shining* (also made for TV) was shot in Denver and Estes Park. And not surprisingly, *The Ellen Hart Peña Story* (she's the ex-wife of former mayor Federico Peña) was filmed in Denver.

The **North Suburban Central** area, bordered by I-25 on the west, the South Platte River on the east, Denver on the south, and 144th Avenue on the north, contains the bulk of the city of Thornton, which has a moderate- to lower-income population and a suburban feel. Some newer developments, such as **Hunter's Glen** and **Thorncreek,** surround a golf course and are more upscale, but the mid-1970s two-story homes still dominate Thornton. Because of its outlying location, prices here haven't climbed as much as elsewhere.

Brighton, the Adams County seat to the northeast, is seeing a lot of growth but still has the benefit of a small-town, rural atmosphere within an easy 15-mile commuting distance to Denver. Here you'll find homes with acreage and space for horses. Some new developments have a minimum 35-acre requirement. Home prices are moderate.

Southeast of Commerce City, the city of **Aurora** has its industrial centers in its northern Adams County side, along the I-70 corridor near Denver International Airport.

Arapahoe County

Most of Aurora lies in Arapahoe County. This is where the bulk of the city's office and research/development centers are found. It's also where the homes are higher priced. A typical, moderately priced Aurora development is **Tollgate,** where the homes are new, the neighborhood is clean, and the lawns are well manicured. The area is close to the Denver Tech Center business area on the south and is well-connected north-south by I-225 to both I-70 and I-25.

Aurora's population is young, with a median age of 31. The city has always suffered from a lack of identity, due primarily to its proximity to Denver. It's known for its flat landscape and lack of mature trees, prompting the nickname "Saudi Aurora." But with a good supply of affordable housing, Aurora is popular with young families looking for starter homes or wanting more room for less money.

The region known among Realtors as the **Suburban Southeast,** roughly defined by the Arapahoe County line, County Line Road on the south, and Aurora on the north, contains most of the region's most expensive properties. The northwestern segment contains about half of Greenwood Village and most of Cherry Hills Village.

The bulk of this area lies in unincorporated Arapahoe County east, west, and north of Centennial Airport. It includes the Denver Tech Center. Home prices here tend to be skewed rather dramatically upward by prestige pockets such as **Cherry Hills Village,** one of Greater Denver's most upscale communities, with residences averaging $1.5 million Cherry Hills Village, for example, has virtually no commercial base, and the only nonresidential features are two private schools and the Cherry Hills and Glenmoor country clubs. **Greenwood Village,** just south of Cherry Hills, wrapping under the Denver Tech Center and up its eastern side, is another highly desired living area with distinctive custom homes. Many are on large lots and are tucked away from the street. Greenwood Village has some condominiums, but single-family homes in some neighborhoods can exceed $4 million.

Move a little to the west, and you'll find the area directly below the city of Denver known as the **South Suburban Central** region, which includes the cities of Littleton, Englewood, about half of Greenwood Village, and a substantial patch

of unincorporated Jefferson County between Greenwood Village and County Line Road, Littleton, and I-25.

The unincorporated part of **South Suburban Central** is generally an area of clean, new neighborhoods with the kind of convoluted street patterns that make life confusing for pizza deliverers but peaceful for residents. It has a country feel, being the last neighborhood south of Denver before you arrive at Douglas County. There are some good shopping complexes along County Line Road, including Park Meadows; the Denver Tech Center is just up I-25; and C-470 provides fast access west and up to I-70 near Golden.

The city of **Littleton** grew from an old downtown established in 1890 on what is now its northwestern edge along the South Platte River. It still has that old, traditional community atmosphere, with ranch homes on big lots, but the city also has its newer areas reaching south to Douglas County and C-470. The South Platte River runs north-south through nearly the entire length of the city, and the extra green spaces make Littleton a particularly pleasant place to live.

Englewood, like Littleton, is one of the southern suburbs with an old downtown established in the 1800s along Broadway. Also like Littleton, it has a small-town appeal. But it's closer to Denver, and its business corridor along South Santa Fe Drive on the city's west side is home to hundreds of manufacturing, industrial, and service companies. Homes are smaller frame structures. On the east side, the city borders Cherry Hills Village.

Broomfield County

The city of **Broomfield** is just north of Westminster, mostly in Boulder County but with a good quarter of its population in the newly recognized Broomfield County. Originally a residential community, it's fast becoming a business-development area thanks to its strategic position between Boulder and Metro Denver and the rampant development of business and industrial parks along US 36. Broomfield is popular because it still retains its own identity, separate from

Greater Denver, with enduring, solid 1950s brick ranches. This is attractive to people who work in Denver and Boulder and want more affordable living. Broomfield's home prices are climbing along with closer-in locales.

Douglas County

Anyone who has lived in Metro Denver for 10 years or more is likely to be struck by the number of new residences in Douglas County, set well apart like estates, speckling the landscape from I-25 south. It's an area of rolling hills and open spaces, with views of the mountains and the feel of the Great Plains—at least for now. Douglas County in January 1999 lost its designation as the fastest-growing county in the nation, but it still ranks among the top five.

Douglas County certainly is the metro area's fastest-growing county, although figures can sometimes be misleading. Because the area had so few residents, the influx of several thousand new residents meant three-figure growth rates. It is a huge area with just a few old and well-established towns like **Larkspur, Franktown,** and the county seat of **Castle Rock.** Otherwise you'll find very little in the way of residential buildings that aren't either ranches, farm structures, or the large expensive homes that are popping up like crazy in exclusive planned communities with names like **Castle Pines Village, Deer Creek Farm,** and **The Meadows.** These are among the 20 to 30 planned communities along the Denver/Colorado Springs corridor that are expected to bring Douglas County's population as high as a half-million by 2030.

Highlands Ranch is the Douglas County community best known by Denverites, partly because it now represents a continuum of the Metro Denver urban fabric. It lies on the northern edge of Douglas County directly south from the city and county of Denver. With nearly 81,000 residents and growing like crazy, it's supposed to top out at a population of 90,000 by 2010. No one will be too surprised if at some point it is incorporated as a city. It's already starting

to look like one, with well-established schools and community centers; a huge central green space, Northwest Community Park that branches through the main, western cluster of the community; and the large Highland Heritage Regional Park on the growing eastern cluster.

Jefferson County

Here is where home buyers can choose from the widest variety of landscapes, simply because Jefferson County has both the bulk of Metro Denver's mountain communities and a large percentage of the area's flatland communities. The mountain communities are a big attraction. After a hot summer day at work in Denver, residents retreat to cool mountain evenings among the pines. Of course, the drive can be less appealing in the winter, when commuters are faced with severe mountain snowstorms. Sport utility vehicles tend to be popular among mountain-community commuters.

Jefferson County's flatland communities, however, still offer the attraction of being near the mountains, and the county in general has a good reputation for quality-of-life factors such as good schools, relatively low crime, and nice neighborhoods. Actually, flatland is a bit of a misnomer here, because Jefferson County's eastern half is close to the mountains and tends to include lots of ridges and valleys. On average, Jefferson County's population is moderately well-to-do and well educated.

Jefferson County South is the county's most expensive housing region, bordering directly on Denver. The vast majority of residences here are in the area bounded roughly by US 285 on the north, Sheridan Avenue on the east, and C-470 on the south and west. Bulging into that area on the northeast corner is the city and county of Denver's Marston neighborhood, which surrounds Marston Lake. It's an unincorporated area, but one that envisions itself as a unique community on the edge of the mountains. It has rejected efforts at incorporation as a city, but it holds its own community festivals and has its own organization of homeowners associations known as the Council of Homeowners Organizations for Planned Environment.

South Jeffco also has some nice housing south and west of C-470; for example, in Ken Caryl Valley on the other side of the Dakota Hogback, where there's a mix of everything from townhomes to million-dollar mansions. **Ken Caryl Ranch** is a stable area with lots of horse property, surrounded by the foothills and tucked away from the big city. North from Ken Caryl is **Green Mountain,** with stunning city views and moderate prices.

The city of **Lakewood** is the giant of Denver's southwest side and the third-most populous city in Metro Denver after Denver and Aurora. Unlike many suburbs, Lakewood is a major employment center, with the Denver Federal Center, strong retail communities, and substantial light industry. At the same time, it also has a lot of semirural areas inside the city limits. Lakewood's older neighborhoods lie to the east, where the city shares about half the western border of Denver. On the west it reaches into the foothills, where its 6,000 acres of parks include Green Mountain and the surrounding William Frederick Hayden Park. Lakewood touches the city of **Morrison,** a small town hidden in one of the red rock-rimmed valleys in the Rocky Mountains' first folds.

North of Lakewood is the city of **Wheat Ridge,** also bordering Denver. It has developed largely since World War II. Before then it was a farming area known for fruits, vegetables, and carnations. Wheat Ridge also has that uniquely rural flavor characteristic of many suburbs here, with older homes on larger lots. Foxes come into the neighborhoods at night from the Clear Creek greenbelt. Deer sometimes blunder into busy Wadsworth Boulevard at morning rush hour. Walkers in serene suburban neighborhoods sometimes see people riding horses.

Driving west on 32nd Avenue and passing out of Wheat Ridge as you go under I-70, you are on the way to the city of **Golden,** on the other side of South Table Mountain. Between I-70 and South Table Mountain, however, you

notice nicely groomed new neighborhoods primarily on the left. You are on the north side of a loosely defined area known as **Applewood,** which includes bits of Lakewood, Golden, and Wheat Ridge but is mostly in unincorporated Jefferson County. Applewood is a name often heard on the lips of westsiders considering a move to a new home, but it also includes older, established homes with mature trees.

Keep going west on 32nd Avenue, around South Table Mountain, past a row of Adolph Coors Co. subsidiary companies, and finally past the brewery itself, and you'll enter Golden through the back door. Largely hidden from Denver by South Table Mountain and scrunched into the foothills on its western side, Golden has kept an identity apart from the rest of the metro area. It has an Old West downtown, and it is a charming small town. Once a Coors-company town, it's now mainly a high-technology and university town, largely influenced by the culture of the Colorado School of Mines just up the hill from Washington Avenue. New neighborhoods have been climbing up the side of South Table Mountain, growing south toward Heritage Square and Morrison and spreading east toward Lakewood. The level of education among Golden's population is one of the highest in the Metro Denver area.

Northeast of Golden and north of Wheat Ridge is one of the larger cities of Denver's west side, **Arvada.** Looking north from the top of the ridge that is the center of Wheat Ridge, you can see the historic center of Arvada, now known as **Olde Town Arvada.** But Arvada has spread considerably from that historic beginning, out to the "horse country" of the far west side. Arvada's central area consists largely of homes typically built in the 1950s and 1960s, but a rapidly growing high-end development called **West Woods Ranch** offers new homes centered around a golf course. Arvada is known for its family-oriented lifestyle and its easy access to Boulder and Denver.

Arvada and Westminster define the residential majority of the area known as **Jefferson County North.** The parts of the two cities in this area—north, east, and south of Standley Lake—

are more like each other than they are like their respective city centers. A lot of new homes have gone in here in the last 5 or 10 years, primarily tract homes with some high-end custom homes and some of the patio homes preferred by empty-nesters. The area has a country feel because you're looking west across the last prairie before the mountains. It's a short shot north on Wadsworth Boulevard to Broomfield and on US 36 to Boulder.

West beyond Rocky Flats and Golden, off Highway 93, there are growing mountain developments up side roads such as **Coal Creek Canyon, Golden Gate Canyon,** and **Crawford Gulch.**

Metro Denver's big mountain communities, though, tend to be off I-70 and US 285. Communities such as **Genesee, Evergreen, Conifer, Aspen Park, Indian Hills, Kittredge,** and **Hidden Valley** offer a lot of new, high-end living across ridge tops with fantastic vistas and in hidden, pine-covered valleys and hillsides. The only drawback is the sometimes hazardous 30-minute commute from **Evergreen** to Denver, 45 minutes to an hour from areas farther out. The bulk of housing opportunities are in burgeoning, although tasteful, developments. Genesee homes are more in the foothills, with better access to Denver.

Evergreen is probably the largest, most-established community near I-70, about 8 miles south of it, actually, on Highway 74. There are more than 9,000 people in the city of Evergreen—45,000 including the nearby communities of **Kittredge** and **Bergen Park**—and there's even a downtown, just below the dam that holds back Evergreen Lake. Evergreen also has shops, restaurants, and the Little Bear bar, which pulls people up from Denver for its great musical evenings and singles scene. Housing here is among the most expensive in the region, ranging well into the millions.

Mountain communities down US 285, in the **Conifer** and **Aspen Park** area, have Denver commuting times closer to an hour, but here you'll find properties in all price ranges, with some horse properties and more available space.

REAL ESTATE RESOURCES

You can get more information on the local real estate market, Realtor licensing and ethics, and other information involving the sale or purchase of homes by contacting the following agencies.

COLORADO ASSOCIATION OF REALTORS
(303) 790-7099
coloradorealtors.com

DENVER BOARD OF REALTORS
(303) 756-0553
www.denverrealtors.org

DOUGLAS/ELBERT REALTOR ASSOCIATION
(303) 688-0941
www.derarealtors.com

JEFFERSON COUNTY ASSOCIATION OF REALTORS
(303) 233-7831
www.jcar.com

NORTH METRO DENVER REALTOR ASSOCIATION
(303) 451-5757
www.nmdra.com

SOUTH METRO DENVER REALTOR ASSOCIATION
(303) 797-3700
www.smdra.com

HOME BUILDERS

Colorado's home-building business thrived during the 1990s and early 2000s before being stalled by the mortgage meltdown of 2008. Based on available space, most new home construction—master planned communities and tract-housing developments—occurred in the suburbs. Single units and smaller townhome or condo developments make up the bulk of city infill projects. Perhaps the biggest trends are the growing number of upscale townhomes and row homes being built on vacant city lots and the pop-top phenomenon in older core neighborhoods, in which new owners remodel small homes into larger modern ones with all the amenities of the suburbs.

On a larger scale, redevelopment of both Lowry Air Force Base, a few miles east of downtown, and the old Stapleton Airport site were major projects that included residential, retail, and parks. Work on Lowry is nearly completed, while Stapleton construction will extend well into the future.

Another trend hitting Metro Denver is the revival of new urbanism, in which communities are built to look like the days of old, with "vintage" housing and neighborhood amenities just down the street. The Lowry and Stapleton sites include new urbanism, as does development in the Central Platte Valley, just west of downtown.

For more information on the hundreds of home builders, call the Home Builders Association of Metropolitan Denver at (303) 778-1400.

REAL ESTATE FIRMS

The following are among Metro Denver's more well-known real estate brokerages.

CENTURY 21 PROFESSIONALS, INC.
www.century21.com
Century 21 is a worldwide company operating in 30 countries and territories. Each of the Denver/ Front Range's 25 offices is independently owned. The general Web site contains links to a complete list of addresses and phone numbers.

CO-KA-NE CONSULTANTS, INC.
405 Arapahoe Street, Kiowa
(303) 621-2555
www.co-ka-neconsultants.com
This offices specializes in ranch and horse property, residential, acreage, and development in the southeast edge of suburban Denver and stretching east into rural territory. Agents help people looking for a rural lifestyle, many with horses and small animals and some looking for multi-acre ranches.

i In the central Denver real estate market, homes frequently sell for at or above the asking price. At best, bargaining is reserved for the overpriced or run-down homes. In general, your dollar buys a lot more square footage, and often lot size, in the suburbs.

COLDWELL BANKER DEVONSHIRE
105 Fillmore Street
(303) 758-7611
Coldwell Banker Devonshire frequently produces several of the top 10 agents in the Denver area. The awards not only say a lot about the agency's expertise, but also about the high-end homes in which it specializes. "Cottages to Castles" is its slogan.

COLDWELL BANKER RESIDENTIAL SERVICES
8490 East Crescent Parkway
Greenwood Village
(303) 409-1500
After a merger in 1999, Coldwell Banker became the largest real estate services firm in Colorado, with more than 900 associates. Each office is staffed by experts who know their area or can help you anywhere across Colorado. This busy Greenwood Village office is in South Suburban Central—an area known for its mountain views and mix of suburban living amid open space. Coldwell Banker is active all over the Denver area, listing new homes as well as resales.

THE KENTWOOD CO.
5690 DTC Parkway, Greenwood Village
(303) 773-3399
44 Cook Street, Cherry Creek
(303) 331-1400
Based in the Denver Tech Center but with an office in Cherry Creek, The Kentwood Co. specializes in upper-price homes and does most of its brokerage in the south metro area as well as some of the more-expensive properties in the inner city. It offers a complete range of real estate

services, including corporate relocations, condo conversions, and new-home sales. The company's 53 sales associates average more than 15 years of experience. Average annual sales volume tops $300 million.

LEONARD LEONARD
420 Downing Street
(303) 744-6200
www.leonardleonard.com

Founded in 1983, Leonard Leonard is known for specializing in the heart of Denver. Owner Sonja Leonard Leonard has built a staff of agents whose attention to detail shows in their high-quality properties. And their open-house tours, which often feature champagne and munchies at every stop, are a fun way to spend a few hours.

METRO BROKERS INC.
4 Inverness Court East #200
Englewood
(303) 843-0100
www.metrobrokersonline.com

Metro Brokers Inc. is a trade association of independent brokers that operate all over the state.

With more than 60 offices and 1,800 agents, they have been working in Colorado for almost 30 years.

RE/MAX
8390 East Crescent Parkway, Suite 500
Greenwood Village
(303) 770-5531
www.remax.com

RE/MAX began in Denver in 1973 as a locally owned real estate office and has grown to become a global franchise network. RE/MAX offices are now open in more than 60 countries on six continents, with more than 114,000 sales agents working from 4,400 offices. Corporate headquarters are located in Greenwood Village, but to find an office near you, it's best to visit the Web site.

EDUCATION

Choices, choices, and more choices. That best describes the educational scene in Metro Denver. Your child loves music and dancing? Denver Public Schools offer the Denver School of the Arts. You have a child who's goofing off and not living up to his or her potential? Numerous private schools offer a low pupil-teacher ratio and individualized instruction. You want your child to have rigorous college-prep courses? Several public schools offer the International Baccalaureate Program. No matter what you're looking for, chances are good that you'll find it here.

Better yet, Colorado's public schools were made more accessible in 1994 by legislation creating open enrollment statewide, meaning you can enroll your kids in any public school at no extra cost. Got your eye on a school with some real nice programs but live outside the traditional enrollment area? That problem has been eliminated by open enrollment. Of course, local children have priority, so it depends on whether space is available.

The state stands at the educational forefront in many ways. In 1993, for example, Colorado became the third state after Minnesota and California to enact charter schools, which are publicly funded but run by groups of parents, teachers, and other individuals who want to devise their own curriculum. Metro Denver now has charter schools in operation or pending in every one of its counties. Many schools are governed by cooperative decision-making teams, made up of parents, teachers, administrators, students, and local businesspeople. And, not surprisingly, in 1997 the end of 25 years of court-ordered busing in Denver Public Schools has already brought a tremendous amount of community support for what will now, once again, be neighborhood schools.

One of the best resources available to parents looking for information about both public and private schools is the searchable online database www.coloradoschoolguides.com by Marjorie Hicks. It lays out just about everything you could want to know about Metro Denver's 15 public school systems, its school districts, and the individual schools and programs within each district, as well as giving complete reference for private elementary and secondary schools in the

area. To purchase a 30-day membership subscription ($20), visit www.coloradoschoolguides.com.

The state of Colorado maintains lots of data about its public schools; it's available through the Department of Education's Communications Center at 201 East Colfax in Denver, (303) 866-6600, www.cde.state.co.us.

Colorado's colleges and universities in many ways stand among the nation's best, and its residents are some of the best educated. Higher education is available in a wide variety of forms in Metro Denver, the most obvious choices being the major institutions such as the University of Colorado at Boulder and Denver, or the Metropolitan State College of Denver. Private colleges and universities are generally smaller but are numerous and diverse. In many ways the most important part of Metro Denver's higher-education establishment is the community college system. At any one time about 40,000 students are attending the area's five community colleges. These are public colleges so well distributed around Metro Denver that no resident is very far from one of them. They tend toward curricula that are career oriented and designed for accessibility by working students.

Our list of colleges and universities is by no means a full account of local adult educational opportunities. Colorado has nearly 200 private occupational schools, ranging from the A-Plus Real Estate School to the Xenon International School of Hair Design. The bulk of these are in the Metro Denver area. Contact the state of Colorado's Department of Higher Education, Division of Private Occupational Schools at http://highered.colorado.gov for more information.

Whatever educational needs and interests you may have, Metro Denver has an abundance of opportunities to offer. We'll begin with the public school systems.

i Regis University's School for Professional Studies (SPS) has new campuses in Aurora and Longmont. The Longmont campus is at 2101 Ken Pratt Boulevard and offers undergraduate classes in business, accounting, teacher education, and liberal arts. The Aurora campus is at 6 Abilene Street, located near Lockheed Martin, Raytheon, and Buckley Air Force Base. It offers undergraduate courses in business, accounting, liberal arts, and teacher education, as well as graduate degrees in business and education. For information about the SPS programs, call (303) 458-4300.

PUBLIC SCHOOLS

ADAMS COUNTY SCHOOL DISTRICT NO. 1
Mapleton Public Schools
591 East 80th Avenue
(303) 853-1000
www.mapleton.us

Adams County School District No. 1, more familiar to most as Mapleton Public Schools, lies just north of Denver and includes part of the city of Thornton and some of unincorporated Adams County. With the third-smallest total enrollment in Metro Denver, the system has an early learning center, a Montessori preschool/elementary school, three elementary schools, six combination elementary/middle schools, two combination middle/high

schools, and four high schools. Although this system has Metro Denver's lowest percentage of teachers with post-graduate (master's or higher) degrees and one of the highest pupil-teacher ratios, it has one of the area's lower high-school dropout rates.

The district provides a lot of special opportunities for its diverse student body, including programs in back-to-basics, learning enrichment, accelerated classes, bilingual and multicultural education, Native American education, and open enrollment for all schools based on availability.

ADAMS COUNTY SCHOOL DISTRICT NO. 14
4720 East 69th Avenue, Commerce City
(303) 853-3333
www.adams12.org

One of Metro Denver's smaller school systems, District No. 14 has seven elementary schools, two middle schools, two high schools, and one alternative high school. It also has a full-time preschool. This district pulls students from Commerce City and areas in Thornton and unincorporated Adams County. It's solidly in the midrange of Metro Denver school districts as far as the education and salaries of its teachers and its spending per pupil. Its high-school dropout rate is the highest, and it has Metro Denver's lowest graduation rate and lowest composite ACT scores in the most recent rankings.

At the same time, District 14 has a gung-ho attitude about the future, with a new commitment to improving its schools under a basic "Reading + Writing x Math" CSAP-driven base curriculum. Adams City Middle School has a personalized alternative instructional program for students at risk of dropping out. Since it was established in 1991, the program has grown to serve 6,870 students and families. With more than 77 percent of its students Hispanic, Adams 14 puts a lot of effort into bilingual education and accommodating cultural diversity.

ADAMS COUNTY SCHOOL DISTRICT NO. 50
2401 West 80th Avenue, Westminster
(303) 428-3511
www.adams50.org

School District No. 50 serves the city of Westminster and parts of Arvada and unincorporated Adams County with one early-childhood program, 15 elementary schools, four middle schools, three high schools, and a career enrichment park. Its average teacher salary is competitive in the metro area and its revenue per pupil is the lowest. Its mission statement is "Push to excel; prepare to succeed."

In 1993 the district began the Graphics Communication Cluster, a prototype for a new method of integrating academic and technical education. Today there are four cluster programs: Graphics Communication, Business Cluster, Engineering Cluster, and Health Studies Cluster. Through these, students are afforded the opportunity to succeed in an applied setting, where they can see the relevance of academics in a real-world environment.

Adams County 50 pushes for technological innovation and offers such features as comprehensive networked computer labs and a computer in every classroom that provides the teacher with classroom management. There are more than 1,800 Pentium-class computers district-wide.

ADAMS 12 FIVE STAR SCHOOLS
1500 East 128th Avenue, Thornton
(720) 972-4000
www.adams12.org
The Five Star Schools, Adams County's largest school district and the seventh-largest in the state, includes more than 36,000 students attending 48 schools in a 62-square-mile area serving Northglenn, Federal Heights, and parts of Thornton, Broomfield, Westminster, and unincorporated Adams County. In addition to 29 elementary schools, it includes nine middle schools and six high schools as well as the Bollman Technical Education Center, Vantage Point Alternative School, and four charter schools—Stargate, for the gifted and talented; the Academy of Charter Schools, a basic school; Colorado Virtual Academy; and the Pinnacle Learning Center.

Per-pupil spending at Five Star Schools is in the midrange in Greater Denver, as are the graduation and dropout rates. Principals work in conjunction with school improvement teams to further student achievement at each school. The district reviewed and approved a strategic plan that sets goals for improved graduation rate and a lower dropout rate. Another district goal is an increase in proficiencies for all students. The district honors the diversity of individuals and believes a student's success is linked to a "responsive school community."

> **i** Colorado high-school seniors have the opportunity to take college courses at community colleges and state universities and colleges. Not only does this provide a challenging academic experience, but it also reduces the duration and expense of college.

AURORA PUBLIC SCHOOLS
1085 Peoria Street, Aurora
(303) 344-8060
www.aps.k12.co.us
Aurora Public Schools covers most of Aurora, which is Metro Denver's second-largest city. The district's mission is to develop its kids into "lifelong learners who value themselves, contribute to their community, and succeed in a changing world."

Strong emphasis is placed on student achievement in basic subjects. The district is committed to preparing students for life in the 21st century by helping them become self-directed learners, collaborative workers, complex thinkers, community contributors, and quality producers. Special services and classes are offered for gifted and talented students, special-education students, and non-English-speaking young parents, preschoolers, and adults.

The Aurora district has a total of 34 elementary schools, seven middle schools, and eight high schools, three of which are alternative high schools. There are also three charter schools, a vocational school, and several specialty alternative schools.

Special classes in 50 skill areas are offered within the district at the T. H. Pickens Technical Center, 500 Airport Boulevard, Aurora. Some programs offer credit toward an associate degree from the Community College of Aurora.

The district has been designated by School Match, an international business relocation firm, as one of 50 in Colorado to provide "what parents want."

BRIGHTON PUBLIC SCHOOLS
630 South 8th Avenue, Brighton
(303) 655-2900
www.brightonps27j.k12.co.us
The closest thing to a small-town, country-school district in Metro Denver, Brighton Public Schools (District 27J) serves about 240 square miles of farmland around the 21,000 population of Brighton, the Adams County seat. As a school district, Brighton's enrollment is the second-smallest in Metro Denver. The district has five elementary schools, two middle schools, one high school, one charter school, and one alternative school. Just about half of Brighton's teaching staff has master's degrees. The dropout rate is the Denver area's second highest. In accordance with state law, District 27J is developing content standards for all academic areas. Included in this effort toward Standards Based Education is the improvement of instructional techniques as well as the assessment of skills and knowledge learned. The average composite ACT score for Brighton students is 17.5. The district's schools offer enrichment programs including bilingual education, programs in basic skills, and accelerated education.

CHERRY CREEK SCHOOL DISTRICT 5
4700 South Yosemite Street, Englewood
(303) 773-1184
www.ccsd.k12.co.us/
Covering Metro Denver's southeastern corner, District 5 encompasses Cherry Hills Village, Glendale, parts of Aurora, Englewood, Greenwood Village, and some of unincorporated Arapahoe County. It includes the rapidly growing and well-to-do communities along the northern edge

District 5 has some impressive statistics, including the state's highest average teacher salary. It has 39 elementary schools, 11 middle schools, six high schools, and one alternative high school. Thirteen Cherry Creek schools have received the John Irwin Award, given to the state's highest-performing schools. In 1996 West Middle School also became a Blue Ribbon School. Smoky Hill High has one of Colorado's International Baccalaureate programs, in which advanced studies give students a jump on college. Every elementary and middle school in the district makes special accommodations for gifted and talented students.

i Metro Denver's largest student populations are not in the city and county of Denver but in Arapahoe and Jefferson Counties.

DENVER PUBLIC SCHOOLS
900 Grant Street
(720) 423-3200
www.dpsk12.org
The Denver Public Schools is the second-largest district in the state, serving 72,000 students. It is home to many high-performing schools and programs that serve a diverse population. The district routinely produces graduates bound for the country's top colleges and universities, and it boasts the 2006 Kinder Excellence in Teaching national award-winner, Linda Alston, a kindergarten teacher at Fairview Elementary. The no-strings-attached, $100,000 grant recognizes an outstanding public-school teacher who teaches in a low-income community.

The district's George Washington and East High Schools were ranked among the nation's top by *Newsweek* for promoting Advanced Placement and International Baccalaureate classes. They ranked 50th and 84th out of 450, respectively. The district is also home to an array of magnet schools, including the Center for International Students, two high-school computer magnet programs, and the Denver School of the Arts, the only one of its kind in the region. With the assistance of Collaborative Decision-Making

Close-up

The Teacher of the Century and Her School of Unlimited Opportunity

Emily Griffith is still Denver's best-known educator, even though she died in 1947. As a Denver public school teacher who taught 8th grade at the Twenty-Fourth Street School during the day, Griffith volunteered at night teaching adults, many of them immigrants, to read and write and acquire basic math skills. But her true goal was to start a school where the age limit was lifted and the hours were flexible, so that a working adult who could spare an hour could come for some job training or self-improvement.

In 1916 Denver Public Schools converted the Longfellow School at 13th and Welton Streets into the Opportunity School. (It didn't become Emily Griffith Opportunity School until 1934, a year after Emily retired.) Her eponymous school, which has touched more than 1.5 million lives since it opened, had a dream to help people help themselves. On the first day Emily sat near the front door and personally greeted each student. By the end of the first week, 1,400 students had registered. School was open 13 hours a day, five days a week. Tuition was free. Emily's goal was to provide training wherever it was needed.

One day a man came to look at course offerings. When he started to leave without registering, Emily asked why he hadn't signed up. "There are no courses for sign painters," he told her. Shortly thereafter, the school offered a course in sign painting. Over the years the course offerings have continued to meet students'—and society's—needs. From radio communications and ambulance driving during World War I to victory gardening and defense work during World War II, the Opportunity School has stayed current with a changing marketplace.

A few years ago, local grocery stores, including King Soopers, Safeway, and Cub Foods, approached the school's administration with a request for a program designed to train workers for bakery and deli work, an area that would continue to grow as more people turned to prepared foods for their meals. Thus was born the food-services department, which operates a bistro and restaurant where students can practice their craft.

Though many courses lean heavily toward technology, the school still offers classes in areas such as cake decorating, creative sewing, floral design, dental anatomy—even aircraft-accident investigation. In fact, just scanning course offerings can be enjoyable in and of itself.

What has remained constant since 1916 are the high-school and continuing education courses for adults who never finished high school and immigrants who wish to become citizens. Each year the school enrolls between 11,000 and 15,000 students and graduates over 8,000. While the list of graduates isn't exactly filled with household names, their stories are the stuff of the American dream: a college dropout who took transportation courses at EGOS, went back to college, then law school, and is now a transportation lawyer; a man who took automotive mechanics classes and today owns his own transmission shop; a woman who took typing classes, which launched her into the business world, and eventually become a state senator; a former mayor's sister-in law who dropped out of high school 24 years earlier and graduated with a GED from EGOS in June of 1997, armed with a certificate in Early Child Care Professions.

Today almost 15,000 students train in 350 classes. Students range from age 17 to 94. Though tuition is no longer free (it was until several years ago), it now costs $1.55 an hour—still a bargain by anyone's standards. Better yet, the school and its students provide a wide range of services to the community at discount prices. Want a filling, inexpensive lunch? Twelfth Street Deli, which trains the food-service students, offers meals for $4.00 to $6.25. Need a haircut? A barber student will cut your locks for $3. How about a manicure for $4? Having dinner guests but don't have a table decoration? Floral centerpieces are $8 to $15.

Teams (school staff, parents, and community representatives) at each school, the district's neighborhood schools are constantly adapting and reshaping themselves to meet the unique needs of the city's many neighborhoods.

DOUGLAS COUNTY SCHOOL DISTRICT
620 Wilcox Street, Castle Rock
(303) 387-0100
www.dcsdk12.org
This district's 42 elementary schools, four charter schools, seven middle schools, eight high schools, and three alternative schools cover a far-flung area ranging from the southern edges of Jefferson and Arapahoe Counties much of the way to Colorado Springs. Douglas is one of the fastest-growing counties in the United States. The district currently has 48,000 students.

The majority of the county's elementary students go to school on a four-track, year-round calendar, a rotation of nine weeks in school followed by a three-week break, throughout the year.

Douglas County has one of the highest graduation rates and the lowest dropout rate. How do they do it? The system overall places a high value on educational excellence. Cherokee Trail Elementary School in Parker was named by *Child* magazine as one of the 10 best schools in the nation. Metro Denver's first charter school, Academy Charter School, is in Castle Rock. Beginning in the 1994-95 school year, the county approved a teacher-compensation plan linked to performance rather than longevity.

Douglas County is one of four school districts partnering in the Renaissance Expeditionary Learning Outward Bound School, which is located in Parker. The K through 12 school has won national grants and acclaim for its challenging learning program.

ENGLEWOOD SCHOOLS
4101 South Bannock Street, Englewood
(303) 761-7050
www.englewoodschools.org
Also known as Arapahoe County School District No. 1, this district educates approximately 4,300 students in 10 schools spanning pre-K through 12th grade.

Englewood was not shy about its educational ambitions when it adopted a student-created name for its only alternative high school: Colorado's Finest Alternative High School. The school was devised by the Englewood School District for kids at risk of dropping out. It received the John Irwin Excellence in Education Award the first six years it was given, and the school was twice named one of the top 50 in the United States by *Redbook* magazine.

The Board of Education recently adopted 10 core beliefs; among them are emphasizing high student achievement, honoring diversity, and valuing every student and family.

JEFFERSON COUNTY PUBLIC SCHOOLS
1829 Denver West Drive, Golden
(303) 982-6500
www.jeffcopublicschools.org
Jefferson County makes up Colorado's largest school district, with more than 84,000 students and a budget of $735 million. Many people seem to want to get their kids into Jefferson County schools.

What is it about Jeffco that makes it so desirable? Well, it's a nice place to live, right up against the mountains with a lot of upscale neighborhoods and light-industry, white-collar employment. Also, the school system has one of Greater Denver's highest percentages of teachers with master's degrees or higher and the second-highest average teacher salary.

Jeffco has a "least-restrictive environment" policy for special-education students that gives primary responsibility for a special-needs student's education to the neighborhood school. The school district also has a Multicultural Learning Center that provides multicultural resources for teachers across the district.

Jeffco pursues these lofty goals in neighborhood schools—93 elementary schools, 19 middle schools, and 17 high schools—as well as a wide range of educational-choice programs. These include open enrollment where space is available, schools within a school, alternative schools, and self-governing charter schools.

LITTLETON PUBLIC SCHOOLS
5776 South Crocker Street, Littleton
(303) 347-3300
www.littletonpublicschools.net
Pulling students from the city of Littleton and the city of Centennial, Littleton Public Schools is another one of those districts that does a good job with its money. The district serves more than 16,000 students in Littleton and Centennial, including 15 elementary schools, four middle schools, three senior high schools, three alternative schools, two charter schools, and three preschool programs.

LPS students consistently rank above state and national averages on standardized tests. Littleton has one of Metro Denver's highest composite ACT scores in recent rankings, the third-highest average teacher salaries, and the third-lowest high-school dropout rate. Of the district's more than 1,000 full-time teachers, more than 64 percent hold master's or doctorate degrees, and they average 12 years of teaching experience.

The district places a high value on small class sizes, which range from 17 to 23 for elementary and 28 to 32 for middle-and high-school classes. School choice is available to all district residents through an open enrollment/transfer policy. LPS also enjoys a high level of community involvement and support.

SHERIDAN SCHOOL DISTRICT NO. 2
4000 South Lowell Boulevard
(720) 833-6991
www.sheridank12.org
Metro Denver's smallest school district, Sheridan has a total enrollment of 1,750 in two elementary schools, one middle school, and one high school. It serves the city of Sheridan, which surrounds the Englewood Municipal Golf Course and pieces of Englewood. The district's graduation rate is the fourth highest in Denver. Not surprisingly, it also has the lowest student-teacher ratio.

PRIVATE SCHOOLS

Not every private school in the area is included here, of course, but you will find the larger, as well as many smaller, schools that come to us by word-of-mouth recommendation. Some accept only one sex, and many of them are religion-based private schools. None of the religious schools profess to turn away students on the basis of their religion or lack of religious commitment. Actually, however, religious schools require students to take religious instruction, and lack of adequate preparation can in some cases disqualify a student. At Yeshiva Toras Chaim School, for example, students need to have a sufficient grounding in the Hebrew language, since the school focuses heavily in Talmud and Torah.

ACCELERATED SCHOOLS
2160 South Cook Street
(303) 758-2003
www.acceleratedschools.org
Students, including the gifted and the learning disabled, study independently through individually prescribed instructional and motivational systems. Heavy use of computer instructional programs increases time spent on prescribed learning tasks and gives immediate feedback with an emphasis on practical business applications. Students on six campuses in Denver and Kansas City can attend part-time or full-time in morning, afternoon, and evening classes. The school offers accelerated reading and college classes for extra credit as well as field trips and other activities. Transportation to and from home is included in tuition. Housing is available for students who need it. The school serves 150 students in grades K through 12.

ALEXANDER DAWSON SCHOOL
10455 Dawson Drive, Lafayette
(303) 665-6679
www.dawsonschool.org
This college-prep school is on a 135-acre campus 35 minutes north of Denver. The school has a need-based financial aid program with more

than $600,000 in grants, which go to 20 percent of the students. Though the school has historically had boarding students, it has been strictly a day school since 1998. The rigorous academic program includes a keen interest in the arts. Alexander Dawson takes part in interscholastic athletic competitions, including canoeing, skiing, and horsemanship. Stables with horses are on campus. The school has a new library as well as a $3 million gym and a $2.7 million arts center. It offers grades K through 12.

BEACON COUNTRY DAY SCHOOL
6100 East Belleview Avenue
Greenwood Village
(303) 771-3990
www.beaconcountrydayschool.com
Beacon Country Day School is a private, nonprofit school on a large acreage in Greenwood Village. The programs use each child's interests to promote learning in classrooms designed for small learning groups. The grounds include a pond and wetlands area for eco-studies. This school also has ponies that the children learn to care for and ride. Offering pre-K through 8th grade, the school has 125 students and is coed.

BETHLEHEM LUTHERAN SCHOOL
2100 North Wadsworth Boulevard
Lakewood
(303) 233-0401
www.bethluth.net/school.htm
Bethlehem Lutheran, a coed school, is part of the national network of Lutheran schools, the largest Protestant school group in the country. It offers quality education in a Christian environment and has received National Lutheran School Accreditation. It has a good music program, computer lab instruction, and interscholastic athletics as well as an advanced reading program for students in 3rd through 6th grades. The school's 365 students are in grades pre-K through 8.

BISHOP MACHEBEUF CATHOLIC HIGH SCHOOL
458 Unita Way
(303) 344-0082
www.machebeuf.org
Formerly Machebeuf Catholic High School, this school emphasizes the students' "responsibility as children of God in a democratic society" as well as preparing them for college. The school boasts that more than 95 percent of its graduates enrolled in college by graduation, and it employs a full-time college admissions counselor. More than 480 students are in grades 9 through 12.

CHRIST THE KING ROMAN CATHOLIC SCHOOL
860 Elm Street
(303) 321-2123
www.christthekingdenver.org
This school, where boys and girls in grades K through 8 wear uniforms, places a high premium on top-quality academic skills along with developing a sense of responsibility all within the framework of the Catholic faith. Along with religion, students are exposed to a core curriculum enhanced by music and art. Extracurricular activities include Junior Great Books, volleyball, basketball, and baseball. The school's enrollment is 250.

COLORADO ACADEMY
3800 South Pierce Street
(303) 986-1501
www.coloradoacademy.org
Founded in 1906, Colorado Academy is in southwest Denver on a lovely 94-acre campus. It's a college-prep program emphasizing a well-rounded education in academics, fine arts, and athletics with a 10-to-1 ratio of students to teachers. Bus transportation is available. About 875 students are in grades pre-K through 12.

COLORADO CATHOLIC ACADEMY
11180 West 44th Avenue, Wheat Ridge
(303) 422-9549
www.coloradocatholicacademy.com
Near the western edge of Wheat Ridge, this coed

academy offers a traditional curriculum and teaches the Catholic faith to 50 students in grades 1 through 12. Students attend weekly Latin mass and daily rosary.

DENVER ACADEMY
4400 East Iliff Avenue
(303) 777-5870
www.denveracademy.org
The Denver Academy applies a structured, closely supervised, and highly personalized approach to educating students with learning differences. This school has a 7-to-1 student-teacher ratio. About 420 boys and girls fill grades 1 through 12. Extracurricular activities on this 22-acre campus include drama and sports.

DENVER CHRISTIAN SCHOOLS
2135 South Pearl Street
(303) 733-2421
www.denver-christian.org
Denver Christian Schools was established by a small group that settled here before World War I, many of whom were from the Netherlands and ill with tuberculosis. Since the first classes in 1917, DCS has grown to four schools at three Denver locations: Denver Christian High School at 2135 South Pearl Street; Van Dellen Preschool and K-8 Campus at 4200 East Warren Avenue; and Highlands Ranch Preschool and K-8 Campus at 1733 Dad Clark Drive. More than 1,000 students study in grades K through 12.

DENVER INTERNATIONAL SCHOOL
1101 South Race Street
(303) 756-0381
www.dischool.org
Denver International School is a multicultural school that attracts students committed to studying in two languages, choosing between French, Spanish, and Mandarin Chinese. Founded in 1977, it offers grades pre-K through 5 and prepares its students to thrive in a global society. More than 200 students study the usual round of subjects in bilingual instruction. Child care is offered before and after school. Language courses and clubs are offered to nonstudents as well.

DENVER LUTHERAN HIGH SCHOOL
3201 West Arizona Avenue
(303) 934-2345
www.denverlhs.org
Owned by the Colorado Lutheran High School Association, Lutheran High has been operating since 1955 on a 12-acre campus in southwest Denver. It was named in 1991 as one of 222 national recipients (four in the state) of the National Exemplary School award for exceptional educational services with outstanding staff in an atmosphere conducive to achieving excellence. There are 230 students in grades 9 through 12.

THE DENVER WALDORF SCHOOL
940 Tillmore Street
(303) 777-0531
www.denverwaldorf.org
The Waldorf movement emphasizes working with the whole child—teaching to the hands, the head, and the heart, according to the school's administration. Contrary to the popular belief that it is an arts program, the Waldorf curriculum is academically rigorous, and by 8th grade, most students have had exposure to chemistry, biology, geometry, and algebra. The arts, both visual and performance, are integral to the program as well and permeate every aspect of learning in this integrated curriculum.

The school seeks to meet the needs of the child at each developmental age and works to establish a balance and rhythm throughout each day, week, month, and year. The school offers pre-K through 12 and serves approximately 300 students.

FAITH CHRISTIAN ACADEMY
6210 Ward Road
(Elementary/Middle School), Arvada
(303) 424-7310

4890 Carr Street (High School), Arvada
(303) 424-7310
www.fca-schools.org
A unique, charismatic Christian school, Faith is

open to anyone interested in a Christian education. The curriculum includes the full range of traditional subjects. About 1,250 students study in grades K through 12. The Ward Road address is for grades K through 5, with grades 6, 7, and 8 just across the street. The Carr Street address is for grades 9 through 12.

FOOTHILLS ACADEMY
4725 Miller Street, Wheat Ridge
(303) 431-0920
www.foothills-academy.org
Valued by alumni and children of alumni, this is one of those schools where word-of mouth is the best advertising. The small and interactive classes expose 200 boys and girls to basic skills as well as art, music, foreign languages, physical education, and an extensive outdoor education program. Foothills emphasizes "experiential learning and exploration," with field trips and visiting artist programs, outdoor experiences, and community projects and services. Once a month they conduct a "mini-society" in which students buy and sell homemade goods, act out the workings of government, and simulate success in the real world. The school offers grades K through 12.

GOOD SHEPHERD CATHOLIC SCHOOL
620 Elizabeth Street
(303) 321-6231
www.goodshepherddenver.org
Good Shepherd is between 6th Avenue and East Colfax Avenue, York Street and Colorado Boulevard. It offers a Catholic education along with a core educational curriculum. The enrichment program is a before- and after-school program, between 6:30 a.m. and 6 p.m., which includes guided study time, structured play time, and extracurricular activities. A Montessori program is also available for age three through grade 3. The school offers grades pre-K through 8 to 280 boys and girls.

GRALAND COUNTRY DAY SCHOOL
30 Birch Street
(303) 399-0390
www.graland.org

Among Denver's premier private schools, Graland has a history of fostering academic and personal growth. Its enrollment is limited to maintain small classes and close interaction between teachers and students. Graland is in a residential neighborhood 5 miles south of downtown Denver. About 600 boys and girls study in grades K through 9.

HAVERN SCHOOL
4000 South Wadsworth Boulevard
Littleton
(303) 986-4587
www.haverncenter.org
This is one of the best and oldest schools in the area for students with average IQs who have been diagnosed as learning disabled. With a better than one-to-one student-teacher ratio, the school offers kids with learning disabilities individualized instruction and occupational, speech, and language therapy as well as self-esteem groups. The goal of Havern is to ultimately reintroduce the child into mainstream education. The school has 10 students in the elementary grades.

HOLY FAMILY HIGH SCHOOL
5195 West 144 Avenue, Broomfield
(303) 410-1411
www.holyfamilyhs.com
Founded in 1922 as a parish high school, Holy Family's mission statement proclaims a Catholic-Christian learning environment that "stresses academic excellence, fosters mutual respect, demands responsibility, and encourages self-growth." Besides the standard high-school core curriculum, there are also courses in subjects such as theology, journalism, advanced computer applications, law, and drama. About 480 students study in grades 9 through 12.

HUMANEX ACADEMY
2700 South Zuni Street
(303) 783-0137
www.humanexacademy.com
This alternative high school is for students in grades 9 through 12 who may not have been successful in other schools. Humanex is dedi-

cated to the idea that every student can succeed in the proper environment. The school has a student-teacher ratio of 7 to 1, a closed campus, progress reports to parents every two weeks, and parent notification within 20 minutes after school starts if the student does not show up. It is oriented to pupils with ADD or ADHD who read at least at the 6th-grade level. Enrollment is at 60 students, male and female.

J. K. MULLEN HIGH SCHOOL
3601 South Lowell Boulevard
(303) 761-1764
www.mullenhighschool.com
One of Denver's more well-known Catholic private high schools, Mullen was founded in 1931 as a home for orphaned boys. In 1965 it became J. K. Mullen Prep, a college-prep school for boys. It has been coeducational since 1989. It's run by the Christian Brothers of St. John the Baptist de LaSalle, a religious teaching order. Today it has a population of more than 1,000 students.

KENT DENVER SCHOOL
4000 East Quincy Avenue, Englewood
(303) 770-7660
www.kentdenver.org
Kent Denver has roots going back to the founding of the Kent School for girls in 1922 and the founding of the Denver Country Day School for boys. The two schools merged to create the present institution in 1974. Its challenging, college-preparatory curriculum produced an average SAT score of 1,246 and an average SAT II score of 1,304 in the graduating class of 2004. Kent Denver has a campus of 200 acres with five academic buildings that include more than 40 classrooms and laboratories; six studios for music, dance, and art; two gymnasiums; six tennis courts; and 20 acres of playing fields. In grades 6 through 12, there are 655 students.

THE LOGAN SCHOOL FOR CREATIVE LEARNING
1005 Yosemite Circle
(303) 340-2444
www.theloganschool.org

A school for gifted and creative children grades K through 8, the Logan School boasts a stimulating academic program with hands-on learning experiences for its 190 boys and girls. To be considered for admission, students must complete educational-assessment and intelligence testing and make an observation visit to a Logan classroom.

MARANATHA CHRISTIAN CENTER
7180 Oak Street, Arvada
(303) 431-5653
www.maranathachristiancenter.org
A Bible-believing, nondenominational educational center with Christ-centered academics taught by qualified, born-again staff, Maranatha was opened in 1980 on an agricultural piece of land that previously had been occupied by a house and barn. Now its 15 acres include more than 60,000 square feet of classrooms, offices, a gymnasium, locker rooms, a learning center, a library, and a computer lab for 860 students in grades pre-K through 12.

MILE HIGH ADVENTIST ACADEMY
711 East Yale Avenue
(303) 744-1069
www.milehighacademy.org
This school dates from a one-room school established by Seventh-Day Adventists in Denver in 1913. The themes here are academic excellence, individual resourcefulness and responsibility, Christian philosophy, and making the world a better place within the student's sphere of influence. About 250 students attend grades K through 12.

MONTESSORI SCHOOL OF DENVER
1460 South Holly Street
(303) 756-9441
www.montessoridenver.org
The oldest Montessori in Denver (there are other independent Montessori schools in Metro Denver), this school has about 275 boys and girls, ages 3 through 12. Like all Montessori schools, this one adheres to a philosophy that allows students "the

opportunity to achieve individually, creatively, and successfully." The school has a wide parent volunteer base and offers a Montessori curriculum including botany, zoology, language, math, art, physical education, and Spanish.

MONTCLAIR ACADEMY
206 Red Cross Way
(303) 366-7588
www.montclairacademy.org

This pre-K through 8th-grade school serves 185 students. The curriculum has a strong liberal arts emphasis with a variety of enrichment programs, including field trips and special classes. The student-teacher ratio is 15 to 1. Enrichment programs are offered after school until about 5 p.m.

MOST PRECIOUS BLOOD PARISH SCHOOL
3959 East Iliff Avenue
(303) 756-3083
www.mpbdenver.org

Students get a standard curriculum here along with religious instruction, including morning prayer and mass once a month. The school also features geography and spelling bees, science and art fairs, speech meets, and a "super citizens" program in which grades 3 through 5 choose a super citizen from their class each month to be honored by the Colorado Optimists Club. Grades pre-K through 8.

OUR LADY OF FATIMA
10530 West 20th Avenue, Lakewood
(303) 233-2500
www.fatimalakewood.com

At this Catholic school, religious instruction is offered in addition to the academic courses. The school has an extensive athletic program as well as special features including a science lab, a reading lab, and a computer lab. About 305 students are in grades pre-K through 8.

REGIS JESUIT HIGH SCHOOL
6400 South Lewiston Way, Aurora
(303) 269-8000 (boys division)
(303) 269-8100 (girls division)
www.regisjesuit.com

Regis has the Jesuit-school mystique of quality education with a public-service mentality. It has earned a U.S. Department of Education School of Excellence designation. Special senior projects, volunteerism, student retreats, counseling, and peer tutoring are among the additions to regular curriculum here, as well as college credit earned from Regis University. Its population is currently at about 1,350, including 500 girls.

RICKS CENTER FOR GIFTED CHILDREN
2040 South York Street
(303) 871-2982
www.du.edu/ricks

As the name implies, Ricks Center is for children who've demonstrated "educational needs in the gifted range." A strong academic curriculum is enhanced with extracurricular activities such as chess, student council, yearbook, and Odyssey of the Mind. The school serves 300 students, grades pre-K through 8, and is part of the University of Denver.

ST. FRANCIS DE SALES SCHOOL
235 South Sherman Street
(303) 744-7231

Since 1904 this Catholic school has been serving the same neighborhood south of downtown Denver, combining religious instruction and experiences with a strong basic curriculum and small classes for its 240 students in grades pre-K through 8.

ST. JAMES CATHOLIC SCHOOL
1250 Newport Street
(303) 333-8275
www.stjamesdenver.org

On Denver's eastern side, just northwest of the former Lowry Air Force Base, St. James provides a values-based education that emphasizes academic excellence, self-direction, responsibility, a genuine love of learning, and the wherewithal to become solid Catholic citizens. The school teaches 175 boys and girls in preschool through 8th grade.

ST. LOUIS CATHOLIC SCHOOL
3301 South Sherman, Englewood
(303) 762-8307
www.stlouiscatholicschool.org

Mastery of the basics is the focus at St. Louis, along with art, music, computer training, and programs such as Junior Achievement, Great Books, and Community Resource. It's a Catholic-sponsored school, but non-Catholics are welcome. There's religious instruction, student-prepared masses, and special sacramental instruction for 175 students in grades K through 8. Extracurricular activities include spelling and geography bees, competitive speech, and competitive sports.

ST. MARY'S ACADEMY
4545 South University Boulevard
Englewood
(303) 762-8300
www.smanet.org

St. Mary's Academy is a Catholic, independent school founded in 1864 by the Sisters of Loretto. In 1875 it awarded the first high-school diploma in the Colorado Territory. Among its features are its Early Learning Center at the Denver Tech Center and the all-girls' high school. St. Mary's emphasizes values-based education, small classes, strong curriculum, personalized attention, and community service. Coed through 8th grade, girls only in high school, St. Mary's serves a total of 785 students.

ST. THERESE SCHOOL
1200 Kenton Street, Aurora
(303) 364-7494
www.stthereseschool.com

St. Therese School includes Catholic teaching with its conventional curriculum. It's staffed by Sisters of Charity as well as lay teachers. It has a reading specialist and full-time teachers in physical education, computer science, and music education for 225 students in grades preschool through 8.

ST. VINCENT DE PAUL SCHOOL
1164 South Josephine Street
(303) 777-3812
www.svdponline.net/svdpk8

A Catholic parish school, St. Vincent was founded to instruct children in the Catholic faith while also providing them with all the standard core academic subjects. Special features include a technology program and full-time teachers for computer education, art, music, and physical education. The student-teacher ratio is 20 to 1. St. Vincent's starts at preschool and goes up through 8th grade. It serves 480 students.

STS. PETER AND PAUL CATHOLIC ELEMENTARY SCHOOL
3920 Pierce Street, Wheat Ridge
(303) 424-0402
www.sppscatholic.com

One of the west side's better-known Catholic schools, Sts. Peter and Paul provides sound academics and Catholic values and traditions to 425 students from pre-K through 8th grade. Features of its integrated curriculum include a literature program, computers, art, music, speech and drama, math, and physical education.

SHRINE OF ST. ANNE CATHOLIC SCHOOL
7320 Grant Place, Arvada
(303) 422-1800
www.stannescatholic.com

A high-quality, well-rounded curriculum in basic academics is accompanied by daily classes in religion. The school describes itself as a "Christian community witnessing to the gospel message of Jesus Christ." Special features include an education fair, a science fair, and a life education program, which tackles real-world issues that students face and will face in life. The school offers a computer lab, science lab, and library to its 473 students in grades K through 8.

SILVER STATE CHRISTIAN SCHOOL
875 South Sheridan Boulevard, Lakewood
(303) 922-8850

Strong in music and orchestra, with daily Bible

classes, Silver State has its own mix of standard educational curricula. The school also participates in interscholastic sports governed by the Colorado High School Sports Athletic Association. Silver State has 195 students in grades K through 12.

STANLEY BRITISH PRIMARY SCHOOL
350 Quebec Street
(303) 360-0803
www.stanleybps.org
Stanley British Primary School (or B.P.S. as it's called locally) teaches 340 students in grades K through 8. Its philosophy is that education should be experiential, and to that end, students study where they are developmentally, rather than strictly by age or grade. The curriculum revolves around core subjects, with the inclusion of study skills. This school relies heavily on parental involvement, both in the classroom and in fund-raising.

YESHIVA TORAS CHAIM SCHOOL
1555 Stuart Street
(303) 629-8200
This private orthodox Jewish high school would be one of many in New York, but here in the Rocky Mountain area it has been unique since its founding in 1967. Half of each day is spent in studying Talmud and Torah, and the other half is spent in secular studies. About half of the 65 male students board at the school.

COLLEGES AND UNIVERSITIES

COLORADO CHRISTIAN UNIVERSITY
8787 West Alameda Avenue, Lakewood
(303) 963-3000
www.ccu.edu
As the only major evangelical Christian university in the Rocky Mountain region, Colorado Christian University offers fully accredited undergraduate and graduate courses with 21 undergraduate majors. CCU also offers programs designed to serve the social and spiritual needs of all students. The university has an enrollment of more than 2,000 students in all programs. The Adult Studies program offers accelerated evening, weekend, and on-site corporate classes (on-site training to company personnel) for adult learners, with centers at Lakewood's main campus and in Colorado Springs, Loveland, and Grand Junction. It offers undergraduate and graduate degrees and a teacher-recertification program, as well as an online MBA program. CCU is a Division II member of the NCAA, competing in men's and women's basketball, soccer, cross-country, and tennis in addition to women's volleyball and men's golf.

COLORADO SCHOOL OF MINES
1500 Illinois Street, Golden
(303) 273-3000
www.mines.edu
"Mines," as it's called, is a school of engineering, energy, environment, and economics nationally known for academic rigor. It was founded in Golden in 1874 because that city was the gateway to Colorado's booming minerals mining industry. A public school, Mines now has about 3,900 students who focus on areas such as engineering, engineering systems, chemical engineering, petroleum engineering, mining engineering, economics, geology, and geological engineering. Degrees are also available in chemistry, geochemistry, petroleum engineering, and physics. Its metallurgical, materials science, environmental science, and engineering programs are among the best in the nation. Not surprisingly, Mines is strong in math and computer science.

Mines also has the benefit of a beautiful location. Golden is nestled against the foothills behind (from Denver) South Table Mountain and retains a small-town atmosphere. The school is a short walk from downtown. Golden is connected by I-70 and US 6 directly into Denver, by I-70 into the mountains, and by US 6 West through scenic Clear Creek Canyon into the Gilpin County/Clear Creek County historic mining areas and mountain communities. Golden claims a higher per-capita concentration of Ph.D.s than Boulder, home of the University of Colorado.

COLORADO STATE UNIVERSITY—DENVER CENTER (CSU)

410 17th Street, Suite 1400
(303) 573-6318
www.learn.colostate.edu/denver

Colorado State University in Fort Collins is one of the state's most highly esteemed public schools. It offers a significant number of majors that are not available anywhere else in the state. It's nationally famous for its College of Natural Resources and its School of Veterinary Medicine. CSU is the state's only land-grant university; its Agricultural Experiment Station and Cooperative Extension form the education/research backbone of Colorado's agriculture industry.

CSU's Denver-area educational and technical services are found in a single location, the Colorado State University—Denver Center. Located downtown on Tremont Avenue between 16th and 17th Streets are services aimed heavily toward downtown Denver's working population. Among the degree programs offered are the executive MBA program, communication management, organizational performance and change, and construction management. Certification programs are offered in construction management, process management, and project management. Offerings include courses in education, vocational education, business and professional, and personal advancement. This campus specializes in customized training for businesses.

COLUMBIA COLLEGE AT AURORA

14707 East 2nd Avenue, Suite 100
Aurora
(303) 340-8050
www.ccis.edu/aurora

This is actually one of 30 extension centers of the Columbia College campus in Columbia, Missouri, but it's a sizeable operation. Some 700 students attend evening and weekend classes here, working toward associate and baccalaureate degrees in the liberal arts, business administration, computer information systems, psychology, criminal justice, history, government, and other subjects. It's primarily adult education, with an average student age of 34.

> **i** The Colorado Free University (which isn't really free, but nearly so) offers a vast array of fun, interesting, and informative classes for busy people. Whether it's computers, yoga, or wine tasting, CFU has something for everyone. Pick up class schedules at grocery and convenience stores.

THE METROPOLITAN STATE COLLEGE OF DENVER

1201 5th Street (mailing)
900 Auraria Parkway (physical address)
(303) 556-2400
www.mscd.edu

Founded in 1965, Metro, Colorado's third-largest college with more than 20,000 students, is a cosmopolitan city college on a 175-acre oasis on the edge of Denver's downtown business district. Half of its student body is of traditional college age (18 to 25), and nearly half consists of nontraditional students—those older than age 25 who have already been in the work force. This, of course, can be a delight to professors who find they are dealing not only with students fresh out of high school but also with professional adults as well. And it's great for students because they can learn from their peers as well as their professors. Metro has a reputation as the working student's college, with an emphasis on applied education, and takes pains to accommodate that student with a lot of weekend and evening classes.

The main campus, the Auraria Higher Education Center, is unique. Metropolitan State College of Denver shares the campus with two other institutions, the Community College of Denver and the University of Colorado at Denver. The three schools together offer a more potent education package than any one could alone because they allow students to cross-register for classes in all three schools and enjoy a combined menu of lectures, concerts, plays, and student programs.

Metro offers a full lineup of NCAA Division II intercollegiate athletic competitions in men's and women's sports. The teams use one of the region's best athletic facilities, the Auraria Events Center, which seats more than 2,300 and is used for a variety of campus-wide events. Metro's basketball team has gone to nine consecutive NCAA tournaments.

Metro has all the elements of a traditional university, such as extensive physical education facilities, one of Metro Denver's best libraries, and a quiet, tree-lined campus. The historic 19th-century Bavarian-style brewery, the Tivoli, which until recently was an independent shopping center, has been transformed into one of the country's most picturesque student unions. The Tivoli houses shops, the campus bookstore, restaurants, an arcade, recreation rooms, and nightclubs as well as student offices and services.

Although there are no on-campus dormitories, many students get assistance from the campus housing office to live on their own in surrounding apartments. Plus, Metro is an easy walk from downtown Denver, the Denver Center for the Performing Arts, Elitch Gardens, Coors Field, the nightlife and restaurants of Lower Downtown, and INVESCO Field at Mile High.

Oh yes, and Metro has classes, too, 2,400 of them each fall and spring. The emphasis at Metro is on individual attention, with an average class size of just 22 students. Each class is taught by a master teacher; no student teaching assistants here. Summer offerings are also available.

Metro has 50 majors, in addition to the individual degree program. Degree offerings cover business, performing and visual arts, liberal arts, natural and social sciences, and specialty areas such as criminology, aerospace, journalism, and aviation and engineering technology.

Metro also operates two other campuses that offer degree programs and specialty classes. Metro South, in Greenwood Village, offers evening and weekend classes to more than 1,500 students from southeast Denver. Metro North, in Northglenn, serves the northern suburbs.

NATIONAL AMERICAN UNIVERSITY
1325 South Colorado Boulevard
(303) 876-7100
www.national.edu

Aimed at the career interests of the nontraditional adult student, National's average student is age 32. The university offers bachelor's degrees in accounting, applied management, business administration, and computer information systems; associate degrees in accounting, applied management, business administration, and computer information systems.

REGIS UNIVERSITY
3333 Regis Boulevard
(303) 458-4100
www.regis.edu

Regis University got a nice big public relations boost in the summer of 1993 when it was chosen as the spot where President Bill Clinton met with Pope John Paul II on the pope's historic visit to Denver. Secret Service helicopters buzzed like flies over the surrounding residential neighborhoods. Regis has been around for a long time, founded in 1877, and it has a pretty 90-acre main campus, about 11,000 students, and a sterling reputation as an educational institution. It's a Colorado Jesuit university, centered around the Ignatius Loyola philosophy of leaders in service of others. Regis pursues that philosophy in three colleges: Regis College, The School for Professional Studies, and The Rueckert-Hartman School for Health Care Professions. Regis College itself is a relatively small school, with about 1,400 undergraduate students studying liberal arts, sciences, business, and education. The student-faculty ratio is 16 to 1.

The School for Professional Studies has undergraduate and graduate programs in business, education, and computer sciences and offers classes in Denver, Colorado Springs, Fort Collins, Broomfield, and Boulder.

The Rueckert-Hartman School for Health Care Professions is particularly well-known among the Metro Denver nursing community. Its graduate and undergraduate programs include nursing, physical therapy, and health care administration and management.

UNIVERSITY OF COLORADO AT BOULDER
Broadway between Baseline Road and
Colorado Avenue, Boulder
(303) 492-1411
www.colorado.edu

Known in the vernacular as CU, this flagship institution of higher education in Colorado was founded in 1876, the year in which Colorado became a state. Today it is a university of international prominence. The university's campus in Boulder has 29,000 students, 75 percent of whom are undergraduates.

The University of Colorado at Boulder, or CU-Boulder, is where the university started, and it's still the state's largest and most important campus. Placed in the beautiful setting of Boulder's University Hill, its 786 acres of rural Italian-style buildings and complexes of Colorado sandstone make it one of the nation's most aesthetically pleasing campuses. A 1991 book, *The Campus as a Work of Art* by Thomas Gaines, ranked CU-Boulder fourth among 50 of the "most artistically successful campuses in the country." Because of nearby skiing and the many outdoor activities available, and because it's often the campus of choice for wealthy students who want an excellent place in which to spend their campus years, some people think of CU as a "party school." But CU-Boulder is far more than the place where actor and director Robert Redford played on the baseball team and waited tables in a local bar.

CU-Boulder excels as both a teaching and a research university. In 2005 *U.S. News & World Report* ranked CU 34th among the nations top 50 public universities offering doctoral programs. CU-Boulder's leading programs include telecommunications, aerospace engineering, and atmospheric and space physics. The department of molecular, cellular, and developmental biology is ranked among the top 10 national doctoral programs by the National Research Council. The chemistry and biochemistry department boasts 1989 Nobel Laureate Thomas Cech among its teaching faculty. Two CU professors won the Nobel Prize in Physics in 2001 for their work on Bose-Einstein condensate: Eric A. Cornell and Carl

E. Wieman. And the 2005 Nobel Prize in Physics was awarded to John L. Hall, a fellow and senior research associate at JILA (a joint research institute of CU and the National Institute of Standards and Technology). CU-Boulder has a separate 147-acre research park nearby that is home to some of its many research institutes.

Programs include the schools of law, business and administration, education, journalism and mass communications, arts and sciences, music, and architecture and planning. The schools offer more than 3,400 courses in more than 170 fields of study to some 29,000 students.

Part of the Big 12, the school's sports program is impressive, too. Between 1988 and 1996 the football team went to bowl games all nine years, then skipped a few years before playing bowls in 2001 and 2002. Its women's basketball team has also made big news, making it as far as the regional semifinals in 2003 for the sixth time in eight years.

ⓘ The Auraria Campus—shared by the Metropolitan State College of Denver, the University of Colorado at Denver, and the Community College of Denver—is a jewel of the metro region not only for its outstanding educational offerings but also for its accessibility to nontraditional students. Night classes have long been a mainstay for working students, and online classes are increasingly popular.

UNIVERSITY OF COLORADO AT DENVER
1250 14th Street (physical address, no
mail delivery)
(303) 556-5600
www.cudenver.edu

UNIVERSITY OF COLORADO DENVER HEALTH SCIENCES PROGRAMS
13120 East 19th Avenue, Aurora
(303) 848-0000
www.uchsc.edu

In 2004, the University of Colorado at Denver consolidated with the CU Health Sciences Center, creating a new university with its main campus at the 175-acre Auraria Higher Education Center, shared with the Metropolitan State College and the Community College of Denver. The University of Colorado Hospital is located at 9th Avenue and Colorado Boulevard, and the Anschutz Medical Campus is located at the 217-acre decommissioned Fitzsimons Army Medical Center in Aurora.

CU-Denver, as it's commonly referred to, has more than 80 undergraduate and graduate programs, and students can cross-register at all three schools. The more than 12,000 undergraduate students at CU-Denver are therefore part of a much larger student body and enjoy more academic and extracurricular opportunities than those provided by CU-Denver alone.

A five-minute walk from downtown, CU-Denver makes the opportunities of a state university available to working students in an urban environment. Strong programs include liberal arts and sciences, business and administration, engineering and applied science, architecture and planning, arts and media, and education.

The Anschutz Medical Campus is home to Colorado's only academic health center and the seat of medical research in the region. The main 46-acre campus offers baccalaureate and graduate programs in medicine, nursing, dentistry, pharmacy, and health-related fields. The center is as prominent nationally in research as it is regionally in medical education and is renowned in numerous fields including transplants, cancer, neuroscience, molecular biology, prenatal care, and cardiovascular services.

UNIVERSITY OF DENVER
2199 South University Boulevard
(303) 871-2000
www.du.edu
Founded in 1864, this is the oldest independent university in the Rocky Mountain region and the reason why one of Denver's main north-south thoroughfares is named University Boulevard. In a residential area 8 miles southeast of downtown, the University of Denver, called "DU" by locals, is a good combination of big-university experience

and small-liberal-arts-college atmosphere. The campus includes 100 buildings on 125 acres. Its Lamont School of Music and its College of Law are on the university's Park Hill campus, formerly Colorado Women's College. The student body counts about 10,400 students. About 4,500 of those are graduate students, and plenty of faculty members are at the forefront of research in their fields. The student-faculty ratio is 16 to 1 for undergraduates. Class sizes average 20 students. Undergraduate degrees are available in arts, fine arts, music, music education, science, business administration, accounting, chemistry, electrical engineering, and mechanical engineering. Campus Connection, a mentoring program, joins each new freshman with a faculty adviser in his or her major area of study.

UNIVERSITY OF PHOENIX
10004 Park Meadows Drive, Lone Tree
(303) 755-9090
www.phoenix.edu
This is the Colorado Campus of the University of Phoenix, which is based, of course, in Phoenix, Arizona, but has more than 100 campuses in the United States and Puerto Rico. It has four in the Metro Denver area, plus campuses in Fort Collins, Pueblo, and Colorado Springs. To attend you have to be a high-school graduate or GED certificate holder and be employed. This university focuses on degree programs and services for working adults. Degrees range from nursing and business administration to educational administration, computer information systems, and technology management. The University of Phoenix has about 4,000 students in Colorado.

WEBSTER UNIVERSITY
9250 East Costilla Avenue, Suite 310
Greenwood Village
(303) 708-8305
www.webster.edu
Webster University is based in St. Louis, Missouri, and has about 15,000 students worldwide; about two-thirds of them are graduate students. The Denver campus in Aurora offers graduate courses

in business administration, business, computer resources and information management, human resources development, and human resources management. All programs are designed for working adults and offered in the evening format. The university has two other Colorado locations in Colorado Springs, one of which is at Peterson Air Force Base.

COMMUNITY COLLEGES

ARAPAHOE COMMUNITY COLLEGE
5900 South Santa Fe Drive, Littleton
(303) 797-4222
www.arapahoe.edu

Arapahoe Community College's 7,500-plus students attend classes on a 51-acre campus adjacent to Littleton's downtown and just east of the South Platte River, which affords great mountain views to the west. It was established as Arapahoe Junior College in 1965, the first two-year college in Metro Denver. It joined the Colorado State System of Community Colleges in 1970 as Arapahoe Community College.

Arapahoe leans toward two-year associate degrees that help students enhance their careers with a degree or certificate, often while working. Some 50 percent of its students are working students. But courses can also transfer to a four-year college or university. The college has more than 70 degree and certificate programs in both academic and vocational areas, with more than 2,400 classes per year. ACC also offers community education classes for the lifelong learner. The average cost of education here is 10 to 50 percent less than most Colorado four-year schools. The college also operates satellite classrooms at the Denver Tech Center and in Parker.

COMMUNITY COLLEGE OF AURORA
16000 East Centre Tech Parkway, Aurora
(303) 360-4700
www.ccaurora.edu

Community College of Aurora has been the community college of Greater Denver's east side since its founding in 1983. It moved to a new 35-acre campus just west of Buckley Air National Guard Base in 1991 and, with the closing of Lowry Air Force Base, opened a second campus there in the fall of 1994, the Higher Education and Advancement Technology Center. Residence halls are available on the Lowry campus. Like other community colleges, it accommodates adult learners. About 60 percent of the students are older than age 25.

Community College of Aurora offers the full range of courses needed by students planning to transfer to four-year institutions with associate of arts and associate of science degrees. It has vocational programs that focus on an associate of applied science degree and training for employment certification. And it provides a menu of courses that serves a wide variety of interests. The college's faculty development program, which trains faculty in better methods of teaching, has won several national awards and has been used as a model for schools across the country.

COMMUNITY COLLEGE OF DENVER
1111 West Colfax Avenue
(303) 556-2600
www.ccd.edu

With about 6,600 full-time and part-time students, this is Metro Denver's "inner-city" community college. It shares the Auraria Higher Education Center's 175-acre campus with the Metropolitan State College of Denver and the University of Colorado at Denver. About 37,000 students can cross-register in the courses of all three schools.

The college offers degree programs in the full range of college subjects, as well as transfer courses for the baccalaureate degree, occupational programs for job entry skills or upgrading, remedial instruction and GED prep, continuing education, community services, and cooperative programs with the other schools.

FRONT RANGE COMMUNITY COLLEGE
3645 West 112th Avenue, Westminster
(303) 404-5000
www.frcc.cc.co.us

The community college of Greater Denver's north

side, Front Range is Colorado's largest community college. It has about 13,000 students at its Fort Collins, Longmont, Brighton, and Westminster campuses. Front Range has more than 100 degree and certificate programs, including associate degrees in arts, sciences, and general studies as well as degrees and certificates in applied sciences.

Front Range offers classes for GED, English as a second language, and literacy and classes for students with learning disabilities. It is the leader among local community colleges in delivering courses at business and industry work sites, including companies such as AT&T in Westminster, Geneva Pharmaceuticals in Broomfield, and Rocky Flats in Jefferson County, where Front Range has 600 employee-students. It is also one of the few places in the West that teaches hearing people to interpret for the deaf. Its nursing program won acclaim as a 1994 program of excellence, and in addition to its vocational programs, it has 60 courses that transfer to four-year schools. Locals can also take a lot of fun lifelong-learning courses such as handwriting analysis and garden management.

RED ROCKS COMMUNITY COLLEGE
13300 West 6th Avenue, Lakewood
(303) 914-6600
www.rrcc.edu

Red Rocks is among the fastest-growing institutions of higher learning in the state, and given its location, that's not hard to understand. Its 140-acre main campus perches on the western edge of Lakewood, in some of Jefferson County's most beautiful natural settings. Since 1969, when Red Rocks Community College was established, its annual student body has grown to 14,000 students on two campuses.

Red Rocks was founded in 1969 as a two-year institution. It also serves northwest metro suburbanites with an Arvada campus. Its largest enrollments are in math, followed by the sciences, computer information systems, English, multimedia, fire science technology, and criminal justice. More than half of the students say they attend for job-related reasons. The college has special programs in construction technology, film and video technology, medical four sites in the nation designated by the assisting, and biotechnology. The Red Rocks Rocks Institute does customized training for businesses. The Red Rocks OSHA Training Institute began in 1992 as one of four sites in the nation designated by the U.S. Department of Labor for OSHA training. A Computer Access Center trains individuals with disabilities to use adaptive computer technologies.

HEALTH CARE

The past decade has brought significant change to Denver's health care scene, due to hospital mergers and major new construction projects. Several of the city's largest facilities have been rebuilt on the Aurora campus that holds the University of Colorado Denver's health care programs. A few more have invested millions to upgrade their buildings.

Metro Denver residents are now well served, with three Level I trauma centers, with two emergency helicopter companies (AirLife and Flight for Life), as well as facilities such as Craig Hospital and National Jewish Medical and Research Center that have earned national and international acclaim for outstanding care and research developments.

In all, Metro Denver has 18 acute-care hospitals and three rehabilitation centers. Two operations, Centura Health and HealthONE, own and operate several facilities. The largest of Denver's hospitals, Presbyterian/St. Luke's, just east of downtown, has 680 licensed beds and nearly 1,600 employees. The smallest, Platte Valley Medical Center, north of Denver in Brighton, has 78 licensed beds.

Because of the city's attractive setting, Denver is able to lure high-quality professionals to staff its facilities. Hospitals and physicians work with university researchers and high-technology companies. The University of Colorado Hospital has been ranked as one of the 25 best hospitals in the country.

Pulmonary medicine is one example of a field in which Metro Denver enjoys renown. Many of the city's major hospitals, including the National Jewish Medical and Research Center and the Swedish and Exempla Lutheran medical centers, originally began as tuberculosis treatment centers back in the days when tuberculosis patients came to Colorado for the healthy air. Research and expertise at institutions such as National Jewish and the Web-Waring Lung Institute are among the reasons why some of the world's most advanced pulmonary-technology manufacturers make their homes in the Denver area.

Denver's other research and medical advancement highlights include the Belle Bonfils Blood Center, the Eleanor Roosevelt Institute, the Barbara Davis Child Diabetes Center, and the C. Henry Kempe National Center for the Prevention and Treatment of Child Abuse.

To insure their health, Denverites, like others across the nation, have turned to managed-care companies that appeal to residents' sense of health and outdoor living through advertisements and policies that stress preventive care and healthy lifestyles.

PHYSICIAN AND HOSPITAL REFERRALS

Clearly, health care choices abound in Denver. To find what's right for you, you can go to research extremes and get a desk directory of Colorado hospitals from the **Colorado Health and Hospital Association,** (720) 489-1630. The agency also maintains a free online directory of hospitals at www.cha.com. Other publications include issue papers on such topics as violence, teen pregnancy, and smoking. **Mile High United Way** is a great place to start when seeking all kinds of community-service information, and medical service is no exception. You can call their HelpLine at (303) 433-8900.

Metro Denver has more than 100 nursing homes and more than a dozen hospices, some operated in association with hospitals. A good number to keep on the telephone if you have kids is the Rocky Mountain Poison Center, (303) 739-1123.

Among the referral services to start with:

ANSWER LINE AT EXEMPLA HEALTH CARE
(303) 425-2929

CENTURA ASK-A-NURSE
(303) 777-6877

HEALTHONE
(877) 432-5846

PHYSICIAN REFERRAL LINE
(800) 362-8677

ROSE MEDICAL CENTER
(303) 320-7673

HOSPITALS

Denver

CHILDREN'S HOSPITAL
13123 East 16th Avenue, Aurora
(720) 777-1234
www.thechildrenshospital.org

The name says it all. Children's Hospital is a health care system caring for kids with the full spectrum of needs from wellness and prevention through the most complex care. Serving a 12-state region, Children's has been an innovator in medicine since it was founded in 1908, with firsts including the largest and most successful pediatric heart transplant program, the nation's first pediatric transport system, and the discovery of toxic shock syndrome. In 1997 it was designated as a Level I pediatric trauma center, the only one in the region devoted solely to children. In 2007 a new 1.44 million-square-foot facility was built adjacent to the University of Colorado Denver School of Medicine in Aurora to enhance treat-ment and research opportunities with faculty and students. The new campus has 270 beds and medical equipment especially designed for children, but its mission remains the same—clinical care, research, education, and advocacy.

Beyond the walls of the hospital, Children's offers pediatric services throughout the metropolitan area, the state, and the twelve-state Rocky Mountain region through partnerships with other health care institutions and clinics. Children's also operates three specialty physician satellite offices, four community-based urgent and emergency care sites, and three specialty care centers. The hospital itself handles more than 10,000 inpatient and almost 350,000 outpatient visits yearly.

DENVER HEALTH MEDICAL CENTER (DHMC)
777 Bannock Street
(303) 436-6000
www.denverhealth.org

This is Colorado's largest public hospital, oper-ated by Denver Health, which also runs Commu-nity Health Services, the Rocky Mountain Poison Center, and Denver CARES Community Detoxifi-cation. The medical center includes 398 staffed beds for a range of inpatient medical and behav-ioral health services. The center runs the Rocky Mountain Regional Trauma Center—the region's only Level I trauma center certified for both children and adults. It also operates Denver's 911 emergency system, paramedic services, and one of the nation's most competitive emergency medicine residency programs.

To a large extent, DHMC is the safety net for Denver residents regardless of their social or economic status. Nearly half of all charges for inpatient and outpatient services come from people without health insurance, and more than a third are from people covered by Medicaid and Medicare. DHMC also emphasizes adolescent and adult inpatient psychiatry and handles some 3,000 childbirths a year. DHMC's Rocky Mountain Regional Trauma Center serves the entire Rocky Mountain region. With more than 3,000 trauma patients annually, it is the busiest Level I trauma center in the area. Denver Health also operates 10 health centers throughout Denver and 10 student health clinics in Denver Public Schools. Denver Public Health monitors communicable diseases such as AIDS, tuberculosis, measles, and hepatitis. It operates several outpatient clinics for diagnosis and treatment of these and many other diseases. Through its Environmental Health Division, Public Health also provides a wide range of non-clinical services such as air and water pollution monitoring, restaurant inspections, licensing for day-care facilities and personal boarding-care homes, and operation of the Denver Municipal Animal Shelter.

DENVER VA MEDICAL CENTER
1055 Clermont Street
(303) 399-8020
www.visn19.va.gov
Through the VA Eastern Colorado Health Care System, the federal government delivers health services to people who have previously served in the military. With 128 beds in use, it provides medical, surgical, neurological, rehabilitation, and psychiatric care. The center also has a 100-bed Nursing Home Care Unit and reaches out to other parts of Front Range Colorado through outlying clinics and a mobile MEDIVAN program. Among their special programs are care and treatment for aging veterans, female veterans, ex-POWs, and Vietnam-era veterans and issues relating to Agent Orange and the Persian Gulf. The center is also a major research site, the 14th largest in the Veterans Administration, with projects including a Schizophrenia Center, a VA Alcohol Research Center, and an AIDS Clinical Trial Unit. A new and long-awaited facility is planned on the Aurora medical campus being built on the former site of the Fitzsimons Army Hospital.

EXEMPLA SAINT JOSEPH HOSPITAL
1835 Franklin Street
(303) 837-7111
www.saintjosephdenver.org
Denver's oldest private hospital, Saint Joseph was founded in 1873 by the Sisters of Charity of Leavenworth, Kansas, and they still sponsor it. It has been designated as one of the top 100 hospitals

in the United States by the Solucient 100 Top Hospitals: Cardiovascular Benchmarks for Success survey, and it has a national reputation for the quality of its heart care. There are 565 licensed beds and 1,300 physicians. It's the busiest child-birth center in Colorado: With more than 5,000 births per year, Saint Joseph is the birthplace of 10 percent of Colorado's babies. The hospital's Maternal/Fetal Medicine program and Level III Neonatal Intensive Care Nursery ensure that babies needing extra help get the best care available before and after birth. Saint Joseph excels in other services including oncology, orthopedics, gastroenterology, and pulmonology. It also serves as the downtown emergency center for Children's Hospital and Kaiser Permanente.

HCA/HEALTHONE SPALDING REHABILITATION HOSPITAL
900 Potomac Street, Aurora
(303) 367-1166
www.spaldingrehab.com
Although Spalding is officially in Denver, it actually has patients throughout the metro area. Its 169 licensed beds are located at other hospitals, in wings or units that specialize in the treatment of stroke, brain injury, chronic pain, neck/back injuries, neurological disorders, multiple sclerosis, and orthopedic problems. Spalding's history dates back to the Episcopal Church's Convalescent Home, which opened in 1914 to serve poor women and children. It was sold, with proceeds going toward a new 80-bed facility that was opened in 1965. In 1988 it opened a hospital-within-a-hospital at Swedish Medical Center, providing rehabilitation services in a hospital setting. That model continues today. Inpatient and outpatient specialty care is offered at the main Aurora facility as well as at Presbyterian/St. Luke's Medical Center. Spalding is a joint venture of HealthONE and Columbia/HCA Healthcare Corporation.

NATIONAL JEWISH HEALTH
1400 Jackson Street
(303) 388-4461
www.njc.org

People with asthma and other chronic respiratory diseases come here from all over the world because National Jewish has an international reputation as a leading—if not the leading—medical center for the study and treatment of chronic respiratory diseases, allergic diseases, and immune system disorders.

National Jewish's pedigree is impressive. It is ranked among the top 10 independent biomedical research facilities in the world and is the No. 1 private institution in the world for immunology research. One of those Denver medical centers that originated to serve tuberculosis patients, it started in 1899 with the opening of the National Jewish Hospital for Consumptives. Today this nonsectarian medical center's staff of 1,100 serves patients on a sort of modified outpatient basis, in which patients usually stay in hotels or in some cases at another hospital. One out of every five pediatric allergists in the United States was trained here.

National Jewish operates a free telephone information service, Lung Line, to answer questions and forward literature on such subjects as acute bronchitis, asthma, emphysema, and pneumonia. Call (303) 355-LUNG if you're in Colorado or (800) 222-LUNG if you're not for the 8 a.m. to 4:30 p.m. service.

PORTER ADVENTIST HOSPITAL
2525 South Downing Street
(303) 778-1955
www.porterhospital.org
This hospital on Denver's southern border is a 369-bed, acute-care hospital that boasts more than 1,200 physicians. A division of Centura Health and a nonprofit organization, it's one of four—along with Parker Adventist in Parker, Littleton Adventist Hospital, and Avista Adventist Hospital in Boulder County—affiliated under Rocky Mountain Adventist Healthcare. It was founded in 1930 by Denver pioneer and businessman Henry M. Porter after he was impressed by his treatment at California hospitals that were owned by the Seventh-Day Adventist Church. He and his daughter gave the church $315,000

and 40 acres to start a hospital in Denver. The hospital's mission is "to serve as a continuation of the healing ministry of Christ." Its specialties include cancer care and cancer support, heart care and healthy heart programs, the Clyde G. Kissinger Center for Sight, the Porter Birthplace, Porter Breastcare, a center for treatment of substance abuse and eating disorders, transplant services, and education programs in areas such as stress management, weight control, nutrition counseling, smoking cessation, and alcohol education. Independence Square helps cardiac rehabilitation patients return to normal activities by simulating situations patients will encounter when discharged from the hospital.

PRESBYTERIAN/ST. LUKE'S MEDICAL CENTER
1719 East 19th Avenue
(303) 839-6000
www.pslmc.com
A division of HealthONE, this huge medical center has more than 1,000 affiliated physicians and more beds (680) and staff than any hospital in Metro Denver. It would be hard to dispute its claim to being the most comprehensive health care provider in the Rocky Mountain West, given its amazing range of services. Among them are the Mother and Child Hospital, the Mothers' Milk Bank, the Sleep Disorders Center, the Colorado Gynecology and Continence Center, the Institute for Limb Preservation, the Senior Citizen's Health Center, the Hyperbaric Medicine Center, psychiatric services, organ and tissue transplants, Addictions Recovery Centers, and a wide variety of women's and pediatric services. The list goes on and on.

i Need specialized medical attention for your pet? Colorado State University in Fort Collins is one of the leading veterinary schools in the nation, and Metro Denverites often take their pets there for chemotherapy or other advanced veterinary needs. Call (970) 297-4477 for information.

The Family Birth Place has been named as one of the top 10 maternity units in the United States by *Child* magazine. Close to Pres/St. Luke's, The Inn at Presbyterian, 2021 High Street, (303) 839-7150, offers convenient lodging at reasonable rates to people undergoing preadmission testing and to families of patients.

ROSE MEDICAL CENTER
4567 East 9th Avenue
(303) 320-2121
www.rosemed.com
Rose Medical Center, also a division of HealthONE, is well-known to many Metro Denverites as the place where their children, grandchildren, nieces, and nephews were born. That's not surprising considering its emphasis on women's health services, parent education classes, infertility, and high-risk pregnancies. The Rose Breast Center performs more mammograms than any other facility in the Denver area. And the Rose Children's Center is strong on inpatient, ambulatory, and emergency services for infants, children, and adolescents. All this is not to say that Rose is just for women and children. Opened in 1949 and named after Denver World War II hero General Maurice Rose, the Medical Center provided the first comprehensive, primary care-oriented health program designed especially for men. The special Suites at Rose continue to provide a distinctive level of care, including private chefs. Among the general list of hospital services provided by Rose's 1,100 affiliated physicians is advanced oncology research and Colorado's first coronary-care unit.

With 420 licensed beds, it was also the first adult acute-care metro medical center to formally affiliate with the nearby University of Colorado Health Sciences Center. Rose is also a teaching hospital. Other special features include a surgical treatment of emphysema program and sports medicine orthopedists, who provide care for professional and weekend athletes alike. In 1994 Rose created what it calls an orthopedic center of excellence, the Rose Institute for Joint Replacement, which is recognized for its model of full-service care. At the new Elaine and Melvin Wolf Ambulatory Surgery Building, Rose offers cosmetic and laser surgery services and a minimally invasive breast biopsy technology that is taught to physicians from around the world.

ST. ANTHONY HOSPITAL CENTRAL
4231 West 16th Avenue
(303) 629-3511
www.stanthonycentral.org
St. Anthony Hospital Central was built by the Sisters of St. Francis in 1893. It operates one of the area's three certified Level I trauma centers and is home base to Flight for Life, probably the best known of Metro Denver's helicopter emergency rescue services. Also affiliated with Centura Health, St. Anthony is an innovator in cardiovascular surgery and services and was one of the first hospitals to provide a chest pain emergency center. It's also performed more than 2,300 operations using gamma-knife surgery, which entails the use of gamma rays to eliminate deep-seated tumors and other malformations in the brain. St. Anthony Hospital Central has 593 licensed beds, and 18,500 inpatients and 34,000 outpatients per year.

UNIVERSITY OF COLORADO HOSPITAL
12605 East 16th Avenue, Aurora
(720) 848-0000
www.uch.edu
University Hospital moved from its old, cramped inner-city location in 2007 to the shiny new Anschutz Medical Campus in Aurora. On the site of the former Fitzsimons Army Medical Center, it joined the University of Colorado's medical schools, a state-of-the-art cancer center, an eye institute, a research library, the Center for Bioethics and Humanities, Children's Hospital, and a growing bioscience research park. Its first phase, the Anschutz Inpatient Pavilion, opened in 2004 as a family-focused community hospital. Those portions of the hospital that provide highly specialized care came next, joining the Anschutz Outpatient Pavilion and the Anschutz Cancer Pavilion on a campus that will consist of more than 3 million square feet of educational,

research, clinical, and support space once it is completed. University Hospital was founded in 1921, performed the nation's first successful liver transplant, and in 1998 was listed among top hospitals in *U.S. News & World Report*. Pushing the medical frontiers, the hospital has developed special expertise in areas ranging from heart surgery to cancer. It's as one of two public hospitals that serves Metro Denver residents.

Adams County

NORTH SUBURBAN MEDICAL CENTER
9191 Grant Street, Thornton
(303) 451-7800
www.northsuburban.com
Since 1985 North Suburban has served the north metro communities of Westminster, Northglenn, and Thornton. It now has 157 beds, and offers women's diagnostic and treatment services at its Women's Center as well as diagnostic, intervention, and rehab treatment through its Cardiovascular Services department. The 26-bed emergency department is rated a Level IV trauma center with heliport facilities and has six beds dedicated to pediatric treatment.

NORTH VALLEY HOSPITAL
8451 Pearl Street, Thornton
(303) 288-3000
www.northvalleyrehab.com
This is a comprehensive medical rehabilitation facility for adult inpatients and outpatients with traumatic brain injury, stroke, amputation, orthopedic conditions, arthritis, neurological disorders, pulmonary conditions, psychiatric disorders, or other disabling conditions. It's a 117-bed facility near I-25 just off the 84th Avenue exit. Comprehensive brain injury services include coma rehabilitation, acute brain injury rehabilitation, and neurobehavioral rehabilitation. Comprehensive rehab includes multiple trauma, neurological, stroke, orthopedic, amputee, arthritic, and neuromuscular rehabilitation. Pulmonary rehab includes ventilator rehab, ventilator management, and pulmonary restoration. There's a substance-abuse program for people with disabilities.

PLATTE VALLEY MEDICAL CENTER
1600 Prairie Center Parkway, Brighton
(303) 498-1600
www.pvmc.org
Platte Valley stays busy because of its proximity to US 85 and I-76. It's also the closest hospital to Denver International Airport. Founded as Brighton Community Hospital in 1960, it came under the management of Rocky Mountain Adventist Health Care in 1980. Although it's one of Metro Denver's smallest acute-care hospitals, it provides a solid spectrum of general hospital care ranging from coronary care and cardiac rehabilitation to perinatal and pediatric services. Its new building more than tripled its size, and its 50-acre campus allows for future expansion. Once completed, the planned build-out will include three six-story buildings and more than 300 beds, transforming Platte Valley into a full-scale regional medical center.

ST. ANTHONY NORTH HOSPITAL
2551 West 84th Avenue, Westminster
(303) 426-2151
www.stanthonynorth.org
One of several major hospitals operated by Centura Health (see St. Anthony Central, in Denver), St. Anthony North was built in 1971 to serve the northern suburbs. This 198-bed hospital is oriented toward the needs of young families in a growing community. The emergency room is one of the state's busiest. Major medical specialties include diabetes management, family practice, pediatrics, cardiology, and obstetrics, with advanced intermediate and intensive-care nurseries. It also plays an educational role, offering parent education classes, wellness seminars, obstetrics classes, sick child day care, and health-promotion activities for businesses.

Arapahoe County

CRAIG HOSPITAL
3425 South Clarkson Street, Englewood
(303) 789-8000
www.craighospital.org
Craig Hospital dates from 1907, when it was started

as a tuberculosis colony by Frank Craig, who himself suffered from the disease. Today Craig Hospital is dedicated exclusively to patients with spinal cord and brain injuries. It has been rated in the *U.S. News & World Report* compilation of top hospitals every year since the ratings began. Some 25,000 patients have been treated and rehabilitated since Craig converted to a rehabilitation facility in 1956. Another of those Metro Denver hospitals with an international reputation in a specialized niche, Craig pulls the majority of its patients from outside Colorado. It supports that widespread patient base with an air-transport team that flies an average of 200,000 miles a year in a specially equipped air-ambulance, a Lear jet, and other aircraft. About a mile south of the Denver border in Englewood, Craig tries to maintain a casual, home-away-from-home atmosphere because it's a long-stay hospital that encourages family involvement in a patient's progress. There is also a Transitional Care Facility, an outpatient and family housing facility, and an in-house cell center for clinical research trials. In these apartment-like units, patients during the last phase of their inpatient stay can work on adjusting to independent life. The units are designed to hold the patient's family members as well, so family can help with the adjustment. Acute-care patients can be managed almost immediately after injury by Craig physicians and therapists in neurotrauma units at adjacent Swedish Medical Center and at St. Anthony Hospital Central in Denver. The hospital is licensed for 93 beds.

LITTLETON ADVENTIST HOSPITAL
7700 South Broadway, Littleton
(303) 730-8900
www.mylittletonhospital.org
A division of Centura Health, Littleton Adventist was opened in 1989 in response to growing development in south Metro Denver, from Littleton and Englewood to Highlands Ranch and Castle Rock. It's affiliated under Rocky Mountain Adventist Healthcare, and is located just north of C-470, near the intersection of Broadway and Mineral Avenue. Littleton features services including obstetrics and gynecology, pediatrics,

surgical, radiology, cardiopulmonary, rehabilitation, and twenty-four-hour emergency care. All of its rooms are private. The hospital's Family Life Center offers a wide selection of classes and programs. This 139-licensed-bed hospital represents an extension of the Adventist healing mission. In 2003 the hospital completed a $38 million expansion that added about 100,000 square feet to its original 210,000-square-foot structure, most in its emergency room area, but also adding a neonatal intensive care unit.

THE MEDICAL CENTER OF AURORA
1501 South Potomac Street, Aurora
(303) 695-2600
www.auroramed.com
Aurora's only full-service hospital, this facility consists of three campuses: the Main campus, the North campus, and the Centennial Medical Plaza. The center as a whole employs nearly 1,200 people and is licensed for 346 beds. The Main campus hosts among other things a Level II trauma center, the Women's Center, and the Colorado Spine Center. A new 84-bed tower for cardiovascular patients was added in 2009. The North campus includes the Sleep Disorders Center and the Geriatric Psychiatry/Senior Care Center. The Centennial campus has day-surgery services, and imaging and lab services.

SKY RIDGE MEDICAL CENTER
10101 RidgeGate Parkway, Lone Tree
(720) 225-1000
www.skyridgemedcenter.com
Sky Ridge in metro Denver covers 57 acres and serves residents of Highlands Ranch, Lone Tree, Parker, Castle Rock, and Littleton. The facility has 156 beds and maintains a Level III trauma center, with twenty-four-hour emergency care and orthopedic surgeons. It also provides cardiac services, has a cancer center and a sports medicine and rehabilitation center, and provides women's and children's services. Sky Ridge also advertises its sleep disorders, bariatric surgery, and complementary/alternative medicine services.

SWEDISH MEDICAL CENTER
501 East Hampden Avenue, Englewood
(303) 788-5000
www.swedishhospital.com

A division of HealthONE, Swedish serves as a regional center for the most complex trauma, neurological, and infertility cases. Swedish received the Consumer-Choice Quality-Leader Award four years in a row between 1996 and 2000, and in 2002 it was ranked among Solucient's Top 100 Hospitals. Because it shares its campus with two major regional rehab hospitals, Craig Hospital and Spalding Hospital, it is well positioned to provide continuum care for victims of spinal cord injury, stroke, neurological disorders, and complex orthopedic problems. Critical health care includes cardiovascular and pulmonary services, oncology services, and emergency and trauma services. Special facilities include the Women's Center and the Oncology Center. The Laser Clinic has state-of-the-art treatment for removing port-wine stains, spider veins, birthmarks, moles, tattoos, etc.

Jefferson County

EXEMPLA LUTHERAN MEDICAL CENTER
8300 West 38th Avenue, Wheat Ridge
(303) 425-4500
www.exempla.org

This community-owned nonprofit health system was founded in 1905. In recent years it has rated among the top 100 hospitals in the nation. Lutheran offers a variety of outpatient and community outreach programs in addition to a 400-bed hospital, inpatient and outpatient psychiatric services, a rehabilitation center, a skilled nursing unit, a residence for seniors, and a full-service home-care and hospice division. It employs 2,500, with 800 physicians, and has a Level III trauma center.

MENTAL HEALTH

AURORA COMMUNITY MENTAL HEALTH CENTER
14301 East Hampden Avenue, Aurora
(303) 617-2300
www.aumhc.org

Thousands of people a year receive help from Aurora Community Mental Health's six counseling centers and six residential facilities and through the Aurora and Cherry Creek school districts. Services include counseling for depression, older adults, divorce, parenting, drugs, and alcohol and group therapies. Also offered are residential services from overnight to long-term adjustments.

COLORADO MENTAL HEALTH INSTITUTE AT FORT LOGAN
3520 West Oxford Avenue
(303) 866-7066
www.cdhs.state.co.us/cmhifl

This is one of two state psychiatric hospitals, charged with providing treatment and services for the mentally ill. It was founded in 1961 and has 410 staff members. Fort Logan houses the statewide program for all deaf and hearing-impaired clients with mental illness. Areas of specialty fall in three treatment divisions: children and adolescents, adult psychiatry, and geriatrics. An inpatient-only facility with 153 inpatient and 20 residential beds, this hospital is based on a treatment team approach—a patient's team consists of a psychiatrist, a psychologist, a social worker, psychiatric nurses, and mental-health clinicians. The team also has special-education teachers for children and adolescents.

COMITIS CRISIS CENTER
2178 Victor Street, Aurora
(303) 343-9890 (helpline)
(303) 341-9160 (office)
www.comitis.org

This privately owned nonprofit has been serving youth awaiting placement into permanent residential homes since 1971. Comitis is a short-term residential care facility with a small emergency housing area for homeless kids. It helps get people off the streets and into low-income housing. Its main mission is to care for runaway and throwaway kids.

COMMUNITY REACH CENTER
8931 Huron Street, Thornton
(303) 853-3500
www.adamsmentalhealth.com
Founded in 1957, this center has been serving Adams County residents with emergency and outpatient mental-health needs. About 4,000 people a year receive treatment for such things as anxiety disorders, substance abuse, and family issues. It also has five outpatient offices, in Brighton, Commerce City, Thornton, Northglenn, and Westminster.

DEVEREUX/CLEO WALLACE CENTER
8405 Church Ranch Boulevard Westminster
(303) 466-7391
www.devereux.org
Devereux/Cleo Wallace Center is Colorado's largest and most comprehensive behavioral health care organization dedicated to the treatment of psychiatric, emotional, and behavioral problems in children and adolescents. Cleo Spurlock Wallace was a local schoolteacher who saw a need for special services for troubled youth, which was why she started the center in 1943. The center provides an inpatient hospital, residential facilities, day treatment, and outpatient services for children and adolescents with behavioral health concerns and for their families. In all, the center has 112 beds. It runs a school certified by the Colorado Department of Education, each classroom having both a teacher and a paraprofessional to integrate treatment into education. Devereux/Cleo Wallace is accredited by the Joint Commission on the Accreditation of Health Care Organizations. John Wayne used to come here for fund-raising events; he was a member of the Sigma Chi fraternity, which selected Cleo's hospital and school as its special charity.

JEFFERSON CENTER FOR MENTAL HEALTH
4581 Independence Street, Wheat Ridge
(303) 425-0300
www.jeffersonmentalhealth.org
A wide variety of mental-health services are offered, including counselors in schools, an older adult program, several residential areas for inpatient services, and twenty-four-hour emergency services. In all, Jefferson Center operates 16 satellite locations in Jefferson, Gilpin, and Clear Creek Counties.

ALTERNATIVE AND HOLISTIC HEALTH

The alternative health scene is growing and gaining notice—and credibility—in Metro Denver. In fact, Denver has more professionals than most comparably sized cities. And nearby Boulder is well-known for its array of alternative healers.

Colorado's alternative health doctors got a boost in 1997 when the state legislature passed a law protecting the ability of M.D.s to do business by prohibiting the state medical board from disciplining doctors merely for practicing alternative medicine. The stamp of credibility was seen as a sign from lawmakers that alternative medicine is a viable option for thousands of people across the state.

Alternative medicine is generally defined as anything outside the mainstream of Western medicine. Services generally include herbology, acupuncture, massage, counseling, hypnotherapy, nutrition, hydrotherapy, reflexology, homeopathy, and chiropractics. Holistic is an approach to healing that views the patient as a whole being with a diverse life and range of reasons

i As with many states, Colorado has varying requirements for alternative practitioners. Depending on the specialty, one may be required to be licensed, certified, or registered. The following listings are recommended as organizations committed to professionalism and overall health.

for ill-health. Holistic practitioners look for the interconnections of a person's health—not just the source of one given problem.

BRIDGES INTEGRATIVE HEALTH SERVICES
8098 West 38th Avenue, Wheat Ridge
(303) 425-2262
www.bridgesforhealth.org
Bridges is the only hospital-based center of its kind in the Denver metro area. It is a joint project of Exempla Healthcare and Lutheran Medical Center Community Foundation. Services range from massage and acupuncture to nutrition counseling, holistic counseling, and a wellness nurse consultation. Its mission is to offer complementary therapies that can be combined with traditional medicine, offering patients the best of both worlds and nourishing the mind, body, and soul. All practitioners meet the professional credential standards for their specialties.

Bridges also offers classes and workshops to the public, including yoga and meditation, as well as lectures on complementary healing topics.

EAST WEST HEALTH CENTERS
8200 East Belleview, Suite 280
Greenwood Village
(303) 694-5757
www.east-west-health.com
This center includes more than 20 practitioners, including an internist and family physician, with both Eastern and Western specialties. Western services include family and sports medicine, preventive medicine, geriatric care, physical therapy, counseling, and OB-GYN. Eastern offerings include acupuncture, herbology, naturopathy, chiropractics, massage, Rolfing, nutrition education, exercise prescription, and stress management.

RETIREMENT

Forget Wednesday-night bingo and mashed potatoes in a dingy dining room. Metro Denver's retirement homes are called communities for a reason: They offer residents a place to recreate, socialize, and thrive. Auditoriums, fitness centers, restaurants, and swimming pools are only a few of the amenities. And with the older generation getting stronger and more prevalent—Denver's age-60-and-older population is expected to climb 13 percent by 2013—housing options are getting better.

Metro Denver isn't exactly a retirement mecca on par with Arizona or Florida, but its sunny, mild climate (belied by our rare but news-making blizzards) has lured thousands over the years, including seniors who want to be closer to relatives or who end their careers in colorful Colorado.

The city and county of Denver has by far the greatest number of independent and assisted-living facilities for seniors in the area, but when you seek word-of mouth recommendations, Denver's outlying areas, and especially the suburban counties, tend to get the most praise. That may not be fair to Denver's senior communities. It may simply say more about life being more difficult for the elderly in an urban setting.

There are a variety of information sources to aid your decision. Referral agencies, such as **Community Housing Services,** (303) 831-4046, are a good place to start. **Community Housing Services** provides free housing referrals to use as a start in comparing costs, availability, and other factors. Another good one is **Senior Housing Options,** (303) 595-4464, a nonprofit corporation that owns and manages assisted-living properties and HUD-subsidized properties.

You can do your own word-of-mouth research by asking other seniors you meet in groups, such as the **American Association of Retired Persons,** (303) 830-2277, and the **Association for Senior Citizens,** (303) 455-9642. The **Area Agency on Aging at the Denver Regional Council of Governments,** (303) 480-6734, offers information and referral services for seniors, as well as a Nursing Home Ombudsman Program. You can socialize with seniors at any of Metro Denver's numerous senior centers. You might also get a copy of The Denver Business Journal Book of Lists, an annual publication of the Denver

Business Journal, (303) 837-3500. We've mentioned it before as a great resource for all kinds of area information. One of its lists ranks the top 25 retirement communities.

The Seniors Blue Book is another source of information for seniors in the Denver metro area. Call (303) 393-1971, or try their Web site at www.seniorsresourceguide.com.

Once you know what part of Metro Denver you'd like to live in and have some communities in mind, call their sales offices for brochures and information packages. Then check them out in person. Arriving around meal time gives you a sense of the staff and how well it relates to residents. Of course, most communities have marketing representatives eager to give guided tours.

Vital to picking the right place is the surrounding neighborhood: whether it's clean, pleasant, and quiet; whether there are parks and shopping within walking distance; and whether the surroundings are congenial to the elderly. Metro Denver's four-lane traffic arteries such as

Wadsworth Boulevard can be tough to negotiate, even for speed-walking teenagers. A more docile setting might be best for those with difficulties moving around.

The following entries represent the more-talked-about examples of retirement communities in Metro Denver. But by no means is the list comprehensive or meant to suggest other places aren't equally good. We have tended to look specifically at places with independent and assisted living in which seniors have their own homes or apartments. These are the midrange of a spectrum of senior living and care options ranging from nursing homes to prestigious single-family developments. Assisted living simply means that assistance is available for such needs as medication reminders; help with dressing, grooming, and bathing; close-by medical and health monitoring; laundry; in-apartment meal services; and rehabilitation programs. Typically, both independent and assisted-living units have call buttons at strategic locations so residents can summon help if needed.

Overall, these senior living communities resemble moderate to upscale apartments or condominiums. The difference is in the community feel, which places more emphasis on communal dining and gathering areas, shared activities, and services. Typically, at least one meal is included in rent, although this may vary. Housekeeping is a fairly standard service. Virtually every community listed here offers a calendar of social activities, many have their own newsletters, and all of them have their own transportation services to area shopping and other attractions. Residents are likely to have their own garage or carport space and storage lockers. Perhaps best of all, someone else cleans the bathroom and does the dishes!

RETIREMENT COMMUNITIES

ALTERRA VILLAS AT CANTERBURY
11265 East Mississippi Avenue, Aurora
(303) 341-1412
www.brookdaleliving.com

Canterbury was the first independent- and assisted-living community for seniors in Aurora when it opened in the late 1970s, and some of the pioneer residents are still there. It consists of two-story structures built around two ponds in a landscaped courtyard with a gazebo. They have 200 unfurnished private or shared one- and two-bedroom apartments for seniors, with on-site meals. This community actually consists of two sections: Alterra Villas at Canterbury, the independent-living section, and Alterra Wynwood at Canterbury, which is assisted living.

Canterbury is owned and operated by Brookdale of Chicago, a company that specializes in developing and managing retirement communities. The community includes a fireside lounge, library, TV and movie living area, a beauty/barber shop, a full-service dining room with soup and salad bar, private dining, complimentary van service for scheduled trips, an ice-cream cart, guest apartments, and a hobby and crafts room.

CHERRY CREEK RETIREMENT VILLAGE
14555 East Hampden Avenue, Aurora
(303) 693-0200
www.cherrycreekretirement.com
Cherry Creek has a nice location in a residential neighborhood, across the street from Aurora's public Meadow Hills Golf Course. The village is in a three-story, buff-colored building with a large circular drive and two atriums for relaxing and entertaining.

Some apartments have patios or balconies. Every unit has a window over the kitchen sink that looks out into one of the halls. They have 30 assisted-living and 185 retirement apartments. Monthly rent covers amenities ranging from continental breakfast and weekly housekeeping to excursions. Meals and other amenities are available at a nominal charge. The village has card and game rooms, an exercise room, library, country store, billiards, an arts and crafts area, restaurant-style dining, and a private dining room. Independent and assisted living are provided. Cherry Creek Retirement Village is owned by American Lifestyles, Cleveland, Tennessee.

THE COURTYARD AT LAKEWOOD
7100 West 13th Avenue, Lakewood
(303) 239-0740
www.thecourtyardatlakewood.com
Three blocks east of Wadsworth Boulevard and a couple blocks south of Colfax Avenue in Lakewood, the Courtyard is in a quiet residential neighborhood. Every apartment in the three-story building has a view of the center courtyard, where there are flowers, rock gardens, and a pond. The Courtyard is managed by two husband and-wife teams who live on the premises.

Beyond the living quarters, the Courtyard's amenities include a giant-screen TV room, large kitchen for group activities, beauty shop, library, billiards areas, and a spa. They have 122 apartments. The Courtyard is owned by Holiday Retirement Corporation.

DAYTON PLACE
1950 South Dayton Street
(303) 751-5150
www.daytonplace.com
Dayton Place is on the western edge of the city of Aurora's south side, just off Parker Road, a major thoroughfare that runs northwest to Denver and southeast past the Cherry Creek Reservoir State Recreation Area. It is a three-story complex with an open feel, in part due to its suburban location and perhaps in part due to its setback on large grounds with meandering walkways, gardens, and outdoor patios. Dayton has a general store, chapel, beauty and barber shop, TV lounges, a billiards room, and a cards and activities room. The have 96 assisted-living and 104 independent-living units called "cottages."

i Check the fine print when looking for a retirement home. Some communities require long-term leases and large down payments, while others are month-to-month. Decide what's best for you, then take the time to ask good questions.

HARVARD SQUARE RETIREMENT COMMUNITY
10200 East Harvard Avenue
(303) 696-0622
www.leisurecare.com
Harvard Square's interiors are bright and open yet reminiscent of the club spaces in an Ivy League university, with dark wood and formal, old world style. They maintain 189 private, unfurnished rooms. The exterior and grounds—overlooked by a second-story deck—also exude a country club air. Harvard Square is in the northwest corner of Denver's Hampden Heights neighborhood, just west of Aurora near the pleasant green spaces of Babi Yar Park and the private Los Verdes Golf Club. Although it's basically an independent-living community, it has a formal Assisted Living Program managed by a professional social worker with nursing support. Under the same roof, Harvard Square also includes a dining room, beauty and barber shop, game room, library, and multipurpose room.

HERITAGE CLUB
2020 South Monroe Street
(303) 756-0025
www.brookdaleliving.com/heritage-club-denver.aspx
Heritage Club has a good reputation for elegant living at affordable prices. The apartments are luxurious. The dining room looks like something in an upscale downtown restaurant with a menu to match, and there's a private dining room for special occasions. Heritage Club has a private library, exercise room with whirlpool and spa, country store and ice-cream parlor, billiards room, cards and games room, arts and crafts studio, and a beauty and barber shop plus shuffleboard, a putting green, and horseshoes pit. The bay windows and balconies are nice features, and the community is in the University Park neighborhood, a pleasant part of the city southwest of Colorado Boulevard's intersection with I-25.

MERIDIAN

10695 West 17th Avenue, Lakewood
(303) 232-7100
www.horizonbay.com

1805 South Balsam Street, Lakewood
(303) 980-5500

9555 West 59th Avenue, Arvada
(303) 425-1900

3455 South Corona Street, Englewood
(303) 761-0300

Denver's western suburbs in Jefferson County have the largest number of retirement communities. One of the most extensive retirement-residence organizations that gets mentioned in a positive light is Meridian, which has four retirement communities in Metro Denver. All are owned by Horizon Bay Retirement Living in Tampa, Florida. Which also owns a Meridian in Boulder and the Village at Lowry, 150 Quebec Street, (303) 364-7149. Each is managed independently, but all are essentially the same: nicely appointed buildings on campus-like settings, with elegant interiors and formal furniture. The Lakewood and Englewood Meridians have nursing-home sections, while the others have independent and assisted living only.

PARKPLACE

111 Emerson Street
(303) 744-1950
www.brookdaleliving.com/parkplace-.aspx

In the heart of Denver, this 18-story independent- and assisted-living facility resembles one of those quiet, elegant hotels that get known by word-of-mouth. Its elegance is immediately apparent in the dark wood and rich upholstery of the lobby, lounge, and formal dining room, and the atmosphere is maintained throughout. It's next to Hungarian Freedom Park on the south side of Speer Boulevard, south of Denver's downtown and not far from the Cherry Creek shopping area. The Cherry Creek greenbelt and its pedestrian/bicycle path runs along Speer Boulevard out front. Parkplace has an indoor swimming pool with a hot tub, exercise room, convenience store, beauty and barber shop, library, card lounge, patio dining area, and auditorium. Parkplace is owned and managed by Brookdale Senior Living Inc., Brentwood, Tennessee.

PORTER PLACE

1001 East Yale Avenue
(303) 765-6800
www.porterplace.org

Porter Place is on the campus of Porter Adventist Hospital in Denver's University Park neighborhood on the northernmost edge of Englewood. In addition to independent and assisted living (with studio, one-bedroom, and two-bedroom apartments), it offers small studio apartments for visiting family and friends of residents, and the facility offers respite care. Porter Place is affiliated with Centura Health, and Porter Adventist Hospital, but that doesn't mean it looks like a medical facility. The interiors are lovely, from the grand piano and high ceilings of the lobby to the pleasant tranquility of the library. There are flower gardens and outdoor patios, activity rooms, a chapel, gift shop, beauty and barber shop, big-screen TV room, parlor, card room, and craft room. Plus residents have access to the hospital's Porter Health Club. A recently completed addition provides assisted living in a secure environment, called Memory Care, in the Elizabeth Rose Wing.

SHALOM PARK SENIOR RESIDENCES

14800 East Bellevue Drive, Aurora
(303) 680-5000
www.shalompark.org

One of Metro Denver's newest retirement additions is Shalom Park Senior Residences. The 41-acre community offers residents lovely grounds as well as an in-house activity department to keep them entertained. There are a total of 104 units, including 44 patio homes and 60 apartments. Any of the 104 units can be assisted or independent living, depending on the needs of the occupants.

SPRINGWOOD RETIREMENT CAMPUS
6550 Yank Way, Arvada
(303) 424-6550
www.springwoodretirement.com
The Springwood Retirement Campus is just off Yankee Doodle Park in a nice residential section of Arvada. Facilities and services include a full-time social director, dining room, maid service, laundry and dry cleaning, general store, library, chapel, hair salon, game room, and exercise facility. Nightingale Lane, and Alzheimer's ward with 28 beds. Lutheran Medical Center provides input to Springwood's health care and health-promoting activities.

Springwood offers a variety of one-and two-bedroom apartments, with two-way intercom and emergency buzzers; it also offers assisted

i If you're in the market for a retirement community, start early. Allow yourself up to a year to compare and visit locations, especially if you need a large space. Many communities have waiting lists for two-bedroom units, which are tougher to come by.

living at its Nightingale Suites. The cottages at Springwood are 1,100-square-foot residences built on a private cul-de-sac. Each includes a foyer, living room, dining room, covered patio, master bedroom with its own bath and oversize walk-in closet, guest bedroom, second bathroom, laundry and utility room, and attached garage.

THE VILLAS AT SUNNY ACRES
2501 East 104th Avenue, Thornton
(303) 255-4151
www.centuraseniors.org
Perhaps the most oft-recommended retirement community by word-of-mouth, Sunny Acres is a large facility on a campuslike setting just south of Stonehocker Park in Thornton. The northern suburbs are quiet areas with good mountain views and a lot of remaining open space, and the landscaped grounds include two fishing lakes as well as gardening areas for residents. To that Sunny Acres adds amenities including home health care, 10 libraries, a 3,000-square-foot fitness center, a whirlpool, pool tables, a woodworking and carpentry shop, lounges, dining rooms including a restaurant, a convenience store, and beauty and barber shops.

MEDIA

Greater Denver is not exactly a media center, at least not in the sense of New York or Los Angeles. It doesn't produce a lot of television programs or magazines, though it does occasionally show up in movies. Still, at least in part because Metro Denver is home to telecommunications industry giants Jones Intercable and Tele-Communications Inc., it may very well become a major stop on the information highway.

NEWSPAPERS

Denver was among the last U.S. cities to have two independent newspapers. That changed in 2009, when the *Rocky Mountain News* published its last edition. The *Denver Post* remains as the city's only daily newspaper. *Westword,* the city's free arts and entertainment publication, comes out weekly. There are also many community papers, too numerous to list here. Specialized publications are always coming into and going out of existence to serve a particular region (downtown) or interest (art).

Dailies

THE DENVER POST
1560 Broadway
(303) 954-1010
www.denverpost.com

The *Denver Post* has a long and colorful history. It was founded in 1895 by Harry Heye Tammen and Frederick Gilmer Bonfils. The early *Post* was a prime example of sensational journalism, relying on stunts and gossip to attract readership. In the 1920s Tammen and Bonfils got themselves entangled in one fine mess, the Teapot Dome scandal. Originally vehemently opposed to questionable oil leases in Wyoming, the *Post* dropped the issue when paid to do so. Tammen died of cancer in 1924, and Bonfils resigned in 1926.

After Bonfils died in 1933, ownership passed largely to his daughters. In the 1960s May Bonfils sold her stock to S. I. Newhouse, head of a chain of newspapers and magazines. Helen Bonfils contested the sale, and after years of litigation, Newhouse finally dropped his bid to gain control of the *Post* in 1973. The *Post* was sold to the Times Mirror Company, owners of the *Los Angeles Times,* in 1980, and sold again to William Dean Singleton of the Denver-based MediaNews Group in 1987.

The *Post* switched from evening to morning distribution in 1982. Notable *Post* columnists include Woody Paige, Dave Krieger, Tina Griego, Mike Litwin, and society man-about town Bill Husted. Daily circulation for the *Post* is about 355,000; Sunday circulation is 475,0000.

Weeklies

In addition to the following non-dailies, weekly newspapers are published for residents of Englewood, Highlands Ranch, Littleton, Evergreen, Golden, Greenwood Village, and Westminster. If you live there or are interested in news about those communities, check for these papers at local newsstands.

BROOMFIELD ENTERPRISE
1006 Depot Hill Road, Suite G
Broomfield
(303) 448-9898
www.broomfieldenterprise.com

This community paper is a subsidiary of the *Daily Camera,* Boulder's daily newspaper. It is delivered free to Broomfield residences and businesses and carries news of Broomfield, Metro Denver's most northwestern community. Regular offerings include news and feature stories, editorials, and classified ads. Coverage is strong on government, business, schools, and sports. The paper also publishes special sections ranging from homes and gardens to election issues.

DENVER BUSINESS JOURNAL
1700 Broadway, #515
(303) 837-3500
www.bizjournals.com/denver
The weekly *Denver Business Journal* covers local business news in depth and includes a small-business strategy section, along with specialized sections that relate to a variety of topics from health care to personal finance. The paper comes out on Friday and is available by subscription or throughout metro Denver by single copy.

MILE HIGH NEWSPAPERS
1000 10th Sreet, Golden
(303) 279-5541
www.milehighnews.com
This company publishes weekly newspapers for residents of Arvada, Lakewood, Golden, and Wheat Ridge, and an online edition. The papers focus on news relevant to these suburbs and include quarterly education sections and a yearly garden insert.

WESTWORD
969 Broadway
(303) 296-7744
www.westword.com
Owned by Village Voice Media, a national publisher of "alternative" papers, *Westword* is known for its muckraking investigative stories and is depended upon for its arts and entertainment coverage. Not everyone admires the weekly paper's zeal in pursuing stories, as is evidenced by heated letters to the editor. But at least a dozen of its articles, such as an investigation of the Rocky Flats grand jury proceedings that examined who should be held responsible for environmental crimes, have won awards and national media attention.

Westword is distributed free throughout Metro Denver and hits the streets late Wednesday afternoon. You can find it in boxes on street corners all over town. Its arts/dining/entertainment listings are superb.

MAGAZINES AND SPECIAL INTEREST PUBLICATIONS

5280
1514 Curtis Street, Suite 300
(303) 832-5280
www.5280.com
5280, "Denver's Mile-High Magazine," debuted in 1993, named for Denver's altitude at 5,280 feet above sea level. It's fresh and independent and has a lively design like any city magazine. It covers things of interest to locals—restaurants, getaways, and interesting people.

COLORADO EXPRESSIONS
New West Publishing
3600 South Beeler Street, Suite 100
(303) 694-1289
www.newwestpublishing.com
Colorado Expressions is the flagship of New West's three magazines. The others are *Confetti* and *Architecture & Design of the West*.

COLORADO HOMES & LIFESTYLES
1777 South Harriston Street
(888) 433-3314
www.coloradohomesmag.com
Colorado Homes & Lifestyles, which published nine times a year, not only includes a wealth of information about home and garden design, but also personality profiles of Colorado residents.

COLORADO PARENT MAGAZINE
5460 South Quebec Street, Suite 130
Greenwood Village
(303) 320-1000
www.colorado.parenthood.com
This magazine includes a comprehensive calendar of events and lists classes of interest to parents in the Metro Denver area. The free paper

comes out the first of each month and can be picked up in about 800 different locations around town, including libraries and bookstores. The folks at Colorado Parent also publish an annual A-to-Z directory of local resources for parents each January.

HIGH COUNTRY NEWS
119 Grand Avenue, Paonia
(970) 527-4898
www.hcn.org
An environmentally oriented newspaper, *High Country News* is published in Paonia, Colorado. The much-praised paper focuses on issues intrinsic to the West, such as use of public lands and water and grazing rights. This sharp biweekly is highly recommended to Metro Denver newcomers who would like to know more about the region they now call home. It's available at the Tattered Cover Book Store (see our Shopping chapter) and other locations throughout the city, or call for a subscription.

OUT FRONT COLORADO
1738 Franklin Street
(303) 778-7900
www.outfrontcolorado.com
A gay and lesbian newspaper, *Out Front Colorado* is published every two weeks (with a break at Christmas). The paper is free and is available at local bars, restaurants, gay businesses, and bookstores. It's noted for its entertainment and nightlife listings. Mail subscription is available for a small charge.

RADIO

Nothing but the Rocky Mountain weather changes as much as Denver radio stations. One day you're listening to jazz; the next day the station has gone country-western. Consider that caveat when tuning in to the stations listed below. For an up-to date list, check the TV section in the Sunday *Denver Post*.

Adult Contemporary
KIMN 100.3 FM
KOSI 101.1 FM
KALC 105.9 FM

Christian
KLTT 670 AM
KPOF 910 AM
KRKS 990 AM and 94.7 FM

Classical
KVOD 90.1 FM

Country
KCKK 1600 AM
KCUV 102.3 FM (alt.)
KYGO 98.5 FM

Hip-Hop
KQKS 107.5 FM

Jazz
KJCD 104.3 FM
KUVO 89.3 FM

Mexican/Spanish
KBNO 1280
KLVZ 1220 AM
KMXA 1090 AM
KXPK 96.5 FM

National Public Radio
KCFR 1340 AM
KGNU 88.5 FM

News/Talk/Sports
KHOW 630 AM
KKZN 760 AM
KNUS 710 AM
KOA 850 AM

Oldies

KEZW 1430 AM
KRFX 103.5 FM (classic rock)
KXKL 105.1 FM (1960s-1970s)

Rock and Progressive

KBCO 97.3 FM
KBPI 106.7 FM
KQMT 99.5 FM
KTCL 93.3 FM

Sports Only

KKFN 950 AM
KLZ 560 AM (ESPN)

TELEVISION

With all the recent mergers and acquisitions in the cable industry, Denver is down to one main cable TV supplier for most of the metropolitan area. Call Comcast at (303) 266-2278 for service information for your area. An alternative to cable is satellite TV. DirecTV operates its national direct-satellite service out of Castle Rock, about a half hour south of Denver, www.directv.com. The area's other provider is Echo Star, in Englewood, (303) 706-4000.

Major Local TV Stations and Network Affiliates

KWGN Channel 2 (Independent/WB)
KCNC Channel 4 (CBS)
KRMA Channel 6 (PBS)
KMGH Channel 7 (ABC)
KUSA Channel 9 (NBC)
KBDI Channel 12 (PBS)
KTVD Channel 20 (Independent/UPN)
KDVR Channel 31 (Fox)
KRMT Channel 41 (Independent)
KCEC Channel 50 (Univision)
KWHD Channel 53 (Independent)
KTBN Channel 57 (Trinity)
KMAS Channels 63 and 67 (Telemundo)

Religious Television Programming

The sermon from the Riverside Baptist Church, 2401 East Alcott Street, (303) 433-8665, is broadcast by KLTT-670 AM at 9 a.m. each Sunday. Check local listings for other religious programming.

WORSHIP

Drive around town on Sunday and chances are you'll find church parking lots full. Denver is definitely a "church town," but in a most laid-back and casual way. Denverites are not only observant (our church attendance average is right up there with national numbers) but also open to new and different spiritual experiences. From traditional services to religious seminars, we fill our spiritual coffers in a variety of ways.

Denver offers every major denomination as well as most of the smaller ones. Catholics make up the largest denomination, though their presence is not a dominant force. Every branch of Protestantism is also represented, and Denver has active Catholic, Jewish, Buddhist, Muslim, and Mormon communities as well. Chances are, no matter what your beliefs, Denver will have a congregation to satisfy you.

This is truly an ecumenical city—one where a great deal of collegiality exists among different faiths. When graffiti on a synagogue made local news, Christians and Muslims took little time to publicly show their outrage. Denverites are church consumers. They shop around, looking for a good fit. And churches here have responded to that trend by being open and hospitable.

Denver's religious diversity dates from before Colorado was a state; by the time of statehood in 1876, 20 religious denominations had been organized in the city. St. Joseph Hospital, the first of Denver's many church-affiliated hospitals, was founded in 1873, and Jews and Catholics as well as many Protestants were conducting services in and around Denver at that time. Present-day Congregation Emanuel can trace its beginnings from its incorporation in 1874 and, even before that, to the establishment of the Hebrew Burial Society in 1859. Similarly, enough Catholics were in Colorado during the territorial period that the Rocky Mountains were removed from the authority of Santa Fe and recognized as a separate vicariate in 1868. The first bishop of Denver, Joseph Machebeuf, was consecrated in 1887.

Today that diversity still prevails, and Denver is a town fueled by religious energy. In addition to the much heralded 1993 visit by Pope John Paul II for World Youth Day, Denverites eagerly anticipated the visit of the Dalai Lama in the summer of 1997. Sponsored by the Colorado Friends of Tibet and the Naropa Institute in Boulder, the Dalai Lama took part in a four-day spirituality fest held in Denver and Boulder that featured other notables such as Joan Halifax and Huston Smith. The Dalai Lama gave two public talks—at Macky Auditorium in Boulder and at an interfaith ceremony at McNichols Arena.

Meanwhile, for your own immediate religious needs, plan to get out and visit some churches or synagogues. In addition to your hands-on research, read the column "How Coloradans Worship" in the Monday *Rocky Mountain News*, which features a different house of worship each week.

Also be sure to check out two of the area's more popular destinations: the Mother Cabrini Shrine and Red Rocks Park. The **Mother Cabrini Shrine,** 20189 Cabrini Boulevard, Golden, (303) 526-0758, is where pilgrims go for prayer and contemplation. The shrine is open to the public daily, and mass is celebrated each morning. Take I-70 west to the Morrison exit 259, then take US 40 (the frontage road) west about a mile. Also in Morrison, scenic **Red Rocks Park** is the site of an annual nondenominational Easter sunrise service that fills the 9,000-seat natural amphitheater to capacity in good weather. Take I-70 west to the Morrison exit 259, and turn south toward Morrison; watch for signs marking the entrance to Red Rocks on the right.

There are also several houses of worship worth a visit (see our Tours and Attractions chapter) for their historical and architectural value.

This brief chapter is merely an overview of the religious scene in the metro area. It would not be practical to list every place of worship in Denver, nor would it be appropriate for us to suggest one rather than another. To find a specific place of worship for yourself and your family, consult the following listing of religious organizations or the yellow pages.

RESOURCES

CATHOLIC ARCHDIOCESE OF DENVER
1300 South Steele Street
(303) 722-4687 (weekdays)

CHURCH OF JESUS CHRIST OF LATTER-DAY SAINTS
Denver North Mission
100 Malley Drive, Northglenn
(303) 252-7192

DENVER SOUTH MISSION
2001 East Easter Avenue, Littleton
(303) 794-6457

COLORADO COUNCIL OF CHURCHES
3690 Cherry Creek South Drive
(303) 825-4910

COLORADO MUSLIM SOCIETY
2071 South Parker Road, Aurora
(303) 696-9800

EPISCOPAL CHURCH CENTER OF COLORADO
1300 Washington Street
(303) 837-1173

FIFTH DISTRICT OF THE AFRICAN METHODIST
Episcopal Churches of Colorado/
Shorter Church
3100 Richard Allen Court
(303) 320-1712

THE GREEK ORTHODOX CATHEDRAL OF THE ASSUMPTION
4610 East Alameda Avenue
(303) 388-9314

PRESBYTERY OF DENVER
(Presbyterian Church U.S.A.)
1710 South Grant Street
(303) 777-2453

REORGANIZED CHURCH OF JESUS CHRIST OF LATTER-DAY SAINTS
Rocky Mountain Mission Center
9501 Lou Drive, Thornton
(303) 426-5900

ROCKY MOUNTAIN CONFERENCE UNITED CHURCH OF CHRIST
1140 West 5th Avenue
(303) 984-9118

ROCKY MOUNTAIN SYNOD/EVANGELICAL LUTHERAN CHURCH IN AMERICA
455 Sherman Street
(303) 777-6700

ROCKY MOUNTAIN UNITED METHODIST CONFERENCE
2200 South University Boulevard
(303) 733-3736

SYNAGOGUE COUNCIL OF METRO DENVER
P.O. Box 102732, Denver 80250
(303) 759-8485

TRI-STATE BUDDHIST TEMPLE
1947 Lawrence Street
(303) 295-1844

Quiet Time

One of the most peaceful and powerful services in Denver is Taize (pronounced TEZZ-ay), a communal meditation hour for people of almost any faith. It's sponsored the second Sunday of each month by The Threshold, a congregation that meets at the Highland Park Presbyterian Church, 3401 West 29th Street, (720) 489-8073. The service has no liturgy, no sermon, no apparent plan. It is held by candlelight and involves meditation and music. A how-to sheet helps first-timers with breathing and meditation. People drive from across town to attend this monthly service.

ADDITIONAL RESOURCES

Faith on the Frontier, a book compiled by the Colorado Council of Churches in 1976, was used as the source for much of the historical data in this chapter. *Denver: The City Beautiful* by Thomas J. Noel and Barbara S. Norgren (Historic Denver Inc.) contains a brief section on Metro Denver church architecture and is a wonderful resource for anyone interested in Denver's architectural history.

INDEX

ABOUT THE AUTHOR

Linda Castrone is a Colorado native, and although she has lived on both coasts and several places in between, she can't escape the lure of her homestate's mountains and prairies. Her first newspaper job (at age four) was selling display ads door-to-door for her father's four-page southwestern Colorado weekly, the *Dove Creek Press*. She graduated from the University of Colorado's journalism school and never looked back, working as a reporter and editor in Boulder, Denver, and Charlotte, North Carolina.